José Esteban Muñoz

A Critical Cinema

A Critical Cinema

Interviews with
Independent Filmmakers

Scott MacDonald

University of California Press
Berkeley / Los Angeles / London

Publication of this book was supported by a grant from
the Mellon Foundation.

University of California Press
Berkeley and Los Angeles, California

University of California Press, Ltd.
London, England

© 1988 by
The Regents of the University of California

Library of Congress Cataloging-in-Publication Data
MacDonald, Scott, 1942–
  A critical cinema.
  Bibliography: p.
  Filmography: p.
  Includes index.
  1. Experimental films—United States—History and
criticism. 2. Moving-picture producers and
directors—United States—Interviews. I. Title.
PN1995.9.E96M34 1987   791.43′75′0973   87-6004
ISBN 0-520-05800-3 (alk. paper)
ISBN 0-520-05801-1 (pbk.)

Printed in the United States of America
1 2 3 4 5 6 7 8 9

For Ian and Pat

Contents

Acknowledgments

Thanks to the following journals for permission to reprint condensed versions of interviews and, in some cases, my introductory comments or portions of them:

Afterimage, for "Larry Gottheim's 'Webs of Subtle Relationships': An Interview," vol. 6, no. 4 (November 1978), pp. 7–11; "Interview with Robert Huot," vol. 7, no. 7 (February 1980), pp. 8–12; "All the Faces Are Us: An Interview with Tom Chomont," vol. 8, nos. 1–2 (Summer 1981), pp. 26–34; "I Don't Go to the Movies Anymore: An Interview with Bruce Conner," vol. 10, nos. 1–2 (Summer 1982), pp. 20–23; "I Never Understood Anything about Cowboys: An Interview with J. J. Murphy," vol. 9, no. 7 (October 1982), pp. 12–18; "Interview with Robert Nelson," Part 1: "We Were Bent on Having a Good Time," vol. 11, nos. 1–2 (Summer 1983), pp. 39–43; Part 2: "If the Vision Is Intense Enough, Everything Is Grist for the Mill," vol. 11, no. 3 (October 1983), pp. 12–15; "Points of View: An Interview with Babette Mangolte," vol. 12, nos. 1–2 (Summer 1984), pp. 8–13; "Raw Nerves: An Interview with Manuel DeLanda," vol. 13, no. 6 (January 1986), pp. 12–15; "Magic Reclaimed: An Interview with Diana Barrie," vol. 14, no. 7 (February 1987), pp. 5–9.

October, for "Interview with Hollis Frampton: The Early Years," no. 12 (Spring 1980), pp. 103–26; "Interview with Vivienne Dick," no. 20 (Spring 1982), pp. 83–101; "Interview with Beth and Scott B," no. 24 (Spring 1983), pp. 3–36. © 1980, 1982, 1983, the Institute for Architecture and Urban Studies and the Massachusetts Institute of Technology.

Film Quarterly, for "George Kuchar: An Interview," vol. 38, no. 3 (Spring

1985), pp. 2–15; "Morgan Fisher: An Interview," vol. 40, no. 3 (Spring 1987), pp. 24–33.

Artforum, for "John Waters' Divine Comedy," vol. 20, no. 5 (January 1982), pp. 52–60.

Film Culture, for "Interview with Hollis Frampton: *Hapax Legomena,*" no. 67 (Fall 1979), pp. 158–80.

Journal of Film and Video (formerly *Journal of the University Film Association*), for "Interview with Taka Iimura," vol. 33, no. 4 (Fall 1981), pp. 21–44.

Millennium Film Journal, for "Film and Performance: An Interview with Carolee Schneemann," nos. 7–9 (Fall/Winter 1980–81), pp. 95–114.

Quarterly Review of Film Studies, for "Interview with Hollis Frampton: *Zorns Lemma,*" vol. 4, no. 1 (Winter 1979), pp. 23–37.

Introduction

The most interesting and useful film-critical insights of recent years, it could be argued, have been coming not from the continuing elaborations of auteurism and genre studies or from the systematic application of recent French theory to popular film, but from that remarkable body of North American films known variously as "underground film," "the New American Cinema," "experimental cinema," and "avant-garde cinema." Many, if not most, of the filmmakers loosely designated by such terms explicitly and implicitly view the dominant, commercial cinema (and its sibling, television) not as a competing mode but as a set of culturally conditioned and accepted approaches to cinema—a cultural text—to be analyzed from within the medium of film itself. One of the goals of these critical filmmakers has been to place our awareness and acceptance of the commercial forms and their highly conventionalized modes of representation into crisis. In this sense, the term *avant-garde,* which is widely used to designate this area of cinema, is a misnomer because it suggests that the films are important primarily because they lead the way for the more conventional forms. No doubt there are many instances where the commercial cinema and, more recently, commercial television have followed the advances of avant-garde filmmakers. But, regardless of the number of such instances, the relationship that is most interesting to me is the opposite one: cinema as a set of commercial forms and mass-audience expectations came first and made possible the development of another set of semicommercial and noncommercial forms that, for our purposes here, can be designated "critical cinema." The critical dimension of the films and filmmakers I discuss is, of course, not their only important dimension. Over the years, the essays and books on this immense area of independent film by

Parker Tyler, Amos Vogel, Jonas Mekas, P. Adams Sitney, Malcolm Le Grice, and others have demonstrated that the films and filmmakers can be understood in a variety of contexts. But in recent years at least, I have found their critical edge especially compelling and useful—and widely enough ignored to deserve comment.

One could sensibly argue that every serious film has a critical dimension; that is, it can be seen as commenting on previous works of its type. Each new film by a recognized auteur reveals dimensions common to the auteur's previous films and deviations from the previously developed auteurist vision; each new instance of a developing genre implicitly comments on the previous history of that genre. Even in noncommercial forms this critical process is often, if not always, at work: recent ethnographic documentaries have functioned as critiques of the limitations of previous ethnographic films. The self-reflexive structures of some of the Timothy Asch–Napoleon Chagnon films about the Yanomamo, for example, are determined in part by the filmmakers' interest in avoiding the frequent tendency of film ethnographers to sidestep the issues raised by the processes they use in recording "primitive" peoples. In fact, the history of the nonfiction film in general can be seen as an ongoing critique of the visions of people and events supplied by commercial cinema. But even if a critical dimension is inevitable, its extent and usefulness depends on the specific film or kind of film. I would contend that the areas of independent cinema discussed here have provided some of the most intensive, illuminating, and useful film-critical insights of recent decades. They have offered many new opportunities for understanding the nature and the impact of commercial cinema.

Critical films have developed a number of distinct approaches to the commercial cinema and the apparatus of viewership that supports it. The first of these, which we can call *mimetic,* involves a partial imitation of the forms and conventions of popular cinema. In some films we recognize elements of commercial movies at the same time that we recognize the discrepancies between the imitated product and the filmic critique of it and the implications of these discrepancies. A second critical approach, the *autobiographical,* is manifested by films that do not imitate commercial film rhetoric, though they do provide viewers with some of the basic elements of commercial cinema: most obviously, narrative and character development. Here the filmmakers use themselves as subject matter: by revealing dimensions of life that are not evident in commercial movies, they attempt to provide more complete and useful visions of human existence, in forms that critique the conventional construction of the life stories of characters in commercial film. The third approach—this one seems most nearly *theoretical*—assumes an awareness of conventional cinema, but instead of foregrounding recognizable characters and narratives, the theoretical films foreground the mechanical, chemical, perceptual, and conceptual structures that underlie the theatrical film experience in general. All three critical modes have developed more or less contemporaneously. In fact, individual filmmakers have often moved from one approach to another and have combined them in some films. Not surprisingly, of the three approaches, the mimetic has the largest following; the autobiographical and theoretical approaches have at most a tiny group of enthusiasts—a situation at odds with the considerable intelligence, ingenuity, and insight evident in so many of these films.

One of the filmmakers who best exemplifies the mimetic approach is George Kuchar. By the late 1950s Kuchar (and his twin brother, Mike) were producing homemade 8mm movies with their neighbors and friends in the Bronx. They had been movie devotees for years, haunting local theaters and internalizing the rhetoric of Hollywood A and B movies. Since they had almost no financial resources, they were immediately faced with the dilemma of how to bridge the gap between what they knew about commercial movies and what they were capable of producing on their own. At first, their little films were the adolescent spoofs one expects from young people who have a minimum of technology and know-how at their disposal and a maximum of excitement about the idea of moviemaking. But soon, the films developed well beyond spoofs, and the gap between what they had wanted to be able to do and what they could do developed into one of the central subjects of their films. They continued to imitate the commercial cinema's more melodramatic genres and rhetorical gestures, but when they cast their films, they could not, or chose not to, fill the roles with actors who looked like their Hollywood counterparts or even acted effectively in such roles, and they did not have the resources for professional-looking sets and costumes or for sync sound. The result was a series of films that referred to the Hollywood tradition of making believable illusions but whose "actors" and settings undercut this tradition. Mostly, the films have been understood as a kind of camp humor, but to see them as only humorous is to miss their critical edge. In the best of the Kuchar brothers' collaborative 8mm films, and in George Kuchar's subsequent, prolific 16mm career, we see not merely the gap between Hollywood film and the Kuchars' ability to imitate it but also the gap between Hollywood's "illusion of reality" and everyday reality itself. Kuchar characters suffer the same sorts of melodramatic traumas as their commercial counterparts, but they must suffer them not as beautiful or handsome stars but as average-looking, everyday people whose fantasy lives have been deeply impressed with the Hollywood illusions. At conventional films we "identify" with heroes and heroines, and we may find ourselves trying to emulate them after the screening; in Kuchar's films we observe people like ourselves trying to emulate Hollywood actors: we become part of a critique of our usual relationship to cinematic characters and realize something of the self-destructive potential of being continually confronted with "realistic" illusions that, by definition, our real lives can never match.

During the 1960s a good many films set themselves in similar relationships with commercial movies. Jack Smith's *Flaming Creatures* is an obvious instance, as are some of Kenneth Anger's films, the productions of the Warhol studio, and the remarkably aggressive early films of John Waters. Like Kuchar (and to a degree as a result of the Kuchars' influence), Waters began making films with friends and neighbors and with almost no financial resources, but with the determination to make kinds of film that would be recognizable, at least in a general sense, to conventional filmgoers. While Kuchar tends to cast average-looking people in Hollywood-type roles and to allow the discrepancy to generate a new kind of understanding of the traditional relationship between viewers and the actors and actions they watch, Waters consistently populates his films with people whose appearance and demeanor are as abnormal as possible, and he designs generally conventional plots, the specifics of which allow these personae to outrage viewers. In *Multiple Maniacs,* as in so many conventional horror films, the central character turns into a monster that is destroyed at the end. But the transformation into a monster is the most normal thing that happens in the film: by the time it occurs, we have seen a long series of outrageous events, including one character eating his own vomit (this is not real, but the idea is sufficient) and the central protagonist (an obese man in drag) experiencing an extended orgasm during a "rosary job" provided by Mink Stole in an obviously real church. We have often understood the commercial cinema to be projecting our cultural fantasies onto the screen, but Waters's films function as shocking reminders that the "fantasies" provided by conventional movies are informed by obvious compromises. For Waters, the "fantastic" is not simply that which is beyond the realm of observable reality; it is precisely those experiences our conventional filmgoing has prepared us *not* to expect. Like Kuchar's films, Waters's are made for viewers who know the movies well enough to be interested in experiencing a new perspective on the act of participating in film.

An essentially related tactic is that so often employed by Bruce Conner. Conner does not imitate conventional melodrama; he recycles material from various highly conventional film contexts (entertainment films, ads, science films, religious films) into new contexts, in which our response to what we see is conditioned in large measure by our sense of the material's original function. Instead of looking at a view of "reality" in *A Movie, Permian Strata, Valse Triste,* and other films, we look at Conner's juxtapositions and reinterpretations of conventional gestures; or to put it another way, these new films make us look critically at aspects of the history of our film viewing. Conner's methods have been imitated and alluded to regularly, by Robert Nelson at the beginning of his career, for example, and more recently by J. J. Murphy (*Science Fiction*), Diana Barrie (*Stay Awake Whenever You Can, The Living or Dead Test*), Morgan Fisher (*Standard Gauge*), and others.

In the mid-1970s some "punk" or "New Wave" filmmakers focused an essentially mimetic approach not simply on the content and rhetoric of conventional cinema but also on the distribution apparatus for conventional movies. In a sense, Kuchar and Waters (and Smith, Warhol, and others) had implicitly posited a new audience for the films they made, a film-experienced audience ready to test its awareness. By the 1970s this audience had become a reality, the midnight-movie crowd. Other filmmakers, however, were not entirely happy with the specialized, marginalized, largely apolitical nature of this audience, and went a step further. Beth B and Scott B and Vivienne Dick decided to borrow enough of commercial cinema so that audiences would be able to relate to their films, but to produce and distribute them in a manner that would be a political critique of the conventional modes of production and distribution. They wanted their films to function on a direct community level. Using simple inexpensive home-movie Super-8 technology, they produced experimental narratives using their friends and neighbors as personae and the real issues confronting their downtown Manhattan neighborhoods—terrorism and police power (the Bs' *G-Man, Black Box;* Dick's *Visibility: Moderate*) and prostitution (*G-Man;* Dick's *Liberty's Booty*)—as subject matter. The mood of these films, and many of their specifics, were recognizable imitations of Hollywood suspense films, especially of cinema noir, but because people saw the films in neighborhood settings (bars and rock clubs) rather than in conventional commercial theaters, the usual viewer detachment from the issues underlying classic cinema noir was, at least in theory, undercut or critiqued. The films attempted to raise issues in a context that itself suggested the depoliticizing function of more conventional viewing contexts. The limited audiences they could reach with Super-8 soon led the Bs to 16mm and toward commercial cinema. For Dick the moment when her filmmaking could function effectively in her East Village neighborhood soon passed, and she returned to her native Ireland.

Kuchar, Waters, the Bs, Dick, and even Conner to a degree have tended to move their viewers into a critical state through the visceral impact of their films, to shock viewers into a larger awareness. Other filmmakers have taken a quieter, more intellectual approach. Yvonne Rainer, Babette Mangolte, Diana Barrie, and other filmmakers have developed critiques of the commercial cinema's representation of gender. In their early features Rainer (*Lives of Performers, Film About a Woman Who . . .*) and Mangolte (*What Maisie Knew, The Cold Eye*) use many of the elements of conventional melodrama but present them by formal means that refuse the viewer's usual privileged gaze at the female protagonists' sexuality. Rainer in particular uses large amounts of text, and both Rainer and Mangolte use highly formalized compositions and long takes to undermine the viewer's easy access to conventional melodramatic situations. In her 16mm films (*My Version of the Fall, Stay Awake Whenever You Can*) Barrie often reverses the gender of conventional narrative situations and redefines the conventional gender politics of viewing such situations. Instead of allowing us to gaze at the sexual involvements of characters in the usual way, these films force us to view ourselves viewing and, thus, to consider to what extent our participation in conventional film viewing automatically reconfirms reactionary patterns of response to sexual difference.

A final instance of the mimetic approach combines elements of a number of the films already discussed. Manuel DeLanda's films partake of the aggressively tacky look of Kuchar's and Waters's work, but they are also intellectual responses to the implicit politics of conventional narrative construction. *Raw Nerves,* for example, uses plot and character elements of cinema noir to examine the technical and psychological construction of the film language normally used in cinema noir films; *The Itch Scratch Itch Cycle* and *Incontinence* set up and then subvert conventional means for conducting a conversation between two people and for moving coherently from one scene to the next.

The mass commercial cinema, particularly in the United States, is so pervasive a part of our film consciousness that even when filmmakers develop and exhibit alternative forms, the dominant cinema is implied by the alternatives. Most of the films I use as instances of the autobiographical critical stance avoid conventional melodramatic forms. And yet, we understand these alternatives because we know—and the filmmakers know we know—the kinds of films that these are alternatives to. Instead of explicitly referring to the dominant cinema, however, the filmmakers tend to establish, or exploit, links between what they are doing and one or more of the aesthetic traditions that have been seen as positive alternatives to pop cinema: most obviously classic poetry, fiction, and painting. One major area that can be included as autobiographical is the tradition of "visionary film" defined and explained by P. Adams Sitney. As Sitney suggests, the films of Gregory Markopoulos, Kenneth Anger, Stan Brakhage, Robert Nelson, Ron Rice, and others often reveal clear links to the western poetic tradition of the creator as seer and mythmaker. Often, these filmmakers attempt to image mental or spiritual states they have experienced or are experiencing. Tom Chomont, who admits a considerable debt to Markopoulos, uses a minimum of equipment and his own humble personal environment to make tiny, finely crafted films that encapsulate a feeling of what it is like to *be* Tom Chomont, to be inside his perceptions and moods at particular times. Chomont has not been aggressive about distributing his films. Because the films are so personal—and because this personalness is a reaction and an alternative to the commercial industry's marketing of the illusion of intimacy—the idea of pushing them seems inimical. Chomont's films, as well as those of the other autobiographical filmmakers I discuss, are available in this country only at distribution cooperatives and from the filmmakers themselves; the filmmakers often appear personally with the films, just as poets traditionally travel to read their works.

A second group of autobiographical filmmakers are sometimes referred to as "diarists": Carolee Schneemann and Robert Huot can serve as instances.

In their films, the direct exhibition of their personal lives implicitly, though often quite aggressively, attacks the ways in which conventional movies "reveal" the personal lives of protagonists. While mass-entertainment films usually pretend to reveal human intimacies, the "personal" details they picture are mitigated both by the star system (we're not looking directly at Marion Crane; we're looking at Janet Leigh *playing* Marion Crane) and by our knowledge of the director's history (we know *Psycho* is a "Hitchcock film," not because it reveals anything particular about Hitchcock's personal life, but because it is part of a larger history of Hitchcock films and film viewing. For Schneemann and Huot the challenge is to reveal and interpret the personal directly and to avoid those forms of detachment that tend to isolate us from real intimacy during conventional melodramatic films. Both filmmakers, though in different ways, reveal particular elements of their lives in part *because* these elements are so rigorously avoided in mass-entertainment films.

In her films (and in her painting and performance, her photo-text pieces, and her writing) Schneemann has always confronted the issue of sex and love, and the particular interrelational involvements that desire and love have led her into. Unlike conventional melodrama, however, where implications or enactments of the characters' sexuality are usually presented as rewards (to the characters and to the viewers) or as transgressions after which the perpetrators (especially the women) must be punished—that is, as part of a filmic control system that mirrors the sexual politics of the larger society—Schneemann's films present evidence of one woman's particular sexuality and its surround in forms that demonstrate the psychological and emotional complexity of her relationships and her commitment to them. In the most general sense, the subject matter of the films may seem related to conventional Hollywood melodrama (and to commercial pornography), but Schneemann's presentation, as well as her choice and organization of imagery, clearly distinguishes her work from these types of films and relates it to painting, collage, and performance: in *Fuses* and *Plumb Line* she paints and scratches over the photographed 16mm imagery; *Kitch's Last Meal* uses two vertically arranged Super-8 images and a collage tape.

Like Schneemann, Huot came to film from painting (both began as abstract expressionists), and especially in his early diaries (*Rolls: 1971, Third One-Year Movie—1972*) he provides images of his personal life with a directness that can seem shocking. Instead of using the Hollywood method of presenting a male protagonist with mannerisms that we are amused by and identify with and involving him in a series of "adventures" leading toward romance and love, Huot records and presents his own adventures in constructing his life. His diaries avoid the conventional narrative curve (excitements leading to climax and denouement); instead Huot organizes the various experiences he records into highly formalized, serialistic structures that demonstrate that many experiences—working in his garden, eating, parental love, sex (both with others and himself), traveling, making art, partying with friends, looking at landscape and cityscape—are central to his life, not just the romantic love and violent action prevalent in the dominant cinema. In fact, Huot's diaries demonstrate that a filmmaker's investigation of his own life and of the implications of his own persona can be as powerful as a conventional action movie, though in a radically different way.

The third, "theoretical" stance involves a considerable number of films in which the elements we think of as standard in the dominant cinema—such as character development, plot, and conventionalized rhetorical gestures—are rigorously avoided or downplayed. The result is a body of work that demonstrates the filmmakers' alienation from the modes of conventional film practice but not from the medium itself. For most first-time viewers of theoretical films, the most obvious element is the very lack of conventional elements: there seems to be nothing to look at. What is there to be experienced, however, is the superstructure of the medium, common to all kinds of film practice. These films attempt to invigorate our awareness of the nature of the cinema experience and, by extension, of the ways in which cinema normally functions in society.

As is true in the other areas of critical cinema discussed above, the theoretical films are very diverse. And yet, certain tactics are common to many of these films. One of the most obvious and pervasive seems closely related to Eadweard Muybridge's method for recording his motion studies: a rigorous grid structure is set up; within it, we are able to measure and contemplate a series of particular developments. During at least one period of their work (both have made other, very different kinds of film), J. J. Murphy and Taka Iimura were two of the most rigorously Muybridgian of the theoretical filmmakers. For *Print Generation* Murphy devised a precise grid structure using fifty print generations made by contact printing a one-minute film made up of sixty one-second images. The point was to discover the degree to which the contact printing process—and by implication, the process of film decay in general—modifies the imagery recorded on film: to what extent is what we understand during a screening contingent on the state of the print we are using? In *Models* and subsequent "imageless" films, Iimura uses various temporal grids and simple mathematical numbering systems to examine the impact on the viewer's consciousness of different densities of imagery presented for different temporal durations. Of course, these theoretical films are meant to be a good deal more than technical experiments. In each case, the filmmaker has created a film environment within which the new formulation of space, time, and imagery functions to make the viewer use the film experience to think about cinema and about cinema's intersection with the "real world" that forms its context.

Other theoretical filmmakers have used films as means of thinking about the process of conceptualization. For Hollis Frampton the most obvious limitation of film practice of all kinds seems to be the failure of filmmakers to provide experiences that are, in any serious sense, direct challenges to the intellect. One might think seriously *about* film but not *in* film. Yvonne Rainer once named a performance *The Mind Is a Muscle:* Frampton's films are calisthenics for this muscle. *Zorns Lemma,* for instance, traces the stages through which our ability to conceptualize develops. *Hapax Legomena: nostalgia* challenges our ability to perceive one level of information, while remembering a second and imagining the implications of a third. *Hapax Legomena: Poetic Justice* develops a labyrinthine intersection of filmic and literary ways of conceptualizing and imaging experience. And *Magellan,* the multipartite epic Frampton began in the early 1970s, challenges the whole notion of film viewing as an individual, discrete, short-term experience: Frampton designed *Magellan* to be seen a section each day for an entire year.

For Larry Gottheim, film has been a means for considering the ways in which the human capability for rational thought informs and redirects the process of nature. Not only does the photographically recorded imagery in his films reflect this theme, but it is also engraved materially and structurally in the films themselves. Often Gottheim's imagery (like Snow's and Murphy's) hovers between representing the physical world outside the camera and theater and indexing the material processes and mechanisms of film: in *Fog Line* we cannot be sure whether the subtle movements we see are the movements of the thinning fog or the dance of the particles of film grain within which the fog is encoded. In *Horizons* the conceptualizing faculty is evident in the ways in which linear organization has informed the fields and roads in the vicinity of Binghamton, New York, and in Gottheim's complex, precise editing of footage recorded more spontaneously. When we experience Gottheim's films, we are thinking about how the film medium extends our thinking processes into the world.

For the most part, the realities of film distribution and exhibition mean that theoretical films can be seen only outside the commercial cinema. The films discussed above (not only the theoretical films but the autobiographical films and many of the mimetic films as well) have had very limited exposure: at some art galleries and museums (the Albright-Knox Gallery in Buffalo, the Carnegie Institute, the Chicago Art Institute, the Museum of Modern Art, and the Walker Art Center, for example), at the few screening houses devoted to these genres of film (Anthology Film Archives, the Collective for Living Cinema, and Millennium in New York; the Cinematheque in San Francisco; the Funnel in Toronto; the Pasadena Filmforum (now in Los Angeles); Film in the Cities in St. Paul; Pittsburgh Filmmakers; SWAMP in El Paso when Willie Varela was running it; and a number of others), and at some colleges, universities, and art schools. For the most part the films are distributed passively by the Film-makers' Cooperative in New York and the Canyon Cinema Coopera-

The first seven pages of Frampton's screenplay in Poetic Justice *(1972), photographed from the book version published by the Visual Studies Workshop in 1973.*

tive in San Francisco (by *passively,* I mean that little or no promotion of films or filmmakers is provided; at most there is an up-to-date catalogue), and by the filmmakers themselves.[1] This separation between conventional movies and the critical cinema has, in fact, been so consistent during the past decade or two that the critical cinema's existence at the margin of the socio-economic system of film has become nearly institutionalized. This development and certain of its implications have been the focus of theoretical films by Morgan Fisher.

Fisher's spare, intellectually dense films often provide implicit polemics about the nature of the avant-garde response to the commercial cinema. *Production Stills,* for example, uses a serial grid structure similar to those used by Snow, Murphy, and Iimura: during a single continuous eleven-minute shot, a series of Polaroid images apparently taken during this long take, are mounted before us; they reveal moments during the making of the film we are looking at. What is unusual, however, is that the mechanisms being used to shoot this minimalist avant-garde film are Industry mechanisms: a Mitchell 16mm camera on a crab dolly on a soundstage, with a Fisher boom for the mike and a Nagra recorder. Fisher's film suggests that even when theoretical filmmakers

1. Two exceptions to passive distribution include the Museum of Modern Art, which distributes selected avant-garde filmmakers, and the American Federation of Arts, which offers packages of specific types of avant-garde films, of the work of individual filmmakers, and of the film programs presented at the Whitney Museum as part of the Biennial.

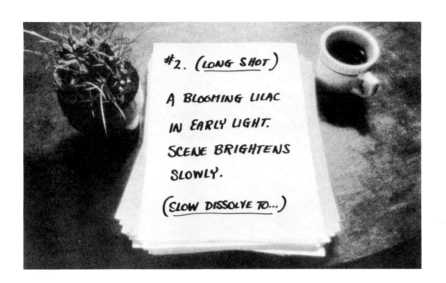

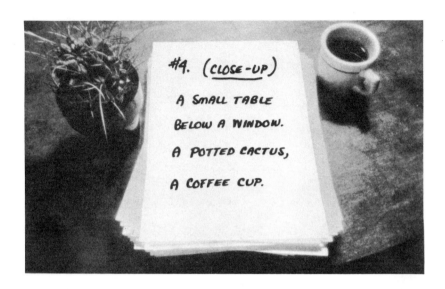

explore elements of the film experience presumably more fundamental to the medium than the articulation of action and character that is the focus of the commercial cinema, and even when they conduct these examinations in avant-garde filmic structures, they must generate their films with equipment and processes devised by the Industry or developed as cheaper, more accessible alternatives to the real thing. Any cinematic critique of dominant cinematic practice, in other words, is inevitably indebted to and part of the dominant cinema itself.

The foregoing review of some of the approaches developed by the film-makers interviewed for this volume may look like an attempt at a history of at least one major area of recent independent cinema. But while I would contend that the filmmakers I have talked with would need to be included in any thorough history of the most interesting and useful independent cinema of recent decades, anyone familiar with this area is well aware that my interviews only begin to suggest the size and diversity of North American independent cinema. In fact, I am continuing my exploration and thus far have interviewed Jonas Mekas, Robert Breer, James Benning, Anthony McCall, Su Friedrich, Lizzie Borden, and Ross McElwee—a promising start for a second volume.

It is my fervent hope that this volume, and any successors, will help to create a climate where the remarkable accomplishments of a massive body of work can be more widely recognized and used. At the moment, the future of much of this work seems tenuous at best. By now, most people working in the area of film study seem to know that a certain amount of avant-garde work exists, but opportunities to see the work seem to be constricting rather than expanding: there is that small network of venues where critical cinema can be seen by the public, and a certain amount of the work is rented for use in colleges and art schools. But one can scarcely call the situation encouraging, particularly given the current tendency to cut back on public support of the arts.

The situation is exacerbated by the widespread inadequacy of good screening facilities for critical films. We have all been frustrated by conditions at commercial theaters, but ironically, they are almost always far better than conditions at the screening spaces available to critical filmmakers at academic institutions, libraries, or art museums. During the late 1960s and early 1970s, when enthusiasm for experimental forms of independent cinema seemed at its highest, there were efforts to design screening rooms with the care normally devoted to art galleries and concert spaces. The "invisible cinema" Peter Kubelka designed for Anthology Film Archives was a relatively well known but largely unsuccessful effort in this direction.[2] More successful efforts oc-

2. Housed for several years at the Public Theater on Lafayette Street in New York, the Invisible Cinema was designed to maximize the viewer's ability to concentrate on the film being presented. The theater was completely black, and the individual theater seats had baffles on the sides to keep audience members from talking to each other. The idea seemed to be to create a space

curred at SUNY Binghamton, at the Collective for Living Cinema, and no doubt in other places as well. But such efforts are isolated occurrences. Some filmmakers have mounted their own campaigns against what they consider inadequate conditions. I have seen Ernie Gehr, Larry Gottheim, and others halt screenings in order to adjust lighting or sound before beginning again. As often as not, this tactic has merely added to the annoyance of audiences whose limited experience with critical cinema makes screenings a frustrating challenge. And yet my sympathies have usually been with the filmmakers in these instances: their hope, I would guess, is that by embarrassing the exhibitor, they can create a climate where more care will be taken with the particulars of film exhibition.

One might ask why we need embrace a critical cinema at all. Since this body of work remains such a marginal part of even educated viewers' experience, since it continually challenges and frustrates those unfamiliar with its mission and tactics, and since it requires screening conditions seemingly beyond the capabilities or the concern of many institutions, why bother with it? After all, the same period that has produced the films discussed above has also witnessed a remarkable flourishing of critical and theoretical writing about nearly every dimension of the cinematic experience. Why not confine our film-critical endeavors to expository prose, a medium we all agree is both sophisticated and accessible? There are at least two answers to such questions. The first is the pleasure and enlightenment that the critical cinema offers. For those of us who have followed its complex history, it has provided at least as much enjoyment and variety of stimulation as any other dimension of film history of comparable size. I would not wish to see only critical films (in fact, as is clear from the foregoing discussion, such an idea is a contradiction in terms: if one is not familiar with the dominant commercial cinema, one cannot understand criticism of it) any more than I would wish to see only documentaries or only animations. But to be deprived of the various experiences available in the critical films would be as depressing to me as to be deprived of any other major contribution to film history. As a film educator and writer, my commitment is to the fullest articulation of cinematic possibilities.

The second answer is the difference between experiencing film criticism in a theater and experiencing it in expository prose. While I cannot imagine seriously studying film without reading and writing about it, I have always felt that the distance between seeing movies in theaters and reading about them in journals and books is a significant problem. There are three aspects of this problem, the most obvious of which is the inevitable gap between what gets

---

where many people could experience avant-garde film, not as a group, but as discrete individuals. In my limited experience with it, however, the Invisible Cinema seemed, if not exactly oppressive, over-determined: I found the desire to peek around the baffles, and in general to be in contact with other audience members, irresistible. See Kubelka's comments in *Design Quarterly* 93 (1974), a special issue on film spaces, published by the Walker Art Center.

communicated during the four-dimensional experience of the movie theater and what can be encoded in writing. The easiest element of cinema for prose to comment on is narrative (which may account for the interest in narrative that has developed during recent decades as film-critical/theoretical writing has proliferated). The subtleties of the intricate filmic structures so common in the critical cinema are, however, exceedingly difficult to describe, much less to analyze convincingly in prose. The act of writing down what one has seen and heard often radically distorts the original experience much like a poor translation does. The second aspect of the problem is that, if one limits film criticism to prose, the theater experience tends to become a sphere of uncritical activity. By writing about movies, we inform each other of what we discover in the films we see, and we hope that some others will read what we have written and will understand and remember it when they go to the movies. But it seems unlikely that we make much impact on the medium itself or its primary audience: only the tiniest percentage of filmgoers read serious film criticism. In effect, our insights tend to be conveniently hidden from the sphere they pretend to critique. The third aspect of the problem is that the act of writing about film rarely helps to shift the process of film production into a more progressive direction. My guess is that the people who make the dominant cinema, who play a major role in constructing the ways in which we come to see each other and ourselves, rarely read serious film analysis and care very little, if at all, about what we find when we decode the ideological implications of the films they make. In fact, despite all the intelligent writing flooding into the editorial offices of academic film journals, the dominant cinema does not seem to be growing more sensitive to the politics of gender that it markets or to other related issues.

While I cannot pretend that the critical cinema can entirely answer such concerns, I would suggest that an attempt to generate a meaningful and effective written critique of the dominant cinema might have considerably more long-term impact if it were more consistently combined—especially in academic settings—with regular screenings of critical films, in theaters designed to maximize their impact. First, by seeing well-made, intelligent critical films in an environment in which one has been accustomed to seeing conventional movies, the viewer develops a more complete awareness of the nature of this environment and of the rigid parameters of its conventional use. If viewers were to have the opportunity to experience critical films with any regularity at all, this expanded awareness would not only begin to inform all of their conventional movie experiences, foregrounding both what the commercial movies do and what they avoid doing, but it would also develop in a substantial portion of the viewers the capacity to have other, more thoughtful kinds of filmic pleasure. And once this process was under way, it would provide a demand for film rentals and print purchases that would assure the maintenance of past accomplishments and provide opportunities for further production. It would, from within the medium itself, invigorate the medium and our ability to critique those elements of it that we are concerned about. Cinema has matured enough to provide its own critique; whether we will be able to provide a setting where this criticism can thrive is another question.

A few comments about my particular choices of interview subjects and the process used to generate the interviews are in order. From the beginning I have seen the process of interviewing as an educative one: I have wanted to talk with those filmmakers whose work I have felt I needed the most guidance with. Geography has also played a role. Living in upstate New York during the 1970s, I was an easy drive from Gottheim in Binghamton, only a few miles from Frampton's home in Eaton, New York, and from Huot's farm in New Berlin, New York; and for a time Murphy was teaching at Hamilton College in Clinton, New York. Since these were some of the filmmakers whose work I was most puzzled and challenged by, they were early interview subjects.

Once the interview process was under way, I found I was learning so much from it that I decided to explore more seriously, and I began interviewing filmmakers living in New York City: Schneemann, Chomont, Iimura, the Bs, Dick, Rainer, Mangolte, Barrie. Of course, I was interested in interviewing filmmakers with some reputation, but I was also determined to talk with filmmakers who were not widely known, even in the world of independent filmmaking. I assumed—and I remain convinced that this was a correct assumption—that, given the nature of making films independently, the most interesting filmmakers are not necessarily those we know about at any particular point in time. Often filmmakers work for ten or fifteen years before their work is seen by anyone other than close friends, or they continue to make interesting work long after critics and programmers have discovered new interests.

As my interviews accumulated, the limitations of talking with people in only one geographic region became increasingly troubling to me. Though the filmmakers I was talking with had come to New York from a variety of places, there were obviously a great many filmmakers who were rarely, if ever, in New York. During the summer of 1981 (with the help of a National Endowment for the Humanities summer grant), I traveled to the West Coast to talk with Fisher, Kuchar, Nelson, and Conner. And during this same period I began making plans to go to Europe: Malcolm Le Grice and others had argued convincingly that the considerable independent filmmaking activity in England and on the Continent had to be seen and considered before one could presume to talk about avant-garde film. Finally, however, I decided against pursuing this avenue, since I could not foresee any circumstance that would allow such an expansion of the boundaries of my activity to be practical: how could I interview filmmakers about highly intellectual films in languages not my own, and how could I free enough time for the many screenings and the study necessary for in-depth interviewing? Further, there was more and more evidence that avant-garde film activity in England and Europe was being documented (or would be) by people with far greater access to and context for the work.

In some cases, I have made plans to do interviews that have not yet been recorded. I've been pursuing Ernie Gehr for years, so far without any real success. In other instances, I've hoped to talk with subjects who were not interested: I was rebuffed by Gregory Markopoulos, for example, in no uncertain terms. And in still other instances, filmmakers whose work is of considerable interest to me were capably interviewed just at the time when I felt ready to talk with them: Sylvère Lotringer interviewed Jack Smith for *Semiotext* in 1978, for example. Finally, there are filmmakers I have so far decided against interviewing simply because, after exploring the available material relating to their careers, I have found that they have written and talked so extensively about their own work that an interview seemed likely to add very little: Stan Brakhage and Paul Sharits can serve as instances. I did begin an interview with Yvonne Rainer, but when the results had been edited, we agreed that nothing of substance was available in the interview that had not appeared in other interviews or in Rainer's own writing.

My interviewing process has remained relatively consistent. I have always assumed that, to be useful in the long term, interviews need to be a good deal more than transcribed recordings of the comments filmmakers make at screenings of their work. For me, an interview must be an index of an extended, in-depth engagement with the subject's films. This involves careful study of all the films a filmmaker has in distribution, as well as material not generally available. Once I have looked at a particular body of work as exhaustively as seems useful, I arrange to talk at length with the filmmaker. In most cases, I have designed my questions so that our conversations will proceed chronologically, film by film, though there have been instances (Conner, for example, and Kuchar) where this procedure has turned out to be impractical. While I always have many specific questions, I rarely try to control the direction of a filmmaker's comments, and I make no effort to limit how much a filmmaker says. From the start, the goal of my interviewing has been to provide a space where filmmakers can have as complete a say about their understanding of their work as they are willing to provide. Once I have transcribed a set of tapes, I edit extensively, using the transcript as the raw material for the interview. I make every effort to produce conversations that capture the specifics of what the filmmaker has meant to communicate and that suggest, in an unobtrusive way, I hope, something of the manner in which the filmmaker communicates. When I have an edited draft of the interview, I send it back to the filmmaker for corrections, additions, and subtractions. In some cases (Fisher, Nelson) the submission of what looked to be a completed interview turned out to be merely the first stage of a continuing interchange between the filmmaker and myself.

The choice of which interviews to include in this volume and which to withhold for another involved several considerations. To have selected the first seventeen interviews I recorded would have narrowed the range of work represented in this volume too radically. To have chosen only the better-known filmmakers would have had a similar effect. I decided finally to include as broad a range of filmmakers and commentary as possible and to withhold a number of important interviews—for a second volume. The order of the seventeen interviews included here corresponds roughly to the order in which I completed them.

Hollis Frampton

When Hollis Frampton died in March of 1984, he left behind him several hundred finished films, as well as many photographs and Xerox works and a distinguished body of writings on film and photography (much of it collected in *Circles of Confusion,* published in 1983 by the Visual Studies Workshop in Rochester, New York). Though he produced memorable work in all these media, Frampton remains most important as a filmmaker. And as a filmmaker, he is probably best known for the almost legendary intelligence that informed his filmmaking. In fact, my decision to do an extended interview with Frampton was a result of his reputation as perhaps the most intellectually challenging filmmaker in North America. While there seems little question about Frampton's intellectual accomplishments, his reputation as a "genius" has probably been a barrier between the films and some viewers, and it has certainly obscured the good (albeit rather dry) humor of much of his work and its frequent visual elegance. Frampton's best work, however, is as enjoyable as it is intellectually challenging.

Much of Frampton's intellectual reputation is probably a function of his being widely read, particularly in areas often outside the purview of visual artists: he was conversant with the history of science and mathematics, for example, and he was fascinated with modern fiction and poetry, especially with Ezra Pound (he spent a good deal of time with Pound near the end of the poet's life), James Joyce, and Jorge Luis Borges. In fact, I have a suspicion that the shape of Joyce's career—his movement from short stories to long, increasingly difficult experimental novels—had a substantial impact on Frampton's progression from short films to the longer experimental works, *Zorns Lemma* (1970) and *Hapax Legomena* (1971–72), and finally to the epic

370-part *Magellan* (1971–80), the title of which seems, at least in part, an allusion to Joyce's *Ulysses*.

Frampton originally came to film from the fine arts, and his background as artist and photographer is evident in his earliest films, several of which include portraits of or appearances by artists who were fixtures in the mid- to late-1960s art scene. *Manual of Arms* (1966), the earliest Frampton film in distribution, includes portraits of sculptors Carl Andre and Lee Lozano, dancers Lucina Childs and Twyla Tharp, painters Robert Huot, Larry Poons, and Rosemarie Castoro, filmmaker Joyce Wieland, filmmaker-sculptor-painter-musician Michael Snow, and others. Huot, Tharp, Lozano, Andre, and Castoro also appear in *Artificial Light* (1969); *Snowblind* (1968) features Snow and one of his sculptures; and *Lemon* (1969) includes the inscription "for Robert Huot."

Frampton's fine arts background is also evident in the structures of his early films, which owe almost nothing to the history of commercial film (except that they imply a rejection of commercial codes) and a great deal to the tendency of many late 1960s painters, sculptors, and other artists to explore fundamentals by limiting the number of elements used in a work and using them in predetermined, systematic ways. *Manual of Arms* presents its fourteen portraits using minimal means (the lighting is simple, and each subject has apparently been given the same basic instructions in the same empty, darkened space) and a serial structure: all the subjects are introduced in fourteen-second shots, each separated from the next by forty frames of dark leader; then the portraits are presented in the same order (the length of each portrait seems to depend on the subject). *Maxwell's Demon* (1968)—an "hommage to the physicist James Clerk Maxwell, father of thermodynamics and analytic color theory," according to Frampton's note in the *Film-makers' Cooperative Catalogue, No. 6*—regularly alternates between footage from a Canadian Air Force Exercise film and twenty-four-frame passages of ocean waves, divided into six four-frame color segments. *Palindrome* (1969) organizes found-imagery discarded by a film lab into a complex palindromic sequence. *Artificial Light* uses the same sequence of imagery twenty times, but in each instance this material is presented in a different way: in one instance Frampton paints on the footage, in another he erases portions of it, in still another he presents it upside down, and so on.

Frampton's systematic approach to film structure reached perhaps its most elaborate exposition in *Zorns Lemma* (1970), where the original twenty-four-letter Roman alphabet is used as the basic module for a complex and fascinating filmic system so different from conventional narrative development that at first viewers tended to be mystified. *Zorns Lemma* remains a monumental accomplishment, and in retrospect one can see the considerable influence of Eadweard Muybridge, whose *Animal Locomotion* series fascinated Frampton ("Eadweard Muybridge: Fragments of a Tesseract," is one of his most interesting essays, and in 1975 he and Marion Faller collaborated on an elaborate joke on the *Animal Locomotion* series, *Sixteen Studies from Vegetable Locomotion*). In order to study the movements of people and animals, Muybridge usually photographed their actions in front of a linear grid; then, once he had made the individual photographs, they were arranged in a grid so that the viewer could see each phase of photographed movement next to the others. *Zorns Lemma* is divided into three sections, each representing a phase in the process of learning (particularly, the process of learning language) that begins in early childhood and continues until adulthood. In the brief first section, a schoolmarmy voice reads verses from *The Bay State Primer,* an early English rhetoric used in New England, while the viewer watches a dark screen. The verses focus on words beginning with successive letters of the alphabet, which becomes one of the central grid structures in *Zorns Lemma.* The long second section begins with a run-through of the Roman alphabet, then proceeds to reveal, in silence, an immense collection of environmental words that are presented in alphabetic sets, one second per word. They form an immense spatial-temporal grid. As set after set of the words is revealed, a second development comes to dominate this central section of the film: gradually each of the word positions within each twenty-four-part alphabetic set is replaced by one-second segments of a continuous action: Robert Huot painting a wall, eggs frying, the pages of a book being turned. A new kind of narrative develops for viewers, who begin to follow the sequential actions (the length of each of which coincides with the time remaining in the central section of the film) and to wonder which letter will be replaced next. When the last letter has been replaced, the middle section of the film ends. In the concluding section, we watch a man (Robert Huot), a woman, and a dog walk away from the camera, across a field, and into the woods, in a series of roll-long shots, edited to look like a single continuous shot. The final section is the first with both imagery and sound: we hear several people reading an eleventh-century scientific-philosophic text: *On Light, or the Ingression of Forms* by Robert Grosseteste. The voices alternate, each one reading a single word at a time. Just as the alphabetic system of the short first section continues during the second section, the one-second rhythm introduced in the second section continues here. The voices read in time to a metronome marking off a one-second beat.

The three sections of *Zorns Lemma* create an experience so different from the forms of narrative that characterize commercial cinema that the narrative implications of the film's progressive structure can be easily overlooked. Instead of identifying with a fictional character and vicariously experiencing this character's adventures, the viewer of *Zorns Lemma* metaphorically relives phases of an educational process that, from Frampton's point of view, characterize contemporary experience. The film is simultaneously a deflected autobiography of Frampton's progress from child-in-the-dark to philosophic thinker and a grid against which viewers can measure their own educational development. In addition, *Zorns Lemma* is a beautiful film to look at. It remains Frampton's most remarkable single film.

Frampton's next work, the seven-part *Hapax Legomena* (1971–72) is, like *Zorns Lemma,* a deflected autobiographical narrative. In this case, however, the subject is Frampton's development from photographer to filmmaker and his subsequent exploration of the new medium. The first three sections of *Hapax Legomena—nostalgia* (1971), *Poetic Justice* (1972), and *Critical Mass* (1971)—are some of Frampton's most impressive (and accessible) films. In *nostalgia* we see close-ups of a series of photographs (mostly his own) as they are burned, one by one, on a hot plate. As we look at each image burning, we listen to Michael Snow read a discussion of the image we will see next. The grid structure so common to Frampton's early films remains evident here: each section is one roll of 16mm film long (approximately two minutes, fifty seconds). In *Poetic Justice* the viewer reads a 240-page "screenplay" one page at a time. A story of a stressed relationship between a photographer and his lover is evident within the verbal and visual labyrinth created by Frampton's ingenious text. *Critical Mass* uses forms of visual and auditory repetition reminiscent of the work of Gertrude Stein (whom Frampton greatly admired) to dramatize a lover's quarrel between a young man and woman. Ironically, Frampton's heavy manipulation of both sound track and image creates one of the most believable arguments I have ever seen enacted in film. The remaining four sections of *Hapax Legomena* are rather unmemorable, especially when compared to the first three. While one can argue for the coherence of the seven-part work, the qualities that give the best of Frampton's early work its power—the sensuousness of the visuals, the rigorously organized intellectuality, the poignant autobiographical implications, the dry humor—are mostly absent in the final four sections.

By the time he was finishing *Hapax Legomena*, Frampton had begun to think seriously about what was to become his largest undertaking: *Magellan,* "a 36-hour film, organized and meant to be viewed calendrically over the course of 371 days" (Jenkins and Krane, p. 115). Frampton worked on the *Magellan* films from the end of 1971 until the early 1980s, nearly completing the epic work. The central concept of *Magellan* is an extension of the Ulysses story. Magellan's circumnavigation of the earth is used as a metaphor for Frampton's quest to aesthetically unite, within a single gigantic work, the two hemispheres of the brain. While I do not believe I have seen all of *Magellan* (since Frampton changed the titles of various sections and the sections themselves as he worked on the film, I cannot be sure that the films I saw during the late 1970s and early 1980s remain in *Magellan*), and while I certainly cannot claim to have explored it in the detail it deserves, I must confess that, by and large, I have found the individual sections of the film much less engaging than the work Frampton did through 1972. It is as if the individual *Magellan* films

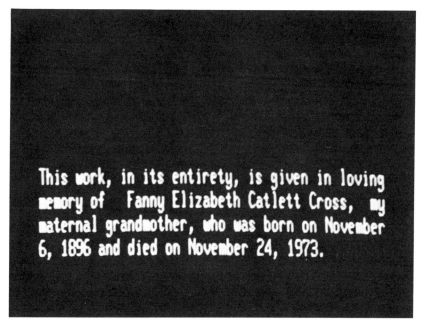

The dedication for Magellan, *presented as an epigraph to* Gloria! *(1979). Frame enlargement by Biff Henrich. © Hollis Frampton Estate, 1985.*

could not, or at least did not, live up to Frampton's grandiose plan. This is not to say that the *Magellan* films are not worth watching or that there are no memorable ones. I admire *Less* (1973), *Straits of Magellan: Drafts & Fragments* (1974), and especially the lovely homage to Frampton's maternal grandmother (and his first computer-generated film), *Gloria!* (1979). But, for all their visual and structural elegance, many of the films seem somehow empty of the personal passion that, deflected or reconstituted, gives Frampton's best early work its power. (For more about the structure of *Magellan,* see Henderson.)

Regardless of how Frampton's career is finally assessed, however, his considerable contribution to North American film history is obvious. He has to his credit not only a sizable body of first-rate films but also a remarkable faith that, despite the dominance of a commercial narrative cinema that ministers, for the most part, to its sense of the lowest common denominator of its mass audience, film artists could and should aspire to forms of cinema that can engage the intellect, the aesthetic sense, and the emotions of film viewers at levels comparable to those that readers are willing to bring to a poet like Pound or a fiction writer like Joyce.

My interview with Frampton was conducted in several sessions beginning in 1976 and continuing until 1978.

MacDonald: Your early films were made quite a while ago. Is it hard for you to talk about them?

Frampton: Well, I like my own early films more than I like a lot of other people's.

MacDonald: In a couple of places you've said that *Manual of Arms* is the first film you will publicly admit to having made. That suggests there are films you don't publicly admit to or don't want to distribute.

Frampton: There were earlier things, only one of which will ever conceivably turn up again. The others are lost. I started making films in 1962, but I wasn't prolific. It was expensive to do. There were three long films and a short one before *Process Red* [1966], which is the earliest finished film I now distribute. The first was called *Ten Mile Poem*—ghastly stuff. It was shot in Brooklyn from the Myrtle Avenue elevated, which has since been torn down. The film was in motion the whole time. It ran from the heart of downtown Brooklyn out to Metropolitan Avenue on the border of Queens. It was probably about twenty-five minutes—rather long—and was shot over a period of three or four months on Saturdays and Sundays. I filmed out the side window, perpendicular to the travel of the train, with moderate telephoto lenses, so that unless a backyard suddenly opened on vistas of laundry, the contents of the frame tended to wipe out, to become abstract, to flatten. The film was in color, silent, and was projected until it dropped dead.

A second film was shot in Fort Green Park, again in Brooklyn, not because I lived there, but because at that time I was seeing a great deal of Carl Andre, who lived half a block away. In the park there was a great set of stairs that went down from the square court in which the Prison Ship Martyrs' Monument stands. The stairs dropped through a dozen levels down to Myrtle Avenue. The film I made there was called *A Running Man*. It was elaborate to do because I couldn't get anybody else to operate the camera, and I couldn't get anybody else to run. I would laboriously set up a shot, put the self-timer on, and do my own running. It was a landscape film that was held together as a picaresque by an unidentified man who ran through the shots, who might appear anywhere in the space, go through it in some way, and exit—all at full tilt. It was about twenty-five minutes long, and ended in a laborious and jerky parody of the Odessa Steps, which was probably as fragmented as the Eisenstein sequence but used just the one runner, who ran up and down the steps, appeared and disappeared, was seen in multiple superimposition, and so on. It was a piece of work in which I was learning specifically about the ways in which film can relate different spaces to each other, or one subset of those ways. It was supposed to be serious, but the effect was ineffably comical: the indefatigable poker-faced runner concentrating so hard, because, of course, there wasn't film to waste. That one got projected to death, too.

Then, in 1964, a huge film in black-and-white negative, all clouds and skies that dissolved from one to another; phrases—typewritten "poetic" phrases—were superimposed. The phrases appeared in different places in the frame. I had it printed on color positive stock—all in Mallarmé azure—a monochrome blue film—very long, fifty minutes. Then I lost the print on the subway and couldn't afford another, and the negative got wiped out, along with a lot of other stuff, in one of those events that seem to happen only to young artists: pipes burst, things got drenched, and so forth. I was quite fond of it, but that's okay.

Finally, there was a very tiny film, in three shots and less than a minute long, called *Obelisk Ampersand Encounter.* First, a slow, very shaky pan down Cleopatra's Needle outside the Metropolitan Museum. Then, in a brief black space on the screen, a male voice that I had clipped out of a junk movie said "and." Then a second image: in a lunchtime crowd on Third Avenue, two people—two friends of mine who I had bribed to do it—collided violently with each other and then went on their way. That was all. My first sound film. Well, I was so dumb in 1965 that I took the material to Movielab to have it printed. They lost my original. I went back to get it, and the counterman said, "We lost it." Very bland. I said, "What do you mean, you lost it?" And the guy answered, "That little piece of shit couldn't be worth very much anyway." So with tears, genuine tears, running down my fresh young cheeks, I departed, never to return to Movielab. So that's the earlier-than-early work. Before that you drift back into still photography, and before *that,* the tail end of infatuations with poetry and painting. All four films were extremely tentative, to put it gently.

I had been aware that there was such a thing as avant-garde film from Cinema-16 days and from film societies in school, where we rented Cocteau's *Orpheus,* but I had absolutely no sense, in 1962–63–64, that there was a film scene. I went to screenings, but a lot of what I saw seemed as though it wasn't going anywhere. With the exception of Brakhage and of Breer (whose work was not seen), there was very little. There were people around, such as Charles Boultenhouse, who made films occasionally. They were pseudo-narratives with tormented protagonists who expressed themselves by breaking glass with their hands. Pretty boring, I thought.

At that time I was nominally a still photographer. There were only one or two places in New York that showed photography. Norbert Kleber had a little gallery, the Underground, in his front hall on 10th Street (Duane Michals first showed there), and there was another place on 10th Street east of Third Avenue that showed photographs. But nobody was particularly interested.

In the late fifties, photography was still locked in the grip of the 8 × 10-view-camera–F-64 school, which included people like Weston and Strand and which had become massively academicized. It had produced such entities as Ansel Adams and Minor White. There was an enormous stasis; photography was obviously something only old masters did. It produced a stasis in me, too, because to a degree I identified with it and got myself up a tree that I was never quite able to climb down until I completely got out of it. Actually, I still do photography periodically.

It may be worthwhile to recall that, from when I got to New York in 1958 until deep into the sixties, there were big doin's afoot in art. Those big doin's had almost exclusively to do with painting and sculpture—and, to a much lesser extent, with performance and dance. Most of the people who started to make films in a serious way around the time I did had matured artistically in some other terrain. There was no hearing for anyone in either still photography or film. It's hard now for newcomers to realize how heroic Mekas's efforts were. It was possible to disagree with him, to scream at him, to feel at any given moment that he was full of shit, but his faith and persistence were the only game in town for years. Jonas not only scrounged screening spaces, he picked up the tab personally and went around and begged people to put up money. It was astonishing.

That's not so long ago, either. I remember when somebody finally got a job *teaching* film. Gregory Markoupolos was hired in Chicago for a year, for a quite princely eight grand; he pretty much played Genius-in-Residence, it was said, and at the end of the year the appointment wasn't renewed. The general feeling was that he'd blown it for everybody. Of course, there were other jobs. I worked in film labs, but heaven knows what other people did to stay alive. Ken Jacobs used to go down to the Fulton fish market and find old fish. Brakhage told me he tried to get a job making pizza! It was a very unpromising situation.

MacDonald: You mentioned that *Process Red* is your first finished film in distribution. How did you get into using multiple modes of presentation? In *Process Red* there is red-tinted imagery of hands doing things, black-and-white imagery of activities on a street, photographic frames of solid white and red, as well as a variety of kinds of direct manipulation of the film.

Frampton: Maybe I can answer the question better if I recontextualize it. Once upon a time it was felt to be important that, in any given work, there be a unity of decorum. A work might not look the same all the time or be the same all the way through, but one general way of making the thing, or one look that it had, should be in evidence. The first modernist art that seized me—during my adolescence—was modern English poetry. One of the striking things about *The Waste Land,* which apparently made it unintelligible at first, is that it tends to shift decorum in every line. Of course, the possibility that a poem could look a different way in every consecutive line turned out to be a tremendously powerful tool for composition. By shifting decorum, a work could also shift place, time, semantic context; it could drag in whole cultures by the bootstraps. It might be reasonable to trace this tendency in Eliot, Pound, and, indeed, even in Joyce (*Ulysses* is, among other things, an essay about shifts in decorum) to the symbolists. So I was coming from there, and, indeed, from a much more general cultural context, part of which had recognized as an option violent shifts in decorum.

Much as we think about painting in the fifties and sixties as having been highly decorous, plenty of work was not. A given painting or group of paintings by Pollock or by Stella might be in the same decorum, but a great deal of the force of Rauschenberg's work depended on violent ruptures in decorum. De Kooning did newsprint transfer. Lay a piece of printed pictorial material down on the paint and peel it off; the solvent of the paint will strip the ink away. Critical effort was expended on turning those into abstract pictorial elements. They weren't. They were illusionist ruptures in the decorum. I remember a series of paintings that Hans Hofmann showed at the end of the fifties or the beginning of the sixties at the Sam Kootz Gallery, which were very loosely painted in dark transparent color and were, for the most part, quite typical of the tendency of action painting to generate deep spaces automatically through semitransparent layers that recede endlessly behind one another. But then, right on the surface, palpably on the surface, I recall primary-color, hard-edged rectangles with strong impasto, which very clearly had been put on with masking tape. They were extremely indecorous spaces.

I certainly was not the first person to physically torture the surface of film, although I may have done it with a larger vocabulary than some, nor was I the first to use open frames of pure color or even to use color monochrome or to mix color and black and white. I may have forced all of them together a little more brutally than others. All I had to lose was the look of its being *recognizably* a film, which seemed to me to be utterly expendable. While there was interesting work being done at that time, there was no contemporary work that I felt had an absolute claim on my attention.

Something analogous to what I felt about film was happening in dance during the same period. There had been something called modern dance that had acquired a vocabulary of its own, a fixed decorum—the bare foot and "floor work" and so forth that extends from the epigones of Graham and Limon to Twyla Tharp, who extends and embroiders balletic diction, or a balletic-and-modern diction. That, too, did not seem to constitute a claim. I remember the first thing I ever saw Yvonne Rainer do. I was in some loft—was it Brooklyn? I don't remember. There were not many people—a small, word-of-mouth crowd. She did a piece called *Three Satie Spoons,* solo dances to *Three Pieces in the Shape of a Pear.* In the middle of it she started making *noises:* little mewing sounds, squeaks, bleats. I was electrified, because it was totally disjunctive within the situation. There she was in a black leotard, doing something that *looked like* a dance. There was music. And then she did something that seemed to have nothing to do with dance, and there was the momentary question, is she going crazy? Is this the moment? Are we witnessing it? Are *we* going crazy? Dance had been mute. The vocal capability of the dancer had been put beyond the pale. No mouth, or at most, the fixed mannequin smile of the ballerina. That brief performance of Yvonne's was totally memorable for me, not so much because of the choreography or the music or the skill of that young person. What was memorable was a violent disruption of, a transgression against, the culturally expected, that had been introduced into the very heart of the thing. What was important was not that she made the specific noises that she did, but that that single gesture broke open the whole decorum of dance. But again, what did she have to lose?

I made most of *Process Red* in about a week, and then I fussed with the poor thing for a year. I just couldn't leave it alone. Matisse remarked that every painting needs two people: one to paint it and the other to cut off the painter's hands when it is finished. As old as I was (I was thirty years old), I still had that kind of relation to *Process Red.* I kept cutting back into it, fiddling with it, caressing it. Finally I just stopped because I had other things to do.

MacDonald: Two other films that you did in 1966—*Manual of Arms* and *Information*—are very different from *Process Red.* A question about the procedure you used in *Manual of Arms:* Had you decided in advance to use fourteen people whom you knew well, and had you thought out ways in which you could capture some crucial aspects of them, or was it more spontaneous?

Frampton: I established a set of conditions within which, nominally, anything that happened would suit me fine. What I had in mind was a series of portraits, but portraits that had to do with the kinesics of the people involved, the way they disposed themselves in a space under very limiting conditions. There was a plain backdrop, one light with a little bounce fill, and a stool. The rule was that you didn't have to sit on the stool, but you had to stay near it. You could do anything you wanted to, or you could leave the space at any time you wanted to, at which moment the filming would stop. That was it. The gestures that I made with the camera and in editing had to do with my understanding of the people involved. Michael Snow comes out a prestidigitator and in the end advertises his *Walking Woman.* Some people I perceived as physically more active and aggressive. Lee Lozano, with whom I was living at the time, talked a blue streak from morning to night. She talked, as most people do, at once to reveal and obscure herself. Her portrait is part of the time her face and part of the time her shadow.

The film has the look of a New York loft, a certain overlay of gritty, claustrophobic funk that permeated that whole period. It's also a formalist's snap-

Michael Snow in Frampton's Manual of Arms *(1966). Frame enlargement by Biff Henrich. © Hollis Frampton Estate, 1986.*

shot album. Those people were friends of mine during a fairly interesting time. We were all lepers, "out-of-it," or what have you, with the possible exception of Larry Poons. I looked at it recently and found it rather touching.

MacDonald: It's very personal.

Frampton: It is, and more openly so than I hoped at the time. I used a severely defined and restricted set of conditions within which improvisations, sheer accidents, indeterminacies, could take place and later, during the editing, be dealt with in second-generation meditation.

MacDonald: The same general approach seems to be true of *Information,* where you decide in advance on a single light bulb, raw stock, and a camera, and then see what you can do with them. Most of the imagery is comparatively complex, despite the simplicity of the means. Were you doing a lot of superimposition in the camera?

Frampton: All the superimposition was done in the camera, at three distances. There were about two takes at each distance. It was highly edited, to break up my characteristic random gestures and make it gesturally more compact. Of course, by the time I had finished performing all manner of rotations and inversions on the order of shots, it came out looking more like uncut footage than the uncut footage did.

Information was intended as half of a collaboration with Twyla Tharp, who was then at the very beginning of her career. That collaboration never took place. I had thought to project the film into the performance space and use it as a lighting system. Since the light beams are narrow, the projected light itself becomes an artifact, particularly if there is a little smoke in the room. In fact, Twyla did use the film as part of a piece. She had it projected *across* the stage, from the wings, so that one saw the columns of light fluctuating. She asked a lot of people to come and smoke so that they could see it. It was done only one time.

MacDonald: You made *States* twice—once in 1967 and again in 1970. Why did you revise that particular film?

Frampton: The revision resulted from a problem with the smoke. The first time I shot *States,* I made the smoke in one of the ways it's conventionally made in the movies, with ammonium chloride, sal ammoniac. If you put a dish of ammonia and a dish of hydrochloric acid next to each other, the hydrogen chloride and ammonia meet in mid-air, combine chemically, and produce a salt in the form of a powdery mist. I used the rising convection currents from four candles to carry the two gasses up in the air and photographed the result against a black background. Well, it did make smoke: four thin, tremulous streamers of smoke that divided the screen into five vertical intervals. In a short segment, alongside the salt or milk, which are the materials for the other two "states," it tended to be invisible. That troubled me because I wanted the "states" to have equal visual density. Finally, I reshot the smoke, thinking I would cut the thing apart and put the new smoke imagery in. I took my trusty hot plate and vaporized ammonium chloride on it. That worked just fine; I had vigorous, swirling smoke, but the scale was marred: the smoke looked closer and overpowered the other two. I had to completely remake the film, using the first version as a recipe. The material was reshot in 1970, and I didn't finish recutting it until 1972. I loathed it; it was one of the most grinding, tedious jobs I've ever done in my life. I was so disgusted that I sent the new original to the lab, asked my timer to look at the print when it was done and tell me if it looked okay, and had it sent directly to the Film-Makers' Coop.

MacDonald: The way you interweave the different states to create a variety of rhythms has always struck me as rather musical. It reminds me sometimes of the Michael Snow piece *W in the D*. Did you have music in mind when you made *States?*

Frampton: I think it goes a little bit deeper than that. *States* was done "by the numbers"; it was one of the few times that I've made a real score, or graphic notation. There's a collision in *States:* three natural substances—all of which happen to be white—are filmed in such a way that their identity tends to be confused and disappear. While I was looking for a way to order that material, I thought about the intellectual artifice of number series and, yet, the manner in which they tend to recur in nature. One particularly interesting series is called the Fibonacci series, in which each term is the sum of the previous two: start with 1 and, having thought of nothing better, write 1 again, add them and get 2. Add 1 and 2 and get 3, 2 and 3 and get 5, then 8, 13, 21, and so forth. The terms get big very fast. The series may be plotted linearly, but if you plot it in other ways, it produces interesting consequences. If you plot Fibonacci numbers as a spiral, you derive the natural spiral of the chambered nautilus. If you plot them as a rising curve on both negative and positive sides of the y axis and drop perpendiculars to x, then for any given negative and positive pair of quantities in the series you get a rectangle that has the proportions of 1 by $1 + \sqrt{5}/2$ the legendary Golden Section rectangle, which is found not only in ancient architecture but also in nature: in the proportions of the entire system of a tree or the Vitruvian man with arms outstretched, for instance.

One problem with Fibonacci numbers is that the series is insufficiently dense: if you say you will put an image at frame 1, frame 2, frame 3, frame 5, and so forth, pretty quickly you have an image out around frame 1,000. To avoid this problem, I took not only the original Fibonacci series, but its first four harmonics. That is, I multiplied each of the numbers by 1, 2, 3, and 4, which in musical terms would give you the fundamental, the octave, the twelfth, and the second octave. Then, in a field 1,000 seconds (or 24,000 frames) long, I allocated three different centers—¼, ½, and ¾ of the way through that 24,000-frame time line—for gas, liquid, and solid imagery to spread out from in both directions. The nice thing about the series is that it's not very symmetrical, which means that the states tended not to overlap each other.

So, while on one hand I had no particular piece of music, nor indeed music itself, in mind, I did use primitive procedures that are typical of music. The Pythagoreans, after all, derived all the tones in the untempered scale from multiplications and divisions of the frequencies of the fundamental tones. That kind of thing wasn't being done in film, but during the sixties there were musicians who were remanipulating the harmonic series in various ways. I'm thinking about LaMonte Young and, most especially, Tony Conrad, who has somehow been typed as the maker of *The Flicker,* period. Conrad did a series of pieces that involved extremely complex relations among tones. For instance, he might take a fundamental tone, calculate its 149th harmonic (which would be beyond the audible), divide it by a sufficiently large number to bring it down into the range of an instrument, and produce a frequency that was distinctly untempered with relation to the rest of the scale but that still had a fixed relationship to a fundamental tone. Playing the fundamental tone against the new frequency produced complex shifting different tones. That kind of activity has been considered perfectly legitimate and straightforward in music but for some reason has been considered overintellectual, or something like that, for film.

MacDonald: In the interview you did with Michael Snow for *Film Culture,* you describe how you made *Heterodyne* [1967]. Your procedure for that film reminds me very much of what you've been saying about *States.* In *Heterodyne* you developed a series of forty frequencies.

Frampton: Yes, that's what they are.

MacDonald: Did you know in advance where those forty frequencies would overlap, or did you discover *Heterodyne* as you went along?

Frampton: Heterodyne was based on prime numbers, each of which is used as a fundamental frequency. Primes are divisible only by themselves and 1, which means that they only interfere where they share equal multiples, and that's fairly rare. In the whole span of *Heterodyne* it happened only once and, in that instance, I left the event out. Did I know what the rhythms were going to be like? Well, as I typically do, I made several models and projected them until I found one that behaved the way I wanted it to. I wanted a sparse, tenuous structure that would *produce* fairly regular clumps of distinct activity but would not have a regular shape.

MacDonald: In both *Heterodyne* and *States* you seem very conscious of darkness as a positive element that a filmmaker can use, as opposed to a state where nothing is on the screen.

Frampton: Yes. There are problems that can be dealt with by annihilation. I don't see why, just because you *can* be seeing something all the time, you *must* be seeing something all the time. I've called these passages "silences"; in doing so, I indicate a debt to Cage. Cage proposed that just because you could be hearing something all the time didn't mean that you had to be. That struck me as a strategic option in film. In any case, because film stock is not truly opaque, you are always seeing something, the outline of the frame at least, and that itself is an enormous cultural icon: it tells you where the image would be if there were one. I am, as I think many filmmakers are, as preoccupied by the film frame as painting has been at various times by the limits of its support. Of course, the film frame is not malleable. There are only a few ways in which it can be manipulated: you can mask or matte or you can do the sorts of things that Paul Sharits has done in putting frames side by side or on top of each other, which expands the film frame but gives you all the problems of the painting frame in return. On the other hand, the time of the thing is malleable, and if you have twenty-four projected options per second, one of those options must be to project nothing.

MacDonald: I've always been struck with how much happens in *Heterodyne,* given the fact that if you hold the film up, the number of frames that are filled in seems relatively small.

Frampton: Once again, the real protagonist, the "first struggler," is the spectator, who is always trying to retrieve why the last event looked the way it did and to anticipate when the next one will come and what it will look like. Given the sense that there are rules, even if those rules are chance, the enterprise that you're involved in, in watching the thing, tends to make it replete. When discrete events do come, of course, they can be quite complex, brief as they are. At that time, I was, once more, listening quite a bit to Webern's music, which is full of clusterings of events within spaces—both "horizontal" spaces, or silences, and "vertical" spaces in which a very brief clump of sonic events will cross four and one-half octaves and five instrumental tone colors, with very large empty harmonic spaces in between. If you listen to a Mozart symphony with about half an ear, you can kid yourself that you're following its drift. With Webern it's an all-or-nothing situation. You have to concentrate to find the music. In a tiny way, *Heterodyne* imitates some of Webern's strategies. I was trying to get my filmmaking procedures back to some level where I felt I could be responsible for them. Webern once complained that people asked him why he didn't use an orchestra, when a voice and an instrument created problems so complex and possibilities so rich that they could occupy him for a lifetime. The same could be said even for *Heterodyne*'s few variables. Paul Sharits uses mostly frames of unmodulated color, and he has a distinguished body of work.

MacDonald: Maxwell's Demon is made up of two kinds of things: the man doing Canadian Air Force exercises and one-second passages of color frames and single-frame images of ocean waves. Even multiple viewings of the film would not necessarily reveal that the one-second passages are organized into six different color units and that the single frames of the ocean are added in a series going from no frames of ocean to all frames of ocean. Do you assume that the viewer will project the film *and* examine it on the rewind? Also, how did you decide on an organization for adding the ocean frames?

Frampton: I have tended to assume a culturally "normal" spectator situation, in which film is seen in a darkened room: the image is in front of you, the projector behind you, and so forth. Because I made this film a frame at a time as physical material, though, there are tiny events that are only fully apparent when you reexamine it as a filmstrip. *Maxwell's Demon* moves from relatively little activity to relatively great activity. The activities of the exercising man, which I took from an instructional film on Canadian Air Force exercises I'd bought for a buck on Canal Street, are graded to change from prone inertness to relatively violent scissoring movements. The one-second units perform a counting operation that follows the same general line: they go from less active to more active but within the frame. The six colors are, of course, the six additive and subtractive primaries. James Clerk Maxwell was responsible for the observation that the impression of any color may be synthesized with only three monochrome colors—red, green, and blue—of which cyan, magenta, and yellow are the subtractive complements (or white light *minus* red, *minus* green, *minus* blue). The six form a six-part wheel, which I exhibit in one second, four frames at a clip. Four frames is long enough to get a clear view of something.

The six parts may be understood as a six-bit binary number. There are 2^6, or sixty-four, possibilities for organizing two kinds of things in groups of six. That in its turn was suggested by sixty-five fragments of athletic action that presumably would have sixty-four spaces between them. It turned out that I had miscounted; there are only sixty-three spaces, and one six-bit binary number is missing. Such things break my heart, but there's nothing to do about them. The film maps sixty-four unique states for one second, which systematically pass from blank color to fully replete frames. In fact, all those segments were shot in the same place at the same time. I single-framed the ocean—with six filters and a white card to put in front of the lens—to a score, an extremely simple one. It was animated "on location," so to speak. I did have to wait around a long time to get a sea gull in that one blue frame. The sound track parallels the water imagery; it also changes from silence to a continuous one-second buzz, the buzz of sprocket holes. I used 8mm sprocket-hole buzz because the pitch is an octave higher than 16mm, and the higher pitch reproduces better on most sound systems. I had seen [Sharits's] *Ray Gun Virus* [1966] by that time, and the sound seemed weak to me.

MacDonald: In the Film-Makers' Coop catalogue you mention that *Snow-blind* proposes analogies for three perceptual modes and three historic montage styles. I think I understand the three perceptual modes—if they are perception while in motion, while light is changing, and while refocusing—but what montage styles are you referring to?

Frampton: The problem was to reconstruct an object that subsists in deep space and is ambiguous: specifically, a sculpture called *Blind* that Mike Snow showed at the Poindexter Gallery in 1967. In classic film editing, there are at least three strategies for reconstructing a deep-space object: one is to look at it and go around it; another is to pass through it; and another is to retrieve the object by retrieving an interaction of something else with it. The third is the most obvious. The last section of the film, where Mike gradually walks out of the piece in that "cubistified" way, is an obvious parody of the typical Eisensteinian gesture of intercutting the same action three or four times from three or four different points of view. I don't think I meant anything more than that. The next time there's a Coop catalogue, if there ever is another one, I'm going to withdraw all those statements. There's a compulsion to write something, but you don't really want to spill the jelly beans, so you try to offer clues. I'm not convinced that it's helpful.

MacDonald: When you made *Carrots and Peas* [1969], did you assume that viewers would become actively engaged with the film—in a physical sense—and listen to the soundtrack in reverse? I've assumed that once the quick alterations of the carrots-and-peas imagery at the beginning of the film are over, after viewers have stared at the single, unchanging image for several minutes, you mean for them to grow increasingly aware that the soundtrack may be English in reverse and curious enough to find out. Am I correct?

Frampton: It's always done, though I must say I did not expect that would happen when I made it.

MacDonald: That's a big surprise to me. Since the sound *is* English and since, specifically, it's someone talking about the Canadian Air Force exercises, I've assumed a connection between exercise as good health, the bowl of vegetables, and an active viewer.

Frampton: Oh, that's nice! For the life of me I never would have thought of it. I thought of the film as a set of ironies upon the form of the art history slide lecture. *Carrots and Peas* goes through its little vocabulary of images; the language is there as a kind of empty sign of the distraction of the lecturing voice, which, if you're actually looking at the images, goes in one ear and out the other. Of course, the first time anybody ever looked at the film out of my control, they immediately ran the track backwards. Although *Carrots and Peas* amuses me, it's not one of my favorite films. It's rather gorgeous to look at, all those reds and greens, which seem—if you just let them blur slightly— like a certain kind of all-over painting. The final tableau tends to look like a Poons of a slightly later period.

I'm fond of taking potshots at painting. As much as I love *some* paintings, as who does not, nevertheless the *making* of paintings is an activity about as arbitrary and ordinary as any I can think of. I find it amazing that it was so hugely cathected at a certain time, since it's fundamentally no more remarkable and interesting than scribbling words on pieces of paper or gluing strips of film together. At the time I made *Carrots and Peas,* I was perennially exasperated by the endless salivation over painting just *because* it was painting. That seems to have subsided in recent years [This naive remark preceded, by a couple of years, the regression of some critical practice to an "oracular" strategy, which proposes to resacralize painting by announcing what the 1980s *will have* shown: that painting, unique among *all* modes of human production, is an entirely self-justifying activity. Meanwhile, here below in the damp savannahs of contingency and contradiction, the voices of film and its companions betray inflections hoarse and odd. —H.F., 1980] Painting is in such sorry shape now that I wish there were something to salivate over.

Transposed to film, the slide lecture becomes an instructional film. I think that instructional films are often astounding, especially if you turn off the sound. They can be crazed. They're meant to be dense and parsimonious and to transmit large amounts of knowledge very quickly. There's a link between track and picture, and if they're deprived of each other and you have to depend on the intelligibility of only one, it can become something rich and strange. The film I call *Works and Days* [1969] was about how to plant a Victory Garden. The sound was a friendly British voice saying, "You do this," and "You do that." I saw it from a different point of view, which was suggested by things that were going on in dance in the work of Yvonne Rainer, Deborah Hay, Simone Forti. They had spent some time developing a choreography of prose gesture, rather than a specialized choreography of movements that you only make when you're dancing. Yvonne had made works that were task oriented—carrying things and so forth. When I saw *Works and Days,* I saw it as a work of choreography, with the rectangle of the garden as a stage and two plain people, costumed as British gardeners, doing astounding formal steps. The gesture of using their feet to put the dirt in over the potatoes and tramp it down was pure Yvonne Rainer. At a time when dance films were—as they always are—an absolute horror, I had found on Canal Street a great dance film that only became one when it had its sound track cut off.

MacDonald: You were speaking of painting a while ago. *Lemon* is dedicated to Robert Huot in a very pronounced way.

Frampton: I'll tell you why it's dedicated to Bob Huot. There are two reasons. One is that it's a film that points towards painting. The light first reveals the form as a sculptural entity and then devours it, transforms it into a graphic sign. Second, at the time that film was made, Huot had started to read *Ulysses,* and having no other warning about it, was reading it as he would any other work of prose fiction. *Ulysses* is funny enough, but I have other interests in it, and at one point I was talking with Bob about a precritical procedure that had been fruitful for *Ulysses* as it might not be for work of different kinds: a statistical study. You can get grants to do such things because they keep eighty-eight grad students working at dumb but marginally sustaining jobs for a year. In this case, it was instructive. One thing discovered about *Ulysses* was that there is an inordinately large number of *hapax legomena,* words that are used in the book only once. Thousands. "Lemon" is a word that occurs only once—as the first word in a section that begins, "Lemon platt . . ."—and I cited that to Bob, along with a few other examples. It created some speculation about how the book was made. Bob said, "Wait a minute, it sounds as though Joyce wrote down a set of words that he was going to use only once; he wrote *lemon,* then the word after *lemon* and the word before *lemon.*" It amused me because it was a painter's way of imagining how a literary work might be made. You make a little green thing up here and you make a big red thing down there, and then you put something next to the green thing, and something around the red thing until this incessant process of occult balance and fabrication of relations has created centers that spread out and meet each other. Since the film was about a painterly conundrum, and because Huot and I had had a memorable conversation about the word *lemon,* I decided to dedicate it to him.

MacDonald: The moving light is the only variable?

Frampton: Yes.

MacDonald: And it was moved in a rather pulsing way?

Frampton: That was a problem. It would have been nice to make some kind of clockwork mechanism, but I didn't have one. I put the light on a wire tether, which was kept taut so it would stay at a constant distance, and I filmed

Hollis Frampton, in Robert Huot's One Year: 1970 *(1971).*

at slightly fast speed. I didn't have an electric motor. I had the seventeen-and-one-half-foot spring-wind Bolex to work with. The light was moved manually, the camera wound between takes, and the light moved back slightly. The manual movement and the lap dissolves that join the takes together show. At the time, I would rather have had it be a continuous take. Now, I don't mind so much. The image goes out of register at the dissolves and then restabilizes, as though it had dematerialized ever so slightly. There are five such lap dissolves; I remember squirming over the extra twenty bucks. Choosing the lemon, of course, was very important. I spent half an hour feeling up all these lemons, looking for the one that would be most breastlike, most splendidly citroid. Finally, the produce manager came over and watched me for a while, wondering if I had a lemon fetish. I bought half a dozen to cover myself.

MacDonald: You've compared *Prince Ruperts Drops* [1969] to a phenakistascope.

Frampton: It's more than a comparison. A painter named Bill Copley decided to publish a box magazine. Instead of getting a printed magazine, the subscriber got a box full of goodies. There were contributions by various hands: some moiré sets printed on plastic slips (I think Gerald Oster was implicated in that, which dates the project); LaMonte Young made a tape that involved bowing a gong—part of the *Dreams and Journeys of the Tortoise.* At first, I thought I would put in a film loop, but film loops have to be projected, so I decided to make a phenakistascope, a protocinematic piece. It's a disk with pictures around the edge, which you view in a mirror through slots between the pictures. In their day phenakistascopes were hand-painted "philosophical toys." They always used cyclic actions—sheep jumping over fences endlessly, children rolling hoops, and so forth. I did not know that in the early nineties someone in France—I conveniently forget his name—had used one of Muybridge's horse sequences to make a photographic phenakistascope. I thought I was making the first photographic one.

I filmed two actions. The film frames were enlarged and cut into radial pie segments. I used a magenta overlay for the lollipop and basketball, so that the black-and-white hand bounced a red ball and the black-and-white mouth licked a red lollipop. I filmed with a metronome to guide the action, so that each movement would be a second long. They went out in the box and that was that. Then I got interested in the footage that was left over. There's something mildly paradoxical about an apparent loop being, in fact, a film document of the actions of performers behaving as if they were in a film loop. For a while, the licking of the lollipop looks as though it could be a loop, but finally, licking a lollipop once per second becomes a gagging thing to do: the mouth doesn't want to do it; the rhythm becomes irregular, and the loop appearance of it begins to break down. It's clearer that there's variation in the bouncing of the ball, because it's very hard to bounce a basketball with perfect uniformity.

The nonloop of the lollipop licking was then looped through three print generations so that it changes parity and acquires grain. It begins to look "antique." I used two generations of the ball bouncing. I was interested in the simple way that these procedures mapped film upon performance, rather than performance upon film. It reminds me of the time when the Kuleshov school had no footage and the actors leapt from one point to another, attempting to perform in the way film montage behaved, to perform "cuts." I felt that *Prince Ruperts Drops* was in the spirit of an experiment of the Kuleshov era. The film presents two rhythmic actions in such a way that the viewer is faced with a problem of separating the performance, the pretext, from what film itself is doing and is capable of doing. I wonder if you like it.

MacDonald: I must admit I don't.

Frampton: I like it for its abrasiveness. The title *Prince Ruperts Drops* refers to a demonstration done in physics classrooms. Prince Ruperts drops are little tear-shaped droplets of glass, about the size of a pea. They're made by dropping molten glass into liquid air. The glass is shock-cooled in a state of violent molecular agitation, so that while the drops look stable, they are in fact under extreme stress. The standard physics demonstration involves taking a tweezers and breaking off the little end of the droplet, at which point it vanishes. The stresses then go out of balance and simply shatter the droplet into very fine dust. A cinematic image can have that same quality. It appears to be a solid, believable entity in the form in which we see it, but if we *think* of it differently, it changes beyond recognition, vanishes entirely.

MacDonald: One of the things that puzzles me about *Prince Ruperts Drops* is that we see three shots of lollipop licking, each of which is also reversed, while we see only two shots, each reversed, of bouncing the basketball.

Frampton: It's that way because bouncing the ball seemed to deteriorate as a believable act more quickly; it took on the appearance of a film loop sooner than the lollipop licking did. It is very apparent that the second repetition seems to present the identical act of bouncing the basketball, but with the left hand instead of the right, which is palpably not possible. There's a certain cumulative trouble in watching oneself watching a highly repetitive, stupid act in two or three very slightly different guises, but that's exactly what I'm interested in: the moment when one begins to watch oneself watching the thing. Is that why Stan Brakhage unconditionally detests *Prince Ruperts Drops?* He hates it so much he can't even remember its name. He alludes to it once every couple of years, and every time he does so, he thinks up an even more outlandish name for it. The last time he thought it was called *Mulberry Street.* Don't ask me why.

MacDonald: Surface Tension [1968] seems different from earlier films in the sense that it uses formally a variety of modes of communication. Later films seem to have more in common with it than earlier films. When you made *Surface Tension,* did you feel you were breaking into a new area?

Frampton: Definitely. Everything before that had been, in one way or another, single-image or single-mode stuff. *Surface Tension* represented a new level of ambition for me. In *Surface Tension* I felt that I was going out on a limb—most especially by letting language back into it. It came very, very quickly. I had the image material for quite some time, and the German voice track, which was simply a digest of what Kasper Koenig had said about his project for three-part film during the two-and-a-half or three hours when I had pixilated him and his ineffable digital clock.

MacDonald: Is it his voice?

Frampton: Yes. I went back a year later and had him record it again. He still had his project firmly in mind, so the recording was done in one pass. I had also transcribed it in outline from memory for the titles, so there are discrepancies between what is said in the German and what the titles say, particularly as regards the lengths of the three parts that Koenig talks about.

MacDonald: I assume that part of your intent was to combine a series of connections between the man talking in the pixilation, the language on the sound track in the second section, and the titles in the third, with other elements that are never joined in any specific sense. Is that right?

Frampton: There's at least an imaginable kind of causal connection between the three chunks of superimposed material—two of which are sound, one graphic.

MacDonald: I see the connection between the German voice in the second section and the titles, but how does the telephone sound fit in?

Frampton: The telephone got in there as a piece of stark realism. While Kasper and I were first filming, his girlfriend was continually trying to phone him. He had agreed to do the thing nonstop and was, as a result, very uncomfortable, because a telephone *must* be answered. I became interested in that sound, which communicates nothing except that there is a message waiting. I had thought about using that sound even before I began to think about incorporating Kasper's description of his three-part film. At the time I filmed him I did not have a three-part film in mind. Initially, I thought that it might amount to no more than a portrait. Kasper was proud of his digital clock—there weren't that many of them around at the time. He was living in an extremely austere, virtually empty loft with the digital clock and a whole closet full of On Karawa paintings. The telephone was "from nature" but, like most truly synchronous sound, was perceived as disjunct. So there is a putative relationship, at least, between the ringing and what Kasper has to say. The telephone does stop ringing, after all, and one then hears a voice.

MacDonald: I've always assumed that the connection was between the visual body language of the first part, the sound track of the second part, and the titles in the third.

Frampton: In the first section Kasper is certainly communicating a great deal besides his plan for a film, including a lot of discomfort at being pinned in that window in a contractual relationship. In any case, I had two blocks of image material: the first very emphatic of gesture and of the passage of time; a second that was much more emphatic of a passage through space. Before I settled on the goldfish as the third, I made a different image: an extreme slow-motion image of a woman on a trampoline, from very low, against the sky; her body came floating up into the blue empty screen and then settled back down again. I still have that stuff somewhere, and I'll make use of it one of these days. It was overpowering.

MacDonald: It had never occurred to me until a moment ago that the various levels in each section correlate to each other. The walk from Brooklyn Bridge to Central Park is a process of physically joining two spaces, just as the flow of language is. In the third part there's an encapsulation of reality both in words and in the tank.

Frampton: The words are in the frame as the fish is in the tank; both are limited to a very shallow depth. There's always a fundamental problem of making a *useful* set of limits for a work. Up to a relatively short time ago that set of limits was, by convention, a narrative. Except in Hollywood at its very droopiest, no one, I think, ever pretended that the story was the whole point.

The presence of a narrative amounted to a kind of visual control structure, so that if the Aristotelian unities of time, place, and manner put it in Paris in 1902 in color, then—without a lot of complicated manipulation—you had set outside the limits of the film the pyramids of Egypt in 1928 in black and white. At the same time, having set limits of linear causality and implied time, you were quite free to explore space and its attributes. Narrative films have organized the surface of the screen in a rich variety of ways. As narrative begins to collapse, I find it striking that film tends more and more towards single images or small image clusters. There's a tendency to control the total shape of the film by drastically circumscribing the spaces that one is likely to see, as well as—in a number of very important cases—to delimit drastically the temporality that one is likely to encounter. One reason that people seeing Brakhage's films for the first time can find them confusing is that the films may be made only of a single complex image—a single space explored in a very complicated way—or a limited cluster of images that appear not to have been made in any linear time. In the films that suggest narrative, that have some of *that* kind of control structure, there's more visual variety, whereas in the films that behave like a suspended instant, there tends to be considerably less variety. Much the same thing is true of my own work. In *Zorns Lemma,* for instance, or certain of the films in *Magellan,* where there is a temporal, or causal, control structure, the imagery tends to be more complex. On the other hand, where there is a decided suspension of time, the imagery becomes more narrow in its range. The four films in *SOLARIUMAGELANI* [1974], for instance, are all made within limited individual spaces, which, however, are woefully difficult to retrieve. It's impossible to retrieve the set of calisthenics, or one entire cow and its behavior, or the method for butchering beef cattle, or the processes of rolling and fabricating steel ingots from those films.

Getting back to *Surface Tension,* it's a film that has at the surface level extremely heteroclite imagery, simple though it is. The problem in putting it together was to find some kind of control structure that would hold it together, that nevertheless was not a direct or obvious narrative. Up to *Surface Tension* the control structures that I had used were linear in one sense or another, like the purely rhythmic control in *States* that allows three different strands of images to coinhabit the time and space of the film. *Surface Tension* was the first time I attempted to make a control structure that would work in two ways; that is to say, when there was no connection horizontally, there was the possibility of supplying a connection vertically, in terms of what was seen or heard simultaneously rather than what had just been seen or heard or was anticipated. The problem of understanding such a film is in discovering the control pattern, which instead of being nominally straightforward, as it is in a flat declarative narrative account of something, meanders.

When I began to think about using sound, it struck me as a surrealist arena, one within which the secret connections among things would be more likely to demonstrate themselves. As I understand it, one of the important elements, perhaps *the* important element, of the surrealist and symbolist heritage is that, once released from the constraint of "making sense," words actually construct or manufacture sense before our very eyes. Clearly, the sense that is made has to do with the way that the words are related to each other *fundamentally.* Symbolist poetry began an attempt to discover the inherent control structures within language, just as action painting was, at least in part, an attempt to discover the inherent control structures within painting. The experiments suggest that these inherent control structures are so rich, massive, and powerful that one begins to understand why people began to write poems "about" things and to paint pictures "of" things—as an effort to limit the choice among those control structures and their actions, to whittle painting down to intelligibility or a small set of intelligibilities. Well, film inherits all of that. By the time it came to me, it had inherited all those cultural constraints that were intended to protect artist and spectator alike from looking through the word into the abysmal intricacy of language or, putting it another way, to make possible a kind of naive "use" of an enormous structure.

All right, back to *Surface Tension:* no sooner had I put things together that looked to be quite disjunct, than they immediately began to suggest and then to enforce internal resonances that were far more interesting and far more complicated than sensical combinations of images. I was starting to reenact a drama that's been reenacted many times. My favorite example is Dali and Buñuel's assertion that the selection and ordering of the images in *An Andalusian Dog* were done on the single principle that they should make no sense whatever. Now, of course, any college junior can undertake a fairly straightforward analysis of *An Andalusian Dog* as a witty, troublesome, short narrative that leaves a few questions up in the air, but not very many. The film now seems haunted by the suggestion that it contains a retrievable narrative, and that suggestion holds one. By 1943 the implicit narrative was so much the only visible part of *An Andalusian Dog* that it got misappropriated in a film like *Meshes of the Afternoon,* which really does look like a story—a little bit science-fictional and a little bit overladen with American-brand Freudianism and one step away from an academicism. At that point it becomes possible, and probably necessary, to reassert once more some of the ambitions that originally produced *An Andalusian Dog,* that is, to begin once more to put together things that have no immediately obvious connection with each other. It will be ten years in the fall since *Surface Tension* was made [in 1968], and it begins to look oddly intelligible, and a film that, ten years earlier still, probably looked very jagged indeed—*Window Water Baby Moving*—now seems as smooth as butter and suggests much more of the time in which it was made than of the manner in which it was intended to be received. It looks more like a home movie than like any great innovation in formal method, and one tailored to some of the cozier domestic sentiments of early sixties liberalism.

MacDonald: I'm very curious about *Palindrome,* which is a film I love very much.

Frampton: You, me, and a couple of gateposts.

MacDonald: You've mentioned that the imagery in the film was created by chemically treating filmstock.

Frampton: Let me be explicit. At the time the material for *Palindrome* was collected, I was working in a lab where professionals brought in sheets and rolls of film for processing. All the processing was done by automatic machinery. The waste at both ends of the rolls, where the machine's clips had been attached, was cut off and tossed into the wastebasket. The physical deformation caused by the clips and the erratic way in which the clips let in chemicals to work on the emulsion produced images. It struck me that by far the most interesting images produced by the process went into the wastebasket. The dull ones were put in boxes and sent back to the customers. I began to collect the waste images and mount them as slides. There was something there, a modulated image that could be decoded as having illusionist content, volume. They just didn't resemble anything specific. The set I chose for *Palindrome* tended towards the biomorphic. They resembled action painting, too, in the sense that while much is made of the emphasis on two-dimensional surface, one can decode de Kooning's paintings or Pollock's or Kline's as containing perspective indicators. In time, I started thinking about using them in a film. It was my second attempt—the first was *Heterodyne*—to make a film that did not proceed from photographed footage.

MacDonald: When I studied *Palindrome* closely last summer, one thing that intrigued me—and after a while began to drive me a little crazy—was that, while it seems to be one of the most completely ordered films I've ever looked at, no matter how many webs of order I deciphered, I still felt as though I was missing the fundamental structure of the whole thing. The general palindromic structure is clear, but in the Coop catalogue you mention that there are "12 variations on each of 40 congruent phrases." I was never able to decipher those, nor was I able—even on a rewind—to figure out any pattern at all in the arrangement of the individual images from one segment to the next. In *Heterodyne,* if you attach yourself to one specific visual event and look at that film on a rewind, you can find its pattern. In this film, I can't, or the pattern is so complex that there's no use in trying.

Frampton: It's probably not important. I started by generating a short roll of images that primed the pump. Forty phrases of twenty-four single frames were generated by animation. Then a set of variations was made at the lab, which produced the following: an image of the original roll (color, single layer); a continuous tone, black-and-white version; a black and white negative; and a color negative. Other sets were produced by printing the original roll superimposed on itself, so that the blocks of image fall on top of each other, but so that we see the images first to last on one level, last to first on the other. A color positive, color negative, black-and-white positive, and black-and-white negative were made in that way. Then came a set made from the black and white; on the forward pass, the original was printed through a yellow filter, and on the reverse pass, through blue; and another done the same way, except with magenta and green filters. Those generated rolls were inter-cut with each other, interwoven around the center point.

Well, why do all that? What is important is not the minute specification of what was done, because other things could have been done. Two general things: first, the palindromicity of the film is local as well as global, and sec-ond, it does have a certain diction that's small enough to be recognizable. We begin to recognize, very quickly, images that we've seen before under a dif-ferent guise, and after a few viewings we develop a sense of where we are at any given moment in the progress of the film. When that last brainlike hemi-sphere appears, upside down and backwards, there's the clear sense, even the first time through, that we are at the end of it. It doesn't have a beginning, middle, and end in the developmental sense. It is immediately the way it's going to be all the time. Nevertheless, it does develop a certain contour of expectation.

At the time I made *Palindrome* I was, as I periodically do, giving thought to serial music. Procedurally, the film is flatfootedly Webernian. One of Webern's mature procedures was to make a *generative* row—often it was a hexachord, in which the last six notes are the retrograde inversion of the first six—and then to manipulate that row rigorously (though I don't think Webern was averse to "cheating" here and there). In this music, one is very quickly aware that some definite set of principles is making the piece sound as it does, and a lot of the energy that goes into hearing it is an attempt to figure out those principles. Unless one spends a long time with the score, and sometimes not then, one can never quite get back the full set of rules. There's always a certain tension, a certain malaise in listening: one listens with a double effort, a double concentration because it seems at once an oddly willful, mutable mu-sic, and yet at the same time it is not the willfulness of a composer, of an artist, that one is hearing, but the generative power of the set of rules, whose consequences are being systematically worked out. That fascinates me.

MacDonald: Artificial Light repeats the same group of shots twenty times, presenting them in a different way each time. Two basic questions: What led you to combine the imagery of a group of artists sitting around and the moon? And how were the twenty variations determined?

Frampton: An old custom in Western art forms, a doctrine, dictates that what shall be said and the manner in which it is said shall mutually reflect each other, shall be in accord. It's a doctrine that is sustained, unvarnished, in Eisenstein's exposition of montage. Surrealism and dada, of course, offered major challenges to that doctrine on a number of fronts—more notably, I think, in performance, poetry, and, particularly, collage than in film, simply because there really never was a continuous body of surrealist and dada film. In *Artificial Light* I proposed to take the surrealist recommendations on disjunction and automatism fairly literally. We start with a fragment of film made in a particular time and place as a kind of cinematic doodle. That fragment sat on the shelf for three years. The zoom on the moon came from a sixty-second black-and-white TV spot advertising an expensive battery-powered kid's robot. It's very hard to throw away a three-foot zoom on the moon; especially if it was obviously made from a still on an animation stand. There was the question of the manners in which the photographic material itself might be obscured, mutilated, rendered invisible. The most elementary is turning the filmstrip upside down and running it backwards. Others were more complex. As usual, it turned out to be unexpectedly laborious to do. The one bonanza in the whole proceeding came when I was aching for a way to get the film finished, to extricate myself from it. Walking down 42nd Street, passing the Commodore Hotel—behold!—I saw lying before me on the sidewalk a piece of 16mm film a foot long. Believe it or not, it was a close-up of the surface of the moon! At that moment the film was finished. Having zoomed the moon during a whole set of disjunctions, I had found the montage piece that provided a final point of *convergence*. I ran home and spliced it in, and the film was done.

In a sense, there's nothing in the film that is not "found": the original situation itself—the young artists sitting around laughing, talking, and drinking wine—is one of those perfect cliché givens, a standard pretext. Two pieces of material were actually found. The forms of obliteration that were practiced amount to a cookbook of things to do to a piece of film. I had been teaching a beginning course at Hunter College. We had very little to work with. In particular, we were cameraless, so the students had to work with either leader or found footage. It constituted a laboratory that quickly reproduced the inventory of ways in which a piece of film may be defaced, some of which have considerable histories. I'm thinking about the dime store "color" photography that was done when I was a kid, which consisted in hand-tinting a black-and-white photograph with oil colors. Everybody's hair came out either dark brown, reddish brown, or yellow; all eyes tended to be blue; all lips, red.

MacDonald: Are you referring to the loop with the brownish tint?

Frampton: No, the sepia-toned one has its own antecedents: childhood memories of forties movies in which Lena Horne and the Mills Brothers were always in sepia tones—black people were brown; white people, grey.

MacDonald: A couple of specific questions about a couple of the passes. There's one where you black out every frame but one every once in a while. The intervals between the frames vary just slightly, from about twenty-one frames to twenty-four or twenty-five frames. Why that variation?

Frampton: It's a cheat. It is intended to look regular and in general it does. When we look at film a frame at a time, especially if there's much motion, we quickly find that most frames do not look like stills at all. Typically, they're extremely blurred. Unless we select carefully, a blow-up will be illegible. The variation in intervals resulted from my attempt to find, within narrow temporal limits, a frame that would be optically intelligible.

MacDonald: There's another pass where every two seconds you insert a yellowish, goldish image that is not optically intelligible.

Frampton: That's a color-negative image of a man operating a bulldozer. During the two seconds that follow it one is diverted from seeing the original loop by wondering what the hell it was that intruded. There's too much in the bulldozer image to be reconstructed, and it's not set off—embedded in black or what have you. I can see the image, but then, I know it's there.

MacDonald: What about the order in which the loops are presented?

Frampton: I don't have much to say about it. I tried to order them in such a way that the film would be isotropic—so that one was, at any given time, equally likely to see color, or physical obliteration, or optical manipulation. I didn't want it to "progress" from a bunch of one thing to a bunch of another thing to a bunch of a third. I suppose the term that has to be used is *intuitive,* although that's an indelibly sloppy word that I dislike immensely. When people say they did something intuitively, it means that they didn't think about it. They did what they liked to do, or what they do automatically, like picking their noses. It's a totally irresponsible thing for an artist to say. On the other hand, simply attempting to keep an apparent progression from developing was probably a better control than assigning them each a number and taking the numbers out of a hat. As always happens with the very elementary uses of chance operations, that would have produced "clumps."

MacDonald: I like very much that the last pass is the basic black-and-white loop. It looks so nice after all the previous renditions. It's so easy to forget now how good black-and-white film is to look at.

Frampton: God, does anybody work in black and white any more? Even I don't. First-generation nitrate prints are of astounding delicacy. Everything we have from the old black-and-white age is struck from tenth-generation masters. As a result, everyone's notion of what black-and-white cinematography looks like has become entirely corrupted.

MacDonald: Well, we're up to *Zorns Lemma.*

Frampton: Groan.

MacDonald: At the risk of driving you crazy, let me ask you some general questions about how *Zorns Lemma* developed. It was obviously a tremendous labor.

Frampton: Yeah, it was. Thank you for noticing.

MacDonald: Could you review the steps that you went through to make it?

Frampton: Very quickly. The film began in the fall of 1962 as a collection—in 35mm stills, not in film—of environmental words. Now, what interested me about environmental words was a very simple thing; namely, that they represented a spatial paradox. Sometimes I try to imagine what it must be like to be illiterate. Of course, it's impossible to imagine. Once we can read, and a word is put before us, we cannot not read it. We are drawn to read it, and when we do, we are not looking at what color it is, or looking at its typeface, unless it's so grotesque or deformed as to make the word illegible. We are reading marks in a fixed order on a surface. On the other hand, in looking at a photograph, one is looking at the representation of an illusionist space within which the shapes of things—their boundaries, their colors, and so forth—are paramount. So, looking at a photograph of a word situated in an illusionist space, be it deep or shallow, involves the perceiver, paradoxically, in two simultaneous activities that seem to be at odds with each other. I was amused by that, and I began to make a collection of the rather brutal confrontations, within the urban environment, between these two mutually exclusive kinds of space that have been violently thrust together by the culture.

I should say also that at that time, as at many other times, I was having a waltz with Duchamp. In particular, during the early part of that fall, I saw *Anemic Cinema* for the first time. I had seen stills from the film, but I had not seen the film itself. In *Anemic Cinema* a number of things are happening. There's the possibility of reading the words and the puns they make, which is confounded by the manner in which they're presented, or one can watch the graphic image, which, because it spirals centripetally, appears to imply a *deep* space—which is, in fact, not there. The film creates an extremely interesting internal decorum. The puns tend to spiral back into themselves, into the deep space that language seems to contain, just as the real spirals create their own deep space.

So I began to photograph these black and whites, though only a few of them actually ended up in the film. That early activity of gathering the stills— a rather rodent-like activity—is marked by the presence of the word *fox,* for example, which was the aerial sign of the old Fox Theater in Flatbush. It is seen in the film as a black-and-white still photograph on one side of which is laid a sentimental bunch of dried strawflowers. It's only there for a second, and there are thousands of others, so if you don't remember it, I won't be surprised. There are things one puts into a work that obviously are strictly for oneself. I made quite a few of the stills. Then at a certain point I decided to do it with film. At that time I was starting to work on other films. At first I thought I would simply animate the words, that I would rephotograph them, but it immediately became clear to me that rephotography looked like just what it was: a filmed image of a flat object. This meant that my treasured spatial paradox was lost entirely. I began to film the words, first of all, in order to retrieve the illusion of space and also, to do it in color. Then, the things that motion could do to combine and separate spaces began to produce palimpsests of complexity within the brief images. So after a long time, and I mean quite a long time—seven years—I had a considerable inventory of imagery.

Frampton's homage to the old Fox Theater in Flatbush, from the second section of Zorns Lemma *(1970). Frame enlargement by Biff Henrich. © Hollis Frampton Estate, 1985.*

There are some aspects of the growth of the finished film that I can construct. First of all, there was a question of what order to put the images in. Well, I did not want to make little concrete poems out of them any more than I wanted to make one of those generically awful films that are animated from still photographs. To make little poems would have enforced that act of reading to the exclusion of virtually everything else, and the deep space would have served as a set of decorations. That meant I had to find some way to have an arbitrary order. Well, alphabetic ordering is extremely interesting because it is at once quite arbitrary, and yet it's something that's given to us by the culture and has a vast history, not the least important aspect of which is concerned with two kinds of books: the dictionary, on one hand, which is the set of all sets of words of which the language is composed, and the encyclopedia, which does a rather odd thing: namely, it proposes to arrange all areas of human knowledge according to the first letters of their names. In order for something to become knowledge in the encyclopedia, it first has to be nameable, then its name must have entered the language via the written word, and finally that written word must have been standardized. The encyclopedia takes many disparate, disjunct things and groups them together, not even as they are related in language, but as they are related according to the precedence of the graphic signs that constitute their names.

When we see and read a written word within the cinematic screen, we tend to equate the space of the screen with the space of the page, so that the succession of images begins to resemble the turning of the pages of a book. It was such labyrinthine thinking that resulted in the image that substitutes for the letter *A:* the image of hands turning the pages of a book. In as many ways as I knew how, I was trying very hard to make the work internally self-consistent and self-generating. The particular book whose pages are being turned, by the way, is a bilingual edition of Antonio Pigafetta's diary of the voyage of Magellan. It's impossible to read the book's title, but *Magellan* was stirring even as *Zorns Lemma* was being made.

That desire for internal self-consistency, or for self-provingness, suggests the possibility, at least, for outrageous hypotheses. There are language-like discourses that carry with them a grand suggestion that they can be internally self-proving, that they can, among other things, get along without the artist. They can get along to a degree without the culture from which they came, transmute themselves as the culture changes, and appear to entrap the new culture in which they will eventually come to subsist if they survive. Music has at various times appeared to be internally self-proving. In other words, according to a fixed set of elements in operation, all the qualities of the work could be demonstrated from within itself and from its parts. One of the strivings of mathematics and one of its grand problems has been to make mathematics internally self-proving and to attempt to find out whether in fact it is or not. Those mathematicians working in what is called analysis, who have addressed themselves primarily to these questions, are a distinguished, particularly magnetizing group of people. In recent times there are two particular mathematicians whose work has given special attention to this question. The first is Kurt Goedel, who devised a method for testing mathematical propositions to see whether they generated certain kinds of symmetries that would suggest whether they could be self-proving. The method is extremely elegant. His finding was that mathematics could not be proved within itself. The other mathematician is Max Zorn, whose work was concerned with the question of whether it was possible to make exact statements about the amount and kind of order that was to be found within sets, including the set of all propositions and proofs that constitutes mathematics itself. The result was Zorn's lemma. There was for a long time considerable question about whether Zorn's lemma is part of mathematics; the answer to that question naturally reflects upon the ultimate horizons of mathematical endeavor. Recently I find that the word is out that Zorn's lemma *is* part of mathematics.

The film seems to have had a sort of parallel history. When it first appeared, it was regarded as an unclassifiable nonesuch, a thing that looked like a film, probably, but did some odd things. It seemed not to make many assumptions about what a film was supposed to be but simply to hold up a set of given assumptions, exercise them in their extreme cases as a test of their validity, and put them back down again without comment. It would appear that since it was finished [in 1970], *Zorns Lemma* has come to be regarded as part of that large body of work called film.

MacDonald: The question for many people is how specifically the film uses the lemma—whether you are making a general kind of allusion or giving a detailed demonstration. I know that some books call Zorn's lemma an "existential axiom," something useful for other proofs but not provable within itself. But it's difficult for us nonmathematicians to know whether the choice of title refers to this quality of the lemma's general position in mathematics or whether the relationship is more specific.

Frampton: Indeed, that has always been the question. That's one I can answer simply: the former rather than the latter. I did not set out to provide a cinematic demonstration of a mathematical proposition. On the other hand, I don't mind that the work should respire that possibility. The irony of the difficulty that this issue has caused appeals to me. We have had any number of films that purport to be demonstrations of the validity of propositions in other language-like activities. And I'm not only talking about literature itself in various forms. I'm also talking about music and the extent to which music has been cribbed, rigorously or sloppily, in film. I happen to be, to a different degree and in a different way, cribbing from another language-like species of endeavor.

MacDonald: Few people have problems with Oskar Fischinger's use of musical methods. I suppose it comes down to the fact that we call music art and we call mathematics something else.

Frampton: I think we should probably refuse to make this kind of distinction. I'm sick and tired of the two cultures, of that gulf between what is called science on the one hand and what is called art on the other. Artists who think there is some great and fundamental gulf between science and art conserve a repulsive little cartoon in which the sciences are cold and unfeeling and the arts are warm and emotional. I get to be typed as an icicle, Frosty the Snowman with his cinematic calculus, which mightily annoys me and hurts my feelings. On the other hand, scientists think of the sciences as straightforward and the arts as abounding in mystery. None of these things is true. In the sciences in particular, and in the queen of the sciences—mathematics—and, indeed, in that celestial, clumsily named intellectual entity, computer science, which has already made mathematics a kind of subset of its own interests, nothing is quite as rampant as aestheticization. Mathematicians are by no means content that a proof "works." They want it to be beautiful, and if pressed, they have clear criteria for what constitutes the beauty of a proof. Since mathematics is now attempting proofs of sets of problems for which

The final "replacement image" of the middle section of Zorns Lemma *(1970). Frame enlargement by Biff Henrich. © Hollis Frampton Estate, 1985.*

there may be no spare, elegant, beautiful, powerful proofs, the mathematical world is in a kind of aesthetic uproar. For instance, the guys in Illinois who used an enormous computer to test empirical cases in the four-color mapping theory, namely, that it's possible to color any map with no more than four colors in such a way that no two adjacent territories will have the same color. This grand problem in topology produced a "dirty" proof, a consequence of which is that they may have discovered a class of theorems for which there is no "clean proof."

Mathematicians are passionate people. The most dedicated of them live in a distant galaxy that is all passion, suspended in a universe that offers only ecstasy. They seem remote and unavailable, and indeed they are. They're in a state of perpetual jouissance, or they're on the verge of it, or they're slightly detumescing from it, or what have you. People who don't realize this cut themselves off from genuine pleasures. I remember years ago trying to get Brakhage to read Borges. Brakhage likes detective stories; why shouldn't he like Borges? Well, he didn't want to read Borges because he had the notion that Borges was "mathematical." So at that point, and he may have changed his mind since, he didn't take the turn that would have led to his getting the most fun out of life. Oh well, enough of that.

I do not think of myself as a sentimental scientist in the manner of Duchamp. I'm a pure spectator. But science has always been for me a particularly suggestive and happy sandbox to play in. I think it's not something to be deeply troubled about. I do admit to using quite simple manipulations of matrices in my work, but much more recently than *Zorns Lemma*. But this is probably about as useful to a spectator as it is to a critic of painting to worry about the length of the handle on the brush.

MacDonald: You were talking about the history of *Zorns Lemma*. . . .

Frampton: With regard to my pursuit of internal consistency, I can point out a few sketchy axes for the choice of the replacement images. Image B is the frying of an egg; it is, after all, breakfast time; we have turned a new leaf in the book, and we're at the start of a new day, and that's all corny enough. Image W is at the end of a day; it's a journey through an urban environment, through night streets where only the lights are visible, and that is the last part of the cycle proper. I did try to take a little care—not quite Joycean care, but a little care—to keep the depicted events in the part of the hourly cycle where they wouldn't seem too outrageous, to present things at appropriate times of day in relation to the frying of the egg and the journey through the night. Another axis had to do with what the activities were. In one way or another, by inference, they are painterly or sculptural. In one case, of course, they're very explicitly painterly. In many cases they are explicitly sculptural. The breaking open of something to reveal its contents, the digging of a hole in the ground, the filling of a container with something. . . .

MacDonald: All the activities are repetitive, too.

Frampton: They're all repetitive, yes, but some of them fulfill themselves, some do not. Some cycles end, others do not. The tree, for instance, that replaces F, is undergoing part of a cycle of activity that happens to have a periodicity far longer than the span of the film, so it appears to be in stasis. Of course it is not. Before our very eyes, even in the actual sixty seconds that we really see the tree, it is going through its own metabolic processes; it's just not doing so very fast. The life of the tree is, let us say, a set of repetitive cycles that nevertheless will, in a relatively short time—sixty or seventy years—have a beginning and an end. The ocean presumably has rolled for four billion years, and we don't know how long that will go on, and that is cyclic in a number of ways. The bonfire will burn itself out. Some of the actions are perfective; others are imperfective, and ongoing, some are cyclic, some are simply repeated, like tying shoes, and cracking eggs, and so forth, which makes up a tremendous amount of life.

I did make quite a few more images than were included. One was an image of traffic passing over a bridge against a facade of buildings, but four layers deep so that it constantly posited—to the exclusion of almost everything else—the same question that Ernie Gehr's *Still* posits; namely, what is the location of the surface that we believe we're looking at? [This image is now in *Straits of Magellan: Drafts and Fragments* (1974).] In most cases I really can't remember the nitty-gritty of my final choices between them. A lot of it had to do with how they looked next to each other. The final replacement image, the red ibis, is sheer pyrotechnics, peripeteia.

MacDonald: A tremendous number of environmental words are seen in windows that simultaneously reflect the real life going on behind the camera. I assume that this is inevitable to some extent, given the realities of where the words would be found in a cityscape, but I also assume that part of it involves an allusion to words being reflective, being condensations of experience.

Frampton: It also involves the question of how the word is related to that mental space in which we can see, in our mind's eye, a cow chewing its cud and the green grass and the blue sky and so forth. It's like looking backward through your own eye, as if one were looking into one of those candy Easter eggs that have landscapes inside them. We can entertain at the same time the word *cow*—a vocal utterance, the name of that creature—and the little candy tableau of the beast in the field. Other effects come from the reflections, too. A word, I forget which one it is, is written in red on a semicircle of bright yellow. That bright yellow placard is then behind a glass window, which reflects the street behind it. Abruptly out of the yellow semicircle a yellow taxicab drives. In another shot, one involving the word *welcome,* a street is reflected. Feet walk into the reflection, as if to walk onto a welcome mat, but they're not in the same space.

MacDonald: Every time I see the first minute or two of the center section of *Zorns Lemma,* I get a rush. There's this wonderful pounding of all this color, all these ways of perceiving, after the darkness of the first section.

Frampton: For those who know Manhattan—Manhattan as it was at that time—the spaces in which the signs are seen come with at least some of those signs. One gets shifted violently all over an urban landscape. This was *not* something I had anticipated, but I was happy about it: traveling from one place to the next, as if by a kind of cinematic sorcery.

MacDonald: Also, in a certain very obvious sense, that imagery is a sort of diary of your moving around during those years; it becomes a record of the process of your personal exploration of that place.

Frampton: Though there's a certain malaise in being presented with the spectacle of a misfit who spends seven years walking the streets, reading the signs. You would have thought I had something better to do.

MacDonald: On the other hand, looking for signs got you out into the street. You had to explore New York further than someone not looking for signs.

Frampton: It also, by the way, conditioned me into an almost incorrigible habit. I still can't keep myself from framing up shots that contain words I wish I had had. It's not as bad as it used to be, when I couldn't go anywhere without doing it.

MacDonald: There's a basic continuity from *Zorns Lemma* to *Hapax Legomena* to *Magellan.* All three works include, either complete or in part, histories of various levels of personal, cultural, and artistic development. I think it's clear in *Zorns Lemma* that there's an educational development involved and that this educational development is simultaneously both your personal development and the overall cultural development of the nation. What I wasn't sure about is whether another kind of development is implicit. The film begins in darkness with just sound, then we get heavily edited visuals, then we get deep space with sound. Was that a conscious recapitulation—at least in part—of film history?

Frampton: It's an inescapable joke, or I find it inescapable, to point once more with a chuckle to the antecedents of the thing one is doing. That's a habit, by the way, that has an interesting background. Art does it all the time, but I probably didn't see it first in art. When I was in my early teens, a man named Sheldon wrote a book called *The Varieties of Temperament,* in which he proposed to investigate the way people behaved according to what has been vulgarly popularized as their body types. It was Sheldon, as far as I know, who coined the words *ectomorph, endomorph,* and *mesomorph.* He invented a pure endomorph named Aubrey, a pure mesomorph named Boris, and a pure ectomorph named Christopher. Notice the alphabetic ordering of the names. These pure body types derive, in fact, embryologically. There's a stage in the development of all vertebrates during which ontogeny is quite explicitly recapitulating phylogeny. One is, for a very brief period, a kind of sponge, a tiny organism composed of three layers. From those primordial three layers everything else develops: the cells that form the innermost layer produce gut and ductless glands; the middle layer differentiates into muscle and bone; the outer layer into the skin, the nervous system, and the organs of sense. To classify adult temperament in that way is to point to embryological origins early on in the development of the individual, to the brief period when the individual was recapitulating the evolutionary development of the earliest invertebrates. The sciences are fond of that sort of thing. In his study Sheldon does it with some wit; he's clearly amused—why shouldn't we be?—by the possibility that the mesomorphic tendency to use noise as a form of aggression has something to do with the physiological dominance of a couple of hundred cells in something the size of the head of a hatpin, phylogenetically very very far back in time and ontogenetically at the very first dawn of the adult walking sentient creature's life. My late childhood and early adolescence were spent reading that kind of stuff, and I suspect that my reading of the texts of art history has been very strongly colored by my reading of the history of science. I don't see very much difference in art-historical speculation and speculation in physiology, for instance, except, of course, that the former has tended to be intellectually sloppier than the latter.

MacDonald: The art-science gap you've discussed is very recent, too. In *Moby Dick,* for example, it's clear that Melville has no problem including both in his thinking.

Frampton: Emerson has no such problems either. These people were inheritors of the Enlightenment, which also had no such problems. There is another thing, though, that I want to bring up about *Zorns Lemma.* It's always a pleasure to cite Eliot. I'm thinking about the moment—and I believe he was under heavy fire about *The Waste Land* at the time—when he asserted that after the writing is done, the writer becomes a reader and is then faced with the same problems any other reader is faced with. There's a short essay about the death of the author in which Barthes talks about the same thing. Well, I believe that; in fact, I believe more. I believe it's obvious that there are things that spectators can know about a work, any work, that the person who made it can never know. And those things are different in quantity and they are different sometimes in kind, as well. So I feel cautious about talking about my reading of my own work. But there is some precedent. Eisenstein was a considerable reader of his own work. There are times, I think, when he overreads, possibly reads erroneously. There are times when he reads extremely well. He appears to have understood certain works very well. Judging from his essays, for instance, I have the feeling that he understood *The General Line* better than anybody else did for thirty or forty years.

With regard to *Zorns Lemma,* I do now have a reading of my own, an alternative reading that I hadn't suspected at all at the time it was made. There has always been a surface autobiography in it that is not particularly oblique. During the long period of time that I spent in New York, there was a shift in my attention. On the 6th of March, 1958, I arrived in New York an aspiring young poet. Well, that didn't last very long. It was a question of being unable to find a meaningful relationship between poetry as it was then practiced and anything I was interested in, rather than a question of finding a relationship between language and something I was interested in doing. I see those as two different problems. The dance with language went on, but I couldn't see any way to make poems at that time. Then there was the shift into the visual arts. When I first went to New York, I fell among painters. During most of the time I lived there, I was primarily in that company. I have accounted for the film on that autobiographical level.

My new reading involves the fact that a couple of years after the film was made, a new kind of traumatic surgery on the central nervous system was first attempted, as a radical treatment for epilepsy. I'm talking about the split-brain operation, in which the two hemispheres of the brain are virtually disconnected from each other by severing a body called the *corpus callosum.* From the unforeseen consequences of that surgical procedure a very large body of observation and speculation has since arisen concerning the differences between the hemispheres of the brain and their functions. There are a couple of things that interest me. First of all, this drastic operation is performed only to alleviate the most violent and uncontrollable of epilepsies, grand mal. Epilepsy is at the high end of a syndrome, a series of disorders that begins with allergic hives, ascends through giant hives and hay fever to asthma, to petit mal and the various photogenic epilepsies, to grand mal, and finally to a rather rare and absolutely incurable degenerative disorder, lupus, so called because the sufferer acquires a darkening of the skin around the eyes in the form of a mask that lends a wolfish aspect to the countenance. The signs associated with that syndrome are all instances in which the body in one way or another harms itself. What it amounts to is that the entire syndrome appears to be concerned with a struggle between the two hemispheres of the brain for control of the body. Of course, I'm cartooning this drastically. The standard reference is Sir John Eccles. He's a Nobel laureate neurophysiologist who was a distinguished professor at Buffalo the first years I taught there, and whose lectures were open.

Anyway, cortically speaking, we are of distinct and separate minds. The functions are not, it would seem, mapped quite as we would like to have them. In right-handed persons, for instance, very distinct mapping of locomotor control right down to pinky fingers was done long before the split brain operation was performed. Obviously, if somebody gets a small brain injury and you find that they can't move their pinky finger, then you can locate the part of the cortex that controls the pinky finger. Generally, it would appear that, in right-handed persons, the left hemisphere is concerned with language and with linear and analytic language-like, deductive activities. The right hemisphere is concerned generally with synthesizing nonlinear inductive activities, one of the chief of which appears, by the way, to be music. Although the left brain is concerned with the dictionary and with grammar and syntax, the right brain nevertheless has its own view of language, engages in its own linguistic activities, makes poetry, among other things. And there's a new hypothesis that meaningful slips of the tongue and those complex allusive puns that pop out of your mouth before you know that you have said them are moments when the right hemisphere seizes the vocal apparatus for its own purposes when the left has its guard down.

There are other complexities to the situation, too. The brain also has an evolutionary structure. It has been spoken of as a crocodile in the embrace of a dog within the embrace of a man. The ancient center brain, which keeps you breathing and turns on your adrenals and so forth, is an organ that deals only in absolute imperatives. When it scratches, you itch, so to speak; its imperatives take precedence over all other functions. The dog is more complex; it can learn things and find its way around and master repetitive sequences, and it knows where home is and comes when it's called and can see motion, and so on. The cortex nominally is us, except that the frontal lobes, which are the seat of whatever is called personality, are directly connected to the old brain and so are responsive directly to its imperatives.

Two pieces of personal information. As a child, and especially as an adolescent, I was an acute hay fever sufferer of the sloppiest kind. I popped pills all day long, and my life, any time there was pollen around, was to be a perpetual fountain of snot. Brakhage has spoken at some length about his asthma. He still occasionally suffers from it. I do not. I haven't had anything like hay fever in years. The other curiosity about my own history is that I'm a "cured" lefty, as my father before me was. In the late 1930s left-handedness was viewed as, if not quite sinister, at least as undesirable. Being left-handed was viewed as a handicap that you should have trained out of you. Both of these pieces of autobiographical information suggest at least the origins of a certain kind of hemispheric conflict. My own reading of the 45-minute central section of *Zorns Lemma,* in which the image that is statistically before one passes gradually from a language-dominated one to a continuous non-language-dominated one, is a kind of allegory, an acting out of a transference of power from one hemisphere of the brain to the other. Of course, that was nowhere within my thinking of the film when I was making it.

MacDonald: Is the hemisphere that is opposite the one involved with language particularly involved with practical tasks? A lot of the replacement images involve practical tasks.

Frampton: No, not especially, but the question of doing practical tasks does relate. I have even been able to perform a few experiments that have to do with this, and I have made some observations. There are certain things that I learned how to do by myself. One of them is the standard operation of making A and B rolls in editing a film. I was not instructed in it. I understood the principle right away, and I figured out how to do it, and I've done it ever since. When students ask, "How do you make A and B rolls," I find that I can do one of two things. Either I can go to the blackboard and give a long demonstration about the principles involved: why one does it, how you situate the two strips of image in order to make a lap dissolve, a straight cut, or what have you. Or I can say, "Watch me," and I can perform that act. But I've invariably found that I can't do both things at the same time. If I attempt to talk about what I'm doing while I'm doing it, I get totally balled up. As soon as I begin to talk, control passes to a different function. Now, during the last year I've spent time with people practically involved with electronic design, and I have noticed a habit among them of incessantly talking about what they do. I ran across a textbook on electronic design that, in its brief last chapter, rather blushingly recommends to designers that they should cultivate the habit of talking to themselves while they're designing a circuit, so that both halves of the brain know what's going on. It's not a very sociable thing to do, because in this culture language is so much an arena of power that any other use of it is viewed as odd. If no transaction is taking place, then language shouldn't be used. That's why people have to talk to themselves in their cars when they're alone.

Well, in any case, that series of discoveries is enormously fertile, and I'm by no means the only artist, or filmmaker, who is excited about them. What I am saying, and I don't propose to work it out in any detail, is that there is the mimesis of a transfer, a balancing out of power within *Zorns Lemma* that I did not consciously put there when I made it and which I now read within it. It's striking that as the film enters the last section, the image is no longer modularized, but, except for the four dissolves, is continuous.

MacDonald: And except for the sound track, which is the remnant of the verbal level.

Frampton: Except for the track.

MacDonald: Judging from the film as a whole, the transfer of power has made progress possible. During the film you go from darkness to illumination.

Frampton: Yes. Now from that I have drawn further speculations. . . .

MacDonald: When you began *Hapax Legomena,* did you know you would do seven films, or did that evolve?

Frampton: It evolved: in exactly what order I can't say, except that by the time I had finished the first three (in the order that they were made: *nostalgia, Critical Mass,* and *Travelling Matte* [1971]), the rest of it was pretty clear. It felt pretty much like a single continuous effort. By the fall of 1971, I was entirely clear about what was to be done.

MacDonald: The title *nostalgia* seems to suggest a strong longing for the past. The tendency has been—I've heard Annette Michelson deal with it this way—to assume that the film is a longing for your years in New York. At the same time, in *nostalgia* itself, you seem relieved that that period is gone. As a result, I've come to think of the title as suggestive of the process that you're involved in: on one level you seem to be destroying some old pictures, but in another sense you're recording them as you're destroying them, so that while you seem to be putting something into the past, you're maintaining interest in it in a different form.

Frampton: But you see, they are not destroyed; they can be resurrected by rewinding the film. It strikes me as historically unfortunate that the word *nostalgia* itself was resuscitated such a short time after I made that film. It seems to be equated with the German word *Sehnsucht,* which means "longing." It is nothing of the sort. In Greek the word means "the wounds of returning." Nostalgia is not an emotion that is entertained; it is sustained. When Ulysses comes home, nostalgia is the lumps he takes, not the tremulous pleasures he derives from being home again. In my film there is a remastering of a certain number of lumps I took during those years as a still photographer in New York. You noticed that there are no triumphs described in the film; it was by no means a time that I look back to in the current pathetic sense of "nostalgia" at all. It was quite dreadful. I didn't find it a picnic to be a photographer, through the sixties, not because photography was disregarded, although of course that was true, but because my predicament was that of a committed illusionist in an environment that was officially dedicated to the eradication of illusion and, of course, utterly dominated by painting and sculpture. At that

A photograph of Frampton burns on a hotplate in nostalgia *(1971). Frame enlargement by Biff Henrich.* © *Hollis Frampton Estate, 1985.*

time I didn't understand how luxurious it was to find myself alienated in that way. Nothing is more wonderful than to have no one pay the slightest attention to what you are doing; if you're going to grow, you can grow at your own speed.

MacDonald: How did you happen to choose someone else—Michael Snow, specifically—to narrate the film? I wonder particularly since you don't identify him in the film itself.

Frampton: No, although he's mentioned. As a matter of fact during the recording of that script, at the end of the passage in which he's talking about the bad show poster I made for him—the last line is "I wish I could apologize"—he looked up from the script and said, "Well, why don't you?" To which I replied, "I wish I could." I almost put it in the film, but I thought better of it because I had already intervened in my own voice at the very beginning.

Well, for a couple of reasons. One is very practical: when I'm in something that feels like an official situation, my voice is essentially a kind of radio announcer's voice (I think I learned to talk as much from the radio as I did from people), which means that it tends to overenunciate histrionically. At one point I did record my own voice reading that script, and it was just awful. Then I cast around for who else could do it. The reason I finally settled on

Mike—except for the possibility of generating a couple of internal jokes—was that Mike has that flat Ontario Scottish delivery. Every now and then, when the Scottish element in that speech suddenly pops forward, I almost expect him to break into a recitation of an Edinburgh menu. His is not, let us say, the standard Minnesota American English that the radio announcer speaks. My tendency is to imitate Richard Burton in the bathtub.

What was most important of all was to sustain a certain kind of distance from that material. The last thing I had the slightest interest in was diaristic memoir, with its drastically confessional tone. If there was to be any sort of personal revelation, that had to be balanced by an obscuring of the same person that proceeded at the same rate.

The film is not about me. So, having fictionalized everything else, it seemed reasonable also to fictionalize the physical organ of speech. It's no stranger than what happens when anyone reads Browning's "My Last Duchess" aloud; one also uses the first person pronoun, but the reader is substituted for the Duke. The voice is simply the vehicle of the fictive ego.

It's interesting how those things now begin to recede into the dim past. The person who made *nostalgia* is not the person who is now talking: all of my material body has been replaced, except for the central nervous system, which I *still* understand to be an exception . . . and that has simply degenerated. They say that after the age of thirty, even without benefit of alcohol, one loses one million neurons a day, most of which, in my case, seem to have spent their first thirty years preventing me from doing the things I really wanted to do, so I'm glad to be rid of them.

MacDonald: One last question about *nostalgia.* The ending, I assume, is meant to be puzzling, in the sense that after the final "Here it is! Look at it! Do you see what I see?" the viewer is faced with, depending on one's interpretation, darkness, the end of the film, or your logo . . .

Frampton: Let me jump in right there. What is seen in the fragment of the photograph, reflected and rereflected in the rearview mirror of a truck, is certainly not my logo. As you may have noticed, that was the last film in which I used either the logo or a title at the beginning. I abandoned them at that point because of a problem they always generated: was the title part of the film, or was it simply a filing system? Was the logo part of the film, or simply a maker's mark? There was always, in my mind, a nascent conflict between the title as a graphic sign, on the one hand, and the illusionist space of the photographic image on the other. Finally, I decided to solve the problem by annihilating it. The only temporary solution I ever had for it was in *Zorns Lemma,* where the end title and the signature are monumentalized and appear to be "made of" something, but that was satisfactory only within the particular context of that film. The darkness in *nostalgia* is there to *separate* the logo from the last image so that your present confusion could be avoided. I may even get around to dropping the logo on that film. It might work better to have it simply trail off into darkness.

I'm thinking about the lost age of radio quite a bit these days. There's a little bit of the same kind of melodrama in that darkness and silence that I remember from an episode of the old radio show *Suspense*. It referred obliquely to the work of a slightly mad physiologist, Alexis Correll, who had drawn all manner of fantastic inferences from tissue cultures and from chemical artifacts that he made, called autosynthetic cells, that met nine (I believe) of the then eleven known requirements for life. In the forties it was somehow believed that monstrous life was about to pop out of a test tube at any moment. This episode was called "Chicken Heart"; it was about a scientist who cultured the tissue of the heart of a chick embryo. As it cultured, this little muscle did not form the shape of a heart but was simply a mass that grew ever larger until finally it escaped from its petri dish and began to acquire whatever nourishment it needed in the environment, until the whole planet was covered with sodden, beating chicken-heart tissue. Very early in the program, as an insistent kind of ostinato background for all the other speeches and all the other sounds, one began to hear very softly the sound of a heartbeat that grew in volume throughout the thirty minutes, until finally the scientist and his girlfriend, the lab assistant—presumably the last people alive—were up in a light airplane, with no place to land, and over the enormous beating of the heart, one heard the sound of the engines drumming and missing, sputtering, and then dying, and that was the last sound except for the beating of the heart which went on all by itself for a good half a minute and then was abruptly cut off for what probably amounted to fifteen seconds, a very long time in radio. There was absolute dead air, the supreme verboten of radio. That silence entirely engulfed the intellectual space of the imagined listener, so that, in a gesture that Cage presumably would like, it was filled with speculations. I admit that in duplicating a gesture of that kind in film, there's an element of shabby carnival rhetoric.

nostalgia pushes the participatory aspects of *Zorns Lemma* a little farther and in a somewhat different direction. Of course, I've always thought of that game-playing aspect of *Zorns Lemma* as the fool's gold of the film. That is also true here. It's a kind of bait, a lure, rather than the whole substance of the film.

MacDonald: Someplace you've mentioned that you don't feel that *Poetic Justice* quite fits into *Hapax Legomena*.

Frampton: Have I said that? I must have been feeling dyspeptic on the day I said that. None of the seven "fits in." I did spend a certain amount of time feeling uncomfortable about that film. Why? Well, except for those few little bits of business in the upper right margin of the frame and the withdrawing of the hand from the lens and so forth, which are very brief, the only motion in the film is that of the eye reading the text, so I could possibly have said that in a moment of distrust of the film's stillness. On the other hand, at one time or another I have felt exactly the same way about every single part of *Hapax*. At various moments I have found each of them uncomfortable, abrasive, trying to my capacity to sustain attention; but while that is true, I have to remind myself that I'm simply getting my just desserts: there's nothing in any of the films, after all, that I didn't put there, and I did include those difficulties, those abrasions, those vexations to the power to attend, so that I have nothing to complain of.

MacDonald: You've published the film in book form too. Was the original conception a book that would be read as a screenplay, or a film?

Frampton: It was a film. The book was entirely after the fact, and it was not my idea. I showed the film at the Visual Studies Workshop in Rochester, and Joan and Nathan Lyons suggested that it might make a book. The irony of the sequence, as well as of the notion, appealed to me. The aspect ratio of the pages of the book, by the way, is not the same as that of the film, and the book is randomly accessible; it doesn't make the same demands on memory as the film does, particularly the first two parts, which are fairly complex narratives. The third and fourth tableaux are simple, so the differences between the book and the film are less pronounced. Anyway, the book came second. At the time it appeared, by the way, there were projects hatched by three different people to realize the scenario.

MacDonald: Is anybody still working on that?

Frampton: No. It's the sort of thing that you come up with after a heavy lobster dinner and preferably walk off before you go to sleep, not because of its complexity or its difficulty but because realizing the scenario would de- stroy its crucial ambiguities. I'm not talking only about the mysterious sexual identities of the three personae of the piece but also of those concerned with scale. "Outside the window is an inverted enamel saucepan"; well, where *is* that saucepan? In the space outside the window. Is it on the sill? Is it a hundred yards away? The difference between the spatial close-up and the psychological close-up is easy to sustain as a tension in language because the declarative sentence itself separates the figure from the ground. It's not so easy to sustain an ambiguity of that type in film. If you're actually photographing, you can't have "six or seven zebras." In the photograph one can always count the zebras. So, for lots of reasons the project was untenable. If anybody ever cared to do it, it might make an interesting film, but, of course, it wouldn't be a film of mine.

MacDonald: The only other place I've seen the second person used the way you use *you* and *your lover* in *Poetic Justice* is in some of Carlos Fuentes' stories and novels.

Frampton: Writing in the second person creates an automatic disjunction between the imaginative space of the work and the real space in which the spectator finds himself. I suppose that's what interests me about it.

MacDonald: It does the opposite of what it seems to do?

Frampton: Yes. One accepts the first and third person as lying entirely within the imaginative space of the text, presumably by convention. It's like the convention of the literary past tense.

By the way, some time ago you mentioned to me that you can remember the imagery suggested by the words of the scenario as completely as you remember the images in a standard film. Well, there are reasons that language has been the dominant code in the culture for so long. One of them is its enormous parsimony. One reads only to recall the set of symbols, or the code, and the code itself indexes the culture. The image does not have that kind of parsimony. Images have been around for a long time, but for only a few hundred years in anything remotely like the plethora that we now have them. For hundreds of thousands of years there was no adaptive value for human beings at all in developing the power to recall unparsimonious codes.

Now, on the other hand, there is a strong adaptive value, a survivor value, in the ability to recall images in their entirety; but we haven't had very much time to select ourselves for that ability. Presumably, if the hard image persists, we will do that in time, though I have a sneaking suspicion that we may not, because electronic imagery, which is for all practical purposes in this culture nothing more than television, has fallen into such a rigid spatial typology that the images are not memorable at all. They are the most evanescent kind of consumer product.

MacDonald: Also, they're repeated so regularly that there's no function in remembering them.

Frampton: I'm positive that you could see the entire spatial repertoire of television ten thousand times in the course of a single day's viewing.

MacDonald: I've looked at *Critical Mass* a lot, and I've tape-recorded it and listened to the tape over and over, and no matter how hard I try, I'm not confident that I know exactly what the changes in organization of sound units are. Is that supposed to be ambiguous? Or is it just a function of my ears not being trained?

Frampton: One of the things that goes on in *Critical Mass* (this is also true of much of the rest of my work and of the work by others I admire) is a process of training the spectator to watch the film. The work teaches the spectator how to read the work. The whole film, of course, was shot as two long takes; the original material is two 100-foot rolls. The sound was continuous; the Nagra was simply left on and that's why you hear the squeals of the slate. Except for that very brief opening passage in which it starts out in sync and immediately disintegrates, it's divided very roughly into fourths, with the passage in the dark forcing two pairs apart. At first, they match, and then in the dark, where there is only sound, each segment of sound, instead of going two steps forward and only one back, is simply repeated exactly three times. When the imagery reappears, the temporal overlap resumes, but the unit of sound cutting is slightly larger. Typically it's about six frames (or a quarter of a second) larger than the image unit, which means that once every four seconds they will coincide exactly. They rotate in and out of sync with each other until finally, they lose sync entirely and are out of step first by one repetition of the word "bullshit" and then by two repetitions of the word "bullshit," which happens to be a particularly easy word to sync on, if you're syncing by hand, which I was. The head-end slate was lost, and in any case, everything had to be laid in by hand. Of course, Frank Albetta said "bullshit" quite a number of times in the course of the improvisation, and if you look closely you will notice that even in the last part, during which the sound is delayed by several seconds in relation to the picture, there is one moment when he says "bullshit" that's in perfect sync.

MacDonald: I'll have to go look at that again.

Frampton: There were plenty of other words, you understand, upon which one can also sync, and there's sufficient repetition in that dialogue that there are plenty to choose from, but *bullshit* seemed reasonable. If something is bullshit, it is false, not real, incorrect, so that in those technical senses—as well as in the sense that for all of its obvious cathexis on the part of the performers, the situation is staged—it is a fiction. The notion of a real argument or a real dialogue is also bullshit. There isn't a grain of truth anywhere in the film.

MacDonald: I believe that *Critical Mass* is the first instance when you've directed an actor and an actress. Did you work with them for a while beforehand?

Frampton: Very little. I spent several days in Binghamton at screenings and workshops. At that time Binghamton consisted of thirty typical state university specimens of immaculate penal modern, rising from a sea of mud. I had an idea of what I wanted to do. I asked around the film department, which was well populated by volatile personalities, for the names of the two people, the man and the woman, that by consensus were judged most likely to fly off the handle. There was virtual unanimity that Barbara DiBenedetto and Frank Albetta were my two best bets. I asked them if they would be willing to do it and gave them a set of conditions—namely, that they had been living together for about six months, that he had disappeared for a weekend and refused to offer any explanation . . . there were a few others—and let them stew in that juice over night. We shot the following evening. It was one take. It was also the first time, and the only instance in a film released so far, that I used lip sync.

MacDonald: They're fantastic.

Frampton: They are. Barbara is a volcano of energy, a young woman with astounding powers of projection. When she finally saw the film, she was, to my regret, deeply troubled by it. I don't know why. If I had delivered myself of an interlude of that magnitude, under conditions of such sanity and control, I would consider it one of the grand achievements of my life. It's a Mediterranean rage. My own bad tempers are essentially Celtic, which means that they go off like Roman candles and are immediately spent. By the end of the shooting—it was ten minutes at the most—everyone in the room was absolutely limp. It was exhausting.

We filmed in March 1971, but it was October before I had anything like a clear notion of how I would edit it. The editing process became a process of decoding, or reading, the footage and the recorded sound, as it has been with virtually all the work I've done since *Hapax*. I didn't spend much time looking at the footage, which is fairly blank. I spent a great deal of time listening to the tape, which became a source of references to the way the film itself behaves. "This is getting us absolutely no place," and lines like that, came forward in high relief.

MacDonald: In the Coop Catalogue, you list Larry Gottheim as sound recordist. Did he have any input into the film?

Frampton: He crewed on the job. At that time I didn't know a Nagra from my elbow. I was the cameraman. I crewed on the job, too.

MacDonald: The imagery in *Travelling Matte* was shot with a portapak.

Frampton: Half-inch portapak, and then kinescoped: rephotographed from a video monitor.

MacDonald: Was the imagery completely planned in advance, or did you put on the portapak and explore?

Frampton: I walked through it three or four times. What was crucial was getting to that pavement with the hexagonal tiles in the middle of it and finding my way back. It's about as uningratiating a landscape as you can find anywhere.

MacDonald: Did you choose Binghamton because of its bleakness?

Frampton: I didn't choose Binghamton; Binghamton chose me. I had never touched a piece of video gear, and two students there absolutely pressed the portapak upon me. They had both worked with Ralph Hocking, who was teaching in the film department (there was a television department at Binghamton, staffed by real, genuine engineers, the usual reactionary situation). The two of them absolutely insisted that I had to do something with video, so I thought for a time about what that might be. They checked me out on the machine, which, of course, was simple to use, and I went and made that tape.

The aspect of that experience which was really overpowering—it took me a long time to assimilate—was not making the tape itself. A portapak is about as cumbersome as a Bolex. What astonished me was that when I returned to my starting point, I rewound the tape and saw the image immediately. Filmmaking is an edifice of delayed gratification; by a kind of inversion of Freud's thesis in *Civilization and Its Discontents,* one is constantly reassured in filmmaking that one is engaged in a civilized activity. That immediate gratification seemed very barbaric. It still does a little bit, although I'm more at home with it than I was six or seven years ago. It's probably a sign of middle age that I can now permit myself a few slightly more immediate gratifications.

MacDonald: Ordinary Matter [1972] seems to place a much greater emphasis on basic film materials than do some of the other parts of *Hapax Legomena.* It also seems much involved with the grainy particle-ized textures of the grass, stones, and other materials that occupy so much of your attention in that film. This led me back to your essay "For a Metahistory of Film: Commonplace Notes and Hypotheses," where you discuss film as the final major contribution of the Age of Machines. Are you trying to draw a connection between a view of the universe as fundamentally mechanistic and particle-ized and film as a material medium that captures imagery in the particles of its grain?

Frampton: Well, now we come to a problem of reading. If you care to expand on that sort of reading, and have the power to enforce it, then it's as good as any other, I suppose. On the other hand, it's not a reading that I can authorize more than I could any other. The film happens to be grainy; it happens to contain mirror reflections that wind and unwind on the rotary sections of the film involving Stonehenge and Salisbury Cloister. It is, however, considerably less graphic and points less to its photographic substance than *Travelling Matte,* which still has the television raster-scan lines in it. I have built into *Ordinary Matter* a montage that equates a set of connections among different kinds of space with the film projector. The film goes from rotary to reciprocating to rotary motion, like a projector.

If anything, I thought I was being rather Hollywoodian in that film, at least in one sense. I was at some pains to hide the spatial transitions between one site and another in such a way as to produce the illusion of continuity. At those moments, for instance, where the camera on Brooklyn Bridge appears to sail right into one of the buttresses, the "buttress" is in fact an entirely different place; at the east end of the Brooklyn Bridge when the camera goes into the dark, that darkness was in fact shot inside a building a considerable distance away. So the construction of the continuous space is the fiction.

If there's any large reference to my customary confrontation of the illusionist and graphic spaces, it involves the sound. The soundtrack is the entirety of the Wade-Giles syllabary of Chinese, minus what are called the "tones" with which those syllables are uttered. There are only four-hundred-odd of them, and if you take tone aside, they make up the entirety of the spoken language, at least in Mandarin dialect. I tried to utter them tonelessly, and they're also reverberant. It sounds like a language; it sounds a little bit like Chinese. At the same time, it is unintelligible to both a nonspeaker of Chinese and essentially to a speaker of Chinese; it is as if one recited a portion of the dictionary. It's like looking at a printed page in an alien alphabet. It may look like written language, but it is, nevertheless, indecipherable.

MacDonald: I was thinking, too, about your use of pixilation. When the amount of distinction from frame to frame is beyond a certain point, the viewer becomes more aware of it as a technique.

Frampton: Well, the usual effect of pixilation is to flatten the space—Mekas's pixilation tends to flatten the space—but that presupposes a hundred percent displacement between frames. I think of the pixilation in *Ordinary Matter* as illusionist. At the time of making the film my notion was to synthesize an impossibly high rate of speed, one that's physically impossible for the body. I think of it not as pixilation (God, I hate the word *pixilated;* it sounds like a cross between *titillated* and *pixie*) but as a kind of stop-motion animation in which the camera, not the subject, moves, in this case through space. In a jittery way, it does a little bit of what Mike's [Michael Snow's] machine in *The Central Region* does: namely, it presents a kind of de-anthropomorphized vision, by transversing the space in a manner and at a speed that a human being could not.

MacDonald: What continues to strike me as reflexive is that the viewer quickly gets engaged in trying to catch the points when the camera is not simply moving through differing spaces but is going back through the same space we've already been through. In all the sections of the film, other than the crossing of the bridge and the spiral into and out of Stonehenge, we see the same spaces over and over—either in multiple prints or in multiple takes of the same walks—but because of the specifics of your single framing, it's very difficult to know when we're moving back into a repeat of our movement across a particular space and when we're continuing to move forward. Since we come to recognize that at any given change of frame anything can happen, we concentrate on trying not to be fooled. We become unusually aware of single framing as a technique.

Frampton: Actually, I used multiple prints of multiple takes. I took three strolls around the Cloister, which I then multiply printed, and some of the other things, too, involved several prints of several takes. There were instances when I set the camera to a slow framing speed and a tight shutter to yield the least smeared image I could get and *ran* with it, staggering up through my hayfield at the maximum possible speed, holding the camera one foot from the ground. There's also real-time footage: the stuff in the dark under Brooklyn Bridge is 24 fps and it was also very highly edited, but that's impossible for the spectator to retrieve because the cuts are all across black. Finally, it all became material for fabricating an impossible continuum.

I should also point out that those three main locations were chosen with an eye to their function in relation to different kinds of spaces. A cloister is, by definition, an enclosure that one sees only from the inside: one looks inward. Stonehenge only appears to be that way. Instead of looking inward entirely, it also very much looks outward, first, towards the larger geographic place in which it's situated—Salisbury Plain, a large and very shallow dish surrounded by forests and ringed by burial mounds that probably predate all but the very oldest parts of the henge; then, historically, towards the sites in England where the stones were brought from; and finally, because it is an astronomical observatory, towards very large astronomical spaces with long periodicities. Brooklyn Bridge, of course, is a monument—one that I've always had a special predilection for—to connecting two places that are otherwise inaccessible to each other. There are plenty of bridges in New York, but I have a particular sentiment for Brooklyn Bridge, not only because of its aesthetic qualities but because of its significance in bridge design. It has a double life: it is, in fact, a functional bridge, but it is also a monument to a certain kind of adventure that was undertaken at the beginning of the industrial age.

MacDonald: When you chose Brooklyn Bridge, were you conscious of a connection between the major technological advance it embodies—it was the first great suspension bridge—and the coming of film? I wonder especially because of the bringing together of spaces that characterizes both the bridge and *Ordinary Matter.*

Frampton: That's interesting. No, I suppose not. The bridge has that same kind of signature, and it's from a not dissimilar time. It also has a peculiar American imprint on it. In a way, Brooklyn Bridge is to the Eiffel Tower somewhat as Edison's cinema is to the cinema of the Lumières. Brooklyn Bridge is at once an adventure of the mind and commands its space as the Eiffel Tower is and does (it's wonderful how much one can see from the bridge and how conscious one is in walking over it that New York is a city of water-ways and islands). At the same time, just like Edison's cinema, it has the marks of profit stamped all over it. It's one thing to discover that one can command a space in a certain way with stone and steel; it is another to take note that there's a good buck in it. Brooklyn Bridge, after all, was financed; it coincides, in fact, quite exactly with—and was a part of—the grand consolidation of industrial capitalism. On the other hand, there ain't nothing quite like it. The first time I walked across the Brooklyn Bridge was unquestionably one of the grand aesthetic experiences of my life—and Stonehenge, indeed, was another.

MacDonald: I had a problem when I was studying *Remote Control* [1972] deciding if the specific TV programs that you collected imagery from to make the basic loop were chosen with a specific purpose in mind or whether they were chosen at random.

Frampton: I had specific purposes in mind.

MacDonald: At times I can identify the shows; most of the time I can't.

Frampton: The real plum was a Ray Milland movie about a man who was able to penetrate matter. Of course, as such things always do, this had the direst possible consequences. He became a murderer by occupying the same space as other people. He reached into their chests and squeezed. Quite gruesome.

Another was an episode of a continuing series with Richard Widmark that involved endless running through halls, up stairs, down stairs, into rooms, out of rooms, and so forth, all at extraordinary speed, investing quite anonymous places far from each other with illusions of continuity: "creative geography" as Kuleshov called it.

Another, which I found particularly interesting, was a spy show in which the spy received his instructions from a central headquarters, literally by remote control. They had a gadget rigged up so that they could see through his eyes.

There were a couple more. Essentially, all of them had to do with the relationship among some sort of active consciousness, the space in which it found itself, and the things in that space—specifically, how much was known or not known about them.

MacDonald: The repetitions of the loop are broken up by series of numbers. In the Film-makers' Coop Catalogue . . .

Frampton: I'm going to stop making comments in the Coop Catalogue.

MacDonald: . . . You mentioned "five ways of knowing," and there are five separate arrangements of numbers within the footage. I've always assumed that the numbers imply different ways in which the same basic material can be edited.

Frampton: Correct.

MacDonald: Did you have five specific filmmakers' editing strategies in mind?

Frampton: I had five strategies that I myself had already used in making films, reduced, as it were, to numerical notation. Of course, in one instance, more is involved than a number.

MacDonald: You're talking about the image of the projected rectangle?

Frampton: Yes. It's in the position of number 1. At least in draftsman's conventions and in projective geometry, dotted lines represent either hidden or imaginary edges. The rectangle that one sees, of course, has the same aspect ratio as the film frame and, depending on how you twiddle your eyes, the dotted lines that converge from the corners of the rectangle can be seen either as being projected from the back towards you or from a point somewhere above your shoulder onto the surface. I thought by assigning a graphic figure to the number-1 position, a sign that had to do with the mechanics and geometry of film (it cartoons—is an index to—the process of film projection from the lens to a 1.33-to-1 screen), I might manage to suggest that it was also imaginable that other such figures might be associated with the other thirty-nine numbers. In the film immediately after *Remote Control—Special Effects* [1972]—one sees only that projected rectangle.

MacDonald: In *Special Effects* you're obviously trying to get the viewer to concentrate on the significance of the frame.

Frampton: The dotted-line rectangle *moves;* at times it partially leaves the frame. There's a signifier in the imagery, in other words, that says the camera was hand held. In college courses, or Brakhage, handheldness usually means "subjective" point of view, looking out through a personal eye. Yet what one sees, looking out through that personal eye, is a signifier that speaks only of the limits of the screen. Let's say that one is attending to a certain space within which, presumably, one expects something to happen.

What I was pursuing, and not at any great length, is that extraordinary determination that consciousness seems to have to find meaning, to decode. When there is very little to decode, that propensity surfaces. The slightest apparent change in point of view or in distance, in the fixity or fluidity of the camera, suddenly leaps into an intense foreground and is decoded as meaning that somehow something has changed, and that change is sensed as meaningful. One of the best remarks I ever heard about the film was reported to me by someone who had brought a friend to see it. This friend said that as he watched *Special Effects,* he wondered what the dotted line was about, and it occurred to him that it was to show where the movie would be if there were any.

MacDonald: How did you choose that particular sound track for *Special Effects?* Is it just a substratum of sounds within which viewers try to hear meaning, the way they try to see meaning in the visuals?

Frampton: I would assume so. That particular piece of sound was pure synthesizer work (not a very complicated patch) made on a Buchla in Pittsburgh. It was one of the first times I used one. It's quasi-musical and not acoustical—not made by rubbing something on something or hitting something or blowing into something. There are moments when it suggests repetitive vocal sounds: laughter or shrieks. I wanted a track that had a certain degree of ambiguity and never resolved itself one way or another. It doesn't stand alone as a piece of music, or even have a sufficient relation to musical culture, for instance.

MacDonald: You mentioned that you do not want to discuss *Magellan* at any length.

Frampton: Not for quite some time anyway [see Simon in bibliography].

MacDonald: Are the short films listed in the Coop catalogue after *Hapax Legomena*—*Apparatus Sum* [1972], *Tiger Balm* [1972], *Yellow Springs* [1972], and *Less*—parts of *Magellan?*

Frampton: Yes, with the moderate qualification that *Apparatus Sum* is a very brief study for *Magellan: At the Gates of Death* [1976]. *Less* is a segment of a section that has no other segments yet, so that its place and function are unclear. One of the things I'm going to do soon is to restructure the mode of presentation of *Magellan*—not the film itself, but only how it's presented—in such a way that its shape can begin to become clearer, at least in skeletal form. *Magellan: At the Gates of Death* is seen, when it has been seen, as a 106-minute chunk. In the calendrical wheel of the whole work, it's divided into twenty-four sections that are seen at considerable distances in time from each other. Much of what I've done so far, with the exception of *SOLARIUMA-GELANI,* is distributed throughout the work; that is to say, sections are factored and interleave with each other. In the next few months, I'll finish certain specimen days in the cycle. A day or a number of calendrical days will constitute a program. Anyhow, *Yellow Springs* is a portrait—of Paul Sharits; it belongs to a particular section late in the film that is a portrait gallery. *Tiger Balm* is also part of *Magellan.* There are whole sections of *Magellan* that are very lightly sketched, that have one or two or three single points; other sections, of course, are more clearly filled out. By the way, you mentioned some time ago that you like *Palindrome.* I'm quoting it in its entirety in *Magellan* as one of the Dreams.

MacDonald: I'm puzzled about why *Palindrome* isn't better known.

Frampton: Well, there is a mechanics to these things. Without question, the film rental market is almost entirely universities. Say you are doing your survey course on the New American Cinema, or whatever it's called, which is still in most places considered an unbelievably outré idea. Which film is going to give you a better handle for a nice nifty class session: *Surface Tension* or *Palindrome?* There is the grimmest possible sense in which the entry of advanced film into the university context has commoditized films. Those things are shown that it's easy to give a lecture about. Now, the easiest films of all to do lectures on are those that have been written about, because you can cop so-and-so's essay on the topic. Speaking from within university teaching and having seen a lot of it, I am not only inclined but entitled to a certain cynicism about the process. There has now been enough written about *Zorns Lemma* that, with a day's preparation, anybody can come up with a coherent, even a blazing, lecture on the subject. On the other hand, it takes a fair degree of intrepidness to take on something opaque about which you may have confused feelings. I mean who is intellectually fearless enough to attempt to hang one on *Palindrome* in front of a bunch of undergraduates?

Of course, not all films invite writing; *nostalgia* does because of its relation to language. *Critical Mass,* too. But if you start heading for *Travelling Matte,* you're on fairly rough ground already, and it at least has the merit of being finished. What the hell are you going to do with *Magellan?* Of course, *Magellan* points at that problem because I'm making it point at that problem. I myself have the fondness that everybody has for things that are clear, for summary works, but it can't all be like that. Indeed, most of it cannot be like that. To use a favorite example of mine, the summary work is like the fictions of chemistry. Inorganic chemistry purports to study such things as "cobalt." Well, in a certain sense, yes, there is such a thing as cobalt, but it is a product of the laboratory. It's a fiction. There is no such thing in nature as the chemistry of cobalt. There is dirt, but nobody wants to have anything to do with the chemistry of dirt because dirt is in fact genuinely complex. So you can teach *Surface Tension* or *Zorns Lemma* because they are like the chemistry of cobalt, but if you're going to get involved with *Magellan,* then, of course, you're up to your eyeballs in the chemistry of dirt.

All this involves the larger and more general problem of developing exegetical tools for unpacking the film image. At this point we tend to forget the history of that sort of critical endeavor. Presumably, any undergraduate junior who has majored in English has the tool kit to pull apart John Donne, but the really difficult and painful problem was the one of building those tools in the first place.

As it is, certain things just get more and more attention, and other things gradually sink into obscurity. Of the films before *Zorns Lemma* that are not known, I happen to have a considerable opinion of *States*. It was a particularly important film for me, but at the same time, it's a delicate reading job to undertake. And then, of course, some things just don't rent often because they're truly forbidding. Although there has been some good writing about *Magellan: At the Gates of Death*—in particular, a fine piece by Lucy Fischer ["*Magellan:* Navigating the Hemispheres"]—people haven't exactly lined up to rent it, maybe partly because they're paternalizing themselves or their audiences and partly because it's oversized and offers very little in the way of immediate seduction.

MacDonald: Is *Zorns Lemma* the most circulated of your films?

Frampton: Probably. *Zorns Lemma,* and *nostalgia, Critical Mass, Poetic Justice, Surface Tension,* and *Lemon.* The summer, fall, and winter sections of *SOLARIUMAGELANI* get around quite a bit. *Tiger Balm* gets around some, and *Maxwell's Demon*—which I think is probably perceived as a filler. That pretty well covers it. There are films that I could just as well take out of the Coop. *Heterodyne* and *Snowblind* are never rented. *Palindrome* rents three times a year in a nation of 240 million. But, of course, *Zorns Lemma* is perfect for your ninety-minute classroom session.

MacDonald: Particularly since it's about education.

Frampton: I know; it's a ringer; it's totally embarrassing. I couldn't have done better if I tried. At the same time, it's an albatross.

MacDonald: During these sessions we've talked about a number of areas from which you feel you've learned a good deal. One is literature, particularly Pound, Joyce, and Stein. I find less and less clear connection between your work and the work of other filmmakers. Are there filmmakers you feel are particularly close to you or whose work has a large part to play in yours?

Frampton: Any more, no. There are people whose work I always find instructive in one way or another. Snow is not about to make another film in the near future, although there are rumors that he's grumbling about it a little bit again, and even rumors of that kind are tantalizing in the extreme. I pay extremely close attention to anything Yvonne Rainer does. She and I share some sympathies. To a remarkable extent, she's involved with language, though in a different way from me. Yvonne has adopted a confessional rhetoric, an overt use of personal material that isn't to be read simply, I think. While the material is personal, or purports to be, it also has a specific formal weight. Also, it's work that transpires within a much larger climate of art. One of the things I've been thinking about recently is Yvonne's leaving off performance. Well, there are plenty of reasons for her to do that; one's interests shift. At the same time, Yvonne's leaving off performance for film is also an evacuation of the performance arena, particularly that portion of it that at one time was associated with dance, although certainly her films enclose and apostrophize performance and performance values. In a way, she has shifted from a posture of visibility to one of invisibility. What is visible about her now is what can be decoded from the work.

I suppose I chose film, or felt sympathetic to it, finally, because much of the art that was being done when I was younger—during my adolescence and during my twenties—was concerned with making the artist visible. The thumbprint aspect of abstract expressionism represented one kind of visibility: only a particular personality, a particular set of anxieties, a particular predicament could have manipulated the surface in quite that way, could have produced that set of traits that, when taken together, constitute an empirical visible style. I have never felt comfortable having that kind of visibility myself. My films put me on the end of the camera where I can never be directly visible; if I do have any visibility, it is always mediated in ways that are open to manipulation. I do know a fair number of filmmakers who have never decided which end of the camera they wanted to be on. The other major filmmaker besides Yvonne [Rainer] that I am thinking of—he also came out of performance—is Stan Brakhage; he'd like to be on both ends: he'd like to be seen and at the same time he would like to be in control of the way in which he is seen. Yvonne seems to perceive the pivot between those two modes of visibility uniquely.

But to get back to your original question. There's a big difference between seeing work and finding it interesting and important, and finding it particularly relevant to what I'm doing. There's a certain point in time when—out of animal necessity—one becomes interested in one's own work. I suspect I've come to that time. I've undertaken a large project, one that only I have any clear notion of. I don't think quite the situation has set in in film that set in by the 1930s among the literary generation of the eighties: they simply couldn't see each others' work for dust. On the other hand, if we haven't reached that point, we're bordering on it. The round of systematic public denunciation of other peoples' work that Brakhage has engaged in during the past year and a half or two years is symptomatic not so much of a specific personal attitude of Stan's as of a tendency among groups of people reaching a certain time in life and a certain stage in their development more or less contemporaneously. It hasn't got to be true, but it certainly suggests itself, that Stan is interested in his own work.

As far as my antecedents go, they are mixed and confused and always did have a great deal to do with language—not just literature but with linguistics and the philosophy of language—on the one hand, and the sciences—especially the exact sciences rather than the social sciences—on the other.

MacDonald: I'd like to raise something peripheral to what you were saying earlier about people teaching films that have been written about. There has been a tendency among many academic film people to redo what is done in universities with literature: specifically, to isolate a few great figures out of a series of generations and then to devote tremendous amounts of scholarship to them. The problem with this, I think, is that a great many very interesting artists tend to get lost during that original, rather erratic selection process and, perhaps, are never found. "Film history" tends to become the history of who is written about.

Frampton: The word *academic,* of course, is a pejorative term. It's characterized by a tendency to limit the territory by proscriptiveness: Thou Shalt Not Do So and So. At the same time, that something is taught or written about does not necessarily mean that it's become academic: it may mean that it's becoming a discipline. There was a time, after all, when what we now call philosophy was not taught, and indeed, that was equally true of literature. I remind myself sometimes that that vast catchall for everything that nobody wants—English—never had a departmental status or was taught as a discipline in any western university before 1911. Universities taught Latin and Greek, the argument being that everybody knew English, so why teach it? There is nothing more academic—in the grimmest sense of the word—than just about any Hollywood film, or, let's say, any commercial melodrama. They are utterly academic. They proceed from the notion that it is known how to make a film. At the same time, there has also been the most extreme resistance to film becoming a discipline, that is to say, something that is to be examined in a general climate of intellectual inquiry. A good part of *that* resistance comes from the avant-grade film community itself.

MacDonald: Are you saying that the avant-grade film community has resisted the academicizing of film or the attempt to bring film into universities as a discipline?

Frampton: I think it has often seen the two things as the same thing. It's a standard confusion. The other arts have, as often as not, felt that way, too. On the other hand, for the sciences, that question has been so irrelevant for so long that we can't retrieve whatever dialogue took place about the entrance of the sciences into the universities; the sciences, of course, are at once disciplines and, in some places, highly academicized. I think right now in some quarters, there is a very specific resistance not just to academicizing film but to film's emergence as a discipline, the argument being, I suppose, that critical scrutiny dries things up, makes them sterile. During the last thirty years film, almost uniquely, has enjoyed a grand period of enthusiasm without much scrutiny of itself, at least on the part of filmmakers. It has had little rational examination undertaken with a view—and this is the point, of course—to extending the range and power of its possibilities. We have seen this same drama enacted before, in the Soviet Union where Eisenstein's efforts to take film seriously as an intellectual discipline were met with cries that he was a chilly intellectual, that he was an engineer. This, of course, was equated with not having the people at heart, on the corny and insulting Stalinist grounds that the people are all heart. If one takes the narrowing of the field of possibilities as a major benchmark of academicism, then it's coming most strongly from some of those who have also preached most violently against academicization. I'm referring very specifically, although not exclusively, to Brakhage's public declarations during the last couple of years, which strike me as academic in the extreme.

As far as making monuments of major figures is concerned, I think the humanities have tended to take as their submerged metaphor what they believe to be the procedure of the sciences. It is believed that the procedure of the sciences is to take typical or illustrative examples and infer generalities from them. One cannot study all cockroaches, one studies a sample of cockroaches and makes stylistical statements about cockroaches. One cannot study all of film; 175,000 or so films have been copyrighted, and presumably that's a drop in the bucket. One deals with the quintessential sample, with the film that seems to point to possibilities for unpacking other work yet to come. Well, anything that is truly a discipline, that is taught and studied, must constantly be under construction because, invariably, one is wrong to a degree. The intellectual tools that one has at any given moment tend to enforce certain readings, to delete certain other readings, to produce an historic order, a finite set of monuments that seem to constitute a tradition. A tradition is that part of the history of a discipline that is perceived as ordered and important, but only at a given time.

MacDonald: Are there filmmakers you feel should be admitted to the tradition now, who have as yet not received anything like the attention they deserve?

Frampton: Strictly speaking, nobody's had it. A few people do come to mind: Ernie Gehr, Larry Gottheim. Jonas Mekas's work has been unjustly eclipsed by his other activities. I don't think it's had the kind of attention it merits, and I certainly don't think Andrew Noren's work has had the attention that it merits. Nevertheless, it's also true that these people are not unknown. It does mean that the difficult and groping first essay and first seminar have not yet been done. I can't think of any utter unknowns who should have their own constellations, because, of course, if I could, I would be madly trumpeting their names. Critical estimate, though, does not begin until the construction of the discipline sets in, so presumably we're only at the very beginning. I cannot think of a single critical examination of an artist making films in my generation, that I would consider exemplary.

Larry Gottheim

Many filmmakers who came to film in the late 1960s and early 1970s seem to have been interested in a return to basics. Like most of us who remember that period, they had experienced the ever-increasing tendency of both the commercial media and the developing independent cinema toward sensory overload. Television ads were condensing more and more information into shorter periods of time; commercial narrative films were becoming increasingly visceral; and many experimental and avant-garde filmmakers were producing heavy-montage "psychedelic" forms of cinema. Larry Gottheim is one of a number of filmmakers who provided filmic reactions against this tendency. Gottheim's extensive academic training had been in comparative literature (he earned a Ph.D. from Yale). He was drawn to filmmaking without knowing anything practical about it, and not surprisingly, in the earliest films he distributes, we can see him learning the elements of cinema in a carefully controlled sequence. If Frampton's work seems indebted to Muybridge's pioneering motion photography, Gottheim's first films—*Blues* (1969), *Fog Line* (1970), *Corn* (1970), *Doorway* (1971), *Thought* (1970, under the title *Swing*), and *Harmonica* (1971)—are reminiscent of the Lumières' early single-shot movies. Though Gottheim's films are much longer than the less-than-a-minute Lumière films (*Blues* is eight and a half minutes; *Fog Line, Corn,* and *Harmonica* are approximately eleven minutes), like the Lumière films, they are exactly one shot long and are photographed from a single, unchanging camera position. Unlike the Lumière films, however, which are simple documentations, Gottheim's exquisite one-shot films dramatize his step-by-step exploration of filmic options (in *Blues, Corn,* and *Fog Line* the camera is entirely stationary; in *Doorway* and *Thought* the camera slowly pans; in *Harmonica* the camera is mounted inside a moving car and the footage recorded in sync sound), and they offer the viewer intellectual and aesthetic meditations of considerable beauty and subtlety.

The focus of the early films, and of most of Gottheim's later films as well, is the interplay between natural process and human rationality—particularly the use of the technological apparatus of cinema to "capture" the physical world. The "still-lifes" and landscapes that at first seem to be Gottheim's central subject matter are dense with subtle indices and metaphors of the mechanisms used to produce the imagery we are looking at. The same approach is evident in his first longer film, *Barn Rushes* (1971, thirty-four minutes); *rushes* refers not only to the weeds we see in the foreground as Gottheim moves by the same upstate New York barn eight times on different days and different times of day but also to the camera's "rushing" movement past the barn and to the completed film's being merely unedited footage (or rushes) spliced together in the order in which it was shot.

This same interplay between technology and nature is evident in *Horizons* (1973) which remains, in my view, Gottheim's most significant achievement. *Horizons* is reminiscent of Vivaldi's *The Four Seasons;* it provides a visual journey through the upstate New York landscape, beginning in summer and proceeding through the seasonal cycle until spring. The seasons are distinguished from one another in Gottheim's overall editing strategy. The summer section presents pairs of shots divided from one another by one-second intervals of green leader; the fall shots are organized into groups of four separated by one-second intervals of red leader; the winter shots are also presented in groups of four, but they are separated by one-second intervals of blue leader; and the spring section presents triads of shots separated by yellow leader. Another structuring device is reminiscent of Gottheim's literary background. Each grouping of shots in the film is arranged so that the individual shots "rhyme" with each other. In the summer section the rhyme is simple—*a a* (that is, each shot contains a visual element that rhymes with a visual element in the other shot); in the fall section, the shots rhyme *a b b a;* in the winter, *a b a b* (a fitting rhyme: upstate winters seem to mark time); in the spring the rhyme scheme is terza rima: *a b a, b c b,* and so on. Since Gottheim's complex rhyme scheme does not announce itself, viewers can experience the film without ever becoming aware of it: the progression of the imagery is itself very lovely. But once we recognize the rhyme scheme, we can see that, like the seasonal structure itself, it extends Gottheim's thinking about human rationality and natural process. A horizon, after all, is a line where—as human perception and thought would have it—sky meets land; and *Horizon* is full of horizon lines. But even while we use the concept of the horizon, we know that there is no such line in reality, except in our conceptualization of it. Similarly, we divide the year into seasons, and yet we know that one season does not stop so another can begin: one season gradually develops into the next. Gottheim's decision to structure footage into rhyming sections is itself a metaphor for the way in which the human mind imposes its logic onto the spaces and processes of nature in order to control and use them.

Horizons was followed by three long films that, with *Horizons,* make up the longer work *Elective Affinities.* In *Mouches Volantes* (1976) Gottheim worked extensively with sound for the first time, making it a central element in another highly structured work. *Mouches Volantes* presents seven lovely passages of visual imagery, photographed around what was then Gottheim's Binghamton, New York, home and during a family vacation in Florida. These passages are separated from one another by passages of dark leader and arranged 1, 2, 3, 4, 5, 6, 7, 7, 6, 5, 4, 3, 2, 1. The sound track is four and a half minutes of reminiscences about blues singer Blind Willie Johnson by his widow, Angelina Johnson, edited from a Folkways record. Gottheim arranges the imagery and sound so that the film alternates between silence and sound: we hear the reminiscences for the first time, juxtaposed with visual passage 2, then with passages 4, 6, 7 (the second presentation), 5, 3, 1. While we repeatedly hear and see the same sounds and visuals, Gottheim carefully arranged them so that a variety of subtle relationships between particular sounds and visual events would become evident. The result allows the viewer-listener to examine a wide range of ways in which formal and representational elements or recorded imagery can interact with formal and representational aspects of sound and with silence. Because the visuals and sounds are so different from one another—especially when compared with the images and sounds in conventional film—many of these interactions are quite subtle; one barely senses a connection before it disappears. (*Mouches Volantes* refers to the "flying gnats" described by H. Von Helmholtz in *Physiological Optics* [1866], which exist in the human eye, just at the edge of perception.)

Four Shadows (1978), the third section of *Elective Affinities,* works with image and sound in a manner reminiscent of *Mouches Volantes* but in a somewhat more complex—and in some senses more literary—manner. Four four-minute passages of imagery—surveyors working in the field across from Gottheim's home, pages of a book about Cézanne filmed in close-up, a series of winter cityscapes, and a family of siamang gibbons filmed at the National Zoo in Washington—are juxtaposed with four four-minute passages of sound—outdoor country sounds, four readings of a passage from Wordsworth's *Prelude* (each by four different voices in succession, including those of filmmakers Vincent Grenier, Heinz Emigholz, Jonas Mekas, Peter Kubelka, Taka Iimura, Alfons Schilling, Babette Mangolte, and Klaus Wyborny), a portion of Debussy's *Pélleas et Mélisande,* and the shrieks and hootings of the siamang gibbons. The eight passages of visuals and sounds are arranged so that each passage of visuals is, in a single instance, seen in juxtaposition with each passage of sounds. Because of the number and diversity of the sights and sounds juxtaposed in *Four Shadows,* the conceptual experience it offers—the primary focus again being the interaction of human logic in its various extensions with natural forces—is remarkably complex. At the same time, *Four Shadows* maintains a tendency in Gottheim's work to move away from the sensual pleasure of looking at beautiful imagery, a tendency which, in my view, weakens the two films that follow *Four Shadows*. In both *Tree of Knowledge* (1980), the final section of *Elective Affinities,* and the more recent *Natural Selection* (1983), the conventional kinds of beauty that made the conceptual dimensions of the early films comparatively accessible have been largely eliminated, and the result is forms of film experience too dryly academic for my taste.

Gottheim's contributions as an administrator, especially during the early 1970s, deserve mention here. He established the film department at SUNY–Binghamton, brought Ken Jacobs to Binghamton to teach, and during the mid-1970s hosted visiting filmmakers (including Peter Kubelka, Ernie Gehr, Taka Iimura, and Nicholas Ray) who made Binghamton for a time one of the nation's more exciting film venues. The influence of the SUNY–Binghamton film department continues to be felt in a variety of ways, most notably, perhaps, at the Collective for Living Cinema in New York, where Gottheim, Jacobs, and a variety of former Binghamton students have played a crucial role.

This interview was recorded during the summer of 1977 at Gottheim's home in Binghamton.

MacDonald: You had considerable academic training at Oberlin and Yale, which led to your earning a doctorate in comparative literature. When you first came to SUNY–Binghamton, in fact, you taught literature. Could you describe how you became involved in film?

Gottheim: It's funny; I was thinking the other day that I'm the sort of person who labors decisions a lot. Even in my films I devise elaborate procedures to slow things down so that I can consider as many factors as possible. I remember reading Kafka's diaries and feeling this great sympathy with Kafka. He was always thinking about marrying somebody and for years wrote these elaborate lists of reasons for and against getting married. Of course, he could never make up his mind about very much. Anyway, although I'm that sort of person, the things that I've done in my life that have made a major difference have been done with almost no thought or preparation or even awareness that a big decision was being made.

The first art that I was involved in was music; I played the clarinet as a child and went to a high school for music and art. I was seriously involved with music and have returned to that a lot. I spend more time listening to music and thinking about music than I do reading or being involved in other arts. In any case, when I was in college, I became interested in other subjects and kind of dropped music. I started writing poetry and fiction; I was writing a novel at one time. During the period when I was deciding whether to go on to graduate school, or what to do with my life, I came to feel that to be a secret poet—you know, somebody who does graduate work in literature but is secretly writing poetry—was to be in an awkward and embarrassing position. I felt that I should make some kind of decision and either get out of the whole school situation and just keep writing or commit myself to the academic thing, which offered real satisfaction, at least when I was in graduate school. So I stopped trying to be a poet or a novelist in the middle of graduate school.

When I got away from graduate school and into the world of teaching and faced the prospect of writing about literature, the more empty that sort of thing became. The people in the literature department saw me as this bright young faculty member who was going to write these articles and this book and do this and do that, and my whole life seemed spread out before me. I had this tremendous revulsion against that, and I guess all of this creative necessity that had earlier come out in music and in poetry just welled up very suddenly and surprisingly, and I have no idea why it had to do with film. I didn't know anybody who was a filmmaker. I was only dimly aware that there was such a thing as independent filmmaking. But for a year or two I found myself longing for some opportunity to learn how to make films, and I realized at some point that that opportunity was never going to arise, that I had to do it myself. I remember going to somebody I knew who had been associated with making newsreels in the fifties. I told him I wanted to get a camera, and he said, "Are you interested in getting 8mm or 16mm?" and I had no clear idea even of what the difference was.

In any case, around that time I went to Willoughby's in New York and for $300 got an old Bolex camera with a single lens, not even a very good lens. It all happened very quickly, and there I was with this camera and two rolls of film, and the only instructions I had were the instructions that had come with the Bolex, and I felt tremendously lightened, tremendously committed to what I was doing. It took a long time to decide what I was going to do with those first two rolls of film, but the transition happened almost overnight. The next year I started wanting to teach courses in film and my every waking moment was involved with film. When people would say, "Oh, I understand that you're interested in film now; are you still teaching literature?" I would realize that only a year had passed. It seemed like forever.

MacDonald: About your first five films: *Blues, Fog Line, Corn, Doorway,* and *Harmonica.* When I describe them to people, they often think I'm kidding: "You *like* a film about blueberries being eaten?" But when I show them to audiences—particularly when I've suggested that you are quite serious and that the viewer has to concentrate to see what's offered—I have extremely good luck with audience response. What sorts of experiences have you had with audiences seeing the films?

Gottheim: To some extent I think these films have aged the way wine ages. They seem to be clearer and to have more weight now on first viewing than they did when I first made them. This is true even with *Barn Rushes.* When you saw *Barn Rushes* when it was still fairly recent, you could hardly see the film: there was so much talking; the audience had so many problems. In the last few years when I've shown those early films, I haven't had that sort of problem. It seems that somehow, even though each audience may be seeing the films for the first time, something has happened in the world to make the relationship between the audience and the films a little clearer.

There is a problem, especially with those films, because they raise a question about what "to see a film" means. To see *Blues* as a film about blueberries, let's say, is not really to be experiencing the film in the way that I mean the film to be experienced. In fact, it may be that the most fruitful way of thinking of that whole group of single-shot films is to see that they have something to do with what it means to experience something. What the films are about more than anything is the experience of perceiving.

MacDonald: All the early films seem to combine examinations of simple natural things and very subtle explorations of properties of film. Much of their interest, in fact, is a function of that combination. But on another level several of the films—I'm thinking particularly of *Blues, Corn,* and *Doorway*—seem metaphoric. In *Doorway,* for example, you could say that a combination of a bleak winterscape and of the pan, which makes that landscape slide from darkness to darkness, seems to take on a fairly obvious metaphoric dimension. It that a by-product of other concerns, or is it something you were conscious of when you were making the films?

Gottheim: I wasn't very concerned, or even conscious, of more literal kinds of metaphors. One thing that I've been involved with for a long time, though, is the way that things in art seem to take on a reverberance. I don't know what the proportion is, but if I were keeping a tape recording of my consciousness, it might be that one out of every million filmic ideas comes to be embodied in a film. Now, why does this one detail or this one procedure or this one constellation of ideas and procedures get to be carried out? As I work, I have a feeling of it being promising; it seems to be holding out the possibility of having these reverberations, even if I don't know exactly what they are. There just seems to be this pressure that leads me on.

For me *Fog Line* has the most reverberations that keep coming. I expect that five years from now, or twenty years from now, I will be looking at *Fog Line* and for the first time will be conscious of some kind of verbalizable significance. I feel that that film, especially, has a capacity of not being exhaustible. This element also has to do with why the early films have been such rich influences on the later films, although that hasn't been conscious either. When

The landscape in Gottheim's Fog Line *(1970).*

I was making *Horizons,* for example, I began to think about lines and horizons and so on and realized that there were a lot of implications in *Fog Line*
that I had been only partly conscious of when I made it. In some cases, I don't
think about even the most obvious things until much later.

MacDonald: The early films seem largely concerned with an almost meditative concentration. While the goal of the meditation seems largely materi-
alistic, at least in the sense that it develops the viewer's sensitivity to perceptual realities both in film and in nature, at times I wondered—particularly in
the cases of *Blues* and *Doorway*—whether there's a kind of mystic tendency
in them. This was suggested to me in both cases by the way that the flicker
created by the sixteen-frames-per-second speed (particularly at the end of
Blues and at the point when the big tree comes across the image in *Doorway*)
seems to hint at something beyond material perception. Do you have any feelings about this?

Gottheim: Yes. This is another area that is very, very important to me, but
it's also true that a lot of my involvement with this sort of question is not very
verbal. I mean some people—filmmakers or other artists—become very involved with a certain specific theory. They might be studying Buddhism or
studying this or studying that, and their work comes to be an embodiment of
their studies. I don't work that way. For me, making a film is like opening up a

veil. I'm seeing something or experiencing something, and I'm not quite sure what it is. Actually, in the period when I was making *Blues* and *Fog Line*, I think that I was very happy to talk about mysticism or mystical things, or at least I had these vague feelings about Eastern religions. These days I tend to talk much more about energy, and I feel that the same thing that I was talking about then is something that's not mystical but is very real, although it's very difficult to talk about. Certainly energy is a very real element in life, not just the electricity that powers light bulbs but the life energy in people that has to do with their relationships to each other and their relationships to nature. In those early years, though, I was much more interested in using films as a way of teaching people how to see. That was an end in itself.

The viewing process that I feel is appropriate for the early films is a creative one. You can't, as you can in some kinds of story film where you know that the film is going to keep providing you with fresh surprises, remain entirely passive. In all the early films there's a sense of having to find a new stance as a viewer. The films are trying to have enough richness and complexity that if you do try a new stance, they begin to reward you, but, at the same time, the films are not saying that everyone in the audience at this particular moment must now start paying attention to a particular detail.

There are moments when you may be more likely to look at one thing than another, but I wanted all those films not to manipulate you or force you or push your attention in a specific direction.

MacDonald: During *Barn Rushes* you shoot from inside a moving car, tracking past the same barn over and over in different lights, and you create a wide variety of views of basically the same scene. Was the imagery collected over a long period of time? Also, did you make many passes by the barn and select specific ones, or did you just decide to use the ones you shot?

Gottheim: Barn Rushes was made in maybe a two-month period. The barn is right near my house; I pass it all the time. I was originally drawn to it because of those movements of light through its slats that you see in the film. The first few rolls were shot as experiments. I made a few hundred-foot rolls just to see what it would be like, not knowing they were sketches for what would become a film. There is this problem of being outside New York City and not being able to take stuff to the lab all the time. So I did three and went to New York, took them to the lab, and brought them back. When I saw the three of them strung out together, as they are when you get back three separate rolls, I started to have this idea of using that as a form. The rolls were very exciting to me, and it began to seem that the difference from one light to another, and from one situation to another, was very strong. I couldn't afford— and it didn't seem necessary—to film the barn hundreds and hundreds of times. Mostly what I did during the next six weeks or so was to go there every time there seemed to be an interesting light situation. There was a very strong selective process going on without my having to film everything, though I did film a lot of material that was finally rejected. Then there was this process of deciding what to include. The order of the film is predominantly the order in which the rolls were shot. The first three rolls are, in fact, the three on that original roll. Deciding that there would be eight was a delicate process; I had to question what contribution each roll would make.

MacDonald: Barn Rushes seems to be a filmic attempt to do a Monet haystack series. What connections and distinctions do you see between your work, particularly *Barn Rushes,* and the Impressionists?

Gottheim: I think the Impressionists had a strong formative influence on my seeing. It goes back to childhood experiences. I have many memories of going to the Museum of Modern Art when I was thirteen or fourteen and seeing Van Gogh, Monet, and others. Their attempts to deal with light and natural scenes at the same time that they consciously dealt with the problems of painting, of art, drew me to them most strongly. Of course, we're using the word *Impressionist* in a very loose way. More recently—in my film, *Four Shadows*—I'm confronting this issue more consciously. In some strange way it has to do with living in Binghamton, where there are elements of nature—not of nature in its grandeur but of nature transformed, at a point between industrial, more modern civilization and earlier, more rural civilization. Artists in the nineteenth century were also responding to this.

MacDonald: Horizons was a much longer undertaking than any of your earlier films. Both in length and complexity it seems to be a much more demanding work. Could you review in detail the steps involved in creating the finished film?

Gottheim: My first idea was of something much simpler and more abstract. As a matter of fact, I remember that I happened to be standing on a hill with Ernie Gehr. He was recording some sheep for a film, which I think never got made. The hill was very green, and it was a very clear day, and there was a clear, cloudless blue sky, and I had this idea of making a film that would somehow involve shots in which the horizon would divide the frame into very clear areas of color. I thought that the form of the film would have to do with these different perceptions of texture and color and so on. It was a very vague idea, but on the basis of that idea I went out to film some horizons. Also, I decided there would have to be some very subtle movement within the shots— say, clouds moving or grass blowing in the wind. There would be a presence of movement, but of a very minimal kind. Though I drove around looking for situations like that, I hardly filmed any. I found myself being very, very selective. I would drive around for hours and not find anything, or I would find something that was somewhat close to what I had originally intended but that also had some element that was a departure. At first I was only using the car as a vehicle for getting around to try to find these places; when I found a place, I would get out of the car and film. Also, although I thought that all of the shots were going to be still—that is, not shot from a moving car—I intentionally did not take a tripod, but held the camera while shooting these fairly static shots because I wanted to be sure the shots would have at least the movement imparted by my own different ways of holding the camera. I also decided right from the beginning that I wouldn't do a lot of recording of any given image but that when I came to something that seemed right in terms of what I was thinking of then that I would take only one shot of it. That way each image I recorded would exist in one place only for a certain moment, and my tremblings, whatever, would reflect my relationship to it at that moment.

I found that I got drawn into this process of driving around and became very preoccupied with going on these long drives by myself or walking around looking for situations worth recording. I found myself being drawn to certain kinds of situations that weren't part of the original premise at all, and at first I rejected them and didn't record them. Then I started to cheat a little bit. I might decide to use most of a roll for filming horizons, but if I happened to find something that interested me, that wasn't part of my original intention, I'd record it anyway. There's a shot in the summer section of the film—it was the first shot that I made from the moving car—where there's a stone wall behind which you can see a cross, which is inside a cemetery behind the wall. I shot that thinking that it wouldn't go into the film, but I was finding myself more and more drawn into a process that was happening on its own. I decided not to stick to a rigorous rule about what constituted the kind of shot I wanted for the film, but if I found myself drawn to something, to trust that, to let myself film it, whether it was a moving shot or a still shot. As a result, the finished film includes shots like the ones that I first set out to get—in which a very clear line of horizon separates a very clear field from a very clear sky—and shots in which there is only the most minimal horizon, in which the whole frame is filled with the landscape and other human material, except for the presence somewhere of a horizon.

Originally my idea involved greens and blues, and I assumed that my shooting would be completed in a fairly short time. But the process was extending into late summer, into autumn. I found that I was drawn into the material in such a way that I hardly understood what was happening. And I was increasingly drawn into the process of going out on these journeys. Mostly I went by myself at the beginning. Later I went with my wife, and still later, other people—friends, students, whoever—would go, and then there would be a kind of interaction that would color that particular day's shooting. But most of the time I was by myself; the sense was of private, lonely journeys out into places that became very meaningful to me personally.

While I had been drawn to *Horizons* as an idea that would be very formal, very pure, I found myself being drawn to things that were colored with certain kinds of emotional and symbolic overtones. I found that I very much liked times like dawn or evening that are more flavored, more resonant emotionally and symbolically. I found also that I wasn't willing to give up this process of going out and recording this material, even though I was then on unsure ground. I no longer had a form in mind. I kept making these images. At times I found myself going back to certain places, certain motifs, but in a different season or a different light. At other times I would deliberately get lost. I would try to find little dirt roads that I'd never been on before and go off on these paths never knowing where I would end up. I didn't know where it was all leading, and even when it was already winter, I wasn't even sure what I was doing. It seemed almost that I had been wasting a lot of time. I began to think, oh, now I've really got to go through the whole year although I didn't know why. It was a way of continuing this activity that was engrossing me, and it also kept me from having to decide what to do with the material. Also, I realized that winter would give me a possibility of getting purer images.

About a third of the way through the winter the whole emotional weight of this experience came crashing down on me, and I realized that I was generating so much material, and such loaded material, that there was no simple form for bringing it together. I finally felt I had to confront this problem of having a large collection of shots. Many people deal with having a lot of material by just editing it in some kind of intuitive way. That was very alien to me. Even when I was recording a still image with just a trembling of the camera, I was still aware that it would be a certain length and that it had a rightness of being that length. Also, when I started doing the moving shots, I was trying to think, where should this shot begin, where should it end? Anyway, I think that at some point, miraculously, the idea of a line, of a line of poetry, began to interest me as an analog to the shot. I began playing around with the possibility. This was partly because the content of my imagery had begun to seem in some ways like poetry. I was reading a lot of things that I thought might help me to find a way of structuring this material. I read Virgil's *Georgics* (I use a motto from the *Georgics* in the film), but it was reading Dante, and the poetic form of the *terza rima,* that pushed me toward the idea of organizing the shots into some kind of rhyme scheme. As a matter of fact, the *terza rima* rhyme scheme was the first one I thought of. There was also an idea of shaping the content of the material in some kind of epic way. Of course, the more I thought about it, the more I realized that while the rhyme scheme in Dante is not secondary, not just a decorative element, yet, if you read Dante in an English translation in which the rhyme is not carried over, you're still getting some of the essential elements of *The Divine Comedy.* In working with something like a rhyme scheme in film, on the other hand, the rhyme scheme itself becomes more essential, so that it's only for lack of a better word that I've used the term.

I finally decided to structure the film into four sections, each section using material from one of the seasons and each section having a different rhyme scheme. I decided that the first section would be two shots that in some sense rhyme with each other; the second and third sections would still use this two-shot pattern, but would use two, two-shot groups in groups of four; the last section, which is the most complex, would use the *terza rima*.

Having decided that the film would consist of this scheme of rhyming shots, I then had this problem of how to separate them. I thought of various possibilities, but I finally decided to separate them, first of all, by a unit of time—namely, one second. Because these shots had different durations—some are rather short, some are longer—it seemed to me that a fixed unit of time every once in a while would function as a reference, a pulse for the time organization of the shots themselves. I also decided to work with colored leader and made various experiments, finally coming up with a different color—one that related to the specific section—for each of the sections.

By the middle of winter I had worked out a formal scheme for the film, and I already had at least half the material shot. Having this formal pattern allowed me to go on through the spring. I also decided not to allow this choice of a general form or procedure to color my shooting. In other words, I completed this process of going out and filming horizons according to the principles that I had been using. It was not until the following summer, a year after I had started filming, that I said, OK now, I have all this material, and I have this concept of rhyme schemes; I'm going to see what happens in working this material into this form.

First, I grouped the material into seasons, in most cases a very straightforward process, though always at the transition from one season to another there was material that could go either way. I made four reels of all the material, essentially just as it had come from the camera, all strung together. Then, I went through a period of excising from those reels shots that I didn't want to look at anymore or that I didn't feel held up as shots. Some things came out just as I had planned them, but seemed weak. I reduced the reel to the material that I felt was the strongest. Also, in some cases when I looked at the material over and over again, I could see that some shots weakened at the end and that by cutting off the end of a shot or by starting it a little later, I could strengthen it. At any rate, there was this period of getting to know the material and tidying it up.

Then I went through a process that sounds very mechanical, but it was very important to me and far from mechanical in its function. I drew cards for all the shots in the order that they occurred on each of the four rolls. For each shot there was a picture, or in some cases several pictures, of the composition and different kinds of notations about what I noticed in the shot. As I drew these cards, I attempted to memorize the material. I was able to work with an analytic projector, so I could project a shot slowly and stop it. What I would do, for example, is look at the card for a shot and try to recreate in my mind what that shot looked like and felt like. I tried to improve my sense of each shot until I felt that I could comfortably look at the card and know everything that happened in the shot, including such things as the shaking of the camera and the different velocities of the car (did it move uniformly or did it pick up speed or slow down?).

Once I had this collection of cards, I went to another stage in which I used a looseleaf notebook. I took a page in the notebook and drew a schema of the first card on that page. Then I went through the whole stack of cards noting on this page any relationship of any sort between that first shot and any of the other shots. Sometimes, a relationship would be very obvious. It might be a shot of the same place. Sometimes, a certain color appeared in a certain place in the frame, sometimes a shape, sometimes a certain movement, sometimes a certain association. On the page with a given card, I might have many relationships; in some cases, very few. Finally, I had this book that noted all of the relationships between all the shots.

Then I went through a process of trying to select out of the many possible relationships the one that I would use. In one case there might be only one relationship that I felt was interesting, so I would choose that one. In other instances, I had to choose the most interesting relationship from among several. Once I had found a suitable relationship, I removed two cards from consideration. Each choice I made reduced the field of available shots to be paired with other shots. I kept paring down and paring down until finally I had made a kind of tentative selection of all of the shots.

Next, I took all the cards and began working to find a possible order for them. I had these regions on the floor and divided the cards according to whether they seemed to belong towards the beginning, towards the end, or at some other point. Within the two-shot groupings it made a big difference which shot came first and which came second. In some cases, the element that constitutes the relationship between the shots is present everywhere in both shots. In some cases, it is only apparent at the beginning or at the end, so that perceiving the relationship depends on the order of the shots.

So I worked out a lot of the editing on the floor with these cards. Then there was this great time, finally, when I was satisfied with the arrangement of things. Only then did I actually put the film together and, of course, I found that certain things worked and certain things didn't work. It was a very, very complicated process to make changes at this point because all the material had been accounted for and paired up. If something didn't work in some region of this first version, it wasn't just a matter of reworking that section. I had to rethink it all. Each of the sections went through several torturous processes of being tried out, taken apart, and reassembled in very different ways. There's more, but I think that gives you some idea of the process.

MacDonald: As a viewer goes through *Horizons,* he or she starts to pick up some of those motifs that you mention finding when you were shooting the film. Some of them seem to have specific sorts of metaphoric intent and, in particular, to suggest the process of making the film. There's a motif, for instance, where you shoot through a window—its individual panes of glass are

Landscape through a window in Gottheim's Horizons *(1973).*

divided by wooden strips. That motif reminds me of the film's organization: shots divided by strips of leader. Was this conscious? Did it come into play during your organization of the units?

Gottheim: No, that particular thing wasn't conscious at that time, although those shots did have a very strong resonance. I hadn't come upon that window and that view during the first summer. The first shot that I had made of the window was in the autumn, and it registered in a very strong way to me. Later, I felt that I wanted it to be a kind of privileged area of material in the film, so I went back the second summer and filmed that material so that it would be present in all the seasons. In other instances, I found myself being drawn to images of cemeteries, of people working the land, and of other kinds of material that were obviously metaphysically resonant. At the same time, I wanted this sort of resonance to be only part of the experience. I wanted the viewer to be aware of shape, color, patterning, and other features. I think all of the material has to do with a lot of issues, and that all of it, in some sense, has to do with making the film. There are many other issues, all of which are vaguely suggested by the title *Horizons*. I'm happy that certain shots have that quality you said, but it wasn't really an intentional thing to use the shots in that way.

MacDonald: Apparently, *Horizons* has been through revisions since you showed it first. Can you explain what you changed and why? Are you satisfied with the film now?

Gottheim: The changes have only been in relation to laboratory work. I haven't made any changes in the actual editing or in the order of things. All my films are problematic in this respect, but *Horizons* in particular involved an enormous process of working with the laboratory to get the kind of print that I wanted. All the material had been shot on the same film stock, mostly with my Bolex. There were a few different lenses, but basically there was a continuity in filming. In all of my work, when I have film developed, if I'm able, I make a work print. I try to have this work print be just a straight, simple print without any filtering by the laboratory, without any changing of the light. If something is overexposed on the original—according to the laboratory—I want it to be just that way on the print I'm using. In this case, I had the entire work print made on the same Ektachrome print stock that I wanted to use finally for the prints of the film. It seemed clear that if a laboratory had made this initial print, they could make a duplicate later if they used the same original material. I felt very comfortable in working with the exact nuances of color and density that were present in this work print.

Well, it turns out that labs are not set up to do that. The most common situation that a lab confronts involves having to match skin tones. If they have shots of a character who appears in the kitchen, they try to even the shots out so that even if different shots were shot in the kitchen on different days, they all look as though they were shot at the same time. The lab times and color-corrects in order to make the film have an illusionary evenness. When a lab is faced with a situation like *Horizons,* it's not willing or able to just match the original. There was this horrible nightmare of getting back the first trial print. I'd given very, very explicit instructions, including a chart that listed every shot and just what I wanted, which in most cases was a print just like the original. Instead, I got back this grotesque distortion; it was incredible. There were other problems that we don't have to go into, but it seems like the more delicate one wants a film to be, the more physical damage and extraneous problems creep in and threaten to destroy the images entirely.

In any case, I went through this very prolonged process of going back to the lab and saying, "No, this shot is too much this way, and this shot is too much that way," and then we would make another version, and another version until finally it began to approach something that I could accept. In some cases it was what my original intention was, and in some cases it wasn't exactly what I wanted, but I could work with it. Finally, I was able to get prints that were fairly satisfactory in terms of color.

This last section was the most problematic because certain things involving color that were being developed all through the film were coming to fruition. There's a kind of tone feeling at the end of the film to which the colors contribute a lot. First, there's an anticipation of an opening up of the color that is deliberately built into the beginning of the spring section; then, there's a kind of retard where it goes back, to some extent, into color areas similar to those in the winter section. In all of the prints, it went too far back; it became too dark. The last change that I made—this is now some time ago—was for the Paris Museum of Modern Art. I made some prints from the internegative in which the last section had this very scintillating quality. I was really very happy with it.

It's only in this way that *Horizons* has been changing. Much the same process has been true of all the films, by the way.

MacDonald: Mouches Volantes is like *Horizons* in its complexity. How did it develop?

Gottheim: Well, *Horizons* was a tremendous thing to live through. There was a big problem of what to do next. I fell into making *Mouches Volantes* in a different way. When I was finishing the editing of *Horizons*—this was in February of 1973—we went to some island off the coast of Florida for a month. I hadn't been filming for a while. I had gone through this whole period of filming for *Horizons,* and then I had been into this process of working with cards, working with projectors, getting to know the material—editing but not filming—and I wanted to begin filming again. I did have one roll of high contrast positive film that I had made before shooting *Horizons.* The silhouettes at the window with the snow in *Mouches Volantes* come from this. I had always thought of going back and experimenting with that film stock some more. I liked the idea of the dense blacks of the silhouettes and also of a character the snow has in that section of totally whiting out the image. I brought a lot of that film stock (it's actually a printing stock) with me, as well as other film, to Florida.

There, I filmed things in a very experimental way. I set myself compositional and light problems. I would take the camera outside and film, changing the focus and darkening the image. I remember filming a lot of material about the surf, thinking it might be helpful, but not having any clear idea how. As a matter of fact, I didn't get any of it developed until I came back. I also brought two rolls of very outdated film in rusty cans; I was interested in using it to see

Wife and child in window, from Gottheim's Mouches Volantes *(1976).*

what it would be like. The other window material in *Mouches Volantes* was shot with that. I never thought that it would be combined with the other things. When I came back, I had quite a lot of the black-and-white high-contrast positive material. I put it all on this big reel, which I looked at a lot, trying to think what I could learn from it or what I could do with it.

Then, there were some other directions, other things I was thinking about. I went fairly far with certain thoughts and ideas that never amounted to anything. I had this idea for a film involving postcards I had bought in Vienna. Also, I had always been interested, in a fairly minor way, in blues. I had this Folkways record of Blind Willie Johnson, and on the other side of the record was this interview with Angelina Johnson. I found myself liking that very much, being sort of haunted by it in a way that I couldn't clearly understand. I played it a lot during this period, and I started to feel that I would like to use it in some way, though at this time I didn't think of it at all in connection with this other material. Also, I had come across this idea of "mouches volantes" in Von Helmholtz's *Physiological Optics;* that was kind of hanging around as a title without a film.

It seems very miraculous to me that all these elements began to lodge together in my mind. It began to seem conceivable to actually make a film called

Mouches Volantes that would somehow include this sound track material and this high-contrast positive material. I began to think of how they could coincide in the same film, and the obvious way was to see if the sound or some edited version of it could be made to go with any of this visual material.

I began to think in a more focused way about something that had interested me for a long time—namely, sound-image relationships in film. It was something that I had never worked with very much, though I had been very interested in films by Peter Kubelka and others who worked with sound-image relationships in formal ways. (Incidentally, I do feel that my interest in this area resulted in *Horizons* having a sound component, even though it has no sound track. It's not in terms of the rhyme scheme so much as in terms of how one is relating to the images as they flow by. There are certain events in *Horizons* that reverberate with a certain sound that changes because of the order of the shots or because of the realization of a kind of rhyme pattern. I could give many examples of it; there's even a playful reference to it in the section in which Peter Kubelka appears playing the flute.) At any rate, when I thought about how I might relate this sound track to those images, I realized that something more complex was going to happen, that the process of doing the film would have to be very intricate and that the film would have to lay out the material so that this intricacy could be experienced.

First of all, the idea of making a fixed soundtrack—selecting a portion of the interview with Angelina Johnson that would function as the sound for the whole film—became appealing. I loved that sound and wanted to work with it. But also I wanted to display the visual sections both silently and with sound. The form of the finished film—namely, that it involves seven visual sections, each seen with and without sound—was not decided in the beginning; it's just that the material that I had lent itself to being in these sections. The arranging of the material so that it would go 1, 2, 3, 4, 5, 6, 7, 7, 6, 5, 4, 3, 2, 1 came out of just trying out the different possibilities in my mind. That one seemed to present itself as a wonderful whole form for the film.

The more I listened to the Angelina Johnson part of the record, the more I realized that three sections were the essence of what I loved. I recorded these three sections in essentially chronological order, though not in the order they were in, in the original interview. I put her story of Willie Johnson's childhood first, the narration of their meeting and marriage second, and the story of his death third. The only sound that I introduced was the sound of my tape recorder going on and off. All the other sounds, like the fading out at the end, all of the other clicks and noises, occur on the record.

MacDonald: Are some of them on your record rather than on the original?

Gottheim: No, they're on the original also.

MacDonald: I'm thinking of that tapping that you match at the end.

Gottheim: Samuel B. Charters, a folklorist, who wrote a very good book about the blues, recorded a lot of this material. I think that during the original time when he was with Angelina Johnson, he must have had a wire recorder; I assume those clicks go back to that time. There are also some sounds that I think come about at a later stage, when he edited his original wire recording, or whatever, in order to make the record. I suppose the fade-out occurred then, and some other things.

OK. I had this sound track and all of this visual material, and I had this idea that there were going to be sections in the film, all of the sections made to go with this sound track. I then had different ideas about what would constitute a section, and for a long time I played with the idea of different formal things. There might be a section in which a lot of the rapid changes in light—from light to darkness, say—would be included and another section in which all of the swinging movements would be included. Different things suggested themselves to me as possible bases for sections. It happened that on this big roll that I was looking at all the time the material was arranged just as it came back from the lab, that is, according to the days on which it was shot. The footage from the day when the kids were climbing on the trees was all together; it began to assume a kind of narrative sense. Other days that were recorded on the film also seemed almost storylike at times. I finally decided to allow that to determine what would be in a section; that is, all of the bees material would go in one section, all of the tree material would go in another section, and so on. Also, by this time I had incorporated the original snow material on high-contrast positive, some other snow material, and the window stuff.

When I had grouped the material that would be used in one section, I pared it down, took out things that I didn't want. Then I made a precise record of what was left. Whereas during the making of *Horizons* I recorded what happened in general without needing to know the particulars except in a kind of intuitive way, in getting to know the material for *Mouches Volantes* I had to be very precise. I had to say exactly at frame such and such this occurs, that it occurs for this many frames, then this occurs. Essentially, I made a frame record of those things that seemed significant or obvious or noticeable. At the same time, I transferred the sound track from quarter-inch tape onto sprocketed 16mm magnetic tape, which has frames on it, so that I could make a frame record of its sound events. I made a frame record for every sound and every syllable. I had evolved a procedure that was incredibly tedious, though in some ways I liked it because it was very homemade and simple. I used strips of graph paper in which each square in the paper was a frame. Finally, I had these long strips on which I had recorded every visual event and every sound event in the film.

Next, holding in my hands a strip of graph paper that represented a grouping of images, I would walk towards the place on the floor where I had the sound track, and I would bring them together. I could line them up very exactly so that a specific sound fell on a specific image event. Then I could look to the right and left of that, and I could see that maybe nothing very interesting would happen through a specific conjunction, or I would see that by lining up a particular word or sound with a particular image, I had created an unexpected conjunction of sound and image, later or earlier, that was really fantastic. I played around with these different possibilities. I soon got to a point that I could see as soon as I put the graph papers next to each other whether something seemed very promising or very weak.

Of course, it was very important that I knew that the material also had to be seen without the sound. A little bit of footage that would work well with a certain sound would be impossible in a visual sense. I wanted people to be able to appreciate what that flow of images looked like visually *and* what it looked like with the sound.

The finished film consists of relationships of all sorts. When I talk about it, the film sounds so complex that I don't know why I ever did it, but I don't think it's a film that immediately strikes one as having resulted from procedures involving graph paper. My process allowed me to develop these systems of formal, emotional, symbolic relationships. In that way I think *Mouches Volantes* is similar to *Horizons* or at least it follows in a similar direction. It presents the viewer with a new kind of experience that's not quite like the experience of other films. I think that's what the importance and the excitement of the film is to me.

Robert Huot

By the mid-1960s, when Robert Huot was beginning to make a name for himself as a painter, his painting was moving away from abstract expressionism and toward minimalist forms that, in some cases, were approaching film: several mid- to late-1960s canvases were long, narrow, modularized strips. Then he and Hollis Frampton became friends, and before long they were collaborating on films: Huot appears in several early Frampton films, and Frampton worked on Huot's *Black and White Film* (1969) and *Nude Descending the Stairs* (1970).

At first, Huot was interested in applying minimalist tactics to film. In *Spray* (1967) he created what Michael Snow called "a fascinating atomized space" (see *Film-maker's Cooperative Catalogue,* No. 6) by spray painting strips of clear celluloid. In *Black and White Film,* a nude woman reveals and then obliterates herself by applying paint to her body. In *Red Stockings* (1969), a single frame close-up of a woman's crotch is embedded in the center of a three-minute passage of Kodachrome red. But it was not until Huot dropped out of the New York gallery scene and bought a small farm in upstate New York that filmmaking occupied as central a place in his thinking as painting. At first—in *One Year (1970)* (1971)—Huot documented aspects of his new life as parttime Lower Manhattan artist, parttime upstate farmer, and strung together the unedited rolls (the only editing was in camera). By 1971–72, he had begun to use filmmaking as a means of reflecting on who he was: the first results were two distinctive, underappreciated "diaries": *Rolls: 1971* (1972) and *Third One-Year Movie—1972* (1973).

For each of these films, and for most of the films he has made since, Huot devised a procedure that he felt would assure him a relatively direct, uncensored look at the central elements of his experience: farming, teaching (in the art department at Hunter College), traveling between New York City and the farm, having sex, looking at scenery, partying with friends, and being a parent. For each new diary film, he devised a new editing strategy that would allow him to use virtually all the footage he recorded and, at the same time, would convey a sense of living through the period of time he had documented.

The year 1971 was particularly intense for Huot: he was struggling to learn how to manage the farm, his marriage with choreographer Twyla Tharp was coming to an end (Huot's need to be out of Manhattan conflicted with her need to work with her dance company in the city), and he and Tharp were adjusting to the birth of a child. As a result, *Rolls: 1971* is at times very beautiful (the roll-long landscape shots are particularly memorable) and at other times quite shocking: sex is not romanticized as it usually is in commercial film—we see it bluntly and in close—and unlike other male diarists, Huot even has the courage to reveal his own masturbation. Huot's willingness to reveal himself at least as fully as he reveals women gives his films a point of contact with Carolee Schneemann's, although Schneemann's *Autobiographical Triology* centers on male-female relationships, while Huot's early diaries are more nearly self-portraits.

By the time he was recording the footage that would be used in *Third One-Year Movie—1972,* several of the personal factors that had made 1971 so intense had been resolved, and this is reflected in the mood of the 1972 diary. Here, we sense Huot's excitement about the potentials of 16mm filmmaking (he uses, for example, a variety of stocks, color and black-and-white negative, double exposure, and painting-on-film) for interpreting the new people and experiences that were entering his life. Even when we see Huot and Frampton killing and butchering a bull, the upbeat mood of the film is maintained by the presentation of this material in color negative. The organization of *Third One-Year Movie—1972,* like that of *Rolls: 1971,* is meant to convey a sense that our experience of time is both progressive and repetitive. We see sequential bits of particular experiences in the same order, over and over, in cycles separated from each other by Academy leader. Each cycle uses one shot of a specific kind of material, and when this material runs out, its position is subsequently occupied by one of a variety of kinds of leader. All in all, I find *Third One-Year Movie—1972* Huot's most satisfying film; it is lovely to look at and provides an elegant self-portrait of a man exhilarated by the adventure of his life—not a Hollywood-type adventure with which we can identify only by fantasizing, but a real-life adventure all of whose elements, Huot means for us to realize, are entirely within our reach.

Huot's next two diaries—*Diary Film #4—1973* (1974; edited by Huot's friend Adam Mierzwa) and *Diary 1974–75* (1975)—are less impressive than *Rolls: 1971* and *Third One-Year Movie—1972;* they are neither as elegant nor as intimate as the earlier films, but in retrospect, it is obvious that the increas-

Huot films himself in mylar, in Diary 1974–75 *(1975).*

ing informality of their camera work (*Diary 1974–75,* especially, moves away from the carefully composed formalist shots of the earlier films in favor of a continuous rush of imagery through the frame) was leading Huot toward a major change in his filmmaking focus, from 16mm to Super-8. Huot had begun recording diary footage in Super-8 in 1976, but it was not until he had access to sound that he began to complete diaries in the smaller gauge. The first of these was *Super-8 Diary 1979* (1980), which was followed by *Diary 1980* (1981) and most recently by the five-projector film *1983 Diary* (1984). The Super-8 films include some of Huot's most impressive filmmaking (most notable, perhaps, are the first four sections of the 1979 diary and sections of the 1980 film) and some of the most impressive Super-8 filmmaking I've seen anywhere. Ironically, the handling ease and lower expense of the smaller gauge have resulted in finished films much less personally revealing than the earlier 16mm diaries and much more consciously directed toward audiences: for example, what sexuality we do see in the recent films is in the nature of performance; often Huot and his wife, painter Carol Kinne, design environments, costumes, and sound tracks for comic, pixilated sexual escapades. The Super-8 films continue to reveal Huot's life, but there is no longer the sense of personal investigation evident in *Rolls: 1971.* In its place is Huot's pleasure in recording the beautiful and enjoyable elements of his life and sharing them with viewers. Central to all the Super-8 diaries is Huot's exploration of sound: each section of the recent diaries has its own kind of sound. At first, Huot tended to "borrow" music from records, but more recently the music on the sound tracks is, as often as not, provided by The Chameleons, a new wave rock band of which Huot is one of the leaders.

My conversation with Huot was recorded in the fall of 1978.

MacDonald: You've been a painter longer than you've been a filmmaker. By the late sixties you were becoming rather well known as a minimal and conceptual artist. Did your filmmaking develop out of your painting?

Huot: I always made things, and that eventually took the form of painting. The tools for building, drawing, painting were available and cheap. They were around home or at school. But actually my official training was as a chemist. I did study with other artists in college, in graduate school, and on my own. My training as an artist is fairly extensive but mostly informal. It's hard for me to say how I got into film. I'd always looked at films. I loved film as a kid. I can remember really getting a kick out of home movies, and seeing cartoon shows—*Felix the Cat, The Little King, Koko the Clown*—at Sunday school, Scouts, or other community events. Going to the movies alone or with a friend was a big event in my life. I remember going to the Saturday movies to see *Abbott and Costello Meet Frankenstein,* and *King Kong,* and all the serials— *The Phantom, Buck Rogers, Batman, Zorro*—and getting Good and Plenty's and throwing them at the screen, all that kind of thing. I can remember seeing a film when I was about thirteen. It was a big deal, one of the first times I brought some friends to the movies at night. The movie was a sort of historic melodrama, and it was in sepia tone. That really knocked me out. Later, I found a sepia-toned stamp that was a reproduction of a Flemish painting—I can't think of who painted it—and I kept that stamp for a long time because it represented that experience for me. So I was a dormant filmmaker, maybe, and that, coupled with my obvious visual involvement as a painter, set me up for wanting to do it, though I didn't really have access to the keys or tools.

Two experiences made the difference. First was a showing of Brakhage's films I saw in the early sixties—probably '61 or '62—that Carolee Schnee-mann put on at The Living Theatre to raise some money for Brakhage. It was the first time I had seen what was called underground film. I was impressed. I identified with it. It seemed like, shit, that's just the sort of thing I would do—not exactly, maybe, but he was a kindred spirit. I didn't act on this in any way, though, until I met Hollis Frampton through Carl André, who was a friend during the minimal period you referred to before. Hollis had a loft nearby, and we met for coffee at Dave's Corner. Hollis was working as a dye transfer technician and photographer, and he was beginning to make films. I think he was working on *Process Red* when I met him. He had equipment and let me use it. He showed me how to make a splice, and that's about all I needed.

I started playing with film because it happened to coincide with some of the things I was doing in my painting at the time. I had been working with linear grids, with square modules. I was dealing with visual experience in a kind of linear-time way, which fed right into the continuity of one frame after another. In some ways I still think of film as this long series of single images that are also one long rhythm. You could tack them to the wall and they'd make a long sequential work—not a painting, but in some ways like those paintings. Even when I did drawings for single-image paintings of the color-field, hard-edge variety, they often evolved out of a series of drawings that were almost like frames of a film. This sequence of frames or images, in other words, led to the development of a single image, and that single image would just stand there kind of ineffable, with no traces of the process that led to it.

Scratch [1967] came right out of looking at commercial films and seeing scratches. I remember seeing a film on 42nd Street. It was not an interesting film, but I got fascinated by a scratch. *Scratch* came out of that experience. It was like saying, well, a scratch can be a hell of a lot more interesting than the superimportant shit that people put into that emulsion. *Leader* [1967] was about light, no light, duration, and a color, a very low-grade color: green machine leader that I thought was very beautiful. A lot of my films are a result of just trying something out. I don't necessarily know what they are going to be. *Black and White Film* was about painting. And about sensuality. The idea of a beautiful woman revealing herself, then painting herself out.

MacDonald: For *Spray* you spray painted clear celluoid strips; when it's projected the feeling is of a multiplicity of textures.

Huot: Right. I wanted to make a film that was just about texture. I tried different spray paints and found that aluminum was the best. I did try to get "dramatic" in it at times, in the sense that some kind of emotion could be evoked by the density or the rarefaction or the speed of it. Sometimes it would go into deep space; at other times it would be like a wall of graphic pulsation. These different rhythms would occur simply through this dumb act of spraying the paint thinly or densely on a ribbon of clear plastic.

MacDonald: In *Red Stockings* you demonstrate the importance of a single frame by using one frame of photographed imagery in the middle of a three-minute passage of monochrome red. Did you assume that the viewer would be able to read that image the first time through? I wasn't able to, but there was enough there to make me want to find out what the image was.

Huot: I could see it because I made it and knew what was there, and I figured that somebody would figure it out. It was a pun, you know. From my point of view, being a straight, somewhat sexist male, the idea of a woman's crotch was, is, a strong and ever-present thing. Anyway, it just seemed like a funny way of demonstrating that, yeah, you could very definitely see a single frame. I don't think there was all that much more to it, really.

MacDonald: When I watch it, the quality of that red does crazy things to my retinas. Was that effect something you thought about ahead of time?

Huot: Sure, I knew that looking at that color for any period of time would do that. And I realized that the colors in that single frame would look funny— very green or something—after all that red.

MacDonald: I think the red alone is interesting, almost a filmic version of optical painting.

Huot: Well, on that level, the pure red experience is maybe just as valid as the rest of it. I was thinking of the film being the image of a woman with long legs, with her legs spread, and the eye starting with her ankle and panning slowly along her calf and up her thigh and to her crotch and then on down the other leg. It's that simple-minded really—on one level, anyway.

MacDonald: Does a similar urge account for *Cross Cut—A Blue Movie* [1969]?

Huot: Yeah. The material was found in the cellar of, I think, 60 Grand Street, where a co-op was being formed. Formerly, there had been some sort of low-grade porn operation, and there were lots of little girlie movies and stuff like that. An artist who lived in that co-op, Mac Wells, found the stuff and said, "You want it?" and I said, "Sure, what the hell?" Hollis and I cleaned it up—not in a moral sense, but it was kind of gunky and dirty and bent up and broken. We just cut out the broken parts and spliced together what was physically any good. One particular part—of the woman wiggling—I thought was kind of humorous, so I intercut it with blue leader. Again, it was a kind of a pun about the idea of cutting two very different kinds of stuff together and seeing what it would be like. An image of a woman wiggling is normally not chopped up in any way. You look at that and you get your titillation. Breaking that shot up seemed to be a thing that normally isn't done, and I thought that was a reason for doing it—to treat a "semi-erotic scene" with an arbitrariness, and a degree of violence to its intent, that would make it another reality.

MacDonald: You seem very conscious there, as you were in *Scratch* and *Leader,* of imagery in the emulsion: the footage of the woman has a lot of scratches and distortion, and the blue leader looks exactly like what it is.

Huot: I was very aware of those physical aspects. Even in the diary films where I appear in an intimate situation, I don't think of that necessarily as me. I think of it as an image. I still make that separation. I think that art and life are very definitely connected and that they feed back and forth, but there's still the difference between a human being and a physical manifestation of that person in a film image: that isn't a woman, it's just silver nitrate on this piece of plastic, and some of it's been scratched off.

MacDonald: In 1970 and 1971 you seem to have become much more involved in film. You had made several short films over a period of about three years, but then in a two-year period you made two long diary films, plus *Nude Descending the Stairs, The Sex Life of the Artist as a Young Man* [1971], *Turning Torso Drawdown* [1971], and *Strip* [1972]. What happened?

Huot: I need to go back in time to answer this one. As an artist, I was pretty naive for a long time about what my art was and where it went in the world. I thought art was a religious activity in the sense that you committed yourself to a life of searching for truth. You knew that things were not necessarily going to be all that good or easy, but at least you had your vision and your medium with which to express yourself, to present your discoveries to whatever other people were willing to look at them. As a child and as a teenager, art had given me a lot of pleasure, but the idea of being an artist wasn't a real issue, because there weren't any artists in my life, at least not in the official sense. There were people involved in art activities. My grandfather on my mother's side was a blacksmith; he played the bagpipes; he read a great deal; he made all kinds of things out of iron. He affected my sense of what a man was very powerfully, maybe as much as, or more than, my father. My father was an amateur singer who worked as an electrical engineer without credentials. He did fairly sophisticated kinds of things but on a laborer level. He was a member of a union, but it wasn't a very strong union. He worked his ass off and was just totally exploited, from my point of view. My mother had a certain creative bent to her, also. She was extremely good at making a beautiful home. She decorated the house, selected furniture, was able to sew, to wallpaper. So there was a creative environment. But there was no "official" artist image in my mind at all.

In college I met an artist named Tom Young. He was a member of the March Gallery on 10th Street—this is in the fifties during the boom period of the New York School. There was this proliferation of galleries on 10th Street and a real society of artists. I met other students in school who thought about being creative people—not necessarily painters, but singers, poets, actresses, and other people interested in the arts—and suddenly found myself part of a small group of people who cared a great deal about the arts. Up to that point, it hadn't dawned on me that I *could* be an artist, and it wasn't until the mid-to-late sixties that I really began to deal with questions like what is the function of an artist in society; what do artists do, really; where do their products go, and who uses them, who benefits from them? I was showing at a Madison Avenue gallery with the naiveté of a teenager. That's the way I look at it now, anyway. I suddenly began to realize that art was hooked to a whole class structure, and I found that though my art was appreciated, the people who bought it dealt with it in a fairly startling way: primarily as a symbol of their own power and their own sensitivity. It became their property and represented how aesthetically astute they were or how important they were. I had thought I was involved in a process of discovery, of making something beautiful, something that would elevate people's feelings about the way they perceived the world and that would sharpen their senses and give them experiences that were stimulating or beautiful or whatever. That was pretty naive. Maybe that is part of it, but in this country, art functions largely as a means of status.

I began to be dissatisfied with my role as an artist in the official system, but I really didn't know what to do about it. I was just uncomfortable. This, coupled with the fact that we were involved in the Vietnam War. . . . Well, to make a long story a little shorter, a group of people formed what would eventually be called the Art Workers' Coalition. It was a sort of leftist-anarchist organization. I started to participate at the second or third meeting and became an active member. We were trying to deal with issues that involved the political nature of being an artist or being associated with the arts. We were artists, historians, critics, whatever, but mostly we were very involved in art. We began to try to affect the shape of the art structure: we participated in demonstrations, for example, to force the Museum of Modern Art to have a free day. We began to talk about artists' rights. I think the women's art movement in New York got a tremendous boost from the Art Workers' Coalition.

Before, I had thought, if I make this beautiful painting, that's it, that's all I have to do, that's the end of it. It goes out and changes the world. Well, maybe it does, maybe it doesn't. American art—abstract expressionism, for example—has been used by government organizations to propagandize "freedom of expression" in the United States. Well, more and more, I didn't want that to happen to my art. I did not wish my art to be used in ways that violated my intent. I became involved in a process of dematerialization. I felt that, possibly, if I made art that was more about ideas and less physically tangible, it couldn't be owned or manipulated. I became what would be called a conceptual artist. But as I began to be involved in the conceptual movement, all that seemed to be happening was that the ideas were being turned into objects by being totally documented. It became chic to own or sell "nothing"—the Emperor's Clothes. So I was very pissed off, and very disillusioned. I stopped making physical paintings in 1968, and I began to do things for people in their homes, in their studios—installation pieces, using a piece of tape, drawing on the wall, or making pieces that existed only in the dark—different things like that. It was anti the power structure; it was trying to take art away from places where it was bought and sold like so much official meat. When the people left the places where I did these pieces, the work stayed there and was painted out, or destroyed, or whatever.

Film appealed to me more and more because I could have a whole four-hour film in just a few cans. There was very little material and a whole lot of matter—and my criticism of art and of our culture is that it's a whole lot of material and very little matter. Anyway, this was part of the attitude: less material, less stuff, and more experience, more information. Film just fit my needs at the time. I was changing rapidly. I had done my journeyman work as an artist. I had proven that I was a good artist, and I had done it in the official way. I had successfully shown in galleries and had reviews and gotten museum shows and all that sort of thing; now I wanted first of all to find out what the reasons were that I was doing it and whether I needed to do it, whether I wanted to do it. So, finally, I just dropped out of the official art world and bought this old farm and began to try to look at myself and the process of living. Film seemed a much more suitable vehicle for that.

MacDonald: The decision to do diary films came mostly out of this urge for self-examination?

Huot: Yes, I think so. I felt that I had made art that was interesting or beautiful or provocative or avant-garde or whatever, but something was missing, and I didn't know exactly what. Eventually, I made the billboard *Less is More But, It's Not Enough* [*Billboard for Former Formalists*, 1978]. That's what I was feeling, but I didn't know how to deal with it exactly, so I started to make the diary films just as a way of beginning to look at what was going on.

MacDonald: You can see a shift in your first diary film, *One Year (1970)*, in the degree to which you were interested in getting rid of formalist concerns and becoming more informal with the camera. Some of the early rolls on the first reel, however, seem to be formal, minimal pieces—very similar to films Larry Gottheim or Barry Gerson might have been doing at that time. Were you aware of that kind of film in 1970, or was that just something you did on your own?

Huot: I did it myself. My only awareness of that sort of thing—of using the single roll as a form—was the Lumière brothers. I was totally ignorant of avant-garde film, except for Brakhage, Snow, Wieland, Frampton, Yoko Ono, and a few other people.

MacDonald: Had you seen Warhol's films?

Huot: At about the same time he did things like *Empire* or *Sleep,* which I think came primarily right out of Cage. Also, I met LaMonte Young through Bob Morris. LaMonte would do very long, very simple things, where the harmonics would start to develop. Terry Reilly, too. I was very aware of music. I didn't study it, but I've listened to a lot of music and enjoyed it tremendously. So I didn't necessarily look to painters for ideas about painting or to filmmakers for ideas about filmmaking. I didn't see anything by Gerson or Gottheim until 1973 at a film festival in London. I was aware of Kubelka. I had seen *Arnulf Rainer,* which I think must be one of the best formalist films ever made. I knew more about Hollywood film and European film, just from going to regular commercial showings. I don't know; maybe I have a sort of dumb arrogance. I just figure, well, I'm going to try it and I'm going to do it. I don't give a shit about the way anybody else makes film. Why should I care? I've made enough art to feel confident as an artist, and I think if you have experience in one area it's not hard to transfer it to another area. Just the materials are different. I was pretty ignorant of underground film really, with the exception of those people I mentioned, and they're pretty good.

MacDonald: Did you make studies for those early rolls of *One Year (1970),* or was it just a process of trying something out?

Huot: No, I didn't make studies. That's *exactly* what I *didn't* want to do. The diary films are not about making studies. The diary films are about setting up the camera and just whatever happens, happens. Obviously, at first I chose interesting or beautiful things to point the camera at. *One Year (1970)* was the first film I made with my own camera—a 16mm H-16 Bolex reflex camera. I was very concerned about doing a good job, so I tried to make very beautiful or strong or interesting or provocative, well-exposed rolls of film, but I wasn't going to change anything, either. I mean, part of the commitment was that there would be no editing, except for splicing the rolls together with flare-ins and flare-outs as transitions. There was a certain kind of realism about the whole thing: on this day I set the camera here, turned it on, and this happened, and that's it. There was no point in changing it. I just wanted to see what it was. But I did intend to make successfully exposed images.

MacDonald: Up until *Rolls: 1971* you tend to be present only as the person turning the camera on and off, but from then on, you and people close to you tend to be very much in the foreground of what happens. How did that transition take place?

Huot: Well, in *One Year (1970)* it was almost a rule that I wouldn't appear. I was interested in what was happening around me.

MacDonald: Are you in that film at all?

Huot: Yes. I was one of the laborers in the scene where cement is being poured into some forms at the end of the barn. I wanted to appear as a laborer, but I didn't particularly want to appear as "me." I had held the attitude that I was an artist, not a performer. I made a kind of class distinction between the two. At the same time, I was somewhat angry and jealous of performers who would go out and perform, and be right up there with everybody looking at them, and getting instant feedback for what they were doing. Here I was, making paintings or films that, once they were out, had a life independent of me, that didn't seem to feed back to me. The illusion was that the artist and the work were separate. Look at what I've *done,* not at me. I had felt it was "incorrect" to draw attention directly to myself. But I was changing, and the result was that I had to put myself into the films.

MacDonald: For *Rolls: 1971* you used a very unusual structure—a combination of two radically different ways of treating the same imagery. You jump back and forth between sections made up of 252 successive one-second images and roll-long, unedited, often single-shot material. What led you to choose that organization?

Huot: Well, I guess it was an integration of *One Year (1970)* and *Turning Torso Drawdown,* in which I got into juxtaposing different images of bodies. For *Rolls: 1971* I took that idea, and applied it to these disparate images that I had gathered over a whole year. Part of the reason for wanting to do that came from a feeling that all these experiences are in our minds simultaneously. You bring to any moment all these other experiences you've had. I wanted to show certain of the full rolls because I thought they were good or interesting as they were, and I wanted also to do this total juxtaposition. I wanted to use everything I shot—100 percent—at least once. I wanted to show real time and also a state of mind. I thought that alternating between slow, very detailed presentations, where you would really look at all of the information, and rhythmic, one-second passages with the juxtapositions of everything would be real in a way only film could be.

MacDonald: A lot of the imagery in that film has a sort of greenish and brownish off-white tonality that you've mentioned came from shooting in black and white and printing on color stock.

Huot: Right. There was some color in the film, so I had to print it on color stock. In the first film there was only one roll of color, so I had the color part printed separately. Even though there's more black and white than color in this one, the way the color is cut into the film meant I had to print it on color stock. The type of emulsion—whether the film is Plus X or Tri-X or 4X—affects the quality of the color. There are things that happen that you don't have all that much control over, and I just accept those things. There's only so much that I can do. I can't keep changing something over and over. It's more important to get on to the next thing than to attempt to make the one definitive statement.

MacDonald: You mentioned that you chose the order of the one-second

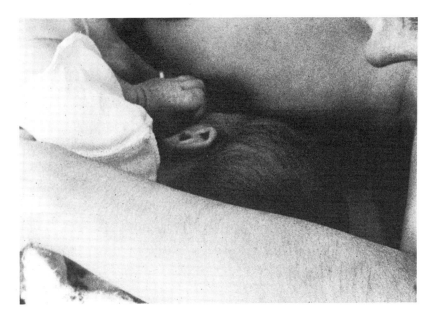

Choreographer Twyla Tharp nursing Jesse Huot in Huot's Rolls: 1971 *(1972).*

units in the one-second passages of *Rolls: 1971* in order to create as many juxtapositions of disparate material as possible. How did you come up with that specific, complex arrangement?

Huot: It came out of experience. *Drawdown* in the name of the film, *Turning Torso Drawdown,* is an expression for a way of matching colors in the pigment industry. I used to work as a pigment chemist. I was involved in research and development and in control and production chemistry. I used to take these formulas and go through them and examine all the steps to see if they were necessary. The results would be made into pigment that would be ground and mixed with oil and made into an ink or a paint. Then we would compare those results by making "drawdowns." This was our method of juxtaposing the experimental colors to one another and to the standard. Of course, I didn't do twenty-three like in *Rolls: 1971.* I might have done three or five. We put the inks in order—say, 1, 2, 3, 1, 4, 5, 3, 4, 2, 5, 1—with 1 being the standard and 2, 3, 4, and 5 the test variations. After placing the inks in a sequence on a special paper, we drew them down across the paper. We could then compare them all to each other. I applied the same system to *Turning Torso Drawdown* and to this film.

MacDonald: Was there a specific reasoning behind the order of the complete roll sections of *Rolls: 1971?* At first they seem to occur in the same order that the units in the one-second sections occur; that is, the snow is the first full roll, as well as the first unit in the one-second sections, and the image of Twyla Tharp nursing the baby is the second in both. Then after a while, the order ceases to be the same.

Huot: Well, it was very simple. I had shot twenty-two or twenty-three rolls that year. Some of them stood up as individual entries, and others didn't. So I used the ones that I thought held up as individual rolls. Those that didn't were cut up. I did use all the information, all twenty-three. The twenty-third was a potpourri of all kinds of things. But I used all twenty-three *completely,* and then I used some a second time, as whole things. The order in which I shot the rolls was maintained.

MacDonald: When I first saw the film, I assumed—I guess because of my experience with certain kinds of longer structural films from the late sixties or early seventies—that *Rolls: 1971* would end at the point when we had seen everything both in one-second units and in complete-roll form. When the black one-second units started appearing in place of the snow, I was very surprised. Did you mean for the end to create surprise, or did ending the film at that point result from something I'm not aware of?

Huot: It was simply a matter of physical considerations. When one kind of material ran out, its place was taken by black leader. I *was* into surprise. All the material in that twenty-third position was chosen at random, so surprise was certainly an element.

MacDonald: I remember that during my second or third viewing of the film, I thought I had figured out the mathematics, but I would get to that last section with all the diverse material, and my mathematics would go to hell.

Huot: Just as I intended—although there is still that simple logic, so that if you know it's random stuff in position twenty-three, you know what's happening.

MacDonald: Third One Year Movie—1972 feels like a much more mellow film than *Rolls: 1971,* both in terms of the kind of organization that you chose for it and in terms of the nature of your presence in it. Did you think of it that way?

Huot: Definitely. I think that my sense of myself as a person, as an artist, changed, and partly because of making the 1971 film. Part of the function of the films for me was a kind of self-examination, an examination of how I appeared. I'm a visual person. I'm very involved in the ways things look. Maybe I wish I were less concerned with the way *I* look, but that's the way it is. My life was going through fantastic changes during 1971. Twyla and I had a child, and we ended our life together. I had built my life in large degree around this farm and a sense of independence—not only intellectual independence but physical independence, the ability to raise my own food, to hunt, to be somewhat independent of the system. I had become somewhat disillusioned with the incredible perverseness of specialization and how it distorts us in terms of our whole persons. Even though my farm is a limited view of the world—very limited—it's a whole world, too. A lot can happen and does happen here. A family can exist here and carry on all kinds of activities. So the farm was something I had focused my life on, at least for this particular period.

Well, all that was changing, and there was an incredible amount of tension. Even though there was this family structure, this seemingly almost idyllic situation, it was under stress, and I was under stress. By the 1972 film a lot of those things had resolved themselves. Twyla and I had separated. I was developing new friendships with many other people, including other women, who I cared about and were important to me. Some of them appear in the film. A crisis like a divorce causes you to reevaluate many areas of your life, and one of the things that I decided was that I had to live more fluidly, more pleasurably. I had to get more out of my life. I didn't want to be so rigid. I had committed myself to certain beliefs, and they didn't pan out. They weren't the way it really was, so even though I was still somewhat traumatized, I was more relaxed and more open, and I wanted more things to come in. I think all those things show in the film.

MacDonald: You mentioned a minute ago that seeing yourself in *Rolls: 1971* resulted in changes in what you did in your life. Could you elaborate on that a bit? Usually people talk about how film comes out of life rather than the reverse.

Huot: Well, I think American artists have become professionals, specialists. That wasn't always true: Charles Ives, who was a great hero of mine, worked as an insurance man—he developed certain fundamental aspects of the insurance business, in fact. He supported himself that way and was in a certain sense an amateur musician, although obviously a great one. Professionalism can be a sort of perversion. I mean, I'm not just a painter, and I'm not just a filmmaker, and I'm not *just* anything. I'm many, many things, and all of those things are working simultaneously. I said earlier that I felt there was something missing in my art. I mean, I could set up a certain set of problems and carry them out and come up with certain results. I learned scientific method at an early age and carried it out and worked at it. It has certainly affected my life. But I'm many things, and when I look at an image of myself—I am egocentric; you have to be egocentric to be an artist—I learn all kinds of things from the way I move, the way I comport myself, from my gestures, my bearing, from hundreds of little things that come across in the image. I didn't know if I was making art. I was just making these films that were about me and my life. I looked at these things, and they meant something to me, and they didn't always mean something that I liked. I wasn't going to change the film, but I could change myself.

MacDonald: One of the things that makes *Third One Year Movie—1972* different from *Rolls: 1971* is your choice of an organization. You begin with a long presentation of various kinds of imagery. Then you generally review that imagery over and over but in shorter and shorter segments, until at the very end you've gone from ten minutes or so at the beginning to the last one, which I think is forty-one seconds long. What did you have in mind when you decided on using progressively shorter waves of disparate imagery?

Huot: Again, it was almost an arbitrary choice. I had made the first diary film by just hooking the unedited rolls together. Then came a much more formal and structural film. For the third one I wanted to retain some of the essence of that juxtaposition structure, but I also wanted to treat the film as it had been made. You know, sometimes you shoot the whole roll of film; sometimes you shoot a series of takes of one thing; sometimes it's a few takes of one thing, a few of something else. I was being much looser about it, and I wasn't trying to think ahead. One of the things about all these films is that I don't start out with a particular thing I want to do. This is what's happening, and I shoot it, and when I get it all done, I say, well, that's enough; now I have to put it together. I had this group of roughly twenty 100-foot rolls—2,000 feet of film, all of which seemed perfectly OK to me. It was exposed well and, again, I was going to use all of it. My solution was something like this: say, for instance, that roll 1 is one shot, roll 2 is two shots, roll 3 is four shots, and roll 4 is ten shots. In the first go-round, roll 1 is all used up, half of roll 2 is used, a quarter of roll 3, and a tenth of roll 4. I just kept going through the rolls until they were used up. If something ran out, I substituted something else. The substitute could be a specific chosen image or a random selection.

MacDonald: Third One Year Movie—1972 seems a culmination of everything you'd ever done before that. This is true, too, to some extent in *Rolls: 1971.* There's not only the single-shot kind of thing you had done at the beginning of *One Year (1970),* as well as more informal types of recording; there's also a lot of work with scratching on the film and types of experiment related to the little films you made before the diaries. When you were making the 1972 diary, were you conscious of bringing together everything you had done up to that point?

Huot: I think what you're saying is true, but I wasn't thinking of it quite that way.

MacDonald: It's one of the things that distinguishes the third diary from the fourth—*Diary Film #4*—which doesn't include some of those earlier kinds of things. *Third One-Year Movie—1972* also differs from the earlier films in that it uses a good deal more color. Was that something that just evolved?

Huot: Right, it just evolved.

MacDonald: One thing that struck me when I was looking at the 1971 film is that a radically feminist audience might have some objection to the way the organization creates juxtapositions of footage of a stripper, of Twyla Tharp dancing, of a cow being artificially inseminated. . . .

Huot: Why would they object to it? Feminists aren't trying to pretend things aren't the way they are; they're trying to change things. You're invent-

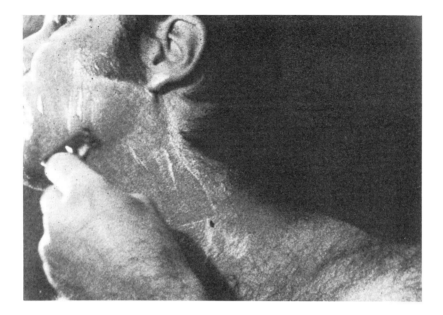

Huot shaving in Rolls: 1971 *(1972)*.

ing a situation. I haven't had any feminists object to that juxtaposition. These things go on in the world simultaneously, and part of the reason for editing the film the way I did is that it represents a certain kind of reality. All these events have occurred, and they exist simultaneously in our minds and in life in some form or other.

MacDonald: A question about the diary films in general: Is the image you create in the diaries the best "you" you can muster, or is it the way you see yourself in normal activities?

Huot: Well, it's me functioning in what I think is a true representation of me. Whether it is or not is something else, but it was an attempt to do that. I don't think I ever attempted to glorify anything, and I don't think I'm necessarily the best, or worst, me in those images. I guess I thought I turned out to be an acceptable human being. Even if I felt *I* wanted to change, I never wanted to destroy or deny what I'd already done.

MacDonald: There's a certain kind of connection between your decision to use all the footage you shoot and your attitude about the past. While you consistently change, you never negate.

Huot: Right. These diary films are a document of interesting things and not so interesting things. They're about making something grand out of the mundane. That's a kind of corny way of putting it. I didn't want to eliminate anything on the basis of an a priori value judgment. I felt it was important for me to have to look at everything, even though obviously I chose to shoot certain things and not a lot of other things. I think there's a lot of value in it for that reason. The diaries contain things that aren't totally entertaining or delightful or fantastic or great to look at or anything like that. Life ain't always that way. The films are more like the tissue of reality, for me, anyway. I wanted to include some of the nothingness, the arbitrariness.

MacDonald: That's especially evident in *Diary Film #4—1973.*

Huot: Yeah, I had done these other diary films, with varying degrees of control and intent and structure. For this one, I wanted certain footage together, but I also wanted to extend the arbitrariness even more, so I asked Adam Mierzwa to edit it. I know this film is not your all-time favorite, nor is it mine, but the job Adam did was fine. I think I could take that footage and make a really superentertaining film out of it if I wanted to, but that really wasn't what I wanted to do. That may be an exaggeration—superentertaining—I'm just saying that the film functions as it was intended to. It doesn't necessarily win great affection, but it showed me something.

MacDonald: It seems a much more detached film, not only because you didn't edit it, but in the footage, too.

Huot: I think that may be so, and what you said at another time about me being probably a little bored when I made it could very well be true. I probably was, but that's OK.

MacDonald: I miss the moments of stillness—the still camera, long-take material—of the earlier films. In this film you're constantly moving the camera.

Huot: Part of what I wanted to do was to break away from all that stillness. I don't want to be known as someone who makes beautiful, well-framed little shots, with *my* signature. I went through that a long time ago as a painter and struggled against it. My attitude about art is, yes, there is a product; yes, I take responsibility for it; yes, I want to share it; yes, I hope you'll like it; but yes, I'm going to change; and no, I'm not going to produce the same marketable product like General Motors does. I'm not a fucking corporation. I don't want to be. I'm a human being. I'm changing all the time, and I'm going to change all the time.

MacDonald: I've assumed that *Beautiful Movie* [1975] is, among other things, a sort of feminist film, in the sense that you suggest that, yes, women are lovely in the traditional sense, but men can be, too.

Huot: Yes. The film starts out of focus and slowly comes into focus through this elliptical matte. A very attractive woman is brushing her hair in this very beautiful setting, somewhat reminiscent of, say, Dutch painting of the seventeenth century—maybe it has a little touch of Vermeer. It's very obviously a classically beautiful situation involving the idea of a woman. The image slowly comes into focus. Then there's this fairly rapid dissolve to a man—not in exactly the same position, because I didn't want it to be too gimmicky—doing a similar thing. Then it goes out of focus and fades out. That simple juxtaposition, it seemed to me, contained a lot of things. Can a man be thought of as beautiful? Certainly men have been thought of as beautiful in other cultures and at other times in Western culture, too.

I don't just want to be a big "heavy" *man* who can drop somebody with one punch or something like that. I don't want to be King Kong all the time. I want to be gentle. I want to be elegant. I want to be attractive. I want to be soft, tender. It's clear that force is generally a rather nonproductive avenue. It hasn't done a whole lot for most people, that's for sure. The old idea of a *Man* is a cartoon, outdated and counterproductive. We need to be all the other things we are. Men, women, everyone will be better off.

MacDonald: For a long time, you made a lot of film and showed it comparatively little. Now you seem more interested in showing your films. Is this a reaction to the films you see dominating people's attention?

Huot: Well, I can't set up a whole program in reaction to something that I think is happening. I don't want to do that, because I would end up being the same as what I'd be opposing. I want to do more than react. The reason I feel like being more public is that I woodshedded for quite a long time. I made a substantial body of work: the diary films, the diary paintings, the Möbius-strip investigations, and a whole lot of other things. I took a position of being pretty much out of view and did a lot of self-searching, a lot of just sitting around thinking without wanting to feel that everything I did had to be shown. So after going through this, I looked around and said, well, OK, what good did it do for Bob Huot to drop out? I saw that it did something for me in terms of the work I had done, but I also saw that if I wanted to have any sort of impact or voice, it would have to be through showing my art. So I will be an artist and will make my films and my paintings and three-dimensional things and whatever. I'll try to use my work for my own ends, my own education, my own fun, but I'll also try to use it as a means of having a voice for myself and my ideas. If I want somebody to hear me, I have to speak out; I have to show my work.

Taka Iimura

When Taka Iimura arrived in the United States for the first time in 1968, he had already completed eighteen films. Most of those that I have seen—*Junk* (1962), *Iro* (1962), *Love* (1963, sound track by Yoko Ono), *Onan* (1963), *A Dance Party in the Kingdom of Lilliput, No. 1* and *No. 2* (1964, 1966)—reveal the influence of the surrealist films of the 1920s French Avant-Garde in their frequently bizarre imagery and unconventional structuring, and in their tendency to include nudity and eroticism, sometimes with a sense of humor. In fact, when Standish Lawder invited Iimura to Yale to present a program of his work, the "outrageousness" of these early films drew a crowd:

> An excited and unruly mob, estimated by campus police at nearly 1,000, prevented the showing of experimental Japanese films in the Art Gallery last night. The crowd began forming in front of the High Street entrance to the gallery an hour before the scheduled 8:30 showing. By 8 o'clock the crowd had grown boisterous and had spilled over into High Street. When a taxicab attempting to pass through the archway sounded its horn, the crowd booed and grew more excited.
>
> Pushing and shoving spread as persons attempted to get closer to the door to the gallery. Several groups of students began to chant, "Open the doors" and "Skin flick." Students near the entrance to the Art Gallery said they were nearly crushed. Shortly after 8, Standish Lawder, faculty sponsor of the Cinema Club, appeared at the doorway. He told the crowd, which had by then become a mob, "You won't find the spectacle described in the lurid, sensationalist *Yale Daily News* article. The films will be cancelled unless you stop this irresponsible mob behavior."
>
> The crowd continued to chant and yell obscenities, threatening to storm the barred entrance to the Art Gallery. At 8:45 five campus policemen stationed

themselves at the door and prevented anyone else from entering the building. High Street was left in shambles. Papers, bottles, and beer cans littered the area.[1]

Once in the United States, Iimura found himself in step with those filmmakers—Michael Snow, Ernie Gehr, Tony Conrad, Paul Sharits, others—who had begun to use film to research components of the cinema apparatus itself, particularly the physiology of film viewing and various elements of the material and mechanical bases of film production and exhibition. Iimura had already begun moving in this direction before he left Japan, as is evident in *White Calligraphy* (1967) for which he scratched into dark leader, frame by frame, the Japanese characters for sections of *The Kojiki,* the Japanese creation myths compiled in A.D. 712 by Hieda-no-Are. In New York, Iimura became interested first in rephotographing conventionally filmed imagery to synthesize new film experiences that lay halfway between the representational and the abstract—*Film Strips I* and *II* (1970) and *In the River* (1970). Next, he began eliminating all representational, photographed imagery in the flicker film *Shutter* (1971), which is reminiscent of Tony Conrad's *The Flicker,* though made in an entirely different way. In 1972 Iimura went even one step further: he turned away from the optical impact of his earliest American films and began to directly address what I assume he had come to feel was the fundamental dimension of cinema: its temporal duration.

In *Models, Reel 1* and *Reel 2* (1972), *+ & −* (1973), *1 to 60 Seconds* (1973), *24 Frames Per Second* (1975, revised 1978), and *Sync Sound* (1975, revised 1978), Iimura eliminated nearly every conventional element of cinema except for enough graphic signs to measure off various durations of clear and dark leader into sometimes simple, sometimes complex sequences that create various kinds of experiences. For me, the films have always been almost-meditative spaces (environments, durational sculptures). But for many viewers the primary (and often, the only) impact of the films is their emptiness of all the visual and auditory "information" that crowd conventional movies: even a film as brief as *Sync Sound* (twelve minutes) can galvanize a conventional audience into outraged howls. And yet, if one is able to accept the idea of a film made out of temporal durations, even the most outrageously minimal of these films can provide various kinds of experience, some of which were evident during a screening of *1 to 60 Seconds* at Utica College in 1976. By the time the film began, the fifty audience members had seen an hour of increasingly minimal films. Much to my surprise, they seemed in excellent spirits and immediately became involved in the quickly passing numbers and passages of dark leader that begin the film. After a few seconds many members of the audience had recognized that the numbers were in some definite order and

1. Excerpts from this *Yale Daily News* story were included in Robert Steele, "Japanese Underground Film," *Film Comment* (Fall 1967).

that the passages of dark leader that separated the frames with the numbers had some specific relationship to the numbers themselves. Various people began to exchange ideas about the specific nature of the progression; five minutes into the film, they had correctly ascertained that the numbers were proceeding in pairs and that the strip of dark leader that followed each second number and separated the various pairs of numbers was exactly as long in seconds as the first of the two numbers in each pair. That is, if a pair of numbers was 10 and 0.55, the duration of darkness that followed would be ten seconds long. Once the audience had established this relationship, they began to debate the meaning of the second number. Finally, someone yelled, "I've got it!" and explained to the rest that the second number in each pair was the total of all durations of darkness up to and including the duration signaled by the first number in the pair. Thus, 10 is followed by 0.55, the total of $1 + 2 + 3 + 4 + 5 + 6 + 7 + 8 + 9 + 10$ (decimals are used to keep track of minutes and seconds); and the pair of numbers that follows 10/0.55 is 11/1.06, that is, 11 seconds of darkness and 1 minute, 6 seconds to this point in the film. Once the relationships were clear, the film became completely predictable. Not only could everyone know in advance each number and the length of each duration, but before long someone had used a calculator to determine how long the film would last. The title had suggested that we would see numbers (and subsequent durations) from 1 to 60; the length of the film is, thus, $1 + 2 + 3 + 4 \ldots + 60$ seconds, or about 30½ minutes (actually about 31½ minutes, since the individual seconds during which the numbers are presented are not included in the duration totals). Since the entire structure was obvious ten minutes into the film, viewers were left with around twenty minutes of numbers and darkness to wait through.

At this point, the audience members began to resituate themselves. Some viewers remained in the theater, either experimenting with their ability to measure time accurately by trying to clap at the very second when the next number would appear or talking with other viewers about the evening's other films (even those not looking in the direction of the screen were able to keep track because of the light flashes created by the numbers after the increasingly long durations of darkness and because of the sound "bip" that accompanies the first number in each pair). Other members of the audience stood outside the theater doors, smoking cigarettes and looking into the room from time to time to see if all was going as expected; still others left the building to get coffee and cold drinks. While almost no one was actually looking at the screen during the final minutes of *1 to 60 Seconds,* everyone I talked with or saw was intensely experiencing the film by remaining acutely conscious of the passage of time and of the stately progression of Iimura's film in the theater. When the lights came on, more than thirty people had reconvened to talk with Iimura.

During the late 1970s Iimura became increasingly interested in video, though he has continued to make films, *Talking Picture (The Structure of Film*

Iimura in Talking Picture (The Structure of Film Viewing) *(1981)*.

Viewing) (1981), most notably. He has also toured with programs of Japanese experimental/avant-garde films.

I talked with Iimura in January 1979 in his apartment in New York City.

MacDonald: How did you get interested in filmmaking?

Iimura: After my graduation from the university, I had no idea what I was going to do. That's a peculiar situation in Japan; you're supposed to have a job. I didn't want the kind of job you go to everyday and have a salary. I wanted to do something else, but wasn't sure what. During my school days I had been involved in editing the college newspaper. I had an inclination to journalism, but that wasn't really my favorite kind of work. I had written poetry in high school; then later, at the university I got into the visual arts and practiced a little painting. Not much. Once I did get into film, these two—poetry and painting—somehow came together. Anyway, I wanted to do my own thing, but I needed a job, so the compromise was to work in the Industry—not at any kind of major studio, just a company that made an occasional promotional film. I did mostly assistant's jobs for about a year after I graduated. I was still frustrated, so I bought a regular-8 camera and projector, and I started making films. My idea was not to make documentaries or dramatic films but to do some kind of poetic film. The first one was called, in English, *Junk*. I went to this Japanese bay, to an industrial beach where there was a lot of junk. Some poor people lived there collecting garbage. I shot some of the garbage and also the kids playing around there. What I tried to do was to make some conjunction between the things and the kids. I also wanted to participate in the film myself. I ran on the beach holding the camera, and I shot my own shadow and footsteps. There was a lot of junk art in sculpture and painting in the sixties. I think the idea came from there, too.

MacDonald: A lot of the imagery seems pretty surreal. Did you have the European surrealists in mind?

Iimura: In a way, certainly. Before I made that film I was quite fascinated with surrealism in Europe. I was interested in dadaism, too. The very first poem I made during high school was a dadaist poem, a little like Apollinaire's visual poems. Surrealism—the paintings and some poetry, too—came to Japan in the late thirties and had some influence. The films, those early avant-garde films from Europe, came later. So, yes, I was influenced by surrealism and particularly by dada. I didn't actually see the early avant-garde films until after I made *Junk* and *Love*. I think it was around 1963 to 1965 when the French Cinémathèque in Paris sent a lot of those films to a film museum in Tokyo. Right after that, around 1966, American underground film came, too. It was one right after the other. I did know about both before they came to Japan, through books and through some issues of *Film Culture*. Around 1962–63 I helped form a small group called Japan Film Independent. We wrote a manifesto that said in part—roughly translated—"The Japan Film Independent is the only place where we can ignore commercial and political conditioning. This is a cinema that is against 35mm feature film. This is a cinema where we have freedom, based on our own standards." Donald Richie was involved. He had a collection of films in Japan, so I visited him and saw a lot of films. The Japan Film Independent had an exposition of films in 1964 in Tokyo. That was our first public presentation. At the exposition I showed *A Dance Party in the Kingdom of Lilliput, No. 1* and another film that may be lost or it might still be in Tokyo. The second film was made with footage I picked out of some trash. It was originally an educational film that recorded a plant growing out of the ground. The content isn't important. I punched almost all the frames with a puncher. I made big holes, so that when it was projected, people could barely see what was originally in the frames. I didn't punch every frame; there were some places where I skipped two or three. When it was projected, there was a lot of flicker from the holes. People got very annoyed and complained. They were afraid they would get hurt by the light. That film was called, in English, *Eye Raping* [1964]. In fact, I had also inserted some porno shots. Pornography was forbidden in Japan; it's still forbidden. You could barely see these frames, though. That aspect of *Eye Raping* was something like Paul Sharits's use of similar frames in *T,O,U,C,H,I,N,G.* The use of holes punched in the film was done before *Eye Raping,* in the forties or fifties by the Italian, Bruno Munari. I was amazed to find that someone had already done that. Munari's a sculptor—pretty famous, I think—but he makes films, too.

MacDonald: A Dance Party in the Kingdom of Lilliput, No. 1, begins with a number of graphic symbols, some of which are used repeatedly during the film. What do they mean?

Iimura: Well, the film is about this Mister K.

MacDonald: K as in Kafka?

Iimura: Right. And also the actor's name is Kazakura. It's all short segments during which Mister K appears at random with letters of the alphabet: Mister K with *C,* or Mister K with *A.* The film was originally conceived to be shown with the imagery in a different order every time. If I did A, B, F, D, C one time, then next time I would splice it together differently. It's not practical, so I don't do it any more. But the film was conceived that way. The other version in distribution now also has scratches on it. In 1966 or 1967 I got this bad print. Instead of throwing it out, I scratched directly on the film. In some cases I show the two versions side by side. They both use exactly the same images but in a different order.

MacDonald: There's an addition, though, in the second version: the image of the actor lying in fetal position.

Iimura: Yes, at the very end. I have a literary source for this film: the French surrealist poet Henri Michaux. He wrote a number of poems under the name "Mr. Plume." The film is not an adaptation of the poems, but I liked their spirit and sense of humor. I read Michaux in translation. Also, I should say that the title was Kazakura's idea. Some people, by the way, relate the scene of the stairway to the stairway sequence in [Fernand Léger and Dudley Murphy's] *Ballet Mécanique* [1924].

MacDonald: Before *Dance Party* your work is dadaist or surrealistic, and you don't attack the illusion of the image that the viewer sees. In this film, especially in the second version when you scratch into the emulsion, you seem to move away from respecting the integrity of the image itself and more into questioning what film is.

Iimura: That is quite correct, I think. The film is quite materially concerned. Also, the segmenting of the chapters questions the temporal order of film. When the two versions are shown at the same time, they also question filmic space. Some of these ideas came later, not at the first stage.

One more thing I should say about that film is that there was a particular shot that was an allusion to Jean-Luc Godard. Around that time he made *Contempt,* and in that film there is a very similar shot to one in my film. It was the shot of Brigitte Bardot lying on her stomach that was used on the movie poster for *Contempt*. I was quite interested in Godard in the early sixties, like every-body else. Also, in *A Woman Is a Woman* he exploited the silent film device of titles. I used this silent film formula, too, though I wanted it to be more fragmented than what Godard did, more chance operated.

MacDonald: I'm very puzzled by *I Saw the Shadow* [1966], and I expect that some of my confusion has to do with my ignorance of Japanese culture. You mentioned in the *Film-makers' Cooperative Catalogue No. 6,* "Paint-ing by Jiro Takamatsu," and I guess I don't understand what kind of painting you mean.

Iimura: He painted shadows on canvas. I used one of his paintings at the end. *I Saw the Shadow* is a very romantic film: a love affair between the girl's shadow and the cameraman who shoots her. I am fascinated with shadows. Film is always a shadow; it's the shadow of the celluloid cast on the screen by the projector. The motion picture, as it originated in Asia, developed from shadow plays, which were performed long before motion pictures were in-vented. You didn't see any real figures, just silhouettes—shadows—moving around on a white screen. The Chinese word for motion picture means "elec-tric shadow picture." Even now, the Asian conception of movies is quite dif-ferent from the conception in the West, where there is less distance between the viewer and the illusion created by the film.

MacDonald: In *White Calligraphy* you scratch *The Kojiki* onto the frames. You mentioned in the Coop catalogue that *The Kojiki* is the oldest story in Japan. Would a Japanese who saw that film know you were using that particu-lar story?

Iimura: Certain characters can be read, but not all of them; it's too fast. Some of the words are repeated, but they're always seen with other characters superimposed. You can guess but never be sure. Anyway, I do not intend the story to be identifiable, except as a movement of light. It's all optical phenom-ena. Even without knowing Japanese, you can read the words as free move-ments of line, although they do have a pattern that originates in the language. Although there are thousands of different Chinese characters, the language has its own rules, so certain patterns are noticeable. Also, *The Kojiki,* like any other Japanese story, uses two different kinds of characters or letters: Chinese characters, which we call Kanji Chinese characters, and the Japanese alpha-bet, which is phonetically written. Chinese characters have their own mean-ing, but Japanese phonetic letters don't, just as individual letters in English have no meaning.

MacDonald: Why did you choose *The Kojiki?*

Iimura: Well, it could be anything, any text. In fact *The Kojiki* is a very long story; I use only a few pages from the very beginning.

MacDonald: Your making a visual event out of the materials of language reminds me of visual poetry—Emmett Williams's meditation poems, for ex-

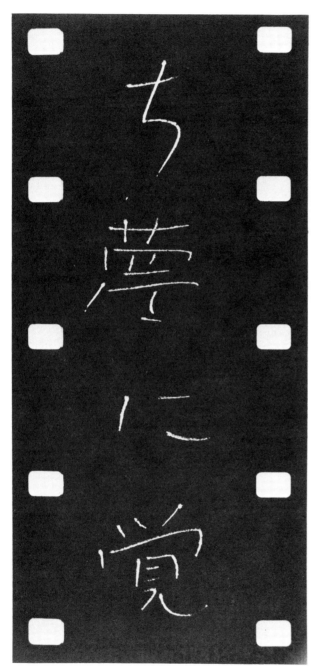

Frame sequence from Iimura's White Calligraphy *(1967).*

ample. Knowing that the markings on the film are characters makes the film more interesting, even though you can't read them.

Iimura: I understand what you mean, but I think it's more like what Mark Tobey did in his painting.

MacDonald: Near the end of *White Calligraphy* you begin to include intervals of black leader, sometimes a frame long, sometimes three or four seconds. Did that have anything to do with *The Kojiki* itself, or were you beginning to be interested in patterns of light and darkness? The ending is a little like a flicker film.

Iimura: It has to do with *The Kojiki.* The story contains poems that are divided at certain intervals. The dark intervals in the film are a translation of these.

All this makes me think how, even in this age of electronic communication, we are bound to writing. Writing in film is, I suppose, a natural extension, like writing on paper. Just the way of reading it is different from what we're used to. In a way, though, we are getting more into reading through light, using the videoscreen and computerized writing. In these, you cannot continue reading as long as you want. There is a time limit. The faster you can read, the more information you can get, so the technique of reading is getting more important.

MacDonald: Can we move on to *Face* and the other later sixties films?

Iimura: Sure. *Face* was my last film of the sixties. It was photographed here in 1968 and completed in Tokyo in 1970. There wasn't much editing. I chose these three girls, including one transvestite, and juxtaposed their faces, adding a sound track of laughing. It's a sort of sexual film. You look at these faces as they act out a sexual experience. I'm still not sure how to place that film in my filmography.

I've withdrawn from distribution the series of films called *Camera Massage,* which were finished in 1968. There are three parts: *Camera Massage No. 1; Camera Massage No. 2: Virgin Conception;* and *Camera Massage No. 3: Summer Happenings U.S.A.* I made these during what was a very confusing period for me. The cultural changes happening here in the sixties were my first non-Eastern experience. When I came to the United States, all of a sudden I was seeing the black riots happening all over. I had known there were such things, but I had never experienced one. I didn't have any idea why they were happening or what was going to happen. When I went to Boston, all I heard on the radio and TV was about the riots. Then I came down to New York and saw all the hippies. To understand change you have to know about the previous stages. I didn't have that kind of experience, so I couldn't understand how those people at Harvard University—I went there first—could not be excited about the riots. I couldn't understand how they could behave in such a calm way.

Also, at that time I made *Filmmakers* [1969], which is a series of portraits of filmmakers: Stan Brakhage, Jonas Mekas, Jack Smith, Stan Vanderbeek, Andy Warhol, and a self-portrait. I visited them, talked with them, and photographed them. It isn't a series of standard portraits, but more like portraits of their environments and of my relationship to them.

MacDonald: Did you choose those filmmakers because their films made a particularly strong impression on you?

Iimura: I thought they were the strongest figures, and I wanted to report about them in Japan. The film is a kind of personal reportage. The sound came later; while looking at the images, I recorded the words of the things that I saw. Most of the shots were photographed without looking through the viewfinder. I tried not to portray the filmmakers as I saw them, but rather as I related with them. If I didn't look through the viewfinder, I could be more in a relationship with the person as the film was shot. All except Andy Warhol. I never met him. I photographed his film *Chelsea Girls* during a screening. Much of the technique of *Filmmakers* is "borrowed." For Jonas Mekas I shot frame by frame, imitating his technique. When I photographed myself, I used a magnifying glass, as I had in some of my other films.

Shutter was quite a change, but before talking about it, I think I should speak about a film installation I did in 1968. It was called *Dead Movie*. It's one of my earliest works to question the whole enterprise of film projection. Also, it's the first to use no photographed imagery, so it's much more closely related to what I am doing now than any other work of that period. I did *Dead Movie* in 1968 at the Judson Gallery, which was the basement of Judson Church, where so many things happened at that time. Two projectors, one with just black leader running through it and the other projecting only light, were set up facing each other. You didn't see any image except the shadow of the projector with the loop of black leader. Since *Dead Movie* I have used this form of having projectors face each other in several film and video pieces. Normally, we regard the projector as just a machine to project film; in this piece it's more than a machine—it's part of the work. Philosophically, this is quite important. It relates to what the filmic system is all about. I try to expose the projection system. I think that film is what happens during a screening, not anything that comes before. So, here, projection itself is the subject of a piece. When people came to see *Dead Movie,* they were disappointed. There wasn't much to see, and they didn't know where to focus their attention.

MacDonald: Dead Movie seems related to the shadow plays you were talking about earlier.

Iimura: Right, except in a shadow play, the shadows move around. Here, there's no moving image except this moving loop of leader. All you see is the film material, the projector, light and shadow, endlessly maintaining the same state of things, like the constant cycle of time. The slow buildup of scratches on the loop is like entropy. When I showed a variation of *Dead Movie* in Austria, I added a third projector, so that next to the projector showing black leader was another projecting clear leader onto a screen. The longer that loop of clear leader ran, the more scratches you could see on the screen. A very old man came to me and said, "This is Zen." Usually I don't like to relate my work to traditional religious ideas, even though I may have been influenced by them. Once people relate a work to a traditional idea, they see it through that idea. They don't see the film as it is. Though I came from a different culture with a long history, I am living in the contemporary world. I am very much here. In this case, I said, "Oh, is that so"; that's all I could say. It could be Zen; it could be something else. I'm indifferent about that. It's a projection piece and, as far as I'm concerned, that is all it's about. There are certain dialectics in the piece; they involve black and clear leader, positive and negative relations, and visible and invisible screens. There is little tradition of such work, though I think it relates to some of Paul Sharits's installations.

MacDonald: For *Shutter* you photographed the light thrown onto a screen by a projector without film in it.

Iimura: Right. It's a process film about the shutter mechanism. In this case, I sketched a diagram, including the fade-ins and fade-outs. At the beginning the fading in and out is rather slow; then it becomes more frequent toward the end.

MacDonald: Were there variable speeds on the projector?

Iimura: No, in this case just one speed. The more slowly I faded in and out, the more you see the flicker of the shutter. The whole impression is softer and less shocking than Tony Conrad's *The Flicker.*

MacDonald: While your work changes quite a bit between 1962 or so and 1971, *Models* (1972) represents several particularly dramatic developments. You reduce what you work with to duration, light, darkness, and different kinds of numerical coding systems. What led to this?

Iimura: Well, *Dead Movie* (now revised and retitled *Projection Piece*) was the first time I used only black leader and, in the revision, clear leader. Using just darkness and light in a film is not new. Peter Kubelka's *Arnulf Rainer* and Tony Conrad's *The Flicker* consist of only black and white. I assume both are photographed rather than made with black and clear leader, though when they're projected, it's quite the same. Also, Hans Richter's *Rhythm 21* uses rectangular black and white shapes, which is different from using clear or black film for its own sake but is a historical precedent. There are other historical precedents in painting and the graphic arts. Richter himself is quite related to the constructivists and to Kasimir Malevich's suprematism—the famous painting, *Suprematist Composition: White on White,* for example. That is one tradition.

For me there is also another tradition, an Eastern one that includes much two-dimensionally organized black and white graphic work, such as Zen painting and geometric architecture like the Katsura Palace in Kyoto, which inspired a lot of modern architecture. When I started *Models,* it was like using both traditions. Although film takes place in time, it has its own two-dimensional space that can be related to these other types of work. The tradition of avant-garde film is dominated by the visual realization of film material. Avant-garde film was started in the 1920s by artists whose primary concerns were visual and spatial. While this tradition is quite strong, however, the visuals that fill the filmic space are only one factor. Another is temporality. This aspect has been neglected. It's always been treated as a kind of supporting factor to the visuals. Although any film work has to have a certain time sequence, temporality itself is never treated as its own subject, except in the sense of rhythm. Richter, Kubelka, and Conrad are much concerned with rhythm. When rhythm gets accelerated as in Conrad's *The Flicker,* it creates optical illusions. The Kubelka film creates afterimages, psychological effects. Although I appreciate their works very much, I try to avoid optical illusions. My concern is not with rhythm but with intervals of time, with concrete duration as material.

I have quite rigorously articulated and measured durations. Henri Bergson, the French philosopher, said that time has no image, that time is something invisible that you cannot materialize like space. We have these three basic dimensions, and time is supposed to be a fourth, but it's quite different from what we ordinarily regard as a dimension. To deal with time in film, I tried to eliminate visual imagery by using black or clear leader, although I cannot totally eliminate all the imagery since black or clear leader project their own images. But I did eliminate the pictures, as distinguished from imagery in general. I chose black and clear leader as fundamental materials: one transmits light, one blocks the light. When you perceive time in darkness or in light, it's quite a different experience. The first reel of *Models* deals with time itself. The second reel deals with certain kinds of logic and time.

MacDonald: Is it fair to say that the first reel tends to involve the viewer in perceptual experiences, while the second creates conceptual experiences?

Iimura: Yes. Whenever timing is involved, we are more in the area of perception; where logic is involved, it's more the area of conception, although time itself involves concept, too. Without the concept of time we cannot have a sense of time. Also, the scientific aspect of time is one thing, and the psychological aspect is another. The scientific aspect is based on physics and on the measuring of time on the basis of cosmology. Since I'm not a scientist or a physicist, I cannot deal much with scientific sorts of investigation, but my method in *Models* is a little like scientific or psychological testing, since I measure each length exactly and then give the exact durations for each sequence. It's quite orderly and very mathematical, so it could be used for scientific purposes. But my films are meant as works of art.

MacDonald: By eliminating all of what you call "pictures" and using just leader in *Models,* as you did in *Dead Movie,* you not only make duration the subject, you implicitly develop another kind of time. Usually, when there is picture imagery in a film, we siphon out all the scratches, dust, and so on in order to concentrate on the pictures. By eliminating picture imagery, you make scratches and other damage that happens during the making and projection of the film more visible than they would normally be. As a result, the film records very subtly the history of its own creation and projection.

Iimura: Right. Especially on clear leader, the more you project, the more scratches and dust you get. It's sort of aging every time you project it, which I like, although it was not intentional. Although I keep *Models* clean, scratches are increasing all the time. If it gets to be too much, then I might abandon the print, but as far as I'm concerned, it's OK as long as the print is projectable. This aging process is what is called "entropy" in physics. It is an aspect of time.

The first reel of *Models* is made up of four works; the second reel also. All eight are made in series. The first reel starts with the measurement I called "2 minutes 46 seconds 16 frames," which is exactly one hundred feet. This is the basic unit, and you see it three times with that title, which, by the way, is also part of the work; it's the verbal expression of what follows.

After the title, the first section involves drawing numbers from 1 to 24 in successive frames and repeating this for the duration of that hundred-foot length. In the second section, successive numbers are drawn once a second for sixty seconds. In the third, a number is drawn each minute; it works out that there are only 1 and 2. The result is three different experiences of the same length. Many people feel that the first one is the shortest experience and that the last one—where you see almost a continuous white image—is the longest. The first, "2 minutes 46 seconds 16 frames," is the basic measurement; all the works that follow in *Models* are based on one hundred feet.

MacDonald: Each work explores a different way of measuring the one-hundred-foot unit?

Iimura: Right.

The second reel deals with logic in terms of filmic time and how it works semiologically. The first work is called "Counting 1 to 100." It has four sections. The first is called "Counting 1 to 100 or 10 Xs." An X replaces each tenth number. The second section doubles the number of X's, although the replacements are not so regular. Then, in the third and fourth sections I double the number of X's, first to forty and then, in the fourth section, to eighty. The more X's, the more difficulty you have in counting. Two systems are involved: counting 1 to 100 and counting the X's. In most cases it's impossible to count both at the same time. It's somewhat similar to the section of Hollis Frampton's *Zorns Lemma* where the alphabet is replaced with pictures. My film, though, is more purely concerned with time, and with systems for counting.

The second work on the second reel is "A Line." There are three parts. I use both positive and negative versions in each section. First you see the title "Positive Version," followed by a line in the middle: ten feet of white line on black is followed by ten feet of black line on white, for one hundred feet. Then you see "Negative Version," which just reverses the order. Both positive and negative versions look the same. In fact, both came from a single line that I scratched on film. In the second section of "A Line" you see a white line on black background on the right side of the image, again for ten feet; it's followed by a black line on the left side, exactly the reverse of the first ten feet. This alternation continues for one hundred feet. Then you see the negative version. The problem in this case is how you see the line. If you count the lines on both right and left, they seem like two lines, but they were made from a single line, and what you see at any given moment is a single line, so they're still *a* line. In the third section the position of the line is the same as in the second section, except that the first white line on black is followed by clear leader where you see no line. It's supposed to be an invisible line—white on white. This is followed by the white line on black and an "invisible" black line on black, and so on for one hundred feet. Then you see the negative version. "A Line" is concerned with the dialectic of positive and negative. Within the positive there is negative, and within the negative there is positive. What I'm trying to say is that eventually those two terms come together. At any given moment you cannot distinguish positive from negative, negative from positive.

MacDonald: You can only distinguish them in reference to each other.

Iimura: Right. I was influenced by the Eastern concept where positive and negative are the same. Whether you say yes or no doesn't matter; eventually they're the same, though to say it like this seems very contradictory. It's not Western logic. People may see this as mystical, but I'm trying to prove that a contradiction exists within the logic of film.

MacDonald: $+ \& -$ is very similar to "Timed 1, 2, 3" on the first reel of *Models,* with the difference that in this case you use the $+$, $-$, and $=$ signs. Did you feel that by setting up a series of basic additions and subtractions, you would be able to more fully engage the viewer? In other words, why change the experience of "Timed 1, 2, 3"?

Iimura: In "Timed 1, 2, 3" the same visual compositions are punctuated by the different sound intervals. In this case time has a very exact equation. I start from $1 + 1 = 2$, and go through the additions up to $9 + 1 = 10$. Then come subtractions. There's a problem with the subtractions, though. Two seconds minus one is supposed to equal one second, but in fact, you are experiencing three seconds. For the subtractions I used clear leader instead of black; when you see the white space, it's supposed to be subtraction, but time is always $n + 1$. It never goes backwards, so all this measurement of time in $+ \& -$ is fictional. Before you see the actual durations, you see all the equations typed out on paper and photographed, so you know exactly what will come next. You have an expectation, and you can try to count the exact lengths.

MacDonald: + & − and several sections of *Models* create a durational experience, but there's also an increased awareness of where you are in the theater. Sometimes, when there are long durations of light, I become conscious of other people and other things around me. When it's dark, there's a different experience of the space. Was that part of your original conception?

Iimura: The very idea of using black and clear leader involves the filmic space. A white frame on the screen reflects light, and, as you say, you become very aware about the space where you sit and watch. When dark film is projected, you are not supposed to see anything on the screen. This also makes you aware about space, but in a different manner. When you feel yourself surrounded by darkness, you are, perhaps, more aware of yourself, since you are not absorbed in the screen. I am always very conscious of this. These films were made to be shown in a theater, which is a ritual space, something like a church, where God is placed in front of you in a space brighter than other spaces. People come to the theater to look at light. This ritual feeling is something I like very much to have with these films. The best theater I have found was The Invisible Cinema at Anthology Film Archives, when it used to be at Lafayette Street. It was designed by Kubelka and was totally black. Even the seats were covered, and you saw nothing but the screen floating in the middle of the air. That was an ideal space for film projection. When I show my films in other places, light leaks interfere.

MacDonald: 1 to 60 Seconds combines both conceptual elements (figuring out the specifics of the progression of numbers) and perceptual elements (viewing and experiencing longer and longer durations). A question about audience involvement: do you assume that a good audience for *1 to 60 Seconds* will stay in the theater and concentrate on the screen, or do you think people can experience that film even if they move in and out of the theater?

Iimura: Well, first of all, I should say that it is fine if you go out and come back, or never come back, or stay outside watching without seeing what's going on. *1 to 60 Seconds* has an exact tabulation from 1 to 60 seconds that takes thirty minutes and thirty seconds to complete. People can predict exactly what comes next: after 22, you expect 23. In fact, it is quite boring; I know that. I experience it myself. Excitement comes from the unexpected, from surprise. This film is quite the opposite. Yet in one sense, there is surprise: you can never predict the exact moment the next number will appear. You can count twenty seconds by tapping the rhythm, but you never know exactly the moment. It's solely up to your own psychological experience. In a way *1 to 60 Seconds* is similar to Andy Warhol's *Empire,* except that Warhol presents a photographed building, uses a photographic illusion. In my case, there is nothing but the numbers, so you are even more aware of temporal duration. The materialization of temporal duration is a quite recent phenomenon in film. While some people use boredom as a kind of artistic strategy, it's still quite hard to deal with. I'm not expressly exploiting the psychological acceptance that we call "boredom," but nevertheless, I know that you may feel bored. *1 to 60 Seconds* is a kind of maximal piece in relation to the concept of time, though it could have been longer. If I'd used one minute as the basic unit, instead of one second, it could have been much longer—like a few days.

MacDonald: Parallel [1974] seems to draw a parallel, which paradoxically creates an awareness of differences, between a photographed line and a hand-drawn line or, in a more general sense, between photographed and handmade imagery. Is this what you had in mind?

limura: Yes. The photographed line stays within the frame; I just photo-graphed a single white line on a black background. The scratched line is scratched onto the frames. It crosses the film frames. I was trying to show illusion and reality at the same time. The scratched line is a materialized real line that runs throughout the film. Although I tried to keep it in the same posi-tion, it is nevertheless moving left or right a little bit or sometimes skipping and jumping, too, so all the frames are different. The photographed line is always the same thing; it's a duplicate all the way through the film. So the one is an illusion of what was originally there and the other is "reality." I tried to show them both at the same time. The argument about illusion and reality is quite old, and people have different interpretations of what reality and illusion are. Film is very much an illusionistic medium. It always shows some type of duplication. When I made a print of *Parallel,* I created a generation gap. When the scratched line is printed, it is a duplication. The photographed line is the duplication of the duplication. No matter how many times you print it, there is always this one-generation gap. In *Parallel* the two kinds of lines are switched back and forth and are presented—sometimes alone, sometimes si-multaneously—for different durations. I thought about the mathematical question of how you can make parallels meet. In mathematics parallels never get together. In this case also, the lines never meet physically; yet concep-tually, when I switch them from left to right and from right to left, they do meet. When the scratched line is followed by the photographed line, or the photographed line is followed by the scratched line, they conceptually merge.

MacDonald: When you look at the photographed line, it gives the impres-sion of a great stillness, which is actually the opposite of the case because the strip of film is always moving. The real line, on the other hand, is always referring to the celluloid moving through the projector, so the viewer is more aware of the actual mechanisms and materials of film. Nearly all your recent films have been made with hands directly on the material. Do you feel that philosophically—or, in Le Grice's sense, politically—illusionary imagery is somehow less significant or further from. . . .

limura: No, I don't think that way. People distinguish between "illusion" and "reality"; yet these terms are mutually referential. If you say that being directly concerned with film materials is a way of avoiding illusion, you are wrong. Material is one of the dimensions of illusion. "Reality" and "illusion" are combined terms. When materialists or structuralists try to say that once they get involved with the filmic material, they are dealing with reality, they are creating another illusion. The projection of the scratched line in *Parallel* is as much an illusion as the projection of the photographed line. It is true that being aware of the film material demystifies the film process. But when you're involved in projection, or even if you look at the film straight—if you're looking at a print—what you see is illusion. You would have to know the process—how both were made—in order to distinguish between them.

MacDonald: Both versions of *24 Frames Per Second* are more complex experiences than *+ & −* or *1 to 60 Seconds,* at least in terms of the information they present to the viewer. *24 Frames Per Second* seems to combine your concerns with duration, with sound-image relationships, and with using light and darkness, sound, and language to measure time. When you made *24 Frames Per Second,* did you think of it as a jump in complexity compared to earlier films?

Iimura: Not really. There are certain complexities involved, and I know that there is also a difficulty in figuring out exactly what is happening. All the events happen within the second, and our perceptions don't usually function in that short a time. The first version—it was made in 1975—is rather simple. You progress from $\frac{1}{24}$ to $\frac{24}{24}$ of a second. The successively larger groups of light frames—or, in the second half, dark frames—move from one end to the other of the filmic second. After a while, you can expect exactly what will come next: after $\frac{1}{24}$ of lightness, you will see $\frac{2}{24}$. First, I show the positive version; then, when it is completed, the negative. The film takes more than twenty minutes. Having the positive version followed by the negative is a formula I have used in other films—*Shutter,* for example. In the revised version of *24 Frames Per Second* I tried to do something else. I put both positive and negative together, so that there is no middle point where you switch from one to the other. In the revised version the two progressions happen at the same time. This dual cycle merges at the end, although the second progression is hard to perceive. Positive becomes negative; negative, positive. Whenever I speak about this piece, I relate it to the ancient Chinese yin-yang symbol, which I tried to translate into filmic time. The revised version was done in 1978; it takes only eleven and a half minutes, so the developments happen in an even shorter time and are very hard to figure out.

MacDonald: I wasn't able to perceive the structure of the new version even when I put it on the rewind. When you sent me the score, though, it became clear right away.

Iimura: It's difficult to perceive during projection; I know that. Whenever I accompany the film, I take the score. It helps greatly, though there is always a problem with comparing a graphical representation and a real-time representation. Each acts in its own manner. The graphical piece is very still, so it's much easier to understand. We're more used to seeing that kind of structure on

Numerical notation from Iimura's 24 Frames Per Second *(1975; revised, 1978).*

paper. When it's presented in time, you have to reconstruct it by yourself. I like both aspects.

MacDonald: Do you still have the first version in distribution?

Iimura: Yes, in the Film-makers' Cooperative. When I showed that version at Millennium, some people got bored and upset.

MacDonald: The first version? That's one of my favorite films!

Iimura: Well, I thought perhaps there was something wrong with the film. Then I got the idea for the second version. Audience reaction sometimes helps me to think, to get new ideas.

Carolee Schneemann

For Carolee Schneemann, film is merely one of the media an artist may work in, and throughout her career she has worked more or less simultaneously as a painter, a performance artist, a book artist, and a filmmaker. She has not made many films, but the three included in her *Autobiographical Trilogy—Fuses* (1967), *Plumb Line* (1971), and *Kitch's Last Meal* (1978)—remain a significant contribution to independent cinema. The most unusual, and least understood, dimension of these films (and of Schneemann's other work, including the film-related box book *A.B.C.*) is the relationship between them and Schneemann's personal life. Conventional narrative films may be generated by the personal experiences of the director (or screenwriter), but once these experiences are fed into the multi-stage processes of Industry production and, transformed by the highly conventionalized codes of representation of the popular cinema, a considerable distance between the original personal experience and what we see on the screen is inevitable. And even when independent filmmakers make presumably noncommercial films about their personal experiences, they usually reflect the traditional assumption that artists must detach themselves from the particulars of their personal lives (that they must recollect their powerful emotions later, in a state of tranquility, as Wordsworth claimed). For example, Jonas Mekas, one of the best-known "personal" filmmakers, rarely edits his diaries until years after the footage is collected. Schneemann, however, resists this assumption of the need for detachment—whether it is the de facto result of commercial filmmaking procedures or the intended result of a film artist's aesthetic commitment. For her, the challenge is to generate films (performances, books, or other works) from *within* the experiences the films are about in such a way that the emotional realities do not get lost in the transition but, instead, can be studied (and modified by the creative process).

There is an implicitly feminist dimension to Schneemann's anti-detachment stance. Though men and women inevitably shape their worlds on the basis of what they have come to feel, most accept the idea that the artist does his work from a position outside his life (the grammatical masculine is used intentionally). In fact, this detachment is often assumed to be—I have often assumed it to be—proof of the artist's seriousness. Yet, despite this "detachment," the resulting works inevitably become evidence of the artist's feelings and attitudes. In a culture where men still tend to be trained to deny their emotions, the assumption that the making of "serious" art must involve detachment implicitly promotes art produced by males.

For a time, *Fuses,* Schneemann's interpretation of her sexual interaction with composer James Tenney, was considered one of the independent cinema's most outrageous films. In the early 1960s Schneemann's erotic openness went so far beyond the limits of accepted public taste that the film was considered pornographic. Now, the film's sexuality seems somewhat less shocking, and yet, even for those who have seen some of the hard-core films and videos that have proliferated since the early 1970s, Schneemann's willingness to take responsibility for her imagery by appearing with the film can seem unusual. The importance of *Fuses,* however, is less its ability to outrage than its presentation of a vision of normal, healthy sexuality between real lovers against which we can measure the mixture of voyeurism and prudery that characterizes the dramatization of sexuality in commercial cinema and the male-oriented fantasies enacted in most pornography. That sex can be and should be a complex psychic and physical exploration between lovers within a particular environment rather than a ritualized series of acts performed for a real (or imagined) spectator is clear in *Fuses,* both in Schneemann's decision to "interpret" the original footage by painting, scratching, and collaging on it and in her refusal to structure the film to minister to the conventional film audience's need for vicarious climax.

While *Fuses* presents an interpretation of a healthy eroticism, *Plumb Line* interprets a period of Schneemann's life when she was recovering from the disintegration of a subsequent relationship. It is as open about the pain of losing a lover as *Fuses* is about the pleasure of having one. And just as *Fuses* was generated from within the erotic relationship it documents (the filming and editing were done during the Schneemann/Tenney relationship), the making of *Plumb Line* was itself a means not only to express the pain of loss but also to recover from that pain: it required that Schneemann manipulate the film and photographic remnants of the relationship into a structure that represented her vision of the experience as fully as the relationship itself had apparently represented her partner's vision of her as a tool for his pleasure. The result is, in some ways, Schneemann's most impressive and accessible—and least appreciated—film.

Fuses and *Plumb Line* include elements of performance—in *Fuses* Schneemann and Tenney perform with the camera, and at the beginning and end of *Plumb Line* Schneemann attacks projected imagery with paint and fire; *Kitch's Last Meal* necessitates a screening-room situation that is reminiscent of her performance work: two portions of *Kitch's Last Meal* are presented on two Super-8 projectors mounted vertically, and the double image is accompanied by taped sound. The presence of the projectors and tape recorder in the screening space is reminiscent of (although more complex than) home movies, a relevant connection since *Kitch's Last Meal* focuses on the domestic aspects of her relationship with filmmaker Anthony McCall. The length of the film (the longest of the several versions lasts for five hours; usually Schneemann screens a 60- or a 90-minute version) was predetermined by Schneemann's recognition that her seventeen-year-old cat, Kitch, could not live much longer: she decided to film the cat and the details of her domestic life that the cat presumably was perceiving, every week until the cat died. The result is a Super-8 epic that allows us to examine a domestic relationship (and dimensions of our lives usually distorted and marginalized by conventional cinema) in a process of transition: McCall and Schneemann stopped living together in 1976, soon after Kitch died.

I spoke with Schneemann in November 1979.

MacDonald: Did you get into filmmaking originally as part of performance?

Schneemann: No. I started making films in 1963. USCO [Us Company—a performance group] asked me two years later to work with a film environment, and I made a piece for Phoebe Neville and myself called *Ghost Rev*. Film has its own complete visual language and in a sense needn't have any kind of action with it, especially a live performance. But at that time I was working with film as an antagonist. I felt that live action could become a nexus through which film imagery was filtered or to which it was attached. *Ghost Rev* was a very aggressive piece. We shredded the screens; we broke through the image; we dismantled its fixity in space. We were wearing white overalls, and in one sequence we intercepted the screen imagery with our bodies and crawled into the audience along the projection beam. The USCO film in this section was a continuous highway going off into the horizon. In effect, we took the linear rush of the highway going toward the distant focal point, turned it inside out, and brought it right back into the audience.

Earlier, when I was starting *Fuses,* I saw film as thousands of frames of paintings passing and was very concerned with breaking frame. I had spent years as a painter trying to get out of the fixity of the rectangle. I was able to do that with painting-constructions cut into layers of materials that are brought forward off the surface or cut through to the back. With film, because of the fixity of projection systems, there are only certain linear directions in which images can move. Things like that really used to bewilder me. That's why a lot of the cutting in that film is inside out and upside down, because I never want to automatically accept technical systems. Any proscriptive orientation, you know, holds within itself its own contradiction.

I also did experiments in a loft with a wonderful, cranky old Bell & Howell projector, one of those cast-metal ones that only take four-hundred-foot reels. It was a beautifully calibrated machine, and it wasn't a sealed, enclosed system: I could get my hands on it. There was a little gear for variable speed, and it had a swivel neck, and I put it on a swivel chair. I used it for the first shots of *Fuses,* or, let's say, the first failures of *Fuses.* One time, for example, I got a whole hundred feet of green back. I didn't know whether that was because someone in the lab considered what was on the film obscene or whether I had used old film stock or had done something wrong. Anyway, I was working in the loft with that material as pure color saturation. I built a wall of white cardboard boxes as part of a construction I was doing (this is 1965) to break down my old sense that film had to be an integral, complete, self-contained image. Why not spread it around the room? Why not see it as another source of moving color, a way of reorganizing spatial dimensions? I would swivel with the swivel-head projector on a revolving office chair so that the green film was projected across the walls of the white structures. Later, I did the same thing with some of the lovemaking images of *Fuses,* and it was always interesting to look at, never predictable or tricky.

But I was always uncertain about this contradiction of what I was doing to film. I had internalized all these very serious, almost religious attitudes about film. I had witnessed the messianic battle Brakhage had had to endure to establish the nature of visual film. That was very serious for me. Anyway, film as part of performance remained something that was in the studio along with all the other rough materials being tried out.

MacDonald: The more I look at *Fuses,* the more obvious it is how much labor of various kinds went into it. I assume there was an original time when you photographed imagery, and this was followed by another time when you made print generations of some of the imagery, and still later you painted and drew on the film.

Schneemann: No. Actually, I worked on that film the way I would work on a canvas. It was like an overall immediacy put into a prolonged time duration, a way of working with film as one extended frame in time. It involved a constant going back and forth and back and forth. Anything that happened at any one place was going to make an effect right through the whole thing. If something suddenly came in at 10 feet, then there'd be a count that would take me to 75 feet, and once I was there, I'd have to go on to 280 feet.

MacDonald: Were you recording footage at the same time that you were editing other footage and painting on other footage?

Schneemann: Yes, right.

MacDonald: So all aspects of it were going on simultaneously?

Schneemann: But not always. First, I started out just learning to shoot. The first roll I ever shot was an incredible, magical reward. I just couldn't believe what came back from the lab. It's in the film, near the beginning: the slow pan of the cat in the window with the leaves behind. Summer green, perfectly in focus, perfect exposure in a traditional sense. Once I had made the identification of aperture and exposure, I had to develop a sense of the camera and me as a meshed system. If I had had to stop and think about it, I'd have lost that propulsion, the rhythm that was coming out of the moment.

Then I'd get all this stuff back and try to recognize what it was so I could know what I was seeing and how I had made it be that way. Of course, I'd have another set of recognitions—not interpretations, recognitions—once it came back and was in its form as a film material. The material would affect other stratas of organization. I might count eighteen beats of blue, four of yellow, three of red. Then, once I had those units set, I'd have to build with that, take that principle right through. During one week I might have been doing a whole rhythmic structure of six purple, two blue, six purple, two blue. How was that going to work with a new phrasing I'd discovered? All of this was still being done within the context of the existing imagery. Once I'd established a certain texture in a certain kind of movement, say, leaves moving left to right, then I might go into something shadowed and dark. I'd have to decide whether I was going back to the window or to the body, and if so, which piece of the body? And once that was decided, then what was the next development?

MacDonald: From the beginning did you know you would paint and draw directly on the film?

Schneemann: Oh, yes. It started right away. I *had* to interfere with it. Especially at that time I had no interest in accepting things on their own, unless that was a decision that came after I had already subjected them in some other way to something that wasn't supposed to happen. The idea that things were pristine and integral was very repellent to me. Now I feel differently. I'm emptying, emptying, taking everything out. The film I'm making is black-and-white stills.

MacDonald: At that time, though, it was important to you to touch the film, to hand-work it?

Schneemann: Of course it was important to me. Anything else would have been the greatest kind of lie and imposition. I was working in a very dusty space. Every day another bunch of spiders had crawled over the table there.

Frame detail of Schneemann and James Tenney in Fuses *(1967).*

The cat was in my lap. Brakhage and Breer and Vanderbeek and Ken Jacobs had given me little verbal lessons, had told me things along the way. But I realized that, given the physical conditions I worked in and my own temperament, what I made could never be pristine; it could never be treated the respectful way that traditionally you had to treat film if you were going to preserve an undamaged image. I felt that all my images had to be available to the natural kinds of damages that would occur in my working situation. Also, I edit in daylight, and I show the films in daylight because I hate being locked up in a black room. I can't stand to work in a synthetic space where I don't have the opportunity to walk around, go outside, pick up the cat, look out the window and see that there's a bunch of birds doing something. I need all that. If I work on a film or a video "properly," I've missed a whole piece of simple natural day or night. I don't want to miss them because I'm making something. I think that comes out of being a painter, where you always have that complete sense that you can make your whole vocabulary and structure of image while you're sitting at your kitchen table with your materials and light is coming in, where you yourself are the complete system. I guess that's why I had to make cameras and light meters and tripods all part of my body. I had to enjoy them in some way. Probably it sounds silly.

MacDonald: No, it sounds. . . .

Schneemann: It's whacky.

MacDonald: Did you use all the footage you shot, once you felt comfortable with the camera? For some time, Bob Huot has, on principle, been using everything he shoots.

Schneemann: No, I wouldn't use everything that came back. When you're self-shooting, you get stuff you really don't expect. You're always a couple of inches off what you want, especially in close-ups. I lost some wonderful material, but I was accepting of that and saw that I was getting back other things that I didn't expect at all. That set off recognitions that had to do with my becoming something permeable through which the film was realizing itself, an idea that has recently gotten clearer and more developed for me. At that time it was very, very important just to be responsive to the fact that what I wanted might not be what I needed. It seems to me now like an apparition or a spirit or a set of forces that use you. The conception of the film becomes the arena in which you and the forces give each other permission to begin making entrances and exists. That's the real excitement of it for me.

MacDonald: Was *Fuses* all self-shot?

Schneemann: We passed the camera back and forth, or in other instances I set it up. Also, Vanderbeek shot one section where we're kissing.

MacDonald: The title. The idea of fusion, or fusing, as the source of the title is obvious, but *fuse* has other sorts of meanings: a fuse leading to an explosion or an electrical fuse. Were all those meanings in mind when you chose the title?

Schneemann: Oh sure. We would always be working very consciously with things like that. Really, the title came out of Jim's studying Greek. ["The word was . . . *physis* (the root of our physics, etc., but possibly also of fuck!). But it was not through any independent knowledge or research of my own into the Greek language. . . . I found it in a book . . . I don't remember the author's name" (James Tenney, letter to author, 18 May 1980). Schneemann is sure that the book was *Eros Denied* (New York: Grove, 1964) by Wayland Young. The relevant comments are probably those Young makes while discussing Skeat's 1887 *Etymological Dictionary,* which includes a list of Indo-European root syllables: "No. 242 in Skeat's list signifies 'grow, become, be, dwell, build.' It underlies, he holds, our words *future* and *felicity* and *fecund,* and also *fawn* and *bower.* It is present in the Greek word *phusis* (nature, or suchness) which gave us our *physics,* and in the Latin *fui,* I was, and *feles,* a cat, or fruitful thing, in the still-used Latin word *fetus,* and in the German *bauen,* to build, with all its countless derivations. Skeat's No. 243 signifies 'enjoy or use,' and is present in *fruit* and *fruition* and the French *froment.* The roots as Skeat writes them are BHU and BHUG. Try making this sound; one blows it out in a sort of generous scattering, or one may feel it as a puff of contentment. It seems to be around today still uninflected in the wolf-whistle, and the exclamation written 'Whew!' If indeed this noise is really the basic noise for all that is constructive, peaceful, pleasant, forward-looking—to be, to grow and to build—one may wonder that Skeat left out the most obvious manifestation of all: *fuck.* The word is central to the whole complex of meanings" (pp. 30–31).]

MacDonald: Have audiences for *Fuses* changed much over the years?

Schneemann: Oh, yes. There was that revelatory time when *Fuses* was first shown, around 1967–68, when not a lot but a certain number of women and a very large number of men in the audience felt that it was giving them back a sort of wholeness. They said it was very positive for them, and women would say that they had never looked at their genitals and had never felt accepting of them and this was a chance to make the kind of integration and "fusion" about self they really wanted. There's a thread of that that keeps going on. There is also tremendous resistance to it—silliness and pain that's masked as a kind of hostility or tacky aggressiveness. One of the most extreme things happened when I was in the audience at Cannes. About forty men went berserk and tore up all the seats in the theater, slashed them with razors, shredded them, and threw all the padding around. It was terrifying, and peculiar.

MacDonald: They came prepared?

Schneemann: I don't know; the theater was full. *Fuses* was on the program of special jury selections, most of which were socially political (it was 1968) compared to *Fuses,* which was sexually political. The people who went crazy were French, youngish; they looked sort of middle class in their dress. I don't know what they were screaming or why. I was very bewildered. I thought at the time that it had to do with the lack of predictable pornographic narrative sequence. There was also a fight at the University of Massachusetts in 1973, where some man in the audience said he didn't get a hard-on, so what's the point to it? And a woman in the back row said to him something like, "You didn't get a hard-on because you wouldn't recognize something that was truly sexual if it sat on your lap." And he turned around and said, "Who the fuck do you think you are? You're just another one of those dumb bitches who . . ." something or other; I don't remember exactly. Anyway, she called him a stupid prick—this is in the university auditorium!—and the professors were banging on the tables, and the students were yelling, and somebody took a newspaper and hit the man on the head with it. Finally they remembered me and shouted, "What do you think about the audience fighting?" And I said, "It seems to be very cathartic for you; it's better than struggling over dull questions."

In 1972 or 1973 at the Art Institute in Chicago there was a group of lesbian separatists who were extremely angry about the film. They said, "There's no role model for us in here, and we don't want to have to look at it." Well, of course, I felt that, first, they didn't *have* to look at it, and, second, they were perfectly justified to object to it, because if they needed a role model, the heterosexual one in *Fuses* was going to be antagonistic. But then a woman yelled to them, "All my life I've been pushed around by fascistic men telling me what to look at and what it means, and I'm not going to be pushed around by fascistic women telling me what to look at and what it means." Big applause from another contingent. And then still another woman put her head up and said, "The role model in the film is the fact that the filmmaker envisions her own life, and we should see it in that way." More fighting and arguing.

About three years ago, in California, *Fuses* was seen as "sentimental shit." You don't usually hear much about what people really say or think about your work. Other things—invitations, phone calls, who remembers your name, stuff like that—are telling you what kind of rating you've got in the art world. Anyway, there was this time in California where, I'm told, people really hated it and booed and walked out. I try to make all my things to go on their own for a long duration; it's up to them to absorb the shocks.

MacDonald: The amount of negative reaction seems strange to me. Just in terms of colors and textures *Fuses* is so beautiful to look at.

Schneemann: Well, it used to be considered too ugly to look at: jumbled, broken, chaotic. In California it seems to have become too beautiful. Perhaps the California people were into leather and straps. A lot of things have been considered indulgent in the past couple of years. Heterosexual love has been a luxury that some women cannot psychologically afford. It's too fraught with compromise and diversion of energies that have to be women-identified among and with other women.

MacDonald: It seems very apparent when I watch *Fuses* that though you and Jim Tenney had known each other for a long time, you were still pretty fascinated with each other. At least on one level, all the different lighting conditions in the film, the different tones, all the different technical things that go on suggest your long-term erotic exploration of each other.

Schneemann: Also there is a prolonged time duration in it. It doesn't have the titillating quality of dramatic immediacy.

MacDonald: It suggests that you can sustain that level of passion over a long period of time.

Schneemann: Hopefully, yes. That's a normal expectation of mine. *Fuses* is, in part, an answer to Brakhage's *Loving,* which Jim and I are in. Brakhage made *Loving* because of his fascination with the erotic sensitivity and vitality that was between Jim and me. That was something very important for him to be seeing and caring about. But I felt that *Loving* failed to capture our central eroticism, and I wanted to set that right. Actually, I hate what happens when I'm in somebody else's work, with the exception of a Bill Brand film, *Split Decision,* which is all invention anyway. I always feel a tremendous distortion has been enacted on me, despite my hope that some coherent self will come through.

Another thing I was thinking about at the time is the issue of equity between couples. There's a tremendous resistance to that; there's always got to be one person on top, right? I always thought it was a particular value that a couple could have this equity between them, and Jim took a lot of flack for that. Men, in particular, thought he wasn't getting the advantages he should. They didn't mean about the sex, but in our daily life. People would be around and see that he was going to do the dishes while I cooked, or that they couldn't come over at a certain time because that's when I was working in my little part of the house and couldn't be disturbed. There was a tremendous amount of hostility towards me, as if he was being victimized by something if I wasn't going to serve him. But it had a double edge; it had an erotic fascination because it was also very sexy. People were always saying, "You can't live like this."

Also, they presumed that influences only went one way. Jim influenced me; I could never in twelve years be an influence on him. Almost no one thought we could both be good for each other. That kind of thing is still going on. I used to watch it with other people. When John and Yoko were first together, the general response, other than that of the fascinated fans, was vicious. All the artists would say, "Lennon is ruining her quixotic imagination," and all the pop people would say, "He's with that freaky avant-garde woman, and she's ruining his mind." Never the celebration of the two of them bringing to each other what they did.

MacDonald: In your book, *More Than Meat Joy* [1979] you include a passage from the text of *Kitch's Last Meal* in which "a happy man/a structuralist filmmaker" says, "you are charming/but don't ask us/to look at your films/we cannot/there are certain films/we cannot look at/the personal clutter/the persistence of feelings/the hand-touch sensibility/the diaristic indulgence/the painterly mess/the dense gestalt/the primitive techniques." In general, were other filmmakers, other artists, supportive of your filmmaking?

Schneemann: Well, it was mixed. You can't, with real equanimity, be acknowledged as having full value when you're moving between other people's disciplines, where their total life intelligence is dedicated to one thing. As soon as you make a move, they say you're being superficial. When I'm choreographing dancers, I insist that I'm a painter. I have to insist on that because that means I'm not assuming that I have the training and the principles to develop or destroy that a dancer would have. I'm not a dancer; I'm a painter working with my body and ways of thinking about movement and environment that come out of the discipline of having painted for six or eight hours a day for years. That's got to be the root of my language in any medium. I'm not a filmmaker. I'm not a photographer. I'm this painter who's working again with extended, related materials. I don't want to feel that as a filmmaker I'm competing with people who have defined that one area as their specific and complete focus.

By the way, that quotation you mentioned is a secret letter to a critic [Annette Michelson] who couldn't look at my films. It's a double invention and transmutation: it's not to a man but to a woman. The projected quotes are from her students. After years of saying she really wanted to see my films and was very interested, there was this festival where she slept through my program. I mentioned to a friend of mine, who was also a student of hers, that I was just astonished that she really couldn't bear to see them. I mean there's a lot of work I can't stand to see, but if I were a critic I think I'd just have to go through it. Anyway, the student said, "Well, look, there are certain films she simply cannot look at: the diaristic indulgence, the hand-touch sensibility," and so on.

MacDonald: While *Fuses* seems to be a celebration, *Plumb Line* seems to be an exorcism or a cauterizing of an experience. Was the film made after the end of a relationship, or was it something that came out of an experience as it was happening, the way *Fuses* did?

Schneemann: It came afterward. I was flipped out at the end of that relationship, to the extent that I couldn't work and was wandering around Europe not knowing who I was or where I was. The only thing that I was kind of clear about was that Kitch was there and was still coherent and sensitive and aware. In those days there were so many people who seemed to think they knew who I was, but I knew that they were following some older illusion. I knew "I" was gone, and I didn't know if "I" would ever come back. That was the worst feeling. The duration of it was tormenting. Every day was composed of these little fissures of hours to try to move through. Tremendous effort was involved in just finding a shoe, getting it on my foot, finding the other shoe, getting that on. Only when I was sort of coming out of it in London—this is after wandering around in France for part of one year and staying in London for another year—I began to think that I had to see what was in this scrap footage and tape I had been carrying with me. I set up a little editing room in the flat where I lived, and started. Friends helped by sneaking me into the BBC at midnight to work with the tape machines there.

MacDonald: Were you conscious of using the making of that film as a means of reestablishing your own equilibrium?

Schneemann: No. It wasn't a matter of I'll do this, then I'll get better.

MacDonald: At first I thought the plumb line was a way of suggesting that by working on this film you were getting yourself back into balance.

Schneemann: Oh, that's an idea. The plumb line really stands for a phallic measure, a phallic exploration and determination of space, which was his most spectacular and particular power over me. His art was really in sex and his sexual imagination, the freedom, the remarkable capacities he had. I thought they were perfectly suited to me, without watching out for how much psychic damage was involved in my vulnerability and his need for power. The film is in some sense a way of righting the balances that I had relinquished to this man, but I wasn't doing it at the time as a way of being cured. I just wanted to examine the material I had. Also, I felt very guilty and very uncertain. I thought, there's no point to this crap; I should throw it away. But I couldn't quite do that, and then I thought, well it'll be something that I explore and it may set off some useful equivalences for somebody else. That was the only way I could justify the content, although the way the film was made was very satisfying to me. I mean both the formal procedures and the fact that the film gets burnt up. I take control of the imagery and its dissolution.

MacDonald: Does the whole film take place in Venice and environs?

Schneemann: I was so lonely and horny apart from him in Venice, and there were all these men following me around, and everywhere spires and towers! But no. Part of it is in London. All the water and hammering and bathing suits is in Amagansett, Long Island. And in one of the opening passages, he's sweeping a loft in New York.

MacDonald: How did you decide on the rhythm created by moving back and forth between the whole image and the quartered image?

Schneemann: It's a little bit like with *Fuses,* only there is a stricter frame grid. Since the original footage was in 8mm, I was able to include four separate images within a single 16mm frame. You start with something you know you want. You see this hunk and say, "That's carrying something for me," and then there's the question of what has to either move out of it or be juxtaposed against it. When you're in there, you're looking at so many things at once; it's so much like painting for me in terms of how my mind is watching ten, twelve units and what's within them and composing them multidimensionally, not just in a sequence but in sequences that break and recur. It's not theme so much as a kind of phrasing, where you just suck out a whole area of yellow so you can concentrate it later on, knowing that it's got to be there and that every-thing else is moving towards that with some kind of visual inevitability. Let's say I have one reasonably controllable unit—thirty feet of something—I'll build out on that for the next sixty feet, doing a set of calculations as to what the permutations seen or implied from that combination are going to be. It's like musical beats; I've got this many counts going here and I know that I want to be able to pull this other thing through two hundred feet later, even though I don't know what's going to happen in between. So I go into a trance; how else can you edit it? It's a "musical trance," and I'm reeling film back and forth. In some cellular way I feel that *I'm* being reeled back and forth. In that sense it's more like dance. Of course, what's happening is that the more I edit, the big-ger the little frames seem to get. The mind's eye blows them up. When I started *Kitch's Last Meal,* the frames were really little; now, I need just a tiny bit of information and they're huge. I'm seeing all that's there, or almost all—enough, anyway. I'm talking about naked-eye Super-8, without a moviola. Partly this came from the discipline of having to print *Plumb Line* in a ma-chine where I could see only a minute aperture and had to make decisions on the slightest bits of information. I was using an old step-printer that belonged to the London Film-makers' Co-operative.

The rhythms are all about the passage through the gate of the step-printer. As I was working, the gate became a vulvic metaphor for how much desire, how much recognition was going to be impressed on the finished film. The plumb line and the gate—not very clear symbols, but they were driving the whole thing for me. I think it's a good film to look at on an analysis projector to see what the underlying rhythms are composed of, because they're very calculated and detailed.

MacDonald: Your methods create a kind of "grip" on the material. That

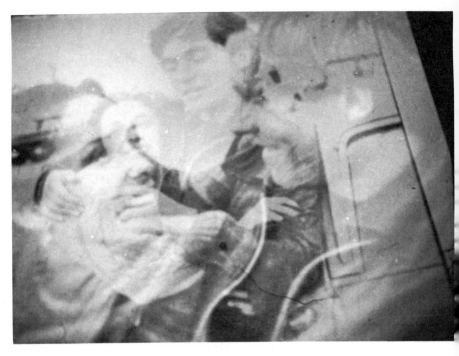

Schneemann and lover in Plumb Line *(1971).*

rigid line down the center keeps everything very vertical and horizontal. Also, at the beginning and again at the end you repeat the same sequence exactly. The formal techniques and the structure seem to be a means of keeping that painful material under control, within clear limits.

Schneemann: I've been working with cards since then, working with the established frame, so that everything is held within and subject to one very specific basic frame convention. All the cards and text pieces I've been doing for the past few years really accept the frame.

MacDonald: As long as there's more than one, and more than one kind!

Schneemann: Oh yes! [laughter] I can't stand just the one. It doesn't work; it's never complex enough.

MacDonald: In *Plumb Line* you seem involved with traditional Venice imagery; were you conscious of that when you made it? I'm thinking of lions and cats, for example.

Schneemann: Well, the original material was just a little touristic, regular-8 film. It wasn't intended to become serious film material. *Plumb Line* was made from scraps.

MacDonald: The sound was scraps, too?

Schneemann: Yes, completely, except for Kitch's chants. The sirens, wailing, the speech when I was crazy were all going on around the loft. I'd wander around hearing the world blowing up continuously. It went on and on—sirens, wailing, screams—which was also how I felt then. The sounds that Kitch made were a web all around me. She liked to work with resonant hollow spaces where, we realized after a while, she could bounce sound. She usually did it late at night when everything was very still. It was uncanny (or uncatty) because it always seemed like she was working. She would chant for sometimes twenty or thirty minutes, always in an enclosed space where she could produce this resonance. In listening to her I had the sense that she was tearing apart the formal fabric between what can be shown and what can't be shown. Through her presence, her cat mind, she was creating some kind of very powerful unknown music. It also seemed an attempt to work with language; she seemed to be playing with wordlike sounds. She would use the same vowels and the same frequency tone projections in different spaces at different times throughout the year, so I hung the microphone out in the hallways where she would be most likely to start chanting.

MacDonald: When I first showed the film to a class, people recognized that it was a cat, but assumed that it was either hungry or . . .

Schneemann: In heat, right?

MacDonald: Yes.

Apparently, *Kitch's Last Meal* exists in various states and stages. The version I've seen is a six-reel, double-projection with sound, but you've mentioned that it's also much longer. Can you describe the different states it's gone through and the state it's in now? Is it finished, or do you plan to make a longer work?

Schneemann: It's all there; I just don't have time to work with it. I'd have to stop everything else. The rest of the reels are in the same basic organization that the ones I show are in. Most of them are edited. The editing was a pretty immediate process. I would do it as the weekly material came back and would develop the double correspondences. Two reels would start to be organized in terms of one another right away. Then, later, that might change quite radically. I might find something from 1976 that really had to work into 1974. It's mystifying when I go through them and see how much work has been done—an enormous amount of work—and how much still remains to do. There's a lot of cutting out, cutting down, necessary, so that what is left breathes enough. Finding the sound tapes that belong with the time of the imagery and cutting them in—that's still left to do. Of course, each twenty-minute section of image and sound is in response or contradiction, extending what occurs in the reels before and after. I can never deal with any new section without going back to the tracks that were laid in the other sections. That's why it would take so much time to completely finish it. I do consider those three sections I show finished. But there are five more double reels, or more—I'm afraid to look. Also, I don't have any money for it now.

MacDonald: Was *Kitch's Last Meal* originally conceived as a double-image film?

Schneemann: Yes, from the beginning. Vertical, too, though I've never figured out to my satisfaction why.

MacDonald: The directions on the film cans even specify the respective size of the two images.

Schneemann: Yes, they can't be symmetrical. That wrecks it. It's an impossible system. What am I going to do with this monster? I've dug myself into another hole. It was supposed to be the efficient film that everybody could see, that I wouldn't have to shepherd around. It's a bit of a joke: here's this five-hour film that can hardly ever be shown.

MacDonald: Every audience I've shown it with has been responsive to what does get shown, though. In fact, when I showed it in Utica, I was a little startled by the audience staying with it for an hour and a half. That's unusual for a non-narrative film.

Schneemann: Yes!

MacDonald: It proves that Super-8 can maintain attention for a feature-length amount of time.

Schneemann: It really takes you over, which has to do with the verticality and the constant permutation of the three parts, the way they feed one another.

MacDonald: I can't remember the film in separate units. Every time I've seen it, I've been completely carried into it, but when I get done I can never remember the differences between sections that I've heard you describe. I look back and forth and I listen and look, and when I'm done, all I remember is this flow of material.

Schneemann: It doesn't matter.

MacDonald: You talk about *Fuses, Plumb Line,* and *Kitch's Last Meal* as a triadic film, as a part of a larger work that in *More Than Meat Joy* you call *Autobiographical Trilogy.* At what point did you begin to think of them as parts of a larger work?

Schneemann: When Anthony [McCall] and Bruce [McPherson] pointed it out to me! And also when I realized I couldn't ever make another personal film, which is an awful position to be in.

MacDonald: When did that realization come about?

Schneemann: Once everything in *Kitch's Last Meal* was destroyed. I had agreed with the film demon that I would make the film on the premise that Kitch was going to die, so that the film was going to absorb from my life something that was already foretold. When I made *Fuses,* it was to celebrate and examine a life process that was continuing. That film was made over a long period of time, too, but even toward the end of the editing I didn't know the relationship with Anthony was going to end. It seemed like it could never end. When I showed *Fuses* in London, Jo Durden-Smith came up out of the audience and said, "I assume that the relationship in the film is ended"; I felt very put out and bewildered by that and said, "Yes, why would you say so?" He said, "I'm a filmmaker also, and film absorbs life into itself." I've always remembered that. Also Stan Brakhage told me how all the places in his early films had been destroyed, how almost all the people in the early films had disappeared or died. He saw some sinister interchange or imperceptible energy that could get destructive. Anyway, *Kitch's Last Meal* was made on the premise that I would shoot so many meals of the cat and *what she was observing* in the course of our life, every week until she died. The cat was already seventeen so it could have been three, six, seven years; it didn't matter. I make these long projections about work sometimes. Well, the cat died in February 1976; Anthony left for his separate life in March; I lost my job in April; and even the freight train behind the house (central to the film) discontinued its twice-a-week run. All the essential elements, except for the house itself and me, were taken out of that context. And I thought, it's done it again!

MacDonald: Fuses is a celebration of a very intense interlocked kind of relationship, and *Plumb Line* is an exorcism of a relationship that went bad. *Kitch's Last Meal* seems—at least to the extent that it's about you and Anthony—to be about a very domestic and intimate but also rather detached and independent relationship. There seems a lot more space between the two of you than there is between you and the men in the relationships portrayed in the other films. Is that a misreading of what's happening?

Schneemann: Well, the real quality of our relationship comes through on some of the other reels. The energy of the intimacy in that relationship is not so explicit in the reels I usually show.

Some people feel it's very erotic. There's no lovemaking as such—a little— and yet that was always very constant for us, even when everything else was disappearing or being denied. Towards the end it was really difficult for him to talk with me, and he couldn't talk about his work at all for quite a while. But the sex always went on very intensely and spontaneously. That made it a little more confusing as to whether we really were not going to go on together, or whether in some way we would. In a way it was less of a brutalizing separation after six years to have that confusion. Also, there was still a lot of care and trust, and we were trying not to be hurtful (which wasn't possible).

MacDonald: Whenever I've seen *Kitch's Last Meal,* you've always been in a maelstrom of activity, trying to get the reels in sync and the sound working. . . .

Schneemann: Yes, horrible!

MacDonald: For me, it has very much the same feel as when I'm with friends, looking at slides or home movies. Your difficulties have tended, at least in the audiences I've been in, to make people more relaxed.

Schneemann: Right. In that sense I like the maelstrom quality of it because it lets the machinery demonstrate itself. It lets the facts of projection be exposed as part of the central process of the perceptual experience we're anticipating.

MacDonald: You would rather have the projectors in the room?

Schneemann: Oh, yes. Well, they have to be anyway because there's never enough throw. I think if I wasn't there it might not be so relaxing—if it was just a projectionist struggling to get this on.

MacDonald: There's something very rigid about the idea that all film automatically has to be in 16mm and projectable from a normal 16mm projector.

Schneemann: Oh, it's insane. Why can't you have two projectors and put one thing on top of another? It's so peculiar, after the sixties where at Expo-67 we saw 360° projection systems and multidimensional screens, on ceilings, floors. Just try and get people to stack two simple Super-8's, and they go berserk. I'm putting *Kitch's Last Meal* onto video. Of course, then they'll have another reason for not showing it.

MacDonald: Was the choice of Super-8 for *Kitch's Last Meal* just practical, economic, or was something else involved?

Schneemann: You mean I haven't already told the story! About the man coming up to me after an NYU lecture and offering me a camera because I didn't have any, and how I assumed it would be something really wonderful—a Beaulieu—and how I went to his hotel hoping that I wasn't going to be made a complete fool of (you know, that he was really offering me a camera, not himself!). He met me in the lobby with this little box in his hand, and I thought, the box is very small, awfully small, and my heart sank, but I thought, maybe that's not the camera, and I opened it up, and there was another little box. It was black, and it had a hole in one end and a hole in the other, and I said, what is it? And he said, that's a Super-8 camera, and I thought, oh christ, just my luck. But I couldn't say no; I couldn't say, "This isn't good enough." I said, "Thank you very much; I'll be happy to see what it does, and it's really kind." And then I got into it; I loved it. It brought me things that I was fascinated to see.

MacDonald: It's very difficult to paint or draw directly onto Super-8 film, which is more fragile and less controllable than 16mm. Did you feel you were done with that kind of work? It had played a considerable part in your earlier films.

Schneemann: Well, I had to recognize that as a value, which I think I did right away. Also, the three-minute duration of Super-8 film immediately established a time structure. All that corresponded to my need for simplification at the time. I wanted to make myself more and more permeable and invisible. It's hard to describe. This camera was a very straightforward, domestic, simple partner to work with, and I wanted to be more and more accepting of the obviousness and ordinariness of things. That was also the premise of shooting according to a diagram of what the cat was looking at.

Of course, what I was finding was actually almost mystical, invisible. What really comes through in that film doesn't have anything to do with what's shown there as image. The rhythms release a deeper level. When I'm seeing it, I'm seeing a whole range of things that I don't carry into a literal formulation before, during, or afterwards. I'm often astonished by what's in that film, but I cannot tell you what it is. It's a mythic film, and all the things you can say it's about only set off something else. That's what it does to you, and that's where I have a lot of satisfaction with it as a work. It keeps exceeding me.

It's such a simple film. You're not really dealing with people (character, personalization). At least when I see it, I don't really feel connected to them. It's more as if the film is some constant motion of particles on which certain moments and pressures of material imprint themselves, and some of those imprints are persons, and some have more to do with elements in the landscape or changes of light. But, again, all the internal rhythms are what's holding it. Also, though issues are imbedded in the sound, in the text, it's not as if you're struggling between the disjunctive imagery and the disjunctive sound. Somehow the disjunctiveness itself lets them all move through clearly and you take what you need. But for all that, the film is cut like a straightjacket. It's very, very fragile. There can't be six extra frames in all the casualness of it. Six or twelve extra frames will knock out a section for me, so that I get crazed when I'm looking at it. I can't wait to get my razor blade at it, can't wait. I've got to get it, or shift it around, or move something from the bottom to the top, or vice versa. Of course, that's when I'm happiest—when I'm all tangled up with the stuff hanging around my neck, and I'm just gone, with my mind hanging into all these different directions in space. I never get used to it. It's always wonderful and strange. Editing is very physical; it's like weaving.

By the way, have I mentioned Ozu? He's a major influence. I was so affected by his films. I learned so much and felt confirmed, able to accept what I was doing. I saw his work very late—*Kitch's Last Meal* was probably three years along when Daryl Chin said I had to go. The particular film I saw was *Spring*. The relationship of the daughter who won't leave her father was especially powerful. In fact, I was hysterical, overwhelmed. Painful, painful. It was such a wonderful work because always you think oh, nothing's happening, this is pleasant, oh, that's a nice bird, oh, someone's walking in from the left, here comes somebody else from the right—and in three-quarters of an hour you're just completely consumed!

MacDonald: In all three of your autobiographical films there seems to be a kind of formal demonstration of the importance of intimate personal experience.

Schneemann: Yes. Perhaps people are unresponsive to that, but then I get very tired of all the alienated, cold, brittle work that many people do.

MacDonald: Have you had reactions from people who feel that the imagery that you're presenting is not important enough?

Schneemann: Of course. Probably most of the male film community feels that. It's a bit of a mystery to me why, whenever there's a show of personal, diary films, everybody's invited but me. I mean I'm not looking for confirmation; there are just places where it seems obvious that my work should be included, even if some people hate it.

Tom Chomont

Tom Chomont has been making short, intensely personal, "poetic" films since the early 1960s. The most interesting of them are finely crafted indices of an ongoing process of psychospiritual self-examination. Working with largely diaristic footage—of himself, his friends and lovers, his environments—Chomont fashions dense, subtle, often exquisite emblems of particular states of mind. In general, his work owes a good deal to the tradition of visionary film as described by P. Adams Sitney, particularly to Gregory Markopoulos, but his interest in commercial film, especially the horror genre, is frequently evident: *Night Blossoms* (1965), for example, centers on a vampire, and *The Cat Lady* (1969) "borrows" a bit of footage from *The Creature from the Black Lagoon* and combines it with homemade footage into a minimal evocation of the genre.

Some Chomont films reveal intense psychic struggles, especially those films he made during the 1960s, when he was coming to grips with his desire to have male lovers. In *Phases of the Moon* (1968), for example, Chomont uses techniques that are a motif in his work—mirror printing and the combination of positive and negative footage and of color and black and white, often in superimposition—to image paranoia, self-involvement, isolation, and loneliness. Though Chomont's films are not plotted in any conventional sense, they do develop characters. In *Phases of the Moon* we often see the protagonist looking through the peephole in his front door; at times this image is mirror printed so that even the protagonist's attempt to look out reveals his self-involvement and his troubled, schizoid state. In the visually stunning *Oblivion* (1969), Chomont uses similar techniques to capture a troubled erotic relationship. A lover lies naked on a bed, deeply asleep, while the filmmaker gazes at his naked body and filmically fantasizes about it. The orgasmic nature of these fantasies is evident both in Chomont's choice of detail (a fountain of lights, for example, is sometimes juxtaposed with the sleeping lover) and, as J. J. Murphy (1979) has suggested, in the overall rhythm of the short film. *Oblivion* is so densely suggestive—so many levels of implication operate simultaneously in dense bursts of tiny shots and frame clusters—that the film almost defies literary analysis.

In other instances, Chomont images blissful psychic states. In *A Persian Rug* (1969), for instance, he uses the complex, spiritually suggestive design of a Persian carpet (or a carpet reminiscent of traditional Persian carpets) as a metaphor for the film, which weaves bits of imagery of a hotel room or an apartment, of the surrounding environment, and of a lover—we see only a foot or a leg—into a filmic "magic carpet" that communicates a romantic, mysterious erotic attachment. As is usual in Chomont's films, formal elements are used to dramatize aspects of the particular psychic state being imaged. In *A Persian Rug* the film frame sometimes seems to function as a rug-like rectangle into or onto which the lover steps. In *Aria* (1971) Chomont images an ecstatic state of mind achieved in an Alpine setting. The title suggests the musical structure of the editing and "air," as in mountain air. *Love Objects* (1971) reveals the erotic interaction among a group of friends and provides a remarkably open statement about the synthetic nature of such distinctions as "homosexual" and "heterosexual." After what I assume is an invocation to Venus, we see the lovers together—first two men, then a man and a woman. As he films, Chomont is in so close that he is part of the lovemaking. At times, in fact, his proximity to the bodies keeps us from being sure whether we are seeing a man or a woman: clearly, for Chomont, the intimacy is the issue; the particulars of one's gender are irrelevant. This idea is emphasized by Chomont's layering of positive and negative, color and black and white: the layers of imagery seem as intricately interlocked as the lovers.

In one sense, filmmaking is almost always a pretentious activity. Industry films attempt to address almost everyone, to capture the mood of an entire nation, to mythify a complex culture; the critical cinema often presumes to offer a critique of this immense commercial enterprise. For Chomont, however, filmmaking is above all an unpretentious act, an attempt by a humble individual to see himself clearly. As intricate and inventive as they are, Chomont's films always have a homemade, handcrafted feel. Chomont has traveled widely; he has lived for substantial periods in Germany and in Holland. But he carries his equipment with him and records and edits (sometimes on a simple homemade editing rig he can carry in a suitcase) wherever he is. Even when he began to explore new processes and new formal issues during the early to mid-1970s, the resulting films did not become academic exercises but remained close to the particulars of his life. When he made *Lijn II* (1972), *abda* (1974), and *Rebirth* (1974) in Holland, he was exploring the optical

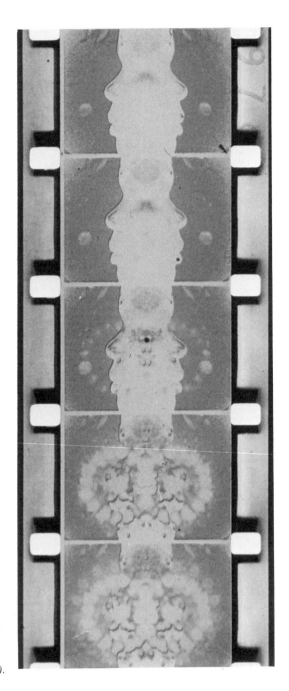

Miriam Israel's face as meditative design in frame sequence from Chomont's Earth *(1978).*

printer and the development process: he printed the films by hand, using buckets and a homemake darkroom. *Lijn II* is a tiny portrait of a friend made on a contact printer from scraps of a film that was lost. *Rebirth* reworks the same brief passage of a man in a bath over and over into an image of a continuous rebirth. In *Space Time Studies* (1977), his longest film to date (twenty minutes), Chomont provides an inventive exploration of reverse: we cannot tell when the characters, friends he was staying with in Amsterdam, were filmed in reverse (or so that when the imagery was developed, their actions would be seen in reverse) and when Chomont directed them to pretend to be moving backwards. As highly formal as *Space Time Studies* is, however, it remains a personal film, a portrait of Chomont's relationship with his two friends and of the environment in which they lived.

Nearly always, the issue of becoming spiritually centered is crucial in Chomont's films. In some cases, it is the primary focus. In . (1974), for example, viewers are trained to search out images of centering, some of which are immediately obvious (circular shapes in the center of the frame); others become apparent as soon as one is aware of the pattern the more obviously circular images create. In fact, Chomont's consistent use of mirror printing (I know of no filmmaker who uses the device as often) is probably a function of this concern with centering: mirror printing automatically creates symmetrical imagery in which the center of the frame becomes particularly dynamic. Like Jordan Belson's spiritual animations, Chomont's films are often reminiscent of mandalas. Unlike Belson, however, Chomont does not see the spiritual as something that develops apart from everyday life. In Chomont's films, the medium of film is a means for bridging the gap between the mundane and the mystical: the strip of celluloid, the image on the screen, become a location where the spiritual and the material meet. In *Minor Revisions* (1979) this relationship is dramatized by the image of an onion being peeled: on a mundane level, the peeling of the onion is a simple act, a diary reflection of the ongoing process of daily cooking (it is also sexually suggestive: the relationship of Chomont and his lover involves their getting together to "peel off" their everyday skins—clothes, uniforms). But Chomont's decision to concentrate on the onion and to reveal it in double, then triple, exposure endows the onion with a deeper meaning: it becomes a metaphor for the film itself and for the peeling away of the surface levels of personality to concentrate on spiritual levels. For Chomont, making films has become a medium for enabling the material and the spiritual worlds to discover each other.

I spoke with Chomont on three occasions during January, February, and March of 1980. Our original interview (published in *Afterimage*, in June 1981) contains a good deal of commentary on *abda, Space Time Studies, The Heavens, Earth, Minor Revisions,* and other more recent films.

MacDonald: Tell me something about your background, especially as it relates to film.

Chomont: The first film I remember was a Castle Films newsreel of Nazi soldiers that my mother and father projected. Later they bought two cartoons by Ub Iwerks—*Jack Frost* and *Puss in Boots*—for my brother and me. When I was four, I was out with my father, and he took me into a cinema in the town where we lived. I remember I could not distinguish the beginning of the film; I couldn't separate the previews from the feature. It was all one thing in my mind, like a reverie, and it took me a while to focus on the screen. I remember just being aware that there were lots of people in the dark room and slowly I felt all of their attention go toward the screen, and so my attention drifted to the screen, too. I remember during the previews the letters coming towards you very vividly. I couldn't read, of course. It looked like some kind of stylized lightning, and this voice like a crack of thunder coming on the soundtrack. Later I found out the film was an Ann Sothern comedy called *Up Goes Maisie.*

My parents had tried to buy a silent projector and got a used one that was broken. My grandfather installed a crank handle, and I remember cranking a Felix the Cat cartoon and watching the whole illusion of the frames—I think I was about three years old—how you could make it into still pictures or go faster and make movement.

When I was about four, I tried to draw a film on a sheet of paper, and when I got to the end of the paper, I drew a spiral that got smaller and smaller. I had the idea it could be projected, and when I went to cut it out I saw that it was too big at the beginning and didn't work at the end.

MacDonald: Did you start making films as a kid?

Chomont: No, I wanted to, and I also wanted to take photographs. My brother did, too. My parents would fool us by giving us the cameras with no film in them—they were afraid we would waste film—and the film would come back and we would look for what we'd taken and it was never there. But I always dreamed of making films. When I was about ten my brother and I got the idea of filming short stories with puppets. We would plan and write little scenarios. We never did them, but the idea was there.

I was always fascinated by dissolves and fades, all those effects that you didn't have in life but that had an expressiveness, that were true in a psychological sense or in a memory sense; events did sort of meld together in the memory and here it was literalized in film. Later I remember liking Jack Clayton's *Room at the Top* because of the dissolves.

One of my sisters gave me an 8mm camera the first year I was in college, an old Brownie with part of the viewfinder broken off, so I had to learn to estimate where the frame really was. I used black and white film, high-contrast newsreel stock; I had to order it because the camera stores didn't carry it. I wanted to be able to walk in and out of buildings filming. I used color too, but only if I knew I was going to be outside in sunlight. Later when I couldn't get the black and white, I began shooting color inside. I think I'd read *Film Culture* already (this is when I was about nineteen), and Brakhage talked about how you could heat film and change the color balance. Even though you lost what the companies considered the real colors, you could get expressive colors.

I thought of what I filmed as a diary. I hand held the camera, and I prided myself on being able to shoot without looking through the viewfinder. I began in 1961 and continued doing that through 1963. Then I took the family's Bell & Howell camera and started buying 16mm magazines. I felt I had to do something more planned, though the diary continued. It may have come out of the fact that when we moved from Illinois to Florida, I felt a loss and afterwards always felt the desire to capture things. I already felt that the most paradisiacal part of my life had been lost: that first house where I first saw films, where I enjoyed everything like a little tyrant who had free time (my mother was confined to bed for some time; my father worked; my grandfather was very indulgent and mischievous), the rabbits, the pheasants, the woods and snow. Suddenly we were in a flat, warm, humid, overly fertile area that was somehow very deathly—everything burning up from the sun. In the diaries I was just making stabs at trying to retrieve things. Even when I made a planned film, I was trying to save pieces of experience.

MacDonald: Did you study filmmaking?

Chomont: Yes, eventually, between 1964 and 1965 at Boston University. Alvin Fiering was the production teacher at the time. Gerald Knox, Tony Hodginson, and Robert Steele were there. The production course was oriented towards social documentary.

MacDonald: Did you make social documentaries there?

Chomont: Well, I tried.

MacDonald: There's still an element of that in your work.

Chomont: Oh, yes. I wasn't opposed to it. I just felt constrained. Finally I dropped out. The only reason I could see to finish was to teach film, and at that time there weren't many places teaching film. Today I'm sorry I didn't do it.

MacDonald: Did you stay in Boston?

Chomont: Yes, for about half a year after I stopped classes. I was working in a cinema as a ticket taker, and I was programming a film series in Cambridge. At the time nobody in the area was regularly showing what was being called Underground, or the New American, Cinema. I thought maybe I could organize something, so through the cinema and the projectionist there I managed to set up a benefit showing of Gregory Markopoulos's *Twice a Man* at the Odd Fellows Hall in Cambridge—which made a very nice poster! I started showing films once a month, then once every two weeks. I had to hire police to be in the hall because at that time it was open to the public.

MacDonald: Who did you show?

Chomont: Oh, Stan Brakhage came in person. He did a show over two hours long including the 8mm *Songs*. This would have been late 1965. We showed Markopoulos (who also came to Boston and filmed there), Robert Nelson, Bill Vehr's *Avocada* and, later, *Brothel,* which turned out to be the film that got me shut down, but that was after about a year.

I had the premiere showing of Andy Meyer's *Match Girl* and *An Early Clue to the New Direction* (Meyer later made films for Roger Corman), and George Kuchar came up with some of the 8mm films, and I showed a mixed program in 16mm of George and Mike Kuchar. And there was a Maya Deren program, a Bruce Baillie program, a Kirsanov program (Kirsanov was a Russian director who worked in Paris), *La Chute de la Maison Usher* by Epstein . . . the standard experimental film society program at the time.

The police tried to intimidate me. They claimed I was showing dirty films and that the hall wasn't licensed to show films. I remember having a 104° fever and getting furious and shouting at the chief of police of Cambridge over the phone (I was very naive at the time, very idealistic), "And you're not going to get away with this!" I just kept calling everyone in the Buildings Department until I determined that the hall was licensed for films. Then not only did they decide it was legal, they decided to send two chaperones—that was for the Jack Smith *Normal Love* rushes. The chief showed up and watched the program, and I remember some people laughing because he apparently didn't see it as at all bizarre. Jack had not included any nudity in what we showed, but I hadn't known that. Now it seems supremely stupid to have taken those risks, especially fighting with the police, but nothing happened until one policeman reported me for showing *Brothel,* and the chief phoned me three days before the next showing and told me they were quarantining the whole hall. They nailed the door shut, put a public notice on it. I had no way to notify people— the posters and the mailing had gone out to the members—so I mimeographed maps of how to get to MIT. (Fred Camper agreed to let us show there.) Gregory Markopoulos was coming with the original rolls of his first portrait film, *Galaxie,* and I didn't want to cancel, so I just went down with maps, and the chief was standing there when I was handing them out. He had his whole regalia on. He said, "Don't ever try to show films here again because I'll close them." They tapped my phone for over six weeks. Friends would phone up and say, "The body's in the trunk" and things like that, but I was very nervous.

With the Swetsof Gallery we did a showing of *Match Girl* and Jean Genêt's *Un Chant d'Amour.* We had two showings because it was a small gallery, and sure enough, at the second showing two plainclothesmen tried to get in the door. Mr. Swetsof was very clever; he just stepped outside the door and slammed it. (He had locked the door on the inside so when he shut it he couldn't even get in himself.) It was very exciting. I'm sure the bravado was inspired by reading about Jonas Mekas and *Flaming Creatures.* [Early in January 1964, Mekas—with Barbara Rubin and P. Adams Sitney—stormed the projection booth at the Third International Experimental Film Exposition in Belgium in order to show Jack Smith's film. In March 1964, Mekas was arrested in New York for screening it.]

MacDonald: Were you doing this by yourself?

Chomont: Yes. I had some backing from the manager of the cinema where I worked for a while, but he pulled out when he saw that it wouldn't be a big-money thing. I did the series for about eleven months. Then I moved to New York.

MacDonald: When did you first start showing your own films?

Chomont: I never programmed my films in the series. The first time I showed publicly was in 1966 at an open screening in New York at the Ciné-mathèque on 41st Street in the old Wurlitzer Building. (Later I was the acting manager there.) I showed *Night Blossoms;* it was demolished [laughter]—a horrible experience. In 1968 Jonas showed an earlier film, *Flames,* and he showed some others later. Vicki Peterson saw some films at Bob Cowan's house in 1969, and she programmed *Ophelia* [1969] and *The Cat Lady* on a program at the Rockefeller Institute. Really, public showings started when I went to Europe.

MacDonald: How long were you in New York?

Chomont: The first time I was here from June of 1966 until August of 1969. In September I went to Europe.

MacDonald: Did you manage the Cinémathèque all the time?

Chomont: No, no. I managed it from about July of 1966 until about March of 1967. I wasn't happy acting as manager of the Cinémathèque; people were always relating to me as the manager and not as a filmmaker. Personal relations had gone very badly. Everything seemed sort of hopeless. I tried to make some films, and they were very depressive, very masochistic, I suppose. I found them too embarrassing and never finished them—they got thrown away. Now I'd like to go back, because it was very revealing material that I just happened to have access to due to the state of mind I was in. Then I got food poisoning: that seemed to snap me out of it. I realized I did want to live, and I began the longest film I'd done up to that time, *Morpheus in Hell* [1967], which turned out to be about sixteen minutes.

I was working in an office then, typing. I began to feel like a machine, and to have these very mechanical rhythm periods in my sleep that were like dreams, and then eventually even when I was awake I would sometimes see landscapes and faces in front of me when I closed my eyes. We would be talked into working until two or three in the morning one night a week, when the deadline came due. Once, I came home and I just stood in front of the mirror and talked to myself, and I said things I didn't even know. The odd thing was that I experienced both talking and listening to the face in the mirror. Some-times I would look at the face and see the lips moving and hear the words coming like someone else talking, as though that face were telling me something. That was part of the beginning of *Phases of the Moon,* which was shot in the same mirror, and the whole idea of the split in the personality that's in that film. Then I began to realize two isn't enough; it's really millions, because all the faces are us: we have to split into more than two—we have to keep splitting until we know all of them. We don't have to, but I felt that way then. I was not religious; I did not really believe in God; I did not really understand metaphysical statements; I had trouble with a lot of philosophical writing. It was a real experience: after splitting in two, it was clear that identity was not as fixed as I had been taught. As I see it today, *Morpheus* is a sort of ego death and rebirth.

I was terrified of going crazy, of being crazy, at the time. I mean all these things half fascinated me and half terrified me because I felt very alone and isolated. When I was making *Morpheus,* I used Tarot cards. I'd had a dream about them, where I was in a hotel that seemed to be in Europe (I had never been in Europe at that time) and there was a cigarette stand where I bought these old cards—somehow I understood they were Tarot cards—and the design on the back of the cards included the word "clairvoyant." I suddenly realized it simply means "seeing clearly." Then I had this urge to get the cards and that became one of the bases of *Morpheus.* Since high school I had approached dreams from a Freudian point of view. I had been determined to see them in a rationalistic, analytical way. I began to let myself just experience the seemingly irrational connections that took place during sleep and in other experiences.

I had a dream where I was in Herald Square (I didn't realize it was Herald Square then), and as I was coming across 34th Street, the sort of steam that comes out of manhole covers seemed to be filling the streets, and I was being engulfed in it. At first I enjoyed it as an unusual experience; then I began to feel that somehow this smoke was going to put me to sleep or suffocate me, and that, in fact, the whole city was either dead or asleep from the smoke, and maybe it was some sort of invasion. I began to run, when I realized it was drifting with the speed of the wind, and I couldn't outrun it, and I was becoming engulfed. I had this panic (by that time I was panicky enough that I was waking up) that maybe I would die in this dream somehow, and I wanted to wake up, but when I managed to open my eyes, I wasn't in my bed—I was up over the bed looking down. It was almost as though the room were sideways, as though the up and down had changed, and I felt like I wasn't in my body any more. It seemed like I could almost see that the sheets went down and there was my body, and I was somehow looking down, and I was terrified. I thought maybe I had died or had somehow become disconnected, and yet that whole idea of myself apart from my body was alien to my concept of reality at that time, and I cried "Help," and in making the effort a melding took place, and I was back on the bed. I'd never heard of out-of-body experiences. I just thought it seemed insane, and I was afraid of being taken over by irrational forces. That was in the time of *Phases of the Moon*. I had shot it but hadn't edited it.

MacDonald: Phases of the Moon puzzled me when I was looking at it. What you're saying makes it clearer. There's a person who seems to be waiting for somebody, or he's closing himself off from somebody. I couldn't tell which.

Chomont: Neither could I! That's exactly right.

MacDonald: I thought he was either waiting for a lover or getting ready to commit suicide.

Chomont: I didn't even think that much was in the film, but that's exactly the state I was in. On the one hand, I had an urge toward self-destruction, and on the other I wanted to get in touch with people. I'd lived for almost a year near Central Park West and never realized it was a gay cruising area, and then one night I was walking and I suddenly realized that men and boys were looking at me, and I remember my mouth just dropped open. I kept walking past my street. I was aroused! Then this one guy came up to me; my face must have looked petrified. I immediately felt he was a hustler. He was living with his mother. I was afraid to bring him to my room, but I finally did. Then he used to come over sometimes, and he began bringing other people. It turned out he took cough medicine (for codeine) as well as seconal; sometimes it was like he was dead. That got into *Oblivion* later. I knew him for over a year on and off; he would disappear and come back.

I had the typical New York door with the chain and all the locks and the peephole, and at night I would hear someone in front of my door. It was like a little broom noise and I began to have this paranoid fear that someone was sweeping some poisonous powder under my door. I would jump up and try to see what it was, and one night I saw this older man in an undershirt and old-fashioned undershorts with flowers. Apparently he had been sweeping his rug in front of my door—I guess he didn't want the dust by his—but all these things made me very paranoid. The superintendent was very nosey, too. I had to smuggle people in, which enforced the isolation. All that got into *Phases of the Moon*.

The other thing it's about is the mechanical actions we do unconsciously. I had become very aware of them because of the typing I was doing. I had begun to feel like an extension of the machine at the office, rather than a person. Then I became aware of the little things that I did mechanically, on a robot level, in my room; my fear—and my longing, at the same time—produced mechanical patterns of looking out the peephole. The whole film had to do in part with irrational things: mechanical movements in a way are not rational. They may have been in the beginning, but then they take over and are simply performed—out of context as easily as in context.

I painted when I was in high school. I never found myself in painting (though I got my bachelor's degree in it), and I had to go through the same process with film. Many filmmakers make their first film, and already it's distinctive. I admire that, but it wasn't me. I staggered around for a long time. I think it was the last half of *Morpheus* where I felt this is beginning to be me, and with *Phases of the Moon* I thought, yes, this is mine.

MacDonald: The man looking through the peephole in *Phases of the Moon* suggests, at least to me, your looking through the camera.

Chomont: That early part where he looks through the door and sees himself in the room was a metaphor for me filming him through the camera—the peephole. Then he's looking out the window, and he's like the spectator looking into the frame. You don't see out; you always see him again and the room, like a reflection, which I felt was reflective of me. Then there's the point where it's like he's kissing himself. His two faces blend, and he's looking through the keyhole both ways; it's like the viewer and the viewed come together.

I couldn't have dealt with all of that in words at the time; if I could, the force of the film would have been gone. It's that buildup of having something you can't quite say with words, or you don't understand in terms of words, which makes filmmaking necessary. That's the whole problem with writing about films, too. You cannot duplicate all aspects of the visual expression.

From the little I've read of semiotics, it seems an attempt to codify visual expressions into symbols comparable to language. I'm always afraid it's not really encompassing the ambiguity of imagery. It seems to me we already have language; we already have a number of codified, highly symbolized forms of expression. Art has always been to me an ambiguous and polymorphous form of expression that resonates and coruscates and transforms. Even when you try to codify, there are always other aspects, other levels, that come into any complex form of expression. I think some structural-minimal films play with that. You narrow down, and then here comes another level: just by narrowing down you pinpoint it more. I'm always afraid words will falsify the image, but, yes, I can say now in words what we said about *Phases of the Moon,* that the window and the peephole are metaphors. To some extent my films were then, and probably still are, therapeutic ways of seeing and dealing with things I couldn't come to grips with in other ways.

MacDonald: Why the subtitle *The Parapsychology of Everyday Life?*

Chomont: It's a pun on Freud. In high school I read *The Psychopathology of Everyday Life,* which is the rationalist approach. He's calling all these irrational, illogical, basically emotional and primal connections that occur as a subtext to the waking, conscious, well-behaved, civilized world—he's calling them "psychopathology." He's making them pathological. In that period I was experiencing these from the other side, the nonrational side. "Parapsychology" isn't negative; really it's not a subtext—it may be the main text, and the "civilized" may be the captioned version of our lives.

MacDonald: Did your interest in superimposition and in using positive and negative come out of your interest in multiple selves?

Chomont: Partly. The way it's used there it did, but the idea originally came to me when I was living in Boston and did *Night Blossoms.* When I was painting, I had the decision of how much of the surface to fill in—you can leave part of it blank. In film it seemed like you really are filling everything in; it's hard not to. I thought the way to avoid that would be to use positive and negative, turn the shadows into flat blank screen and make it so that the colors would be like drawing. I wanted to do that in *Night Blossoms,* but the expense of making negative to combine with the positive just seemed too much at the time.

MacDonald: As you say that, I think of *Ophelia.*

Chomont: Oh yes. That's the most extreme of the early films; the screen's practically all white; the colors are very slight and give a daguerreotype look. You see a lot of the grain. It was a very dark image, which I made into a negative and then used the negative to blank out the screen and allow traces of the image to come through. I wanted to move the light to give it a watery look, but I don't think that came off so well.

It was filmed in a bathtub. It came from the Millais painting of Ophelia for which, I had read, he had asked the model to lie in a tub of water heated by candles. Somehow looking at the picture you feel the posedness of the subject in the water, and I wanted to do something stylized like that and use the film emulsion as the water—the figure (Carla Liss) coming in and out of the emulsion. It's like washing the emulsion off the film, then sketching in.

MacDonald: I've never seen anybody else do that.

Chomont: Aspects of it have been done. For example, shortly after I made *Oblivion,* which I thought was the most exciting thing I had done using that method, I saw *T,O,U,C,H,I,N,G* by Paul Sharits. He intercuts frames of pure color and of black-and-white negative and positive. The effect is similar. Solarization and some video effects resemble it, too.

MacDonald: You use the sound of the sprocket holes, which gives a one-second pulse. Is that automatic, or did you do something to get that pulse?

Chomont: It's just the sprockets. The regular pattern of the edge numbers and letters probably causes a pulse. I didn't originally think to make *Ophelia* a sound film, but somehow I thought of *Ophelia* and *The Cat Lady* as one film in two parts. When I decided to show them together, I realized sprockets would be very nice because they give a somewhat mechanical feeling that goes with that textural feeling of the emulsion.

MacDonald: In *The Cat Lady* I presume that you combined a shot you took of somebody you knew and some found footage from a sci-fi film.

Chomont: That's about it, except for one random image taken from the room where I filmed Carla Liss. Originally I filmed more; it was going to be an homage to horror films. I've always had a predilection for horror films, especially the more fantastic and spooky ones. Carla always seemed to me to be a rather glamorous figure. She'd been in a number of films around that time—Andy Meyer's and George Kuchar's. Her work with film and mixed media has been exhibited in New York and London. She was also the director of the London Co-op at one point.

MacDonald: In a number of your films, including *The Cat Lady,* there's a surprise at the very end, where the film seems to break from what's gone before.

Chomont: Jonas [Mekas] once wrote some very complimentary things about my short films, but he said my longer films tend to break down and fall apart. (Reading Jonas's "Movie Journal" column in the *Voice* from 1960 on, by the way, was an enormous source of inspiration and encouragement to me.) In a sense, Jonas was right, but what he noticed was something I've meant to do, starting with *Morpheus.* The whole structure begins to unravel, as if to say the experience doesn't really end, this is just where I'm ending the film.

MacDonald: After *Ophelia* and *The Cat Lady,* and with the exception of *Re:Incarnation* [1973], you don't deal any more with sound.

Chomont: No. I keep thinking to, but it's a whole thing in itself and re-quires so much equipment—to do sync sound anyway. I'm not opposed to sound, though there are films (like *Oblivion*) that I've never, ever thought should have sound.

MacDonald: Oblivion and *Phases of the Moon* are in the tradition of trance film and psychodrama. *Oblivion* often reminds me of Kenneth Anger's *Fireworks.* How much of that tradition had you seen when you made those films?

Chomont: Oblivion was shown with *Fireworks* recently. The first experi-mental films I saw were mostly trance films or reactions to trance films, but by *Oblivion* I wasn't really directly concerned with that. *Oblivion* was a diary to a large extent—a diary and a portrait and a confession. The first films, like *Anthony* [1966] and *Night Blossoms,* are rather like trance films; that's part of the reason I didn't think of them as my own.

MacDonald: Did you shoot *Oblivion* over a long period of time?

Chomont: No. I think I shot it on two separate evenings, but it had ele-ments of many of our visits: we would sit and talk; he would smoke; at some point one or both of us would feel aroused—usually he would start to take off his shoes when he wanted to have sex; that's in the film where his hand un-tying his shoe is blended with a pan of his body on the bed.

MacDonald: One of the things I noticed about *Oblivion* and several other films is a tendency to use synecdoche; a detail of something that's happening takes on multiple dimensions. It's interesting because what tends to be diaristic for you, with that condensation, has a different effect on the viewer.

Chomont: Yes. I felt that this material was highly personal, and I was con-scious from the beginning that there had to be some formal side to it. The experiences themselves had broader meanings of identity and role-playing and the face as a mask, things like that. I wanted to give the whole film the feeling of being between sleeping and dreaming, and waking. All the imagery had personal meanings, but of course I didn't use everything I filmed, and I had

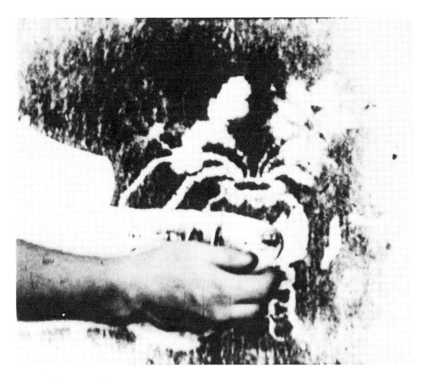

From Chomont's Oblivion *(1969).* © *1969 Tom Chomont.*

symbolic meanings in mind. The apple was symbolic: besides having the Biblical reference that J. J. pointed out (Murphy, 1979), it had an erotic look—the redness, the dimple, the stem, all of that.

MacDonald: The fountain of lights seems suggestive, too.

Chomont: That's from a store on Fifth Avenue. At Christmas they always used to have these canopies made of strings of lights and a light fountain over the main doorway. I filmed that and thought of it as the nervous system and the circulatory system.

MacDonald: It suggested ejaculation to me.

Chomont: I masturbated a lot in that period, and I became very aware of the connection between ejaculation rhythm and pulse. I thought of it as all those things; I didn't know what it would mean to someone else. I was trying to mix carnal and metaphysical elements, though it wasn't clearly formulated in my mind.

There's always a tension for me between the fact of seeing someone from the outside—as a body, an object—and seeing the identity dissolution that usually takes place during sleep. If it happens when we're awake, it's disturbing; we want to avoid it. I was trying to deal with that. Sex fantasies tend to objectify other people's bodies and sometimes their personalities, too, and I suppose it's evil in a sense because it can lead to the manipulation of other people. That was a tendency in that relationship because he took so much of those drugs. At that time, I think he had trouble accepting his sexuality. He said it was easier to accept performing sexual acts for money, but the fact of the matter was he would sometimes take the money he earned and go buy another prostitute to have sex with him as he wanted it. Twice he asked me to pay him to have sex and I thought, "This is a very bad precedent and besides I can't afford it." Well, I resisted it, but I was aware that it appealed to me to just say, "OK, what will you do for this much?" After many years of trying to follow what I was taught—not to do certain things sexually—I had a lot of very intense fantasies. During this time I began to act out my fantasies, and, in doing so, the experience became more important than the fantasy.

When something sexual seems impossible or unthinkable, fantasies are horribly exciting, horribly intense; yet I think that's the beginning of seeing other people as part of your own concept of reality, and that makes it hard to break through to other people as they really are. I guess I can think of it like a time warp, where other people are us but in another place and time; in a sense *Oblivion* is a view from the evil side, the side of desiring to manipulate another person's body and person. (Of course, that's involved in any portrait or likeness.) I thought of it at the time as simply accepting the fact of being turned on by other guys, confessing that, and trying to show something of it. It brings up the whole question of sexual identity, of role-playing. At times his body is like an object, as the apple is an object containing life, so this whole border between objects and definitions of things comes in too.

MacDonald: A technical question: near the beginning the image breaks down into three levels . . .

Chomont: It's just an A and a B roll; the A roll has a red filter; the B roll has a green filter, and where they overlap you get yellow. The reason I did that was for the 3-D effect. Actually I just filmed everything twice from a slightly different angle; if you wear red-and-green glasses, momentary stereoscopic effects slide in and out.

Something I was thinking about at the time of *Oblivion* is the relationship of the right and left hemispheres of the brain to the right and left eyes. I had forgotten that both right and left eyes connect to both hemispheres; there's a crossover point and somehow the information exchanges, but seeing stereoscopically does seem to have something to do with the two hemispheres. I understand they say in psychology—in meditation people told me this many times—that the right tends to be the verbal side of the brain and the left tends to be the instinctual, intuitive, irrational side.

MacDonald: You were talking earlier, in connection with *Oblivion,* about splitting into various selves. Is the 3-D process used there a metaphor for the idea that if you separate into separate selves and then come back together, you get more perspective, more dimension than if you'd stayed the way you were?

Chomont: That was how I originally conceived it. As the film came out, it seemed less important than that. I still would like to use 3-D that way. Also, I'd like to get the viewer's eyes to perform certain movements in the course of seeing the film that would have a soothing and unifying effect, that would be like visual exercises in meditation.

Visual meditation exercises are based on locating a central point in your visual field. I think it's a point that infants must look at a lot, even before birth. In fact, the first time you see it consciously—from all I've read and from my own experience—tends to call up pre-birth memories. It's there all the time but we just don't look at it. If you start looking at it again, like with your eyes closed, or even with them open, it can start to radiate light, because you're concentrating so much energy that the visual field just starts to light up, and you can pull energy from that. I first saw it as the two eyes on someone's face coming together. I associated that with the two hemispheres and the two sides of the face, and I thought, this is like unification. I associated the center point with a flame; eventually I saw this point all on its own, eyes open, eyes closed. A lot of people who are brought back from death describe having seen an intense light. That's what it was like the first time I saw it—a star that got more and more intense and it was like I could go into it and leave everything, but in part of my mind that was like death and I was afraid of it. On the other hand, I felt, well, it's coming anyway . . . but I couldn't accept death, and this seemed like a failing. It seemed like acceptance was the reality, and the rest is striving. In meditation they describe people who do accept that state and "die" and their striving is over; the rest of their life is simply to help other people complete the cycle. I couldn't do it, but I know it's there.

Of course, we're more than two brains; we're much more, much, much more. It's like the yin and yang. Many people react to the yin and yang because they think it's a reinforcement of polarized masculine and feminine characteristics (which some of the literature is), but what it really is, is the idea that everything can be considered as having two aspects, and from that you can keep dividing infinitely until you get down to the molecules, the atoms, below the atoms to the energy. We're already divided into at least two and we can keep working from there down to our cells if we want to. Somehow film seems to have all that in it, at least metaphorically; you can become conscious down to the movement of the grain. A lot of what was going on in independent films and in reviewing when I began making films seemed to be involved with that kind of awareness.

MacDonald: I've assumed that the title of *A Persian Rug* refers to an analogy between the structure of the film and of Persian rugs.

Chomont: It was an intuitive title, and it really referred to my having just read Indries Shah's *The Sufis*. In the house where I was staying when I did the filming, and where part of the filming was done, there was some kind of oriental carpet on the floor. I didn't know if it was a Turkish rug or a Persian rug, but as a reference to Persian Sufism I called it *A Persian Rug*. The traditional

Persian rug is a religious form that is an homage to Allah. There are very traditional designs, but the rug maker always weaves an imperfection, an asymmetrical or irregular place, to say that only Allah is perfect. I thought of those things with the film, but the title was intuitive.

MacDonald: One of the things that led me to think of the connection is that the first time you actually see a rug, it fills the frame, and then simultaneously you see a foot protruding onto the rug and into the frame. The rug and the rectangle of the image function the same way. I even thought of film as a magic carpet.

Chomont: That was intended. At one point, the film is so overexposed that the only image you read is the rug and the feet; you don't really see the floor.

At this point I'd like to say that I never faded in the lab in any film; I do all fades and all changes of exposure myself. None of my films are timed. I want the lab to do what's called a one light print, preferably along the lines of a workprint, because I want everything the way I photograph it. I avoid laboratory-done things. If I can work on the printer, I'll play tricks with it, but I want to do it myself.

MacDonald: When you made *Oblivion* and *A Persian Rug,* did you construct the films as you were shooting, or did you do random diary recording and then later decide to use that?

Chomont: In those films it's a combination. Sometimes I head out to get certain images. Sometimes I make images without knowing how they will fit in. Sometimes in editing I change my idea. In the beginning it was often a big struggle for me to get over my preconceptions of how I was going to do the film and accept what I really felt was the best way to do it—especially after film school, where you're supposed to plan everything.

I started using splicing tapes because I could change what I had planned and done without losing frames. Also, I like the whole feel of splicing tape. You put it on and smooth it and trim it; it has a very handcrafted feeling to me. In film school splicing tape was considered unprofessional.

MacDonald: A question relating to the idea of handcrafting films: do you work wherever you are?

Chomont: Yes. When I was traveling I had an old rewind mounted on a board. I did *Portret* [1971], *Love Objects, Research* [1972], all those films, on it. It was made in Czechoslovakia and had collapsible rewinds. I carried that in my bag and would just pull it out. If I couldn't edit in one place I'd carry it to the next. I'd always carry some little 100-foot reels so I could work in short segments. *A Persian Rug* was filmed in Orselina and in Locarno. Then I went to Zurich and started editing it there, moving from one pension to another. It's nice to go into a real workshop and sit down, but, of course, they're only open so many hours. I'd rather be here and get out the clothes hangers, put up the film, and take down the pieces I want.

MacDonald: In *A Persian Rug,* and in other films you use a limited number of images, or kinds of image, and then reiterate them in different contexts. Is there a background for that way of constructing a film?

Chomont: Probably the biggest single influence on my editing is Gregory Markopoulos. He doesn't do variations so much as progressions, at least in the films of his I'm familiar with. I did a transcript of his film *Twice a Man,* where I actually made note of each shot: the number of frames, the content of the shot, and when it was repeated. It took some months to do and made a very big impression on me. I saw the film as precisely musical, precisely rhythmical, though he told me he didn't count frames, but did it by feeling.

MacDonald: Life Style [1978] seems to have come out of a time when you were involved in a lifestyle that involved a lot of drugs and hallucination.

Chomont: It was about a couple I lived with in Brugge (Ioanna Salajan and Richard Lamm). They were into macrobiotics and yoga, but I talked to them a lot about hallucinatory experiences. I had been afraid of hallucinations from LSD and mescaline, more from LSD.

The people in *Life Style* had never taken LSD or mescaline, but they described equally fantastic experiences they had had just through meditation, and I had many of them. The difference was that you could stop it. Ioanna (especially) and I, and Richard and I would look at each other's faces, and I would see other faces—sometimes animal faces, sometimes fantasy faces. They had explained to me that the whole body tends to have a right/left dichotomy. (Palmists say the left and right hands express the innate and the actual character of the person and the differences between them.) During that time a psychology magazine published photos where they duplicated one side of a face to be both sides, to show that each side actually expressed a different person. That was all very interesting to me because I had done that in *Phases of the Moon* two years earlier, where the man looks in the mirror and his face is the same face overlapped. I'd been doing a lot of things with the mirror-image type of thing. I filmed *Life Style* during that period [early 1970], and there is a lot of hallucination, but it's supposed to be about meditation.

MacDonald: Is that true of *Portret,* too?

Chomont: Somewhat. I associated it with Mallarmé's interest in developing certain poems so that they would be completely rounded. I wasn't interested in symmetry but in a rounded form that could be approached from either end. I suppose I would trace that back to reading about Alain Resnais and Alain Robbe-Grillet wanting to have the reels of *Last Year at Marienbad* projected in different sequences. They felt there was no beginning or end to that film. That appealed to me. Also it was influenced by Renaissance and Mannerist painting. For instance, I realized that angels at the top of a painting were—if you turned the painting upside down—quite clearly painted from models lying on sofas or rugs. After I'd finished *Phases of the Moon,* I saw *2001* and what intrigued me in that film (which, on the whole, didn't impress me much) was that, due to the lack of gravity, you had compositions where there was no strict up or down. I thought of *Phases* and *Portret* that way.

MacDonald: Many of your films are very personal and very intimate, and yet up to *Love Objects* you generally present eroticism in a deflected way. The viewer understands the eroticism by reading metaphors or by uncovering an-

Joe Glin in The Heavens *(1977). © 1977 Tom Chomont.*

other level of the film. What happened that you decided to make this very direct, sexy film?

Chomont: When I was at the Museum of Modern Art in 1975, someone in the audience was saying, as I understood him, that compared to *Love Objects, Oblivion* seemed to be inhibited about sexuality and nudity. That may have been influenced by having some films seized by a laboratory simply because of nudity. To get them back I had to cut out whatever the lab found offensive, which included any trace of pubic hair. I was very upset by the experience, but I was also very determined to get around that whole thing, and it made me more obsessed with the question of nudity. What would have been incidental became more of a key issue. I suppose it led to my wanting to do it once without feeling any restraints.

Eroticism in itself is at the edges of sex. That's a problem that porno films have made clear—showing sex is not necessarily erotic, and sometimes there can be difficulty in making it erotic. I don't think *Oblivion* should have any more sex. I played with that idea in preparing the film, but it didn't seem right. For *Love Objects* I had had the idea to make a film simply about genitals. I wanted to explore their forms and eroticism, to work with them as image. Then while I was living with the people doing yoga, we got into the chakras, and I began to think of this new film as dealing with the first chakra, the one at the base of the spine that is most connected with the earth and decay and fertility, or the second chakra, which is sex. The title "Love Objects" came to me because I thought I would show the genitals simply as plastic forms. When I actually started filming the people, I couldn't confine my interest to the genitals. Then the idea crystallized more into the whole juxtaposition of the metaphysical concept of love and the physical organs. There are continuing references to the alchemical allegory, *Les Noces du roi et reine*. Originally, I wanted the people to pass the camera around during sexual contact, to film me setting up equipment—to break all the barriers and eliminate the voyeuristic aspect of filming sex, but most of the people felt uncomfortable taking the camera, and I ended up doing only one sequence that way.

MacDonald: There's a place where you see a man and a woman together for the first time, and it takes some time before you realize that it isn't two women. The confusion seemed purposeful.

Chomont: Oh yes.

MacDonald: The sequence near the end with the two women and the child, in the context it's in, seems related to incest.

Chomont: Well, I wanted to have a child in the film because I really think all of these feelings go back to childhood and are even clearer in childhood— more felt, but not conceived of. I wanted him to be the child in all of us.

One of my first realizations about my own sexuality came from my recognition that as a child I desired both my mother and my father. This happened when I was visiting a friend of mine in Boston. We took mescaline, and I wasn't ready for it. A guy was giving a very tense rap, and I was getting very upset. My friend and his girlfriend went into the bedroom; he got very sick, and his girlfriend was lying with him on the bed. I knew I wanted to go in and lie with them, just hold onto them and be comforted, but I couldn't. I was having all this guilt, and I remembered wanting to go into my parents' bedroom when I was afraid as a child, wanting to lie between them. I realized that a child is both sexes, he's both the mother and the father—together they're the child's identity. It's only gradually that the child is persuaded to identify more with one or the other.

MacDonald: I think that idea does come across in the film. Of course, it's one thing to say that children are very erotic, which they are, but children in an erotic context is still taboo.

Chomont: Well, I certainly do not mean to encourage sexual relations with children. I've heard gasps when the child's face first fades in, especially because it fades in just after the ejaculation in the previous sequence. I hadn't quite calculated the shock effect, but I was happy about it because I think it's good to realize that eroticism is continuous with those childhood feelings of wanting physical intimacy and the warmth of other people.

MacDonald: Your films seem to be the way they are because of where your life was either personally or financially.

Chomont: There are a lot of factors connected with doing even the plainer, more self-contained films. I used to have the idea that Mallarmé (as I understand it) expresses about a true poem being something very self-contained. I thought that I was sealing the personal things into a container from which they would never leap back to their origins. It's surprising how personal the films look now, and I'm sure that's part of their tension.

MacDonald: When I first saw several of your films together, I found it hard to know where one ended and another began. It was especially hard because the films are so dense.

Chomont: It took me a long time to understand that experience, though I understood the statement. The first time I showed a program of my films, in Munich, someone attacked me for trying to brainwash him. It was so important to me then how people were going to react, but going to Europe and doing eight showings in a month was very good, because I began to see how varied people's reactions can be. I began to take it all the more as part of the whole experience. Either I had to stop making films or I had to deal with the fact that some people—maybe a whole audience—would get very upset. When I started out, I thought, "Well, I'll just do what I want." Then I realized how much the audience mattered. You wonder, "Why am I making these things that are lying around the house if I'm not showing them?" It's odd, too, once the films have gone into the world, they begin to have life of their own that may not have much to do with my original ideas.

J. J. Murphy

From the moment when J. J. Murphy began making films as an M.A. student at the University of Iowa, he seems to have been much less interested in expressing himself through the medium than in setting up filming procedures that would allow him to step aside once the filmmaking process was under way and see what the cinematic apparatus could show him about itself and about the world it recorded. In *Highway Landscape* (1972) and *In Progress* (co-made with Ed Small, 1972) he carefully chose a single positioning of the camera—in *Highway Landscape* a ground-level view across a two-lane highway, in *In Progress* a view from a window of a rural Iowa landscape—and he chose a single tactic for recording imagery—for *Highway Landscape* one long (six and a half minutes) sync sound shot, for *In Progress* a few seconds of imagery recorded every day for nine months. In *Highway Landscape* the result is a dramatic interaction between the simple roadscape and the approaching-disappearing sound of the vehicles that flash through the space delineated by the film frame. *In Progress* is a lovely and fascinating landscape film that reveals not only the myriad changes that take place over a period of months but also the degree to which our sense of the space is created by the amount and quality of light available during the seconds when the camera is recording: sometimes we see into the distance; sometimes we see only the yard in front of the window; sometimes the buildings at the opposite end of the yard seem larger, or in a slightly different place; sometimes we are conscious of the dancing grain of the filmstock, sometimes we're not.

In the other early films—*Ice* (1972) and *Sky Blue Water Light Sign* (1972)— the same urge to allow film to discover itself is carried out in a different way. To make *Ice* Murphy projected Franklin Miller's abstract film *Whose Circum-*

The campsite in Murphy's Sky Blue Water Light Sign *(1972)*.

ference Is Nowhere onto one side of a block of ice and recorded what one could see through the ice from the opposite side, in a single continuous take. The sound track is a tape recorder recording under water. The result is a transformation of Miller's film into an abstract experience of a very different kind. *Sky Blue Water Light Sign* also made a new work by transforming a work that already existed, though in this instance the original work was a film-like light sign for Hamms beer that Murphy had seen in an Iowa City bar. By matching the film frame to the rectangular area on the sign through which a celluloid loop of an idealized North Woods scene continually moved, Murphy's single-shot record of the sign entirely transformed it. Instead of seeing imagery move through a rectangular space, we experience a continuous panning movement to the right, as though the camera, not the sign's imagery, is moving. And because film projection enlarges the imagery far beyond its original size, Murphy's new North Woods scene is not immediately recognizable as what it is: viewers tend to be confused about whether the landscape is real or not. Like Gottheim's early one-shot films and the roll-long shots in Huot's early diaries, *Sky Blue Water Light Sign* is reminiscent of Lumière, but in its transformation of an everyday object into a filmically mysterious one, it is equally reminiscent of Méliès. *Sky Blue Water Light Sign* is simultaneously documentary and fiction. In another sense, its implicit antecedents go much further back, to the panoramas that fascinated European and American audiences during the first half of the nineteenth century.

Murphy's first long film, *Print Generation* (1974, fifty minutes) stands in relation to his early career the way *Zorns Lemma* and *Horizons* stand in relation to Frampton's and Gottheim's careers. For *Print Generation* Murphy wanted to conduct an extensive investigation of the ways in which the process of contact printing (and, by extension, any form of photographic printing) affects the quality and intelligibility of imagery. First, he made a one-minute diary film from sixty one-second bits of material he had recorded during a visit to filmmaker-friend Norman Bloom's cabin in Vermont and at his mother's home in Bayonne, New Jersey. He provided the film lab with careful instructions to generate contact prints beginning with a print of the original diary and proceeding with a contact print of the contact print, a contact print of that contact print, and so on, until the original imagery had completely degenerated. He arranged the fifty resulting print generations so that during the first half of the film we move through twenty-five generations, from the most to the least decomposed prints and, during the second half of the film through the other twenty-five generations toward the most fully decomposed prints.

The finished film is interesting on several levels simultaneously. Most obviously, perhaps, the film demonstrates that, indeed, the degeneration of prints does affect our sense of what we are seeing, in dramatic ways. The first half of the film presents viewers with a series of mysteries to solve, and in some instances we cannot clearly or completely identify what a particular image is until we have reached the final few, least degenerated prints: in other words, two or three print generations are often enough to obscure the nature of the original material. A second level of discovery activated by *Print Generation* relates to Murphy's long-time fascination with ethnographic cinema. Early in the film, as we begin to try to decipher the imagery we are seeing, we tend to make guesses that must be continually revised as further imagistic information becomes available: these guesses are, in essence, projections onto scintillating abstract dot patterns. In other words, watching the film allows us to study not only how the printing process affects filmed information but also the way in which we identify imagery (the nature of our response is, of course, considerably affected by Murphy's soundtrack: a one-minute tape of ocean sounds, recorded and rerecorded in a process analogous to the generation of the visual imagery but arranged in the finished film in the opposite configuration—from original to decomposed sound and back to the original). A third level of discovery results from the partially decomposed imagery being a good deal more exciting to look at than the original diary loop: in fact, the middle portion of the film is quite stunning, and in a way very different from any other film imagery I've seen. *Print Generation* not only offers us an opportunity to inform ourselves, but it discovers deep within the film emulsion itself new forms of visual pleasure.

Murphy's fascination with the process of Polaroid photography was the impetus for his next long film, *Movie Stills* (1977), though, again, the imagery from this new film involved a transformation of a previous film, a home movie made by Chuck Hudina. Murphy studied the home movie until he had discovered sixteen frames that he felt could encapsulate the original footage into a mini-narrative: he made Polaroid shots of these frames and filmed them as they developed, in continuous roll-long takes. The resulting film provides a lovely meditation on a common photographic process, though, as in *Sky Blue Water Light Sign,* the inevitable enlargement of the Polaroids by movie projection puts us back in touch with the quiet mystery of the Polaroid process (and implicitly of the development process of other forms of photography), which—for me, at least—has usually been more interesting than the photographs that are its result.

After *Movie Stills,* Murphy became increasingly interested in narrative. The short, comic *Science Fiction* (1979) involved a procedure reminiscent of the work of Bruce Conner. Murphy re-edited an old, faded science film so that we see only those portions of the original where narrative elements had been used to illustrate scientific principles. The result is a surreal adventure on a flying train. In more recent years Murphy has begun to make more conventional storytelling films. The first three—*The Night Belongs to the Police* (1982), *Terminal Disorder* (1983), and *Frame of Mind* (1985)—are different from Murphy's early work in obvious ways: the films make up a visually distinctive, expressionistic, noir-esque trilogy about the precariousness of individual lives in a world of dangerous, manipulative social and political forces. But as different as they are, Murphy is not breaking from his earlier concern with the filmmaking process as a form of personal and cinematic research. By the late 1970s, Murphy apparently felt less challenged by the idea of making additional structural films than by seeing what he could learn—about film, about himself, and about functioning in the world—from making accessible narrative films about issues that concerned him. Judging from the trilogy, he has been learning a good deal.

Murphy and I talked in June 1980.

Murphy: OK, so what's the question?
MacDonald: The question is how did you get into filmmaking?
Murphy: By accident.
MacDonald: What was the accident?
Murphy: I'm from a working-class background. Art was not part of my upbringing. In high school, I had the idea that the most important thing was to experience life directly. I thought books were a vicarious experience and that movies were a lazy person's vicarious experience, so therefore I was opposed to both books and movies.

I really became interested in film as an undergraduate at the University of Scranton. (By then, I had changed a great deal and was interested in learning about everything.) I remember going to see Polanski's *Knife in the Water* and being fascinated by the fact that there was virtually no action—the film worked on a psychological level. It seemed totally different from Hollywood. I hadn't the slightest idea what I thought about it, but it definitely made me want to see more European films.

There was an English teacher at Scranton, named Quinn, who started a film course during my second year. He showed Eisenstein, Pudovkin, classic films. I continually asked him for books. I also began going to movies all the time, sometimes four or five times a day. In my last two years, I ran the film seminar, which involved programming the films each semester and running the discussion group afterwards. When Sheldon Renan's book on experimental film came out, Quinn gave me a copy, and also Gregory Battcock's book. I saw Warhol films and some other experimental films in New York City, and I began reading Jonas Mekas's columns in *The Village Voice*, which were very influential. I didn't pretend to know what cinema was, so I just accepted experimental film as a different kind of film. I was terribly impressed by Warhol.

MacDonald: Which Warhol films did you see?

Murphy: Mario Banana, which is three or four minutes of Mario Montez very suggestively eating a banana, and *My Hustler.* They were at the Hudson Theater. The usher kept shining a flashlight to make sure people weren't jerking off—the audience was all men. I also saw *Chelsea Girls, Lonesome Cowboys,* and *Four Stars.* The literalness of Warhol's films seemed important.

I did see other films, such as Isadore Isou's *Venom and Eternity,* which is extraordinary. I remember seeing films by the Kuchar brothers, Marie Menken, Kenneth Anger, Richard Preston, and Peter Emanuel Goldman's *Echoes of Silence* and Ron Rice's *Senseless.* I would go to screenings at the Wurlitzer building, the Gate Mini Theater, the Cinémathèque—wherever experimental films turned up. I also went to a couple of Ken Kelman's history of cinema lectures, and I was very enthusiastic about them.

I wanted to bring experimental film to Scranton, so I went around the college with a can and somehow managed to collect $200. After one of Kelman's lectures in New York, I approached him and asked him whether he would come to Scranton. I explained that Scranton was a very straight place and why I was bringing in a lecturer—he'd written articles and was very distinguished in my mind. He said, "Why don't you get in touch with Ken Jacobs—he'd be very good." I said: "No, no. I would like you." Well, we went out for coffee. Actually [P. Adams] Sitney had recorded the lecture, and so we all headed out for coffee, and we ran into Taka Iimura on the street. I must have known something by then because I knew he was a Japanese filmmaker—maybe I had read about him. I used to be so hungry for information that I'd go to screenings and try to listen in on people's conversations. There just wasn't very much information except for Mekas's columns. A couple of people at Scranton had seen some experimental films, and we used to talk about the ones we saw, but nobody really knew anything.

Anyway, I called Kelman later and he decided on a program. It was—I hope I can remember this—*Prelude: Dog Star Man, Scorpio Rising, Mass for the Dakota Sioux,* and I'm sure there was at least one other. I was sure *Scorpio Rising* was going to cause problems, but it turned out fine. Kelman was very unassuming; he made it seem like the most natural thing in the world to be showing that film. These football players came in and sang all the songs in *Scorpio,* and the hipper people started screaming, "Shut the fuck up!" I was embarrassed about bringing Kelman into this situation, but at least the screening was well attended. And it was a wonderful lecture, really fantastic: he talked very slowly and there were long pauses where he would stop and drink his chocolate milk for maybe a minute in the middle of some very important idea. He would lean back and seem to pull the thoughts out of his head and set them floating in the room. He had to catch a very late train afterwards, but it didn't seem to bother him. He had never mentioned money, so I just gave him all the money I had collected. I remember he didn't even look at it—just put it in his coat. It struck me as a beautiful gesture.

MacDonald: How did you come to go to the University of Iowa?

Murphy: Wait, there's another thing that's probably important. When I was twenty years old, my brother bought me a Super-8 camera for Christmas; he'd come home on leave from the army with a lot of money. I didn't have a projector, though, so I could never look at anything I shot. I just went out and shot trees and reflections in puddles, the typical things people do when they first get a camera. It never dawned on me to tell a story. But I knew a guy who had access to a projector, and I told him that I could show him my films sometime, so he got it all set up. When I showed him the films, his reaction was extremely negative. I remember being crushed, and yet I was absolutely convinced about what I was doing and continued to go out and shoot occasional rolls. I can't say I learned a lot technically, but the camera was certainly important—not in any decision to be a filmmaker, but as a first experience.

I'm leaving a lot of things out. I was also writing plays and poetry and was very involved in working with emotionally disturbed kids. That had an enormous effect on me. I really thought it was what I wanted to do. Most of the people I saw doing the work were totally unqualified and shouldn't have had anything to do with children. What happened was that what I had been assuming would be my avocation suddenly became more important, and I thought about going to graduate school in film. Someone showed me an article about film schools and it said that the University of Iowa was a good place. So I went to Iowa, but not for a couple of years.

MacDonald: What did you do?

Murphy: Taught high school in New Jersey. Mostly English. I did teach a little film.

MacDonald: Highway Landscape is the earliest film you distribute. Was it made in Iowa?

Murphy: Yeah.

MacDonald: Can you talk about what led up to it? With the exception of some of Warhol's, all the films you've mentioned seeing are a long way from a single-shot film made with a camera looking across a highway.

Murphy: The first film I ever did was about a demonstration. I shot the footage with my Super-8, and I edited it and put a soundtrack to it at Iowa. It was sort of a documentary, but it ended up being a humorous film because the draft card turn-in was so anemic that the narration is all about what the film doesn't show. The other films before *Highway Landscape* were really experiments in editing, and I always saw them as preliminary. I tried to edit footage together to learn about editing, and I always ended up feeling very unhappy, feeling that if I was going to make films, I was going to have to change my own consciousness.

MacDonald: Highway Landscape, then, was an attempt to start from scratch?

Murphy: I don't know if it was as conscious as that. I did have the feeling that I was making my first film. It was in 16mm, and I actually had a $100 budget. I knew I wanted to make a film, but I didn't set out to make a one-shot film.

MacDonald: What happens on the highway, including the guy who yells out the window at you, wasn't choreographed in any way, right?

Murphy: Right. After *Highway Landscape* I decided I didn't want to make films in courses anymore, even though Franklin Miller (who was the instructor for the film class at Iowa and who I have very fond feelings for) was really wonderful. He was perfect for me: he left me alone, and he always took me seriously.

MacDonald: It's an unusual and distinctive first film. You create tension between the image and the sound. The soundtrack will indicate that a vehicle is about to pass through the image, but since the sound is monaural, one can't tell which direction the vehicle will come from so one searches the image as the sound gets louder, wondering when the car or truck will come through and from which way. It's a technique James Benning has used a lot since then, particularly in *One Way Boogie Woogie.* Was that tension something that you wanted to explore?

Murphy: I was interested in the relationship between sound and image, and that's in the film. I do some thinking about my films before I make them, but there's also an intuitive element. I've heard George Landow say that his films represent his unconscious, that he hasn't the slightest idea what he's doing when he's making a film—except afterwards, when he's simply another viewer.

MacDonald: Do you feel that way? You always have very strong feelings about what the works are or aren't.

Murphy: I mentioned Landow because I think there is an element of truth in what he said. My films aren't totally worked out before they're shot—that happens in the process of making them.

MacDonald: I guess the question is, what process led to the unusual action of setting up a camera in a bizarre position and using one very long take? It's an action that doesn't exactly promise anything acceptable.

Murphy: You mean it doesn't sound like an interesting film?

MacDonald: I mean I can understand why someone might make a fast-moving narrative about cowboys. . . .

Murphy: I've never been able to understand anything at all about cowboys.

MacDonald: There's a paying audience that's interested in Westerns.

Murphy: I *never* thought anybody would be interested in my films. I certainly never thought, "What is an audience going to think about this film?" I always thought *Highway Landscape* was a good film, but I wasn't sure that other people were going to recognize it as such.

MacDonald: What do you mean by a "good film"?

Murphy: I found what I saw on the screen interesting. I don't know if I mean anything more. It's hard—this is 1980, that was 1971. In 1971 there was a certain outrageousness in *Highway Landscape*. In *Visionary Film* Sitney talks about Warhol influencing structural film. I think he's absolutely right, but at the same time what Warhol was doing was very different from what I was doing. *Highway Landscape* is a very carefully composed film that's trying to work almost solely through composition and sound. There was certainly a sense of being outrageous, and a lot of people—the other people in the class—thought that it was ridiculous. The film affronted them on many levels: perhaps they'd spent $500 making complicated narrative films, and mine was so simple that they felt it made fun of them. I had the idea and just wanted to make the film; I never thought of the audience. You could say the same thing about *Sky Blue Water Light Sign*. The word that keeps coming to the tip of my tongue is "dadaist," but I don't want to confuse things: they're not dadaist at all, but . . .

MacDonald: The urge is similar?

Murphy: Yes, but there's also something very aesthetic about the film—I had definite formal concerns. I wasn't about to make a sloppy film. I spent hours composing *Highway Landscape*.

MacDonald: In terms of things like how far the camera was from the road?

Murphy: Of course. But part of it was that I had never shot a film before, and I just couldn't get it right. I had a lot of anxiety about shooting that film. It's funny because now I'm interested in questions of film language, and montage is very much involved. The films I write about—such as Chris Mac-laine's work, Ron Rice's *Senseless,* and David Brooks's *Nightspring Daystar* and *The Wind Is Driving Him Towards the Open Sea*—are montage films. But in the sixties, there was a limit to how much montage you could take. I became interested in film in the late sixties and began making films in the seventies. "Structural film" didn't mean anything to me. I knew the cosmic films from the West Coast and the heavy montage films. My reaction was to slow things down so that I could really see—I'd had enough of being blitzed. People who are beginning to make films today will react very strongly against my films, and they should.

MacDonald: When I first looked at *Highway Landscape,* my training as a literature teacher led me to see thematic patterns: the camera pointing across the highway toward the natural backdrop, with the dead animal in the foreground, seemed to suggest a conflict between technological change and natural cycles. That sort of reading used to bother you a good deal; I presume it still does. Do you think it obscures the formal level of the work, or that it's just completely irrelevant?

Murphy: When I visited Larry Jordan's class at the San Francisco Art Institute [April 1980], he was interested in the film on the level of the death of the animal. Out of habit, my reaction was to sidestep that reading, because it does bypass the formal elements, which are extremely important to me. The formal elements *are* the way that film works; it doesn't work through statement.

MacDonald: But you could argue that if it works by composition, what ends up *in* the composition implies certain meanings. That approach need not negate a concern for the formal elements, but . . .

Murphy: If the film was about ecology, it would be in every library in the country. It's not. I'm not denying that there's a dead animal, but if you reduce the film to saying it's a tragedy that animals are killed on American highways by cars that go too fast . . . that sort of response is really frustrating. It's not that it's not true; it's just that the issue is more complicated. I used to drive cars, and I will in the future.

MacDonald: Are you worried that the potential meaning of the imagery will get reduced to a preconditioned pattern of response?

Murphy: Absolutely. That's why I insist on the things it's doing *as a film.*

MacDonald: In other words, the formal decisions are ways of catalyzing new kinds of meanings?

Murphy: Of course! The other approach simply fits the film into an old habit of seeing. Thematic interpretation comes from literature: it's been carried over to conventional narrative films, but it shouldn't be grafted onto experimental films, which are often a conscious reaction against such conventions.

MacDonald: A lot of people reject formal film on the grounds that it's film about film, a "masturbatory exercise." You're suggesting that formal film does go outside itself: by changing the way a viewer sees a film, you change the way the viewer sees and thinks, in general.

Murphy: Sure, but then what's wrong with masturbation? If people were just masturbating to the point where they couldn't get into anything except themselves, that would be different, but ancient views about masturbation be-

come an automatic way to dismiss reflexive films. Reflexivity has been important—examining the image and seeing how images are put together has been
absolutely vital. I just heard something on the news about a study done at
Purdue University, which concluded that something like 85 percent of the
people who watch TV misunderstand what they see (maybe my figure is
wrong, but it was phenomenally high). I think that's true: most people don't
understand what they're seeing. Society is dominated by images used in the
most manipulative way—by advertising, by politicians. To me it's important
work to learn to see more critically.

MacDonald: Was *Sky Blue Water Light Sign* made quickly?

Murphy: In one morning. I had watched that sign for months, and it turns
out that I wasn't the only one. Bette Gordon told me she wanted to make a film
of it, too.

Sky Blue Water Light Sign is dedicated to Norman Bloom, who was and is
very important to me, both as a person and a filmmaker. We were always
friendly, but it took a while [1971–72] for us to become close. The whole
summer after I finished school [1972] we hung around together. He helped me
get a job working on a Warner Brothers project. Franklin Miller was also an
important influence, and Ed Small, Judy Briggs, and Sherman Paul. One's
life is full of important influences.

MacDonald: Do people who live in places where the light signs are dis-
played have a different response?

Murphy: They tend to laugh faster. A lot of people read it as a simple recording, a pan of a landscape. They don't even have problems with the geometry! Someone once said to me, "You should have pulled back at the end of *Sky
Blue Water Light Sign* and shown people sitting up at the bar. Then it would
have been a great film." To me it would have been an anecdotal film—a joke.

I always thought of it as very funny, although it was a private film. I never
planned to show it and didn't show it for at least a year; I never thought that
anyone would want to see it.

MacDonald: Where did you get the sound? It's not real water, is it?

Murphy: Of course it is.

MacDonald: That's a real creek? It must be the juxtaposition with that image that makes the sound seem canned.

Had you decided to make a landscape film when you and Ed Small made *In
Progress,* or was it that particular landscape that prompted you?

Murphy: It was really Ed's idea to make the film. He was helping me move
into the farmhouse, and he looked out the window and said, "What a terrific
view! I've always wanted to make a landscape film. Would you like to make
one together?"—and told me his idea for the film. I hadn't made any films and
he was older than I and my first filmmaking instructor, so I was flattered.

MacDonald: Did you ever have the urge to manipulate the things outside
the window as the shooting progressed?

Murphy: Absolutely not. As a matter of fact, there's one section where the window screen comes on and then gets taken off, which seems very mysterious. What happened was that the other person who lived in the house took the screen off. Of course I realized it was off, but in order for it to be on, I would have had to tell him to put it back, and I wasn't going to manipulate the film, even though as a result things might look inconsistent and a bit strange.

MacDonald: I've always assumed that the title *In Progress* has a double meaning: on one hand, the landscape is continually changing; on the other, the title suggests that the film itself is in a state of transition.

Murphy: Actually, Ed gave it the name because he kept showing it while it was in progress. Somebody would come over and he'd ask, "Can't we show the film?" I would always be opposed, but I didn't have any more right than he did to make that decision, so we'd show the film. Then in 1972 there was some sort of film competition, and we submitted the film. Ed told me that you had to give a title on the entry form, and he had put down *In Progress.*

I see the film as a dialogue. At least that's what it was for me. Making a film over the course of eight months raised issues that we discussed throughout. How much of the film should be manipulated? Should things be polished? Should it be mathematical? (Ed's camera was available; it had a built-in intervalometer, which would have made it possible to be much more precise about how much footage we took each day.) Should it have sound? How much should it deviate from the original concept? When the shooting was finished, Ed wanted to polish the film. I think he felt it could be stronger if we selected the best material and made a fine cut. I always saw the film as a notebook, very rough and casual and unpretentious. Its rawness seemed to me its strength.

MacDonald: Were you very casual about when you shot, or was it a matter of looking out the window and saying, "Oh, this might be a nice thing to add?"

Murphy: It was always random. There was a basic idea to shoot in the morning, though there generally wasn't enough light in winter, and we had to shoot in the afternoon then.

MacDonald: It was shot in Super-8 and then blown up to 16mm?

Murphy: Yes.

MacDonald: Did you and Ed share the shooting?

Murphy: No, because Ed didn't live there.

MacDonald: So you did it?

Murphy: Yes, though eventually I was forced to move out. There was an agreement that somebody else would keep shooting, which was another idea I liked. I remember in a *Village Voice* review—the film was shown on a program at Film Forum—the reviewer said that although she liked the film the most of those on the program, pointing a camera is not the equivalent of directing a film: therefore, the film was a failure. All of which meant that she didn't understand the aesthetics of the film, which had nothing to do with directing.

MacDonald: Are you ready to talk about *Print Generation?*

Murphy: Perhaps.

MacDonald: Obviously, it was a much larger undertaking than your previous films. You've called it "a process film," specifically in reference to the process of contact printing. What was it about contact printing that interested you enough to make it the subject of your first long film?

Murphy: At some point anybody who makes films is forced to think about that process. I'd always been aware that every print is different, even if you have two prints made at the same time, despite all attempts to make the procedure very rigorous and exact. It was mysterious to me. That was certainly one aspect of it. Also, I had been showing various films in film history classes and the actual print I was looking at always struck me. So many prints of classic films are generations away from the original. I remember one version of Eisenstein's *Potemkin* that had a section so grainy I became more interested in the grain field than the actual film. I had been curious about what would happen if you made prints of prints of prints of prints. A number of people told me afterwards that they had had similar ideas, so the idea isn't unique.

MacDonald: There's Ian Burn's *"Xerox" Book,* which begins with plain white paper and goes through one hundred generations of xeroxing.

Murphy: It's in *Conceptual Art,*[1] right? Ed Small subsequently told me about it.

MacDonald: But that's radically different from what happens in *Print Generation,* which involves an exploration of the material that the imagery is made out of.

Murphy: Burn's piece is more conceptual. Similar things have been done in photography, I've seen other Xerox things, and there are other films that have generations in them.

MacDonald: It's obvious that some of the things that happened as you made successive generations were predictable. Had you fooled enough with generating prints to know pretty much what you would get?

Murphy: I couldn't look at anything while making the film. It was all or nothing.

MacDonald: You had to generate all the prints before you could see what happened?

Murphy: Yes.

MacDonald: How did you know when to stop? You didn't go all the way to the theoretical end: there are still some red dots in the most decomposed imagery, and you could have continued until everything was gone.

Murphy: The sound had pretty much gone at the point I stopped; it degenerated much more quickly than the image. I knew that would happen because I had done a preliminary experiment in Missouri. That was one consideration. Another is that it would have taken another ten generations for the picture

1. Ursula Meyer, *Conceptual Art* (New York: Dutton, 1972), pp. 94–95.

to go to blackness, and I felt that it wouldn't add anything interesting—the imagery had become abstract enough. It was also a question of money. If it had been just money, I'm sure I would have done it anyway, but there were maybe five factors that conspired. And I felt somehow that it was finished at fifty generations. I had thought the film would be a full hour long, yet I don't think it would be any more interesting if it were actually ten minutes longer.

I had made arrangements with an industrial lab. They would do my film only when they did runs, which made it a very slow process because they didn't do a run every day—it depended on business. The head of the lab, a wonderful man named Harvey Wheeler, was very helpful. We had a long conversation about the film before I did it, and we fixed a price. He knew I was teaching at the University of St. Thomas [Houston, TX], so I didn't have trouble establishing credit. But when the film was finished (it took several months), it was shocking to owe $2,000.

MacDonald: There's a paradox in the film: while the original motivation for making it has to do with the decomposition of film imagery when prints are made—which is normally thought of as a problem—in this film the decomposed imagery is more interesting than the original imagery. You find something positive in what is usually seen as negative.

Murphy: That was the difficulty in making the film. I must have talked to the guy in the lab for two hours to get him to understand what I was doing. It wasn't that he was stupid; he was trained to maintain image quality, and I was asking him to do something he had spent twenty years trying to avoid. At the time I thought it was crucial to involve the people in the lab in the film and that it would be an educational experience for me to learn from the lab. They thought I was a very strange person at first—they had all these little jokes about me. I hoped that *Print Generation* would be a film they could get into: it's the ultimate laboratory film.

MacDonald: Did they see the finished film?

Murphy: Yes, they liked it. They all had things that they especially liked. They would huddle around and watch it; when other people went by, they would call them in.

You mentioned that the film is more interesting when it's more abstract. That's my perception of it: the most representational sections are not the points of high interest for me.

MacDonald: For the viewer there's an interest in seeing what the images are. What looks like one thing turns out to be something else twenty generations later. There's a conceptual irony in the decomposed imagery, too: what would normally be viewed as decomposed imagery becomes part of a new film; degenerated prints become originals the minute they're used in a new work. *Science Fiction* raises that issue, too.

Murphy: It's hard to imagine that the actual physical material of film—the color emulsion—has so much energy inscribed in it.

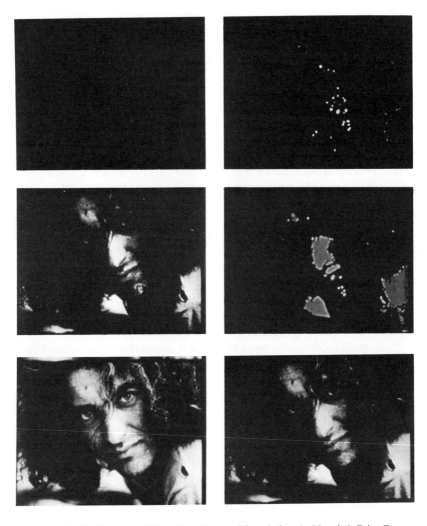

Stages in the development of filmmaker Norman Bloom's face in Murphy's Print Generation *(1974).*

MacDonald: The process that you put the sixty one-second images through is one thing, and obviously that was a major part of the conception of the film, but the nature of those sixty images is another question. Did you choose the imagery to undercut whatever expectations viewers would develop watching the film? As the imagery forms, we make guesses about what it will be, but when we do see it complete, it tends to be much less dramatic than the process might lead us to expect; it's mostly simple, diaristic shots of people and landscapes. Was that part of the thinking that went into the arrangement of the shots?

Murphy: It's hard to answer with the question phrased that way. It interests me to reveal the magic of the ordinary. I wanted very casual and banal imagery so there would be a tension between it and the film's mathematical structure. I felt then, and I still feel, that it's a crucial aesthetic choice to use ordinary imagery—as opposed to carefully composed, dazzling shots—because it's the *process* of the film that's interesting, not the images. I wanted that to be clear. The simplicity of those personal images allows you to realize that what you're seeing isn't the result of the images but the process.

MacDonald: Did you shoot the sixty images with this film in mind?

Murphy: I shot them specifically for the film. I wanted a variety. If blue was prominent in all the shots, the film would have gone out very quickly, though I certainly wasn't sure which images would be the most prominent or which would last the longest. I did suspect that it was related to the layering of color emulsion, which turned out to be true, but there was a lot I didn't know. I just tried to pick different kinds of shots.

MacDonald: They seem arranged with rhythm in mind. There are times when certain kinds of motion are carried through a series of images.

Murphy: When I edited, I thought about how the shots went together.

MacDonald: Obviously, you could have arranged the fifty generations in a variety of ways—most complete to least complete and back again, least to most and back, or in a checkerboard structure. You've mentioned that you had considered other kinds of arrangements—even double projection, so that one version would go from composed to decomposed to composed, and the other image would go the opposite way. What was in you mind when you finally decided on the present arrangement? Do you still consider changing it?

Murphy: No, those were just weird ideas. When I first made the film, I had it on two separate reels. I wanted it so that people could decide how they wanted to show it. But as a result, I was always writing long explanations of this and that. The long directions on how to achieve the possible options became just as directive as imposing my own choice.

MacDonald: When I first thought about the film's structure, it seemed a reflection of the way an experience is often lived: there's conjecture in working up to an experience, the experience itself, then finally the memory of it. Was that something you had in mind?

Murphy: No. In a sense, contact printing determined the structure of the film. To have intercut the A-wind and B-wind imagery in the same left-to-right configuration, I would have had to turn one of them over [contact printing produces a mirror image], and then they wouldn't have had the same focus. The soundtrack worked the same way. To use two tape recorders to record and rerecord was a perfect analogue, because it produced two different

188 A Critical Cinema

tracks. But to answer your question, the way it's arranged now seemed right
me. I always showed it to myself like that, even though I had an idea that oth
people might feel differently. I see the film more in terms of energy build
up to a point and then dispersing.

MacDonald: You don't mean that the energy is highest at the point wh
we see the finished imagery, though.

Murphy: No, I think that each reel has that buildup and a dispersal.

MacDonald: The reason I got into the structure as a model for the psych
ogy of experience is that the second half is so obviously involved with me
ory: there's the irony of having waited so long to find out what a certain ima
would be and forgetting a few generations later what it was! It's startling
realize how fragile our mind's hold on that kind of connection can be.

Was your decision to have the sound work in the reverse direction from
images intuitive?

Murphy: I thought it would compound the degree of difficulty. If the sou
ran the same way as the image, the sound would get lost. That still happe
but not as much.

MacDonald: Any particular reason for ocean sounds?

Murphy: I'm not sure that I would use ocean sounds today. It might
interesting to use a sound that would go through greater transformatio
A few people have mentioned that—Phill Niblock, for one. At the time
seemed like the ocean was the right sound, though it wasn't that I had expe
mented with a lot of different sounds. I think the ocean sound goes with
film poetically; the associations you have with the ocean make sense w
the film.

MacDonald: I was very powerfully affected by *Print Generation* whe
first saw it. *Movie Stills* affected me differently, more like your other film
Several weeks after I saw it, I found that I was starting to think about
issues it raises. I had a nice time thinking about how the film hovers betwe
our conventional filmic categories.

Murphy: I was terribly excited by the film when I first saw it. For me,
been a richer film than *Print Generation*—it's pushed me into other areas a
interests.

MacDonald: What was it about that original Chuck Hudina footage th
interested you?

Murphy: Tess Gallagher showed me the footage a year before I made
film; I knew when I saw it that I wanted to make a film from it. She had ask
Chuck to take footage of her horse Angel Foot, and most of it was shots
Tess and Angel Foot. The part I used was the last two rolls. What fascina
me was that the people in the footage weren't totally in control of what w
happening; it was a home movie, but at some point it turned into a narrati
I started thinking about what narrative is and what narrative does—h
something becomes narrative.

About eight years ago, I saw a film by Morley Markson called *The Tragic Diary of Zero the Fool*. He went to a mental institution to make a film with the institution's dramatic group—they'd written a script. The film starts off as a conventional narrative, although as a viewer you're certainly aware of what's happening. In the course of the film the people start flipping out of the narrative: because the film is very personal to them, they start falling out of their roles and begin relating to each other. Their lives are bound up with their performances. For instance, the woman in the film sees it as the one chance in her life to create real beauty, and when that idea is threatened—as the film begins to fall apart—*she* begins to fall apart. What you have is a narrative film that is transformed, as you're watching, into a psychodrama. That film had an incredible effect on me. It's interesting to wonder at exactly what point it becomes a documentary of people trying to act in a narrative film.

The Hudina footage was interesting just because it starts off one way and then, very minimally, turns into something else. In no way are the two films analogous: the Markson film knocks you over. But both place our nice theoretical categories in crisis. I was interested in using the footage to try to determine whether these distinctions could be analyzed. Could I say, "It's at *this* frame that it happens?"

During the same period, I did a similar project with a photography student of mine. It led to making still photographs of people playing pool and plotting all the changes in where they stood and what happened, image after image. I wanted to see whether you could tell anything about what was happening between people, whether there was a story in that.

MacDonald: Whether you could read their body language and their positions in relation to each other?

Murphy: Right. I've had an interest in anthropology, and I've done a certain amount of reading about proxemics and kinesics—nonverbal communication. I feel that as a filmmaker I can't help but be interested in those areas. It's always been puzzling to me that so many filmmakers aren't.

MacDonald: I've often wondered whether you were trying to get a series of images that would reflect the essence of what you felt was going on between people, the way Ray Birdwhistell does in *Microcultural Incidents in Ten Zoos* (1971).

Murphy: That's a nice film. I've always felt that it's an experimental film—he uses a lot of the techniques.

MacDonald: But what you're doing in *Movie Stills* is different. You're constructing a skeletal narrative, or the potential for a skeletal narrative, rather than trying to deduce the essence of the original situation.

Murphy: Well, I certainly respect Birdwhistell's work and his notational system. Kinesics has discovered lots of things, but I'm not sure *Microcultural Incidents* is scientific. It is a research film, but there's a point where I have to say it's also fictional. He makes up more than the available visual information can support. It's like the Balinese films that Margaret Mead and Gregory Bateson did: they're perhaps the first attempts to use film to record objectively and to gather information so that the films can be studied as evidence, but today Mead's conclusions seem clearly her own fantasy. I remember watching one of those films a couple of years ago and laughing at the discrepancy between what you're seeing and what you're hearing as the explanation.

This relates to what I'm writing about now. David Brooks, in *The Wind Is Driving Him Toward the Open Sea,* uses all the techniques of documentary, yet the film winds up being fiction because the main character is never shown— he just doesn't turn up. You have to rely on what other people say about him, but you have no basis on which to judge that information. Brooks uses cinema verité in a totally fictional way: the film is ultimately a critique of the filmic document as evidence. Perhaps I was drawn to write about that film for the same reason I was drawn to make *Movie Stills.*

MacDonald: Like *Movie Stills, Science Fiction* uses a previous film as its raw material.

Murphy: What I did in *Science Fiction* was to change a science film into a narrative film by taking the narrative elements of the original film, which were really illustrations of concepts, and presenting them in a different context. It's supposed to be funny. The sounds are from a sound-effects record. I did what the surrealists did: I wrenched things out of one context and put them into another. Joseph Cornell does it in *Rose Hobart;* he takes a Hollywood film and reworks it. I don't really think of *Science Fiction* as a surrealist film—I haven't suddenly taken up surrealism—but the visuals have humorous aspects because of that surrealist tactic and because of the sound. When I was working on it, I was very conscious of playing all kinds of little . . . well, I don't want to use *games* because I've recently been accused of gamesmanship. I just had fun with it. For example, I continually change the train sounds. To catch the things I did with the soundtrack, you'd have to listen in a way that most people don't. It's like *Sky Blue Water Light Sign:* since the image looks slightly representational, many viewers assume it *is,* and the sound helps that reading; if the film had been silent, people would find it more difficult to read the image representationally.

Vivienne Dick

One of the more provocative developments of the 1970s was the use by a group of filmmakers in New York of inexpensive Super-8 technology to reject both the big-budget, mass-entertainment assumptions of Hollywood and the artistic pretensions of the formalist cinema that fascinated and frustrated many critics and viewers during the late 1960s and the 1970s. In their determination to produce watchable films by working with their friends and neighbors in their own neighborhoods, these "no wave" filmmakers were reminiscent of some of the earlier 8mm filmmakers whose work had surfaced during the early 1960s—the Kuchar brothers and Bob Cowan, for example. But unlike the Kuchars, whose work parodies the rhetoric of Hollywood cinema without explicitly critiquing the politics of commercial film, Vivienne Dick, Beth B and Scott B, and other no wave filmmakers were interested in using small-gauge filmmaking to make direct, politicized commentaries on and in their immediate surroundings. In some ways, the five distinctive films that Vivienne Dick produced in New York before she returned to her native Ireland—*Guérillère Talks* (1978), *She Had Her Gun All Ready* (1978), *Beauty Becomes the Beast* (1979), *Liberty's Booty* (1980), and *Visibility: Moderate* (1981)—revealed her to be, as J. Hoberman (1982) has suggested, the quintessential no wave filmmaker.

Guérillère Talks is a series of eight portraits of independent women Dick knew in Lower Manhattan, each portrait recorded on a single, unedited roll of Super-8 sound film. The rolls were simply strung together to make the completed work. *She Had Her Gun All Ready* and *Beauty Becomes the Beast* are probably Dick's most widely seen films. *She Had Her Gun All Ready* is a dramatization of interrelational power politics between a bullyish woman

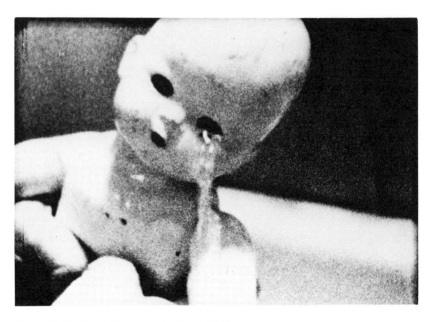

From Dick's Beauty Becomes the Beast *(1979).*

(Lydia Lunch) and her wimpy companion (Pat Place), presented in a visually anarchic, hand-held style. *Beauty Becomes the Beast* is a study of influences on a lower-middle-class American girl growing up in New York City as seen at various moments between childhood and adolescence. Both films have a raunchy, chaotic feel that is reminiscent not only of the 8mm melodramas of the Kuchars but also of film noir and pornography.

Liberty's Booty hovers on the edge between documentary, diary, and narrative dramatization. We meet and listen to a number of women, some of whom are prostitutes living on the Lower East Side as they candidly discuss their experiences and attitudes. Instead of assuming the usual "detached" position of the social documentarian, Dick approaches the women simply as people she knows (she met them through friends) and allows them to have their say, while giving us a sense of the way they live. Though we know from their own comments that at least some of the women are prostitutes, we have no way of knowing whether the other women are or not, and while we know that one location is the house of prostitution, we cannot be sure whether all the apartments we see are used this way. Our uncertainty of the boundaries between the practice of prostitution and "normal life" is precisely the point. The film reveals a practice that is outside the laws of a social system that itself has evolved gender definitions that make the practice almost inevitable. *Liberty's Booty* is full of such ironies. At one point we see one of the prostitutes with a trick, and though we may rightly assume that the scene was dramatized, we are no more sure of the line between fact and fiction here than we are with any other aspect of this issue: after all, the interaction between prostitute and trick is inevitably a performance of one sort or another, as is much of the interaction between men and women in "normal life." Dick's unsteady camera, her abrupt transitions, and the mixture of moods are appropriate for the contradictions and complexities of her topic.

Though all of Dick's films politically contextualize her personal explorations of the life around her, *Visibility: Moderate* is her first film to deal with the political situation in her native Ireland. As is true in *Liberty's Booty*, Dick uses her filmmaking to draw us into the complexities of a real environment rather than to announce any conclusions. *Visibility: Moderate* records the activities of a young woman (Margaret Ann Irinsky) first on the observation floor of the World Trade Center in New York and subsequently on a tour of Ireland. The woman innocently explores locations familiar from romantic stories about the Irish—such as the Blarney Stone, the lakes of Killarney—then she goes into Dublin, where she comes to have a sense of the social and political realities of contemporary Ireland: she meets a young man who explains some of the history of the Irish-British struggle; she sees an anti-British demonstration, visits a punk club (The Resistors are playing).

Visibility: Moderate is shot in a Super-8 style reminiscent of the travel diaries many of us make as tourists. By using this informal type of filmmaking to record more than what Dick calls "Tourist Land . . . this fantasy land where everything has to be beautiful and fabulous," she reveals the degree to which we participate in filmic conventions that can blind us to as much as they reveal. For most of us, Super-8 is essentially a personal home-movie medium, but we usually use it to record only beautiful locations and happy moments that create a fantasized ideal of our personal lives; this "personal" Super-8 filmmaking is little more than a homemade version of the predigested world view promoted by commercial television.

In a sense, Dick's significance during the years she spent in New York may have been due as much to her being a role model as to the films she produced. She made it clear that her commitment to using Super-8 as a means for community consciousness-raising and political development was far more important to her than making "great films" or developing a career either in the art world or in conventional filmmaking. She lived on almost nothing, in a tiny, ramshackle apartment, seemingly oblivious to any concern with living more comfortably. I spoke with her in May 1981, not long before she returned to Ireland.

MacDonald: You didn't start making films until fairly recently. What did you do before then, and how did you get into making films?

Dick: Well, I used to take black-and-white photographs and make the prints myself. After I was in New York about a year, I heard of Millennium and realized that all this equipment was only a few blocks away. I went and joined up, and I liked it because it was just people fooling around with cameras. Everyone would look at everyone else's film; it was really good for a start.

MacDonald: This was when?

Dick: 1976. I went to Ireland and made this fifteen-minute film. It was the first film I ever edited. I wanted to film my mother, because she was dying. It was easier to shoot film with family, although I found that they would clam up whenever the camera was on. I started shooting when they were a little bit drunk, and it was easier. Then I stopped for almost a year. In the spring of 1977, on my birthday, I met all these people who were talking about making films, people like Eric Mitchell and James Nares. They were getting together to talk about a film grant. Someone had a projector and someone else had this or that, and they helped each other out. They wanted to have actors and make up little stories. That seemed like a great idea to me. The people at Millennium were all into shooting the beach at Coney Island or the Staten Island Ferry or Central Park or pigeons. These were the first people I met who were talking in a *live* way about making films. I'd been to Anthology to see films and I liked some and hated others, but the atmosphere that pervades that place—and Millennium was the same way—is so heavy. These people took making film lightly; it was fun.

MacDonald: Guérillère Talks is the earliest of your films I've seen.

Dick: I just started shooting. I didn't really know what I was doing. I would do one roll with each person; they could do whatever they wanted in front of the camera. We'd choose a location, and the camera would either remain steady or I'd play around with it, experimenting. It was an easy way to start. I picked people I was interested in—sometimes people I didn't know, like Lydia. This film was an excuse to go talk to her; I was very curious about her—I'd seen her in Teenage Jesus. We became friends, and I went to a rehearsal of a new band—Beirut Slump—and she asked me to play. I met all those people that spring: Pat Place and Adele, Anya, Lydia.

MacDonald: I assume that *She Had Her Gun All Ready* is about either a failing relationship or the difficulty of relationships. I get a bit lost, though, in the middle section, where the Pat Place character is either being followed by the Lydia Lunch character or is hallucinating that she's seeing her.

Dick: She's haunted by her. She feels taken over by her and is anxious to get away. It's like when you meet someone you're very impressed by and start to feel overpowered, menaced. After she's so paranoid at the lunch counter, she goes out and makes a phone call. She's so nervous that she puts in a penny instead of a dime twice before she realizes what she's doing. When she does get through, it's like the wrong time—the person she wants to talk to is just about to go out the door. I'm very interested in that. You know, where you're just out of sync, your timing's off in every sense. Or, when things are right, and all kinds of funny coincidences happen. It can be really extraordinary sometimes. Toward the end the Pat Place character starts to realize that she can be strong after all, and the situation reverses.

MacDonald: So then she's following the Lydia Lunch character?

Dick: Yeah, stalking her.

MacDonald: When the Pat Place character is at the World Trade Center, are you making a statement about this kind of relationship existing because of, or in a context of, the sorts of things the World Trade Center represents?

Dick: I don't know. When you improvise, things happen that are coincidental but can fit in perfectly well with some idea you have.

MacDonald: You and the Bs are talked about as "punk filmmakers." Are you comfortable with that term?

Dick: I think people will just get tired of using that term after a while. I really don't care one way or another. The last film I made [*Visibility: Moderate*] could never be called a punk film, or even the film before that [*Liberty's Booty*].

MacDonald: Is there a punk visual style?

Dick: That's something people have made up, "punk style." I want to make films that are different; you can call them whatever you want. *Cars* by Tim Burns was the first Super-8 feature I ever saw. It was a pretty funny film—real messy but real funny. I also saw the films Eric Mitchell made. Scott and Beth were making *G-Man* then, too; I was pretty impressed by that.

MacDonald: Did you originally want to work in Super-8 rather than 16mm, or was the choice economic?

Dick: It was economics maybe first of all. But it seemed like Super-8 was much more modern. You had to wind the 16mm camera, and there was no sound on it. And all that cutting and everything. Super-8 was just much handier. And Super-8 has its own qualities, too; it does have a look about it.

MacDonald: All your films up to *Visibility: Moderate* center on women. Now that I think of it, I can't think of men in them, except indirectly—as tricks in *Liberty's Booty,* for instance. Women seem to be functioning within a world that's dominated by men, even though we don't see them.

Dick: I was focusing in on women for a change, that's all. I was more interested in filming women, and found it easier as well.

MacDonald: In *Beauty Becomes the Beast* I'm clear that Lydia Lunch is playing a character who we see as a child and who we see later as an adolescent. But there are other characters I'm not clear on. When she's at home, she apparently has a sister.

Dick: A friend or a sister.

MacDonald: Hoberman talks about the film being about the way in which women grow up in this culture, the way they're created to be incompetent, in part because of influences like television and . . .

Dick: Education, school, parents, *all* authority figures. The Son of Sam stuff on the TV in that film is like a terror tactic.

MacDonald: A terror tactic against women?

Dick: Yes, like the Atlanta killings of black kids. It's the same racist thing.

MacDonald: The film gives a general sense of the influences that are acting on this person, but it's not as though everything is intricately put together in a normal kind of narrative way—is that right?

Dick: I don't really know. When we were shooting it, we weren't following a book on how to make a film, and I was going on instinct when I edited—it worked or didn't work. I think it pretty much does work. But it's not all that self-conscious. See, I want to make movies that are a little looser. That's why it's difficult for me to write scripts. You have to have a plan if you're going to get money, but I don't want to be hemmed in by it, trapped by it. I'm still learning. I'm still fooling around. I have to try out things that maybe are silly, like that scene in *Beauty Becomes the Beast* with all the ghosts. That's almost embarrassing for me to watch, but on another level it isn't silly.

I think that films, or whatever you're doing, should push beyond. You shouldn't be scared by conventions. You have to have room so you can get really wild or crazy. I'm not anywhere near there yet. I want to make films that will be outrageous, and I haven't. I hope I'll be able to do it. I hear music like Public Image; that's pretty outrageous. I think the last album [*The Flowers of Romance*] is really great music. They're using all these Third World sounds. We're mostly trapped in a white supremacy civilization, in the dominant culture idea, and we're ill from it.

MacDonald: In both *She Had Her Gun All Ready* and *Beauty Becomes the Beast* you list the Bs as helping you.

Dick: They used to let me use their projector, sometimes a microphone or a camera guard.

MacDonald: Were they working with you during the filming?

Dick: No, except when I shot that scene with Lydia and the ghosts. They helped me out with that.

MacDonald: You were in *Letters to Dad.* Did you work on other of their films?

Dick: No. I used to edit over there and do sound work. Scott showed me how to do some things.

MacDonald: The day after you showed *Liberty's Booty* in Utica, one of the students in my class said it was a documentary, but done from the inside rather than the outside. I think that was a good point. You can feel that the filmmaker sees herself as being a part of the same community that the people in the film are in, that you're not coming in to examine a group of women who you feel are completely different from you. What was your feeling about making a film about prostitutes?

Dick: They knew friends of mine, and we were talking about prostitution quite a bit. I was very interested to meet them, curious about them, of course, but also interested in what they had to say. I found them really vocal; they were very interested in doing the film and in bringing out stuff that they thought should be said about their work. Another thing, it's not limited to houses of prostitution—it moves to other people's apartments. People get confused and think, oh, they're all prostitutes; *she's* a prostitute, *she's* a prostitute. . . . The whole point is that they may or may not be. How do you know who's a prostitute and who isn't? Most people who work as prostitutes are not your stereotype at all. The whole work situation in New York makes everyone a prostitute—in the other sense, anyway. We're all prostitutes to somebody. The film is playing with all that.

When I was a kid, prostitutes were really outside of society. Today, too, they have no rights, even though they're just like anybody else. Like she says in the film, it could be your sister—it could be anybody.

MacDonald: In a number of places you show males, tricks. Were they actually men who had come for prostitutes?

Dick: They were actors. Whenever you see a movie with prostitutes in it, the camera and the male director always examine the prostitute, the way she looks and this and that. She's this object or something. This film is different: the prostitutes are people telling me what they think and talking about the men and how *they* look, what it's like to be with them and how stupid a lot of them are. This idea of going to a prostitute to get off is such a peculiar thing. You hand over some money and pretend you control someone for an hour. It's an indication of some sort of warped repressive sexual thing; it reflects a kind of organization outside of the society, but it's all part of the American system.

It has to do with pretense, too. If you're a prostitute, you're putting on this act. You can't be real; you have to suppress that because it's not going to do you any good. And the tricks enjoy or even believe the pretense—it's always seemed peculiar to me.

MacDonald: At one point one of the characters says that prostitution should be decriminalized but not legalized. How do you feel about that?

Dick: Well, when I was there, all of them I spoke to had that opinion. They feel that if it is legalized, there will be far more control over them. In Nevada prostitution is legal, and you have these really sordid hotel complexes full of women, like barns or something. Men go on tours. It's really weird. There are rules: if you get a job, you have to stay there, and your hours are long, and there's a boss—a pimp boss. I suppose when it's just decriminalized, they can't quite set up those kind of places. The women are still sort of half-independent. These women don't have pimps and don't want pimps. They *had* pimps; they got rid of them. If it's legalized, the mafia will take over.

MacDonald: During the opening credits you do an animation where the Statue of Liberty becomes a hootchy-cootchy dancer, then a rifle-wielding revolutionary. Were you thinking of that in connection with the women speak-

Greer Lankton and her doll in prologue to Dick's Liberty's Booty *(1980). Photo by Beate Nilsen.*

ing out in the film? Did you think of your giving them an opportunity to talk to an audience as a kind of revolutionary feminism?

Dick: Yeah, of course. When I make a film, I'm always thinking that it's going to be a revolutionary something or other. Otherwise, I'm not going to bother doing it. And it has to get more revolutionary; it's not revolutionary enough.

MacDonald: When I talked to the Bs about *G-Man,* Beth said they wanted to make a film that would combine different areas of filmmaking: documentary, formalism, narrative. . . . *Visibility: Moderate* strikes me as working that way, too.

Dick: All my films do. They're part documentary, part improvisation, part whatever.

MacDonald: Visibility: Moderate seems an attempt to do a travelogue— or, you mention on your poster, "a tourist film"—that, unlike all other tourist films I've seen, deals not only with the romance or beauty of a country but also with the political and economic realities.

Dick: Tourist Land is always make-believe land in a certain way. You work most of the year, and in America you get two weeks off, only two weeks.

Sometimes you get a month. You escape into this fantasy land, where every-thing has to be beautiful and fabulous. If it's Ireland, you see lush green coun-tryside and horses and carts and the Blarney Stone. The tourist in the film is completely vulnerable to leprechaun land. She sees this Broadway-stage Irish scene, and she's taken in by it as if it's the real thing. Irish people have a strange impression of American tourists. A lot of them come over with such a weird conception of Ireland. You can tell when they come to a bar. The Irish people in bars pretend they know relatives and get the Americans to buy drinks. It's totally unreal; it's all memory and myth.

MacDonald: Are there filmmakers around who you particularly like or ad-mire or learn from?

Dick: I'd say some of Maya Deren. Ken Jacobs's *Little Stabs at Happiness* is a good film, though I really can't understand someone making films like that and then doing structural films, which I find pretty constipated.

MacDonald: I think it *can* be constipated, but it's not always.

Dick: Yeah, well I haven't seen the films.

MacDonald: So Maya Deren, and who else?

Dick: I like Jack Smith's films, the ones I've seen.

MacDonald: Flaming Creatures?

Dick: Yeah, and other bits of things that he shows. *Baby Doll* is a great film, and *Peeping Tom* and *Juliet of the Spirits.* I like those Kuchar films we saw the other day [several of the Kuchar brothers' 8mm films made between 1957 and 1963]; they're a little bit slow moving, but they're pretty funny. I'm kind of sick of the John Waters thing. It just reached the point where it's pretty boring for me. At the same time, there are things about it I really like. Mortville [Waters's trash village in *Desperate Living*]. His sense of humor.

MacDonald: You started showing your films in clubs, but recently you've shown a lot on the independent film circuit—Millennium, Anthology, the Collective. What kind of audience do you like best?

Dick: Well, generally the people who respond best are people who are not film critics or conscious film buffs. The people up at City College were a really great audience. When I showed in Ireland, it was good, too. I showed to this audience that had come to see Shell Shock Rock; they didn't even know a film was going to come on. I was really happy that they could understand. One thing about showing your own films: you're always there in the audience, and even though I've seen them a million times, I still enjoy sitting in the audience and hearing people react. The last time I showed *Beauty Becomes the Beast,* everybody thought it was hilariously funny.

MacDonald: Do you plan to keep traveling with the films? One of the problems with Super-8 is that it's still fairly hard to distribute.

Dick: I'm hoping it will go into this lower-power TV thing. That's where to go, not just here but all over Europe. I think people will start giving money to make films for cable TV, and we'll make better ones. And music—we'll be able to go to the studio and make our own music, our own soundtracks, our own programs, have our own TV station. There's a million things you could do! There's so much money wasted on bad films I can't believe it. You can open a TV station with $50,000. Beam it to the satellite.

Anyway, I haven't shown enough in places like City College. They were asking questions all through the film and laughing. That was really great.

MacDonald: What's been your worst audience?

Dick: Cal Arts [California Institute of the Arts, Valencia, California]. Some people aren't able to respond to anything—they're so frozen up inside. They have to tick their brains around to try to work out this and that and this and that. Is this a correct response? Is it OK? Is it the right thing to do?

MacDonald: For a relatively young filmmaker—you've made and shown just a few films—you've been getting a fair amount of recognition. Do you have any feelings about why that is?

Dick: I think the films are quite good. They touch on things that people are interested in. Not enough. I think I could be a lot better. I'm scared about professionalism, scared of writing scripts, and all the business of it. The ideal thing is to work with people who relate to what you're doing—not just hired people, stationmen. You really have to get along with the people you work with so they're in touch with what you're all doing together. No ego trips and carrying on. No bullshit. Collaboration's such a great thing, but you've got to find the right people.

Beth B and Scott B

For five years during the late 1970s and early 1980s Beth B and Scott B (Scott Billingsly) collaborated with each other—and with other punk or "no wave" artists such as John Ahearn, Vivienne Dick, Lydia Lunch, and James Nares—on a series of Super-8 and 16mm films. Like Vivienne Dick, they were dissatisfied with both the commercial cinema and the experimental/ avant-garde scene: they found conventional movies and movie theaters too safe and the leading experimental/avant-garde films and screening venues too arty. They began to make short, powerful, technically funky Super-8 films and to develop new kinds of screening situations for them. In many ways, their first three films—*G-Man* (1978), *Black Box* (1978), and *Letters to Dad* (1979)—remain their most interesting.

In *G-Man* (the film was shown in versions of varying lengths; the final version was thirty-seven minutes), Bill Rice plays Max Karl, the commanding officer of the New York "Arson and Explosive Squad," a law-enforcement body dedicated to stopping terrorist acts. But we also see him in his private life as a "trick" who hires a prostitute specializing in dominance to brutalize him. For the Bs, Karl's schizoid life is a metaphor (based on Beth B's experience as a receptionist in a brothel and on the Bs' video interview with a real bomb-squad commander) for contemporary lives in general. And the film's raw, gritty imagery and semi-synced sound are less limitations than means for undercutting the slick images of law-officer heroes promulgated in Hollywood. In *Letters to Dad* nineteen men and women make brief speeches to "Dad," looking directly at us as though we are "Dad." When the end of the film reveals that the characters have been reciting portions of letters written to Jim Jones in the hours before the mass suicide at Jonestown, our previous identity as "Dad" and the apparent sanity and clarity of some of the speeches create disconcerting implications.

Perhaps the most arresting dimension of the first three films is the Bs' use of sound: it is not simply an accompaniment, as in most films, but an environment that immerses the audience in the mood and meaning of the Super-8 imagery. The centrality of sound in the early films was due, in part, to the Bs' interest in having the films screened at New York rock clubs, where unusually good sound equipment was available, and audiences expected powerful sound. But even when the Bs presented their films at college campuses, they demanded special sound systems. Their use of sound as visceral environment is most central in *Black Box,* a Kafka-esque parable about the societal oppression of individuality. A young man resists the advances of a young woman, apparently because he is too distracted by *Mission Impossible* on TV (a black box); their bedroom is a claustrophobic space (another black box) with a single window looking out at a large Big Brotherish wall painting. When the young man goes out to buy cigarettes, he is captured by thugs and taken to a room where he is tortured by being beaten and hung upside down and is then confined to "the Black Box," the ultimate in torture chambers (which is modeled on "the Refrigerator," an American-designed torture chamber, made in Houston and used by regimes in Iran and Latin America). Until the young man is put into the Black Box, the skeletal narrative holds the viewer's attention in a relatively conventional way, but once the Black Box is used to torture the man by alternating between earsplitting noise and silence and between darkness and light, the audience becomes part of the action: the noise in the Black Box is noise in the "box" of the theater; when the Black Box lights up, the theater does too. Our identity as potential victims is communicated quite directly. Of course, when the theater lights come on, we are released (or release ourselves), but the young man is still in the Black Box: our momentarily privileged position is confirmed, though its fragility has been memorably demonstrated.

The Bs' success in getting their work shown to club audiences emboldened them to try a larger project, *The Offenders* (1979), a weekly Super-8 serial about groups of New York street toughs trying to find ways of staying alive. Later recut into a ninety-minute feature, *The Offenders'* raucous technique has a comic-book feel. The film has interesting moments but lacks the power of the first three films. Their next feature, *The Trap Door* (1980), was shot in Super-8 and blown up to 16mm. It focuses on Jeremy (John Ahearn), a young man who, unlike the lawless characters in *The Offenders,* does what he is told. As a result he is manipulated at work by his boss, by women, by a salesman, and finally, by Dr. Shrinkelstein, a mad psychiatrist and hypnotist (played by filmmaker Jack Smith, in an inspired bit of casting). Dr. Shrinkelstein explains to Jeremy that the secret to life is that "you've got to be a bigger creep than the guy next to you," and describes the "trap door to oblivion" one can fall through if one forgets this important lesson. At the end of the film Jeremy

Bob Mason as young man tortured in the Black Box, from the Bs' Black Box *(1978).*

falls through the trapdoor: the bottom of the film frame. While *The Trap Door* maintains something of the rough feel of *G-Man,* it is a more conventionally skillful film, especially in its frequently inventive compositions.

Two years elapsed before the Bs completed *Vortex* (1983), their first 16mm film and their final collaboration with each other. They had ceased to be interested in the democratic implications of inexpensive Super-8 technology and were becoming increasingly interested in making more conventional films for more conventional screening situations. *Vortex* is a film noir, loosely based on the bizarre later years of Howard Hughes. While the film is often visually arresting and includes some solid performances (Lydia Lunch stars as the film-noir detective persona), it has neither the creepy power of the raw early films nor the conventional narrative skill of more effective Hollywood noir films.

Since finishing *Vortex,* the Bs have worked separately—Beth on music videos and a 35mm feature *Salvation!* (1986), and Scott on Super-8 shorts. While it is too early to be sure, my guess is that the nature of the Bs' relationship fueled their best work: they seemed to be able to bounce off each other— as they often do in the interview—in ways that enabled them to make the best of their individual skills.

I talked with the Bs in the fall of 1980 and again just before *Vortex* was released.

MacDonald: How did your work together begin?

Beth B: We . . . fell . . . in . . . love. It's really true!

I had done a short film in Super-8, but it was just an extension of other things I was working on. I worked a lot with video in Germany and did drawings and some sculpture.

Scott B: I'd been involved primarily in sculpture and, then, desiring to get into something that was more public and less object-oriented, I moved into architecture. I designed and built a house in Arizona on commission.

Beth B: We'd met before that but were not collaborating. We knew each other for about a year while we worked on separate projects. . . .

Scott B: And then we started thinking in terms of collaboration as a way of breaking down the individual star quality of most art endeavors. We did a performance piece together that was practically a ritualized marriage ceremony, although we didn't realize it at the time.

Beth B: We were very romantic . . . then [laughter].

Scott B: Both of us were moving toward a medium that wouldn't be something done in a strict art-world context. Film was the obvious thing. I'd always wanted to work with film.

Beth B: Also, film was an economical medium to use—much more so than video for us. To make film, all we did was pick up this silent little Super-8 box Kodak camera. We'd had no training at all with film, but we had ideas that we felt could be directed through film to larger audiences, which was a very large part of what we wanted.

Scott B: To a certain extent our earlier films were a comment on our backgrounds in art.

MacDonald: You mean *G-Man*?

Scott B: *G-Man* in particular was trying to break away from a heavy concern with form and style and break into something that had a real gutsy, political, content-oriented thrust that at that time we didn't think art was able to hold. Maybe that's becoming less true.

Beth B: There are more artists now who are working with information and trying to get messages across to people. We approached *G-Man* with the idea of putting out a lot of information. We did research on different aspects of terrorism. We tried to shape that information into a narrative. Also, we tried to combine documentary, narrative, and experimental film. We approached *G-Man* trying to bridge the gap between those three aspects of film.

MacDonald: Did you divide the labor or did you presume that both of you would work on everything?

Scott B: We both did everything. Recently we've begun to be more specialized. We've found the simplest way is to decide ahead of the shoot who's going to do what, but still, in terms of concept, writing, directing, and shooting, we've got an equal division of labor.

Beth B: With *G-Man* there might be a subject I was especially interested in, or one that Scott was especially interested in, and we would work independently on those. We collaborated on other material all the way through.

MacDonald: I know of at least three versions of *G-Man.* J. Hoberman's piece in *The Village Voice* [May 21, 1979] describes a seventy-minute version. The version I studied was forty-five minutes long. The version you showed at Utica College was shorter still. I presume the shortest version is the one that you now show.

Scott B and Beth B: Yeah.

Scott B: We came into *G-Man* with an extremely visual sense of the film. We found after we had shot it and completed it that it didn't hold together in a linear sense. Also, in terms of pacing, we had all this material that was interesting, but it didn't build the way we wanted, so we started to pull things out and reshuffle the order so it would move properly.

Beth B: We ended up taking out a lot of narrative material that had to do with the life of the character Max Karl, the commanding officer of the Arson Explosive Squad—scenes with him and his family. After we had shown *G-Man* awhile, we felt that all we really needed to show to get our point across was him in his two positions: as commanding officer of the Arson Explosive Squad and as a participant in a dominance session in a whorehouse.

MacDonald: Some of the reactions to *G-Man*—and to *Black Box,* too—suggest that you have a love affair with violence. After looking at the film, I feel that's pretty silly, but I've presumed that one thing you're trying to suggest is that the various things that are going on in the film—the arson investigation, and terrorism, and prostitution—are integrally related in a single system.

Beth B: Sure.

Scott B: I think most of the feelings about the film's violence came out of people's perception of the new wave music scene and social atmosphere. People connected us with that.

Beth B: Also, at the time that *G-Man* was made, low-budget Super-8 films weren't coming out. *G-Man* was a very distinct break from what was going on in independent film, and we did not approach it in a conventional way. Instead of showing the film in controlled situations where we'd try to hustle some institution, our idea was to get the film out to as many people as we could. I think the approach that we were taking was very different. There was a whole new crop of artists, filmmakers, musicians coming up at the time, and people had a certain fear of that. When something new is happening and there's a new surge of energy, people get confused about how to categorize it or how to understand it, and they try to stick certain connotations or stereotypes on it.

Scott B: One thing that we were trying to get at was the idea that essentially control *is* violence. Whether it's enforced with violence or with the threat of violence, that's the nature of power. We were using this arson and explosive inspector to try to show the contradictions of a structure that gives someone that kind of power. Essentially people can't deal with all that power all the time. Some men who go to a whorehouse for dominance sessions are people who during their everyday lives have an immense amount of control. They go in wanting release, wanting to give that control to someone who will degrade them as they've been able to degrade other people during the course of their jobs. That applies to what we were perceiving about terrorist activities at the time: in a sense a terrorist takes the whip out and whips society for having too much control.

Beth B: I worked at a whorehouse as a receptionist, and I was really shocked to see the number of men who came in for dominance sessions. I had always thought that it was a rarity, a specialty thing, but actually about fifty percent of the men were coming in to be submissive. We thought that was interesting and important to get across to people. Also, a lot of the people who came in were very respectable people—judges, politicians, executives.

MacDonald: The sections on Max Karl are obviously based on your videotape *Inspector Howe* [1978]. Was *Inspector Howe* made as research for this film?

Scott B: Well, we used it for that, but we also showed it on cable television as part of a weekly news program, *All Color News*.

Beth B: The group of people we were collaborating with on *All Color News* was Collaborative Projects, who put together the Times Square Show and *X Magazine*.

MacDonald: One of the things that *G-Man* is about is the way financial success and violence feed on each other.

Beth B: The relationship is more specific than that. This man's job is dependent upon a continuation of terrorism. Without terrorism the commanding officer of the Arson Explosive Squad would not have a job. That dependency is very interesting.

Scott B: Also, the media vision of who would go out and bomb something is different from what we've been able to gather. Most people who are involved in terrorist activities come from very middle-class backgrounds and are educated. They are able to set up a totally separate life and be completely straight and successful at it, while on the sly, they're involved in sabotage. In the most brutal way, they're living a schizophrenia.

Beth B: But most people live schizophrenic lives on some level. Our films deal with the contradictions within people's lives and within society. One thing is publicly professed, but privately something else is happening. We're interested in the hypocrisy that exists and why it exists, and whether it's conscious or not, and whether it's profitable to certain people. I think a lot of the reason it does exist is the pressures that are put on people publicly.

MacDonald: You mentioned that you saw *G-Man* as a combination of documentary, narrative, and experimental film. *G-Man* is full of formal, self-reflexive techniques. The long pan across downtown Manhattan has a formal impact that's similar in a general sense to the zoom in [Michael Snow's] *Wavelength*. The first time I saw that pan, it seemed impossibly long. Had you seen much experimental film?

Scott B: Not much.

Beth B: Hated it!

Scott B: We still haven't seen *Wavelength*.

Beth B: We saw one of Snow's.

MacDonald: Which one?

Beth B: It was inside some school room . . .

MacDonald: Back and Forth [↔]?

Scott B: Is that what it's called, *Back and Forth?*

Beth B: I really don't like those films. I get bored. No information is coming across, except for formalist ideas.

Scott B: When I was still in Madison, festivals of avant-garde films came through. I saw early Brakhage and Anger and *Flaming Creatures* . . .

Beth B: Anger I like. I saw *Scorpio Rising* when I was in school.

Scott B: Snow's film seemed standard for the art scene at the time. It was exactly what we *didn't* want to do.

MacDonald: Despite your feelings, I'm sure that your films will be seen as reactions against formalism that bring with them a lot of the same sorts of extensions of technique that formalist filmmakers explored.

Scott B: Well, I think a lot of those people were coming out of art backgrounds similar to ours. Maybe they had similar visual concerns. We had the sense, too, that the films we were able to do—shooting in Super-8, shooting with our own money—could never be done in any other way.

Beth B: So you see having money as being a burden [laughter]?

Scott B: Well, in a sense, because you have a certain responsibility to make it back.

Beth B: Not just that. If you're funded by someone or backed by someone, you have to satisfy their needs and ideas as to how the film should be done and what they're going to get out of it.

Scott B: When Buñuel first showed *L'Age d'Or,* the guy who backed the film invited all of his friends . . .

Beth B: Big premiere!

Scott B: And nobody would talk to him afterward, so he canned the film for years. That's what happens. We didn't feel the lack of money limited us so much as it gave us an opportunity to deal with things that aren't dealt with in film.

Beth B: It gave us a lot of mobility. We could put out whatever we wanted, and we had complete control of what we were doing. We still do.

MacDonald: I presume that from the beginning you assumed that in your films sound would be more important than it normally is.

Scott B: Sound is just as important as the image. When you watch television or Hollywood films, you're empathizing with whoever the main character is. We didn't want to get our audience involved that way. We felt we could hold the audience with the sound, by making it extremely visceral.

MacDonald: I don't know very much about the events at Jonestown, but I understand that for *Letters to Dad* you arranged for the actors to read letters written by people who had died there.

Scott B: After the suicides we were really interested in the whole situation. That one person could have that much control over a thousand people! We started collecting all the material we could get, with the idea that eventually we'd be able to make a film.

Beth B: It related to material we had been dealing with before that. We wanted to take a very different approach, one that would be direct and simple, without being sensational.

Scott B: We gathered all the letters we could find (a huge number of them actually got published), and we just circled or underlined the ones we thought were the best and gave them to the people who . . .

MacDonald: The best in what sense?

Scott B: The most characteristic, or the . . .

Beth B: The ones that gave the most insight into the writers' psychological states. Some of them are just phenomenal, very childlike, like confessionals.

Scott B: They felt totally lost on their own and believed Jones had the answers.

Beth B: We're thinking about dealing with a cult situation in one of our next films.

Scott B: One thing that was remarkable about Jonestown was not pointed out, except in one article I read. The methods that were used in getting people to believe in the structure were classic brainwashing techniques.

Beth B: Torture and brainwashing.

Scott B: Not torture.

Beth B: Torture, come on!

Scott B: Torture was used as a last resort, but it was more the classic sort of wearing people down physically by poor food, lack of sleep, and a constant battering of ideas that was developed in China after the Revolution. I'm not sure, but my guess is that those stories are inflated in terms of what actually went on.

Beth B: I doubt it!

Scott B: I think the most insidious and freakiest aspect of the whole thing was the practically scientific use of peer pressure. The American understanding of that situation is based on Western ideals that people are individuals who have their own opinions that they will maintain, once they've been raised with them, for the rest of their lives. The Eastern concept is that the community has control over the opinions of each individual.

Beth B: It's also that you're living and working within this community, trying to further its ideals for the good of the whole community, and, as a result, for your own good. The concept within Jonestown was "We are doing this because the rest of the world is evil and bad and our community is good and peace loving"—similar to Evangelist philosophy.

Scott B: The lack of understanding in the West of how people can be totally changed, in terms of their opinions and beliefs, is one of the reasons why I think the whole Jonestown situation was unreal for most people who heard about it. Practically anyone who would have been there would have ended up the same way. It's not as if those people were all crazy; it's the situation that was crazy. And it was powerful enough to control them.

MacDonald: A while ago you were explaining that you circled or underlined certain passages from the letters. Then what happened?

Beth B: We invited a whole bunch of people . . .

Scott B: At half-hour or twenty-minute intervals . . .

Beth B: But they all would come at the same time!

Scott B: And when they got here we'd give them the letters and they'd choose one.

Beth B: We told them to choose a line or a phrase they could relate to on some level . . .

Scott B: And we said to make it as long as you can remember.

Beth B: We didn't want them reading. We wanted them to say the lines and to repeat them as if they were trying to convince themselves as well as other people.

MacDonald: The repeating gets more evident as the film proceeds. The most heavily repeated line is, "I never realized how enslaved by capitalism I was until you freed me."

Beth B: That's Tom Otterness. Actually we had everybody repeat their lines; then we edited the film to build the way it does.

Scott B: The situation in Jonestown was very weird racially. They had eighty percent blacks and twenty percent whites. But almost all of the ruling committee of the town was white. There were some very strange racial tensions. A lot of Jones's appeal, you see, was his idea of a mixed society.

Beth B: He had adopted thirty racially mixed children.

MacDonald: By having the people in the film look at the camera, we become Dad.

Scott B and Beth B: Yes.

MacDonald: We're supposed to be aware that we're all part of systems where we brainwash each other?

Scott B and Beth B: Right.

Beth B: Also, we wanted it to be very direct.

Scott B: There's as little artifice as possible. The only thing that we added to the image was the lighting. We used just two lights and tried to light everybody in keeping with what they were saying. We wanted to keep the visual interest, but also to make them look like normal happy people.

Beth B: The person sitting next to you could have been involved in Jonestown. In many cases, the things they say are not that unusual. They're often very funny. We have audiences where everybody is laughing through the whole film. Then, when the title card comes up at the end, and they find out where the statements come from, they're totally shocked.

MacDonald: Black Box is pretty clearly a parable about oppression.

Beth B: There's a school in Kansas now where they have a black box.

Scott B: They're calling it "The Box."

Beth B: If a child in school behaves badly, they put him in this isolation box. They're trying to get more of them to put in different schools. That's really scary.

Scott B: It's indicative of the direction in which our society is moving; it's becoming more authoritarian.

MacDonald: The origin of your use of the Black Box has to do with "the Refrigerator," doesn't it?

Scott B and Beth B: Yes.

Scott B: We first read this article in *Skeptic,* a real interesting magazine that no longer comes out. They described this isolation device that was being used in Brazil called "the Refrigerator," which combined heat and cold, brightness and darkness, and loud noise and no noise. It's a combination of sensory overload and deprivation. I think it's probably not as effective as simpler methods.

Beth B: It was a replacement for the Tiger Cages. They thought that the Tiger Cages were too inhumane! The Refrigerator not only breaks down your physical self, but your mind, your whole system.

We were trying to build the box and at the same time make a film. We made it a generalized situation. You don't know where it's taking place. You don't know who this guy is. We wanted to relate it to people's own individual levels of understanding. We didn't want to give any relief at the end. That was very important. You don't know what's going to happen to this guy; it's not like, "Oh, he dies, and don't we feel sorry for him," or, "Oh, he escapes, and don't we feel great!" A lot of meaning can be lost by giving a final answer, because in my mind there is no answer. I don't want to give people answers. I want to have people continually asking themselves questions, asking other people questions, and not feeling self-satisfied.

MacDonald: As the film ends and the lights come on, the guy's still in the Black Box. We were in the black box of the theater, but the lights are coming on and we're leaving—which is our luck. Our escape is our potential for developing the awareness that the film character doesn't have.

Scott B: Essentially what got him into that position in the film was his lack of initiative.

Beth B: Even at the very beginning when he's in bed with his girlfriend, she's the aggressor.

MacDonald: He's already distracted, by the sign outside the window, by

Mission Impossible on the TV, by his need for a cigarette. It's as though he's halfway to the torture chamber already. His whole life is a black box.

Beth B: The film relates to the idea of control, not only on a governmental level, but also in terms of people's relationships with other people, relationships within love affairs, and so on. Mind control by authority figures does exist and will exist in the future. It's not going to be resolved by one action or a series of actions. But it's something that people need at least to be aware is happening so that they don't get sucked in like the character in the film.

Scott B: When we first started dealing with that material, we felt that it was something we hadn't come into contact with. And yet torture and very blatant mind control techniques are used not only in Communist countries but are fostered by the United States and are used as an aid to prop up regimes that support our life-style.

Beth B: To make money so that Americans can live comfortably. There was no awareness within the news, or anywhere else, of these things going on until the situation in Iran came about.

Scott B: We shot *Black Box* very quickly, whereas *G-Man* was shot over a period of almost a year. We wanted to do *Black Box* specifically for a club situation, where we'd have a good sound system and an audience that was used to rock and roll . . .

Beth B: Where it was a loose open arena for people to talk, to react to film. It was our reaction against certain gallery and museum situations.

Scott B: Well, it was also what was available to us . . .

Beth B: And what was available to show Super-8. But the atmosphere did influence our films at that time.

MacDonald: There's an independent film circuit in New York—Millennium, The Collective. Are those places you would not want to show or . . .?

Beth B: We have shown there.

Scott B: Those places have good screening situations, but they're geared primarily toward a different kind of film, a very personal type of filmmaking.

Beth B: Audiences come there with a certain aesthetic in mind.

Scott B: They come to see Art, which is not the attitude that we want people to come to see our films with. We want them to think it's an open situation where anything can happen.

Beth B: We wanted to get away from the formal films and the formal painting, *and* from the formal spaces: the white walls, the rigid wooden chairs, No Smoking, No Drinking, No Eating; you sit and analyze; you intellectualize. There's no communication. People should use film to communicate, because these days there's not much communication between people. People watch more and more TV. All that is is manipulation. It makes them sit back after they've been working all day and just say, "Oh, ah, feed me!"

Scott B: In a sort of Brechtian sense we want people to have fun while they're watching our films and at the same time feel a burr that will make them think.

I was starting to say that *Black Box* was the first film that we did very quickly.

It made us realize that with Super-8 we could shoot a film and show it immediately. We had a date for the show and we just started. We figured out exactly what we wanted to do ten days before the screening, shot it in three days, got the last piece of film back the day we showed it, and did the sound track that afternoon. After that we realized what would be feasible, and we set up *The Offenders* to run as a serial and planned to shoot a new part every week.

Also, working in Super-8 enhances the sense that film is a throwaway. You're doing it for this moment, and you're going to do the best you can, but you can't get it perfect. There's no way in hell that you can ever get Super-8 to be the way you really want it. What we've been running across recently, especially with *The Trap Door,* is trying to get it perfect and running into . . .

Beth B: He's been making me ill [laughter]!

Scott B: I'm a perfectionist, so the experience with *The Offenders* was really refreshing.

Beth B: But now you're trying to get back into your perfectionism!

Scott B: There were two main reasons why we thought a serial form was viable for *The Offenders.* We felt very comfortable in a cabaret situation, and we were interested in doing something that was to be continued so that we could build up an audience over a period of time. Also, it was a matter of lack of funding: we were able to pay for the next part of the film with receipts from the previous part. That was the only way we could actually do the film. We showed the original the entire time! We felt that we were using Super-8 in the best way it can be used. With the possible exception of videotape, you can't work that quickly normally.

Beth B: At the beginning of *The Offenders* we really weren't that sure of how things would proceed from day to day, but after the third week, it turned into a schedule. We would usually script one day, then shoot for maybe two days, drop the film at the lab, get it back the next day, and then use the weekend to work on the music.

Scott B: We didn't have time for reshoots. Either we got it or we didn't.

MacDonald: Was there any time for rehearsal?

Scott B: We generally do rehearsals on the set. In the past we've scripted all our films the night before we were shooting; we'd give the actors the script at midnight or 1:00 A.M. so they'd be able to read it over before they had a good night's sleep [laughter]! The next day we'd walk it through—how long depended on who the performers were. There are certain advantages to the way we shot: a feeling of spontaneity, for one thing. There are certain compromises, but we could do things you could never do with 35mm or 16mm—like the shots on the streets.

MacDonald: Is there any possibility of distributing *The Offenders* as a serial?

Scott B: It's a possibility, but we'd have to recut it again.

MacDonald: It doesn't exist as a serial anymore?

Scott B: No. It would take a lot of time and some money as well. At this point we'd rather put our energy into new projects.

MacDonald: The first time I saw the film, at the Times Square Show, the Times Square atmosphere made the film seem very threatening. Because you just carried that camera around in a real city, the film has the ambiance of being in the real place, which gives the film a feeling that things *can* happen even if we don't actually see very much violence.

The violence in *The Offenders* is funny, too. When the two guys get to the park bench and chop off the man's hand to get the briefcase—an unbelievably grotesque act of violence—the way the hand sort of bounces makes that violence clearly unreal. It takes place in a real place and we understand the plot motivation for it, but it's like cartoon violence, rather than normal commercial film violence.

Beth B: The characters themselves are like cartoon characters.

Scott B: When we shot that scene, rather than focus on the hand, we had the one guy stand in front of the camera, so that you can't even see the chop. We used catsup for blood, rather than stage blood. We didn't want to use a visceral effect in order to sell the film, which is what most film violence today is used for. We were using it to give an idea of the conflicts within those situations or those characters. Most film violence resolves a conflict; ours . . .

Beth B: Creates other conflicts. Also it's a comment on how the oppression of one group of people becomes activated toward another oppressed group or person.

On several levels our films are reactions to television. TV presents a certain surface of images, and the people see them but often don't see what's under them, what's really going on there.

People are really attracted to the sensationalism of violence. I'm more interested in getting ideas out clearly than with hyping violence up.

Scott B: The violence in *Black Box* is turned on the audience. I think the spectator aspect of film viewing is really crucial. At this point there's really only one film that plays that for what it can be worth: *The Rocky Horror Picture Show*, which I think is a movie that's going to be imitated in the future. That's one of the main directions where film can go.

Beth B: I think the strongest thing a film can do is create a reaction the way that *The Rocky Horror Picture Show* does, where you get an involvement of the audience with the film, or the way *Eraserhead* does, where people get really grossed out, or the John Waters films, or *Black Box*, where some people *run* out of the theater because they can't stand being in there. Any type of reaction that gives people an awareness of themselves and what they're feeling.

Scott B: But film should act as a catalyst for people to reassess their position, their lives . . .

Beth B: Sure! You're obviously going to reassess if you react strongly to what's happening on the screen. But it's not often that films do that. I'm not talking about an ideal situation; I'm talking about film generally. It's valuable if a film can create a reaction in an audience. Most films don't create *any* reaction. Films that provoke a negative reaction sometimes make me think more.

MacDonald: Some people who make Super-8 films do so because they accept, even want, to make more intimate films for small audiences.

Beth B: We want to reach the largest number of people we can. I think it's disgusting that Hollywood entertainment extravaganzas—the most surface-oriented films—are the films that reach people. The main problem with Super-8 from our point of view is that you just cannot get it out to a large number of people, because there's no distribution, and it's limited technically.

Scott B: Part of our reasoning in dealing with Super-8 is that it's important that people who are not part of the Industry, who are not part of the power structure or the economic elite in this country, can make films that do get out. With Super-8 you can communicate ideas almost as effectively as with 35mm. You can't reach the same sorts of audiences, but you can at least get your ideas out.

Beth B: People tend to be shocked about where we have been able to get our films shown. When people realize what can be done, I think there'll be more independents making films.

MacDonald: I think that your films get part of their mood from the audience's consciousness of Super-8 home movies.

Scott B: Particularly with *The Offenders* and *The Trap Door* we used that to our advantage. We play with the fact that we're a low-budget operation, and we make a comment on the whole nature of filmmaking by saying, "Yes, we're going to make an extravaganza out of this spaghetti."

Our main concern from the beginning has been maintaining the integrity of our vision, of our perception of things. By working with Super-8 for as long as we have, we've been able to work out some of our ideas and create a base for ourselves. By maintaining control this far, we feel we'll have more room when we do start working with greater amounts of money.

The Offenders captures the community that we were involved with at that point. Everybody was desperately broke and looking around for any way to get by without having to do a regular job. It was like taking the fantasies we all had about robbing a bank and getting some easy money, and just trying to concretize them into a film. The way the film was made—on a very low budget, plotted pretty much as it went along—reflected our situation.

Beth B: A month after we finished the film there was a crime wave in New York. There were ten bank robberies a day. We filmed some of the newspaper headlines after we finished the film and, when we recut *The Offenders* into a feature, we included them. So the film flowed with the energy in New York at the time.

MacDonald: What led you to call yourselves "B Movies"?

Scott B: "B movies" implies a certain amount of creative control. The directors who made B movies generally had more control over what they were doing than the A-movie directors, because the A movies had to have a much stronger commercial potential. Most of the directors we have appreciated have made B movies. Like Fuller . . .

Beth B: Huston . . .

Scott B: Fritz Lang and Luis Buñuel. "B Movies" was a play on our names and on the kind of films we like to watch on television.

MacDonald: You've been filmmakers for only five years and you've made relatively few films, and yet you're rather widely known. What sorts of things have you done to get the films out?

Beth B: You can't make a film and put it in a theater and expect people to come not knowing what it's about or where it's coming from.

Scott B: We view publicity and all of the accoutrements to the film—the photographs, the press releases, the posters—as part of the film. We try to make what we're saying with the film carry through into everything that's related to it. We do our own posters and our own publicity.

Our attitude is to treat Super-8 professionally, which tends to make other people look at it professionally. We do let people know we're around. We didn't realize when we first started working on films that 50 percent of making the films is business.

Beth B: We never learned *that* in art school [laughter]!

MacDonald: The Trap Door seems to involve the feeling that society's goal is to rigidify everything to such an extent that there is no room for even the slightest deviation.

Beth B: The main character in *The Trap Door,* played by John Ahearn, is the antithesis of the characters in *The Offenders. The Offenders* shows people who do not have the desire to fit into society and are able to find another way of surviving. It's about people who create their own values to suit their own lifestyles.

Scott B: If Jeremy were only more cutthroat and a little less concerned with what was right and wrong, he'd be able to handle the situations he finds himself in. It's Jeremy's inability to get past the idea that you've got to be a good guy and follow all the rules that causes his defeat.

Beth B: But there's more to it than that. It's not just his lack of insight. The people around him really don't give a shit about the next guy.

MacDonald: The system he lives in is totally exploitive, with moral-sounding rules.

Beth B: Right. It's not only Jeremy's inability to see that; it's that the people on the other side of the desk are taking advantage of his inability to be ruthless.

MacDonald: You were saying earlier that the shoot-from-the-hip tactic of filming *The Offenders* is a reflection of the lifestyles we see in the film. In *The Trap Door* you work in the opposite way.

Beth B: Well, actually we wanted the film even more stable than what we ended up with. We were limited by the two-and-a-half-minute Super-8 rolls. All the shots should have been incredibly long and stable. We had wanted a situation in which you would feel as though nothing could move.

MacDonald: Also, either Jeremy's on the edge of things, or if he is in the center of the frame, there's a distraction between him and the viewer. There's a whole series of tactics that keep him from seeming to have any power.

Beth B: He's always in the wrong position in terms of the camera and of the situation itself.

Scott B: The stable camera was very much a part of the idea that these situations he comes into are already established, and he's falling away from them the entire time. We wanted the feeling that each shot is a trap in the same way that his being in those situations is a trap.

MacDonald: A lot of the visual situations in *The Trap Door* force viewers to consider what our own position is vis-à-vis the film. When the woman seems to address us at the beginning, we're thinking, "How am I involved?" It's only later that we realize she's really talking to Jeremy, but we also realize that in another sense she really is talking to us. Or the scene where we see the angel start to shake on the table. We don't know why it's shaking, and it takes on a symbolic meaning before we realize, "Oh, it's just the subway." In both instances we raise questions and suggest meanings and then pull back so we can see what the narrative function of the situation is.

Beth B: That can create a double or a triple meaning. You realize what a detail means to you; then later you find out what it means in the film, which in turn might alter your earlier ideas.

MacDonald: Hypnotism seems to be a major motif in the film. At the end there's the long scene where Doctor Shrinkelstein tries to hypnotize Jeremy with the Maria Montez medallion. I assume that the casting of Jack Smith was meant to be recognized, at least by some portion of the audience, as an irony on the idea of psychoanalysis.

Beth B: Well, Jack always says he wishes he could go to a therapist and be in psychoanalysis, but he can never afford it—so he does theater.

The whole film centers around professionals. It's difficult for Jeremy, and for people in general, I think, constantly to have to confront professionals, specialists. You can't ever get enough knowledge to get beyond where they want to keep you.

Scott B: Basically we wanted to deal with authority. The characters embody some of the essential authority figures in society.

MacDonald: There's a connection between the professionalism idea and the verbiage. It's language that defines the specialist.

Scott B: Part of what happens when you're watching the film is that the words create a story on their own. In earlier films—*The Offenders,* for instance—we use characters and action in order to portray conflicts between the

Dr. Shrinkelstein (Jack Smith) hypnotizes Jeremy (John Ahearn) in The Trap Door *(1980).*

mature, older part of society and the younger, more energetic part. The characters on the screen embody differing philosophies. In a sense, the trap of *The Trap Door* is that those conflicts and those battles aren't visual so much as verbal, and they don't become clear until the battle's already been lost. Part of Jeremy's downfall is that he doesn't quite grasp that all this verbiage is the front on which the battle's being fought.

MacDonald: In *The Offenders* your style was an expression of your identification with some of the situations in the film, whereas here your style as professional filmmakers is part of what seems to oppress Jeremy.

Scott B: Well, in a sense we were approaching the film that way, with practically no sympathy for Jeremy.

MacDonald: Vortex seems much of a piece with *G-Man* and *The Offenders,* in terms of its crime-world aura and the way you approach composition and lighting. And like *Black Box* it has a relentless nightmare mood.

Beth B: We wanted a very isolated feeling through the whole film. You don't know where it takes place. You don't really know who these people are, or what the company they work for is.

Scott B: It all takes place in the dark, in interiors. We were thinking of it as an amalgam of all of our earlier films.

Beth B: All the people in the film are in this pit, and the only one who climbs out of it is Angel Powers, the detective. Not that she's happy when she climbs out of it. She's the survivor. The film is about how far people will go for the sake of power.

Scott B: Right, and impose on other people's lives to get it. *Vortex* stemmed from the story of Howard Hughes and how his whole empire had been essentially taken over by his aides.

Beth B: But it had been built upon the mystique of this very powerful man, who eventually couldn't even deal with the outside world. He had to withdraw and become a recluse. Things swarm around the Fields Company in the film. It's involved in everything from surveillance techniques to brain implants and religion.

MacDonald: One of the things that struck me about your early films was that their power came not so much through the story as through the mood. What made those first films interesting to me is that you used Super-8 for subjects and approaches that Super-8 was theoretically not supposed to be able to handle. It was like using the negative aspects of the gauge positively. Sixteen-mm is pretty malleable. You can do pretty much what you want. It doesn't bring with it automatically any of that homemade quality. Did you use such obvious play money to try to maintain that quality?

Scott B: More important than details like the play money is casting Lydia in that sort of a role. As soon as she walks in, she's a wrench in the works. She's never really quite believable as a detective. There's always an edge.

Beth B: Also, we set up a lot of the scenes so that they feel like theatrical settings. We used long takes, instead of doing a lot of cutting, to help build that theatrical sense.

MacDonald: Did you use a carefully worked-out script?

Beth B: We had a very tight script.

Scott B: With 16mm you have to have things worked out in advance.

Beth B: We had a big crew, too big a crew—it was ridiculous for us. The transition was horrible.

MacDonald: What were the costs?

Beth B and Scott B: About $70,000.

Scott B: Our original idea for the film was much more modest. We started out figuring that we were going to be able to do it for very close to $20,000. Then we were able to get a lot of people to work on a deferred basis, very good technicians, crew, so we went for the highest quality we could get. The whole thing has been an immense learning process.

Beth B: With Super-8 we worked with everybody on a trust basis. With 16mm you're confronted with contracts and how much money will be deferred and how much money is being put in and where it is going to come from, and it's checks and balances everywhere you go. . . .

Scott B: Our original motivation for getting out of Super-8 was that we were spending at least 50 percent of our time distributing our films. We were getting by on it, but it wasn't enough so that we could fund new films. We figured to get into 16mm so, hopefully, we wouldn't have to deal with the distribution on a booking-by-booking basis. We figured that would give us more time to make films, which is what we want to do. But now we end up spending 50 percent of our time raising money!

MacDonald: The Trap Door struck me as on one level a personal film that had to do with what I felt was a quandary for you as artists and filmmakers. Which was the more dangerous route: to be professional and a sellout, or naive and idealistic and exploited? In *Vortex,* the characters, like you two, are involved in the process of dealing with the big business world. It's as though you're hoping that a certain directness of confrontation will get you through as the survivors.

Scott B: I wouldn't say that we actually identify directly with the Angel Powers character . . .

Beth B: But sure there can be a connection there. We don't want to be co-opted.

MacDonald: Do you fantasize about where you'll be in five years?

Beth B: No way!

Scott B: Yes, I fantasize about it. I'll be making films without having to deal with all the other shit—that's my fantasy, just to be able to be concerned about the artistic stuff.

Beth B: That's a ridiculous fantasy, Scott. Being a director you can't stop dealing with the technical bullshit and the people.

Scott B: I don't mean the technical side of it. I mean the aspect of having to put a package together.

Beth B: We're still going to have to put a package together.

Scott B: I know, but that's my fantasy. I'll have enough money to do what I envision. Not that I want $20-million budgets.

And I fantasize about making a film during which the audience can actually make choices, where the audience's interaction with the film affects the film. Essentially that's why video games are popular. Whoever's playing has control over what actions the characters in the games take. Maybe it will bring a whole new structure into film. But maybe video games are it, and it'll never transfer to film.

MacDonald: As you've tried to reach larger audiences, your film language seems to be growing more conventional. This language has an impact on the kind of characters you can develop and the kind of world you can show. Do you see that as a problem?

Scott B: The dilemma really is to make a piece that's a whole, that works as an integral unit and has a solidity.

Beth B: The question is how big do you want to get? If you want to do *Star Wars* or *Chariots of Fire,* then, yes, you have to sacrifice in terms of subject matter and social commentary. In the society we're living in, the media's manipulation of people teaches what to like, how to see. Every step of the way people are taught how to relate to things, and you're not going to change that just by one film.

Scott B: There are films that ask very hard questions.

Beth B: Nowadays? Name one made in the last few years.

Scott B: Well, I think things are going to change.

Beth B: [laughter]

Scott B: I think there's going to be room for stronger films. I think it's basically a problem of marketing. If you do something that hits home, that says something about trying to survive in society, people aren't going to be able to put a top on it. It's important for filmmakers and people who are involved in culture in general to open people's minds up.

Beth B: Except the problem is that most films that would do that would not be commercial. Scott, look at the films that are being made, and look at the film *Pixote*. That was an incredible statement, and what happened to it? I understand exactly what you're saying, but when you're making films saying that things should change, you've got to deal with the Industry having taught people that you go to cinema to escape your horrible lives, you go to the cinema because we're going to entertain you and alleviate your problems for a couple of hours.

MacDonald: Some filmmakers I've talked with are suspicious of the whole new wave, punk movement in film. The suspicion is that new wave artists are less concerned with any ideological commitment than with manipulating their images so that they can work themselves into power positions in the commercial industry.

Let's say *Vortex* is an immense success and opens at theaters around the country . . .

Scott B: And Hollywood producers come to us and say, "Why don't you make a film for us?"

MacDonald: You're going to say yes, right?

Scott B: It depends on what kind of a deal it is.

Beth B: It depends *com-plete-ly.* No way we're just going to say yes to Hollywood producers.

Scott B: Getting back to the point you were making. I think that that sort of attitude has been around ever since *avant-garde* was coined as a word. Essentially, to be an avant-garde artist you need to remain on the outside of current events. You're always starving, always struggling to get your statements out. Essentially, you're always powerless. That ideal has been around for over a century now.

Beth B: A complete myth.

Scott B: What that has done is make it so that the best minds, the best people, who aspire to be avant-garde make things or experiences that very,

very few people understand. Art becomes something that has no real impact, something that doesn't reach people because it's so refined in its thrust. It's a way of saying, "The world out there is corrupt, and I refuse to take any part in it. I'm going to make this because I feel that this is pure and clean." But life *is* dirt and grunge, along with all of our ideals.

Beth B: A very important reason why both of us got involved with film was that we felt that whole attitude was full of shit. I don't want to make something in my little closet and show it to this little art world so that a few people can see it and someone can collect it, and so a few people can pat me on the back and be my patron or whatever. That's why we got involved in the rock-and-roll scene. There was an incredible energy, an incredible response and reaction coming from people, from young kids. To me young kids are critical, and theirs are the minds that are going to be shaping this world. I just don't see that avant-garde film or being an avant-garde artist is effective.

Scott B: The avant-garde is constantly trying to reinvent the language, whether it's in film or painting or whatever, and it has impact that way. But there are languages effective for constructing stories, and there are very strong things that you can say in these languages. We don't have to reinvent English to talk to other people.

MacDonald: I wonder.

John Waters

John Waters's cult status among midnight-movie buffs as the "Master of Sleaze" and the moderate commercial success that has gone with it may seem to locate hm in a different sector of film history from the other filmmakers in this volume. During his first ten years as a movie maker, however, his approach was essentially the same as that used by several of the filmmakers I have interviewed. Like the Kuchar brothers, Robert Nelson, the Bs, and Vivienne Dick, Waters made his early films with minimal amounts of money by using his friends as cast and crew and his own neighborhoods as locations (Waters has consistently—seemingly as a commitment—made his films in and around Baltimore). Further, Waters's films seem very much a part of that crucial strand of experimental/avant-garde history that includes Salvador Dali and Luis Buñuel's *Un Chien Andalou* and more recent American films such as Ken Jacobs' *Star Spangled to Death* and *Little Stabs at Happiness,* George and Mike Kuchar's raucous melodramas, Jack Smith's *Flaming Creatures,* Kenneth Anger's *Scorpio Rising* and *Inauguration of the Pleasure Dome,* some of the Warhol Studio's films, Robert Nelson's *Oh Dem Watermelons,* and the Bs' *Black Box.* All these films rebel against the bourgeois canons of filmic "good taste," developed and ministered to by the commercial film (and TV) industry. And, like George and Mike Kuchar's films in particular, Waters's six features—*Mondo Trasho* (1969), *Multiple Maniacs* (1970), *Pink Flamingos* (1972), *Female Trouble* (1974), *Desperate Living* (1977), and *Polyester* (1981)—rebel by borrowing Hollywood-type plots and presenting them so that they undercut exactly those viewer expectations these plots have created.

From the beginning of his career, Waters and his collaborators (including

Divine, Mink Stole, Mary Vivian Pearce, David Lochary, Edith Massey, set
and prop designer Vince Peranio, and make-up artist Van Smith) realized that
what Waters came to call "shock value" was a way of overcoming the inevitable difficulties of making feature-length, sync-sound narrative films on
picayune budgets. During the 1970s, many independent filmmakers—and
most of the filmmakers in this volume—came to accept that by making the
kinds of films they felt committed to make, they would probably never develop large audiences. But Waters and his collaborators seem never to have
accepted the idea that they would be osbcure. The whole point of making
films was for the films—and the group of friends who made them—to become a focus of attention—famous, if possible—and to do so entirely on their
own filmic terms. The bottom line was that the films should develop a paying
audience large enough to support further production.

The peculiar kind of shock that Waters's films deliver is radically different
from and in some senses more complex than, shock delivered by the suspense
and violence of effective horror or gangster films. During most films that
scare us, we maintain a kind of double consciousness: simultaneously we have
to remind ourselves that what we are seeing is not really happening *and* we
know that the entirety of what we're seeing is a fabrication. *The Texas Chain
Saw Massacre* may have been inspired by real murders, but we know that we
are not actually seeing the murders as we watch the film—even though the
events may "scare us to death." Waters and his collaborators had neither the
money nor the technical skill to make convincing conventional violence.
What they did have was a willingness to put themselves on the line to create a
different form of shock. The most famous example is the concluding scene of
Pink Flamingos, where Divine (he plays a character who is determined to
maintain her reputation as "The Filthiest Person Alive") collects a handful of
poodle shit as it comes out of the poodle, puts it directly in his mouth and
grins and gags at the camera. An even more remarkable instance occurs in
Multiple Maniacs, the earliest powerful Waters film, when Divine is led to a
Catholic church by "the Infant of Prague": Mink Stole comes out of a confessional and gives a "rosary job" to Divine, who—as is customary in Waters's
films—loudly, seemingly endlessly, screams her orgasm (Mink wipes the
rosary beads off afterward). One of the most striking dimensions of this
scene—I've never seen it without my hands over my face—is that it clearly
takes place in a real church. The scene may not be "believable" in the way the
shocking actions in commercial films usually are, but we can see that the filmmakers are doing outrageous things in order to give their movie impact. Or to
put it another way, in Waters's films we are as likely to be shocked by what we
can see was done to make the film as by the outrageous actions of the frequently repulsive characters as characters.

But shock value itself accounts for only part of the impact and interest of
Water's films, which are full of raucous humor and anarchic elegance. Often,

the humor is a function of Waters's willingness to use dialogue that conventional directors would be afraid to use and his ability to do so with considerable imagination: in *Female Trouble*, when Dawn Davenport's boyfriend Gator suggests that her daughter, Taffy, give him a blow job, Taffy screams, "I wouldn't suck your lousy dick if I was suffocating and there was oxygen in your balls!" In other instances, humor is a function of Waters's ability to develop funny situations. The series of vignettes in *Female Trouble* dramatizing Dawn Davenport's high school experiences, Christmas Day with her parents (when they give her the wrong kind of shoes, she tears down the Christmas tree), and her attempts to make a life for herself in the late 1960s are as amusing and insightful as anything I've seen on that period. Usually, humor and shock occur simultaneously, and this is often the result of Waters's willingness to refer to a mundane reality that the whole history of conventional film and TV have managed to avoid. When Dawn Davenport is raped by a guy who picks her up hitchhiking (he is also played by Divine), Waters reveals that his underpants are badly shit-stained. We cringe and laugh, even though we know that the underpants are just a prop, because we cannot believe a filmmaker would refer to such a personal detail.

While Waters is clearly delighted with the moniker, "the Master of Sleaze"—having such a moniker seems to suggest that, like "the Master of Suspense," he's earned a crucial place in film history—his films are not all that sleazy. They are shocking and outrageous and gross, but they have too much good humor to be really sleazy the way cheap porn is, for example. And besides, like George Kuchar, Waters has a remarkable design sense: his films—especially *Pink Flamingos*, *Female Trouble*, and *Desperate Living*—are often quite stunning. Divine's trailer and Connie and Raymond Marble's apartment in *Pink Flamingos*, the trash village in *Desperate Living*, and Divine's costumes, hairdos, and make-up in all the films are distinctive and memorable. At first, one may laugh at the idea of Dawn Davenport (in *Female Trouble*) as "the Most Beautiful Woman in the World," but by the end of that film, Divine's courage and skill, Van Smith's costumes and make-up, and David Lochary and Chris Mason's hairdos have rendered Dawn beautiful, in a new sense of the word. Waters is committed to a definition of physical beauty that centers on imagination and distinctiveness rather than on adherence to an Industry-promoted standard. No contemporary actress has more style than Divine at the end of *Pink Flamingos* and in many scenes in *Female Trouble*.

In the long run, what comes through Waters's films is his energy, his courage, his persistence and an unwavering determination to develop a large audience without suppressing his hostility toward the viewer complacency ministered to by most Industry films. In his attempt to invigorate the experience of moviegoing, he has been willing to offend just about everyone. But he has remained dedicated to his work and his co-workers. Together they have proved they can do amazing things with very few resources. But ironically, when Waters had by far his biggest budget—for *Polyester*—he made his least

Divine at his most divine in Pink Flamingos *(1972).*

exciting film since *Mondo Trasho* (though Waters' decision to center that film around a scratch-and-sniff card with gross smells to accompany the characters' gross actions was inventive and amusing). It remains to be seen whether Waters can maintain the integrity of his anarchic vision in the midst of financial success.

I spoke with Waters in May 1981, soon after the completion of *Polyester* and the publication of *Shock Value* (1981), Waters's charming and troubling personal reminiscence.

MacDonald: How did you get started?

Waters: I went to the movies constantly as a kid. *The Wizard of Oz* was one I went to over and over and over. I always rooted for the witch; I used to identify with the witch. I always liked the villains in movies; they were the only ones I was interested in. They were the best parts, the ones that everybody remembered. I used to run to see the films that they told us in Catholic school we'd go to hell if we saw. So, really, the nuns got me interested in making movies. Especially *Baby Doll*—if you saw that one you'd go straight to hell. I saw it a lot of times. When I was about twelve I started getting *Variety* and I used to make up lurid advertising campaigns for films I would think up. I was also a puppeteer for kids' birthday parties. I got hired to put on shows, but the shows started getting so weird that the parents stopped hiring me. I started putting fake blood in, and that ended my birthday-party circuit.

I used to sneak to this hill near a drive-in and watch films like *The Mole People* and *I Spit on Your Grave* with binoculars. As soon as I could drive a car, I started going to drive-ins all the time. At the drive-in I saw films like Herschell Gordon Lewis's *Blood Feast, 2000 Maniacs, Gore Gore Girls, Color Me Blood Red,* and early Russ Meyer stuff like *Lorna, Mud Honey,* and *Faster, Pussycat! Kill! Kill!* Those films were my *Citizen Kane.* I even got arrested in a drive-in, which I fondly remember. I think everybody should be arrested before they're twenty, or something's the matter with them, and their parents should worry. I think it's part of growing up. I was obsessed by William Castle's movies. Odorama in *Polyester* is an homage to him.

MacDonald: I don't know William Castle at all.

Waters: He did *The Tingler, House on Haunted Hill.* He had all these gimmicks: skeletons came out, buzzers went off under your seat, there was "Chicken's Corner" where you followed a yellow line to a cardboard booth set up in a corner with a nurse in it—if you chickened out, you could get your money back. In *13 Ghosts* there were glasses—if you looked through the red, you could see the ghosts but if you looked through the blue, you couldn't.

I also went to see Fellini, Bergman, that kind of stuff, but I liked the exploitation movies best. They were real low budget so they had to do something that nobody else could do in order to get people to come see the film. I wound up making exploitation films for art theaters.

MacDonald: I was going to ask about Bergman because the village in *Desperate Living* reminds me of scenes from *The Seventh Seal.*

Waters: I think it's more like Oz. The end is like, "Ding, dong, the wicked witch is dead."

I was very influenced by the Kuchar brothers, very much, and early Warhol films, and Kenneth Anger. Really, George and Mike Kuchar influenced me more than anybody. Then all these movies came along that I really don't like, like Stan Brakhage and films with colors jumping around. I think that killed the underground movement. Everybody thought, oh, there's underground films, let's go see. And when they just saw colors jumping around, after thinking they were going to see something risqué, they stopped going and went back to the safety of regular movie theaters.

When I was about sixteen, I made this black-and-white movie called *Hag in a Black Leather Jacket* [1964]. I knew *nothing* about how to make a movie. I was getting in a lot of trouble with the police—nothing serious; I wasn't a murderer, but you know, underage drinking, car wrecks, stuff like that. My grandmother always knew I was a show-off, so she gave me a movie camera. It was just a Brownie. I knew a girl who worked at a camera store, and she stole film. The first movie cost $80, and it grossed $100. A success! Instead of putting it in my closet the way a lot of people do, I opened it in this coffee house. It looked just terrible to me. There was no editing; the film went right out of the camera onto the screen. It was about a Ku Klux Klan guy marrying a white girl and a black guy. We filmed on the roof of my parents' house. It was very much pop influenced: the girls wore American flags and tin foil, that kind of stuff. It was terrible. But I felt like doing it.

After that I went to New York University, very briefly. I got kicked out in 1966—marijuana, which was a big scandal then. I don't even take drugs now, but then, Big Deal. It was in the *Daily News.* I never went to classes anyway. The first film class I went to I had to watch the Odessa Steps sequence [from Sergei Eisenstein's *Potemkin*] over and over. I just went there to be in New York. I went to movies every day on 42nd Street.

MacDonald: Do you think film should be studied at all, and if so what should be studied, and how?

Waters: I think films should be studied, but in a movie theater, not in a classroom. That first day at NYU, I realized that their sense of values about film was going to be so academic that I would be completely bored sitting through the course.

MacDonald: So it was more the course than *Potemkin* that turned you off?

Waters: I'm not crazy about the movie. I'd much rather see *Mud Honey.* I'd rather see a new turkey than an old classic. I had absolutely no interest in *Potemkin.* I lived by stealing textbooks and selling them back to the bookstore. When I got kicked out, I went home. NYU recommended extensive psychiatric treatment and all this ridiculous stuff. I hung around with Divine, David Lochary, Mary Vivian Pearce, Mink Stole. We had grown up together.

MacDonald: This was in Baltimore?

Waters: Yeah, in the suburbs of Baltimore, but we all went downtown and hung around. We thought we were beatniks. I used to wear sandals that laced up to my knees and Levis with bleach and paint on them. I actually owned bongos. So we made this film, a home movie called *The Roman Candles,* [1966]. It was heavily influenced by [Andy Warhol's] *Chelsea Girls,* which was two films shown at once, so we showed three. It was mostly about a lot of drugs. Divine in drag, all the girls I knew modeling clothes they stole from boutiques. We opened in a church and got a lot of media attention because they thought, oh, underground films, some forbidden thing. We put the Kenneth Anger film, *Eaux d'Artifice,* with it so people would come—we exploited Anger's name. It went over well, and we showed it a couple more times at different underground theaters in Baltimore. By that time we were all going to Provincetown in the summer.

I borrowed some money from my father—he said, "Don't ever tell anybody I lent it to you"—to make this movie called *Eat Your Make-up* [1968], which was the first film I did in 16mm. It was black and white, silent with taped rock and roll. To this day I'm the only one who can show the movie. It's so closely synchronized that I have to use my own tape recorder. It almost drove me crazy. That film had a plot, and we built sets. The best part in it— it's not that good—is when Divine is Jackie Kennedy and we do the whole Kennedy assassination. Divine had on Jackie Kennedy's exact outfit, and we had a Cadillac and a motorcycle with police. I filmed on the street where my parents lived, and since the assassination had happened just a year earlier, the neighbors didn't think it was too funny. We opened that one in a church, too, with a world premiere and everything. I entered it in a film festival. In the middle the judges started screaming, "Get this shit off!" They didn't even watch it all the way through, and they called the church and said, "Don't let him show this movie because it's pernicious." I remember that word; I had to look it up. But the reverend said go ahead and show it, so they called the IRS. The IRS came and wouldn't let me charge admission, so we had to ask for donations at the end. I think we showed it one more time, in Provincetown— at another church. I wanted to do it in the actual church part, where the audience would be in pews, but they wouldn't let me.

MacDonald: Was it clear to you when you were making these short films that you wanted to make longer films?

Waters: Yes, but I was just learning how. I didn't know anything about making films. This man at the Quality Film Lab in Baltimore knew I didn't have money, and he would give me pointers. I used my friends, who I was trying to build into some kind of stars. After that we made *Mondo Trasho,* which was silent, except for music, and a few lines we put on at the end. It was my first feature-length film. Now that I look back, I can see that it should be about half as long, but there's no point going back and changing it. We got arrested making the movie—the whole cast—for conspiracy to commit indecent exposure.

Remember where the guy's hitchhiking nude, and Divine pulls up in the Cadillac? We filmed on the Johns Hopkins campus without asking permission. We just pulled up. Some campus policeman saw the guy nude, raced down, called the police. With Divine in drag, a nude guy, the rest of the cast, and the camera equipment we sped off in the Cadillac Eldorado convertible trying to escape. He had gotten the license plate, and the police saw us driving away and pulled us over. They arrested the actor, and the next day they came and arrested all of us, which was ludicrous. We were all in a paddy wagon, and looking back on it, it was fun, but at the time. . . . The Civil Liberties Union handled our case, and it turned out all right, making *Playboy* and the front page of *Variety* and therefore creating a lot of interest in the film. We opened in the church where we always opened and did very well, and we showed it in Provincetown. Then the Film-makers' Distribution Center got it shown in L.A., and *Variety* and *Show,* which was at the time a pretty good magazine, gave good reviews. I made enough money to pay my father back.

MacDonald: How much did *Mondo Trasho* cost?

Waters: $2,500, for a feature-length film. I still get rentals for it today.

MacDonald: One thing that struck me when I saw the film is that you tend to make virtues of necessities. In a lot of places you use the same people more than once—you do that in *Multiple Maniacs,* too—but instead of trying to disguise the fact, you let it become a joke rather than a weakness.

Waters: Right. We had *no* money. I don't remember if anybody worked at the time. Those were drug days, not that anyone was a drug addict, but it was the sixties. We lived in this place that had a plumbing school underneath it. To get to our apartment, you had to walk right through the plumbing place. Divine would walk through in full drag—a gold lamé toreador outfit—while these student plumbers would be working on their pipes. We called it a gutter film because it really was filmed in gutters, alleys, and laundromats. We'd go to the laundromats because they had neon lighting so we wouldn't need lights. After we got arrested, we were always looking over our shoulders. We were so paranoid, we'd jump out of the car, film the scene, and leave.

MacDonald: Even people who have seen later films are shocked by the scene at the very beginning where the guy kills the chicken.

Waters: I'm shocked when I look at it now, especially because he keeps missing! I've only killed chickens twice. On the other hand, I eat chickens— how do you think they get to your plate? They don't have heart attacks.

MacDonald: I assume the idea of the scene was to wake the audience up.

Waters: Well, no. It was a joke on the *Mondo Cane* movies, which always had things like that. We bought the chickens at a place called "Freshly Killed Chicken." You go in there, they kill the chicken, and you go home and eat it. The same thing happened to this chicken, but it got to be in a movie. The beginning *is* a little much; the ASPCA wasn't around.

That was the first film where Divine was really Divine, trashy and with tight clothes. Divine and I both idolized Jayne Mansfield. Mary Vivian Pearce, the blond, looked like that at all times—that wasn't a costume. I loved how she looked. Everywhere she went was like a *riot*. Bonnie—her real name is Mary Vivian Pearce, but no one's ever called her that, except in the credits of my films—had absolutely no desire to be an actress. She sort of dreaded doing the films. She's in *Polyester* for a minute as one of the nuns. She lives on a very fancy horse farm and exercises race horses. We used her to promote *Eat Your Make-up*. I had gotten the idea for *Eat Your Make-up* from those candy lipsticks—the make-up you eat up, they said. I used to hand people a flyer; she'd hand 'em a candy lipstick and say, "Eat it, read it, and come." People thought we were giving them acid and would say, "No, no, get away from us!" but it was good promotion, and we didn't have any money for advertising.

MacDonald: At the very end of *Mondo Trasho* there's a sequence where she's standing on the sidewalk that seems a reaction against stereotyping and movement politics.

Waters: Well, I never took politics too seriously. I went to all the riots and stuff, but just to meet good people. It wasn't like I had any deep political convictions.

MacDonald: The amateurishness of *The Diane Linkletter Story* [1970] appears to be a comment on all the media moralizing about that event.

Waters: The only reason *The Diane Linkletter Story* happened is that right before we were going to do *Multiple Maniacs,* I had to test the camera. I read the morning papers, and she'd jumped out the window, so we just did it. It was the only movie I ever improvised.

MacDonald: You made it that day?

Waters: That day—talk about bad taste! It's a film I don't really talk about a lot, for obvious reasons. It's really not even a film; it was a joke between ourselves. And talk about *me* being in bad taste: that record Linkletter put out was in worse taste than anything I could ever think of.

MacDonald: Multiple Maniacs seems to be the first of your films that's full strength.

Waters: I look back on the film that way. It still plays. It only cost $5,000, and it's technically terrible, but I like the movie. I like the nastiness of it. Divine threatens Reagan's life, which really gets a laugh now. I was obsessed by the Manson case. I still am. At the beginning of the movie Divine claims she did it, because Manson hadn't been caught yet when we were filming. Then at the end David Lochary finds this newspaper headline. That's because Manson had been caught that same day and we had to work it in. Nobody could upstage Charlie Manson.

MacDonald: There are unbelievable sequences in *Multiple Maniacs*. The "rosary job" is probably more outrageous now than it was then.

Waters: I think I finally worked Catholicism out of my system with the "rosary job." We went to this church. Somebody knew a guy there who used to let Black Panthers have meetings; I figured he might go for it. We didn't tell him what the scene was, but he didn't seem to care. I mean he *saw* Divine. A friend of mine took him into the other room and had this political discussion with him while we filmed the scene. I haven't seen him since, but a friend did recently—he said to this day the guy prays that nobody connects the scene with that church. We opened the film in another church, and the reverend was in hysterics. There are a lot of off-the-wall priests.

MacDonald: Watching the film, you realize it's shot in a real place, which changes the whole effect of that scene.

Waters: It looks as though we snuck in there.

MacDonald: Like guerilla moviemaking. That sequence is almost unbelievably abrasive—it's the one thing of yours I've ever hesitated to show . . .

Waters: The censor board in Baltimore just busted it last year. We went to court, and the judge said that his eyes were insulted for ninety minutes but that it wasn't obscene.

MacDonald: Ironically, the stations-of-the-cross sequence actually comes across pretty powerfully.

Waters: Yeah, I think that works. We filmed it on an old dirt road in the country; we rented all the costumes and just went over and did it.

MacDonald: I assume the carnival-of-perversions sequence was done that way, too.

Waters: That was on my parents' front lawn. The neighbors were watching through binoculars.

MacDonald: When you were making *Multiple Maniacs,* were you thinking of confusing the audience's usual way of identifying with film characters? There's a wonderful device near the beginning where you show the perverts, then you show the incredible reactions of the other people, and their reactions are so much more obnoxious than the perversions that the audience tends to be on the side of the perverts.

Waters: I always try to confuse the audience, by making them laugh at things that they feel unsafe laughing at. Also, I don't know if you recognize them, but the people that are supposed to be the straight people in the beginning are Mink Stole and Mary Vivian Pearce, who also play the perverts, but in wigs and different clothes.

MacDonald: I didn't recognize them.

Waters: The "perversions" were all the standard, cliché things suburbanites were uptight about—drugs, homosexuality, all things I figured you could laugh at. It's hardly threatening.

MacDonald: Did you have an audience in Baltimore right away?

Waters: We had an audience, yes, but they didn't always like the films. I also had an audience in Provincetown. Then *Multiple Maniacs* got picked up by this guy, Mike Getz, at Underground Cinema-12, which had a number of theaters across the country. It showed on that circuit at midnight shows. He paid well. I went to Los Angeles for the L.A. opening, and we got a good review. I went there because the Manson trial was opening at the same time. The first two good reasons to go to California.

Then I moved to San Francisco. *Mondo Trasho* and *Multiple Maniacs* played a lot at the Palace Theater in North Beach, where the Cockettes started out. They flew Divine out and they had about 500 people at the airport to greet him. It was the first time Divine became Divine in his other life. He was a hairdresser and he hated it, so it was a real escape for him. His whole life changed. He realized he wanted to do this for a living. He doesn't walk around as Divine usually—those are his work clothes.

We kept trying to make the films look a little better so people could watch them and get through them. We just hoped there was an audience for them, which I always suspected there was. I had always had a reaction against hippies; I was never a love child. I knew that violence was the one sacrilege, so I wanted to play violence for laughs. *Multiple Maniacs* was made to offend hippies.

MacDonald: When did you start being able to pay actors and crew?

Waters: With *Pink Flamingos*. They all had percentages, and the main people still get money. I ran a bookstore in Provincetown every summer and then got unemployment every winter, so I had something to live on while I made movies. I used to, well, sell amphetamines, too—we all have different ways.

MacDonald: Did you have the characters use their real names because it was easy and you figured nobody would know who they were?

Waters: I thought that the best way to make them famous was to use their real names, not just in the credits, but in the movie, so you'd remember them.

MacDonald: The killing of the cop is a good example of a certain kind of violence that exists in the films—the act is violent, but not at all visceral.

Waters: It's so fake that you can't take it seriously.

MacDonald: The effect on me is that it frees me to laugh at something in which the violence, if realistically portrayed, would be much more questionable in its impact. Were you trying to make things as violent as you had the means to do, or were you consciously trying to make the violent acts not look really violent so that they'd have this kind of double effect?

Waters: It was just badly done.

MacDonald: Did you rehearse a lot?

Waters: Yes, I always do. I rehearse for at least a month or two before starting. It's hard to *believe*, I know, watching *Multiple Maniacs,* because a lot of people forget their lines—but on these tiny budgets you have to rehearse.

MacDonald: Have you been responsible for all the writing?

Waters: I've done all the writing for all of them. I guess that's why I still like *Multiple Maniacs* so much: it was the first film in which we could talk.

Divine raped by Lobstora in Multiple Maniacs *(1970). Photo by Lawrence Irving.*
© *New Line Cinema.*

That's also the first film that Vince Peranio did. He's done all my sets since
then. He made the giant lobster and he's in it—you can see his feet sticking
out. I got the idea for the lobster from these postcards of a giant lobster they
sell in Provincetown.

    MacDonald: That film seems full of all sorts of allusions to other movies,
particularly to monster movies.

    Waters: At the end when the National Guard kill Divine, it's like *Gorgo*—
only it's Divine. In that last scene there's a blind man you see every time they
come around the corner. That's because he was a ham, and I couldn't get him
out of there.

    MacDonald: From what you've been saying, I assume that you always
wanted to move in the direction of more polished, slick films.

    Waters: We always tried to make them look as good as we possibly could.
I *never* thought, "Let's make it look technically fucked up." I did the best I
could do at the time. Each time we got a little more money. *Multiple Maniacs*
cost $5,000, *Pink Flamingos* cost about $10,000. We had one light with an
extension cord that ran a mile from the house to the trailer. The trailer cost
$100, we got it in a junkyard. Vince painted it and redid it, bought the fur-
niture in junk shops. We had to walk through mud for a mile to get up to
where it was hidden on this friend of mine's farm. I had no work print for that
film. I edited the original. When I look back, I can't believe it. Every time I

had to watch a cut, I put it through the projector; and it's not scratched. How that's possible, I don't know. It was filmed single-system sound, with a newsreel camera borrowed from a TV station.

MacDonald: It seems like the most Baltimore of the films.

Waters: All of them have allusions to Baltimore.

MacDonald: How does Baltimore feel about you?

Waters: They've been very good to me. The mayor tells me to keep making movies. When we made *Polyester,* they gave us cops, buses, everything. They really stood behind it. I really love Baltimore. There's a great tolerance for eccentrics there. I think they like the fact I've stayed. I think they figure that they're for anything that comes out of there. They have a good sense of humor about the whole thing. That time we got arrested was just a fluke; it wasn't an organized effort against me or anything. I've really had no trouble there, except with the censor board.

MacDonald: Which films have had censorship trouble?

Waters: All of them except *Polyester.*

MacDonald: I assume that you've had censorship problems all over.

Waters: No, not really. *Pink Flamingos* was busted in Hicksville, New York, and found obscene. We had a $5,000 fine. But that's the only other place in the United States we've had trouble. We had a lot of problems in Europe. *Pink Flamingos* was banned in France. In Italy *Desperate Living* was heavily cut. I've had censorship problems with *Pink Flamingos* everywhere in Europe, and in England and Australia. This *is* the freest country.

MacDonald: Do you feel any of that freedom threatened these days?

Waters: You mean by the Moral Majority or something? No. I'd love it if they picked me as a target; it would help the movies. That's the reason Russ Meyer hired pickets. I'm sure the Moral Majority never goes to the movies. I've never met a person I had any respect for who they could influence in any way. Let them stick to television; that's more their speed. No, I don't feel threatened. *Polyester* is a pro-abortion movie.

MacDonald: Is *Pink Flamingos* the first film that Van Smith did make-up and costumes for?

Waters: Yes. David Lochary did Divine for *Mondo Trasho* and *Multiple Maniacs.* Van came in with *Pink Flamingos.*

MacDonald: Did they have training?

Waters: No. David was a beauty school dropout.

MacDonald: How about Peranio?

Waters: He went to the Maryland Institute College of Art, but not for set design. He was a painter. He does lots of movies. He did Linda Blair's movie, *The Private Eyes.*

MacDonald: Who is the man/woman who exposes him/herself to the David Lochary character in *Pink Flamingos?*

Waters: She's a woman now. She's married and runs an all-male construction crew. She's real happy. She was the first sex-change in Maryland that welfare paid for. She had to buy her own breasts, but they paid for the rest.

MacDonald: Pink Flamingos was the first film Edith Massey had a big role in.

Waters: She was the barmaid in *Multiple Maniacs.* That's where I discovered her. She worked in a wino bar that we used to hang out in because drinks were 10¢. I thought, "God, she looks so good!"

MacDonald: Somebody told me she runs a second-hand clothing store? [Massey died in October 1984.]

Waters: Yes, it's in Baltimore—"Edith's Shopping Bag."

MacDonald: How much direction do you give Vince Peranio about designing sets? I'm thinking of the scene in *Pink Flamingos* where Mink Stole and David Lochary are in bed making love to each other's feet and there's this red and blue color coordination.

Waters: Oh that was just Mink's bedroom. The furniture was moved around, but it was all just Mink's stuff. Vince didn't do anything in the Marbles' house. It was just where we lived. You can see the same movie posters on the wall in *Multiple Maniacs.*

MacDonald: Female Trouble is dedicated "For Charles Watson."

Waters: He was in the Manson family. I visited him in prison. He made the helicopter in the credits. I told him I thought crime is beauty. He certainly didn't believe that; he thought I was nuts. I used to see the celebrity criminals in the visiting room. Timothy Leary was there at the time. I just exaggerated all that to think up *Female Trouble,* and that's why I dedicated it to Watson. It was hardly a commercial thing to do.

MacDonald: I became interested in your films because when I saw them, it wasn't a matter of liking or disliking them, it was just that something happened. I've gotten so used to paying $3.50 or $5.00 to be bored to death and to forget the movie within an hour.

Waters: I make films to make people laugh. I hope with my sense of humor that I can get other people to respond to them. That's the total reason. You can read a lot into a film, but I'm really not trying to say anything. Well, obviously I am or I wouldn't make movies, but I have no great message, and I'm not trying to change anything. The films are my vision of what I see that makes me laugh.

MacDonald: Do you feel your films are art films?

Waters: That's a word that really makes me uncomfortable. It's a word I don't use, except as Mr. Linkletter's first name. I hate to hear filmmakers say, "My art should mean this and that."

MacDonald: Your statements about Herschell Gordon Lewis and Russ Meyer are not just that you like them or that you laugh at their films; you see something in their work that you make a value judgment about—you talk about them being great filmmakers.

Waters: They are, because they do make me laugh *and* because what they did was completely outside of the mainstream: they made something original. You can look at a Russ Meyer film today and instantly know it's a Russ Meyer film.

MacDonald: How do you feel about Mel Brooks?

Waters: I don't think he's very funny. He's too involved with Jewish humor, too ethnic. I wouldn't like a whole movie that just made jokes about Catholicism.

MacDonald: Woody Allen?

Waters: I like some of Woody Allen. I wish he wasn't in the movies though. I liked *Interiors* the best. If it had come out without his name on it, *Interiors* would have been a big art hit.

MacDonald: Of all your films, *Female Trouble* seems the closest to making a definite statement.

Waters: It's exaggerated so much, though—everything I do is. When it first came out, a lot of people didn't like it. *Pink Flamingos* was a tough act to follow. People expected that I was going to try to top myself, but how could you after that? I figured it would be a dead-end street to keep trying to make things more gross. In *Pink Flamingos* the shit-eating thing was really a publicity stunt. I had to get people's attention some way. I figured if I did that, no one would ever be able to forget it, and that it would be a first and last in film history. It was the first idea I had for the whole movie. I had $10,000 and I knew I had to compete with regular movies. You have to go way out on a limb and give 'em something that the studios would never want to give them. With *Female Trouble* I tried to make the ideas a little weirder than the action. As I told you, ever since I was a child I've been a fan of villains, so I'm also attracted to murder trials, which I go to all the time. *Female Trouble* was a reaction to going to a lot of murder trials.

MacDonald: You seem to be posing a definition of beauty that works off the standard definition. In this culture being "beautiful" is looking like whoever happens to be in style. In *Female Trouble* being beautiful is looking the most unusual or distinctive.

Waters: To me, beauty is when I'm walking down the street and I see somebody and I think, "Oh my god, look at that person!" *That's* beauty to me, because I notice it. I certainly don't want to make movies that star people who look like everyday people. To me the people in my films look glamorous. Also, it's good to hire fat people because they take up more room on the screen—you don't have to spend money on sets. All my films are based on reversals—good is bad; ugly is beautiful. I always try to cast heterosexual people as homosexuals and homosexuals as heterosexuals to further confuse people, because I think confusion is humorous.

I like *Female Trouble* very much. I guess if I ever made a personal film that's it. When I went to high school, the girls were like they are in the film,

Divine with facial burns in Female Trouble *(1974). Photo by Bruce Modre.* © *New Line Cinema.*

and I loved to watch them with their beehives. They used to stab each other with rattail combs. And my Christmas tree really did fall over on my grandmother. Nobody pushed it, but I remember her pinned under it. Many of the images in that film are based on real things, except they're exaggerated. I used to play car accident as a kid, but not the way Taffy does!

MacDonald: How did you finance *Female Trouble?*

Waters: Well, *Pink Flamingos* made a lot of money, and I put all the money that I made from it into the new film and borrowed some money from a man who ran a cinémathèque at the University of Maryland, and from another friend who was rich. *Female Trouble* cost $27,000. It was really hard to get that money, but it's never easy. You've just got to keep working. It took three years to raise the money for *Polyester.* That's the worst part of filmmaking, the part I hate. It's the most depressing part: you feel like a used-car salesman, and you go around with your synopsis and talk to people, some of whom you don't even know—they're just rich. *Polyester* was financed by New Line Cinema, which distributes all my other films. Michael White, who did *The Rocky Horror Picture Show,* liked the script, and I raised $50,000 from friends. The hard part is all the lawyers and the contracts. It was easier in the old days. The more money you have, the harder it is to make a movie, because you're trying to make it better and you're trying to do more things and there are more people involved, more equipment, more everything.

MacDonald: You talk about the films as comedies, which obviously they are. Are there comedians you particularly like?

Waters: I think Fran Lebowitz is funny, and I think the movie *Modern Romance* was funny. I think a lot of things are funny, but the things I find the funniest are the ones that aren't supposed to be funny, like *The Other Side of Midnight* and *Mahogany.*

MacDonald: Are you conscious of trying to visualize standard clichés?

Waters: I *love* clichés. They're in every one of my movies. Clichés obviously have something or they wouldn't have become clichés. I especially love a cliché that has something wrong with it: that makes a joke. Tab Hunter and Divine in *Polyester* running through the fields in slow motion is a cliché, but not exactly, because it's a three-hundred-pound drag queen and Tab Hunter.

MacDonald: With the way the camera is set up, at the end of *Female Trouble,* the viewing audience is, in a sense, part of Divine's audience; so she's attacking us, too.

Waters: I think if you were in a movie audience, you would love it if somebody in the audience got shot by one of the performers. You'd still be talking about it. As long as it wasn't *you.*

MacDonald: In that scene Divine is a lot like you as a filmmaker. People come "to be shot at" by you.

Waters: I agree with that.

MacDonald: Or to shoot at themselves. In *Polyester* the number 2 comes on and we *know* the smell, but we scratch and sniff the card we've been given anyway.

Waters: It's like that with the skunk, too. You see the skunk and then the number comes on and you think, "Oh, no!" But, it's like you paid to get in, so you go ahead and scratch. At least you know you have the choice: you don't *have* to scratch.

MacDonald: Why Divine in that box of fish? That part of her performance seems strange.

Waters: You know, I don't know. I think part of that was influenced by Russ Meyer. Vixen does a dance with fish in *Vixen.* And there's the negative cliché about whores smelling like fish.

MacDonald: Carolee Schneemann did a performance in the late sixties called *Meat Joy,* which involved rolling around with fish.

Waters: I remember that. Fish are just so weird looking. Divine and I used to do shows in California, and every time we would make a personal appearance, Divine would throw mackerels at the audience. Whenever we had a job, we said, "Just make sure there are three fresh mackerels in the dressing room." That was our star demand.

MacDonald: Did you perform?

Waters: No, I would come out and talk. Then I'd introduce Divine, and she'd come running out. It always worked for some reason.

MacDonald: In most of the films, and in *Female Trouble* and *Desperate Living* especially, women, or men enacting women, are the center of attention.

Waters: That's why some women say my films are a put-down of women, which I *totally* disagree with. I like aggressive women. I have a lot of friends who are aggressive women, and I get along with women very well. Dave Lochary died after we made *Female Trouble,* and I didn't know who I could replace him with, so I figured I'd make a movie with women, about lesbians. Gay papers really came down on me, and I thought, there are so many lesbians working on the movie!

MacDonald: Were you worried about making a film without Divine?

Waters: Well, in a way it was a challenge. Divine was going to do it. It wasn't like we had some big fight or something, which everybody thought. Divine was doing this play and had a contract. So, no, I wasn't nervous about that. I was nervous because that was the first movie we made with an outsider—Liz Renay. I didn't know how she would fit in; the same with Tab Hunter, though I wasn't that nervous about Tab.

MacDonald: How did you come across Liz Renay?

Waters: I read her book, *My Face for the World to See,* and I just couldn't believe it; it's hysterical.

MacDonald: In *Desperate Living* and in the other films, did you tell people to exaggerate their acting?

Waters: Oh, I always encourage hamism. A lot of people complained that there was so much screeching in that movie, but that's how desperate people talk.

MacDonald: In the early films—*Multiple Maniacs,* for instance—the gross stuff is horrendous; in *Desperate Living* it tends to be much more simple. The effect is weird; it's like being grossed out by very ordinary things because they're in a context where you'd never expect them. In *Desperate*

Living, when I saw Mole walk out and clear her nostril, I was really shaken.

Waters: Well, I got that idea from seeing people do that on the street. It offends me, too—I can't believe people have the *nerve* to do that.

MacDonald: I've wondered whether you're offended by those things or whether you're . . .

Waters: I'm not for snot liberation, if that's what you mean. When I do college lectures, the students that pick me up always say, "Oh, we've got this sleazy terrible place." I don't want to go to those places. Take me to the Ritz! These things are my fantasies for films, but they're not my fantasies for my life!

Also, a lot of people assume that all the people in my films are like the characters. They're nothing like them. They lead fairly normal lives. In a film something can be funny when in real life it isn't. I think a perfect example is in *Polyester* when the trick-or-treaters come and kill somebody because they don't have an apple. I think people will laugh at that; I've seen them laugh at it. But in real life you wouldn't laugh at it, not if somebody did it to you. I like to see violence in movies, but I have no desire to see a snuff film. Why is something funny in a movie but horrible in real life? I'm not sure I know.

MacDonald: You're very open about the processes involved in making the films, but even after reading *Shock Value,* I know relatively little about you as a person.

Waters: Right. I have to keep something private. I would never reveal the private lives of people I work with. Everybody in the book read the book, and I told them, "If there's anything you object to, I'll take it out." Who wants to dig up the dirt about their friends to make money off it? When I read Shelley Winters's book, I was so embarrassed for her. Do you know what I mean? I respect the people I work with and my own privacy.

MacDonald: Often you seem to admire people who do the opposite of that.

Waters: Right. I admire murderers, but I'm not a murderer. Because I admire something doesn't mean I have to emulate it. I don't think there's any shock value in our personal lives, anyway: they'd be boring to read about.

MacDonald: What about your interest in the personal lives of people you go to trials to see?

Waters: Well, they have become public figures. If I was arrested for murder, I guess everything would have to come out.

MacDonald: You are a public figure.

Waters: I'm not a public figure about my personal life. Generally when people ask me personal questions—they don't very often—I say I've tried everything but necrophilia and coprophagia, and I like kissing best.

MacDonald: Most Hollywood films seem to aim for one very simple, very specific reaction. In your films the viewer laughs and gags simultaneously. Because of that I think it's more complicated to talk about your films than about most narrative films.

Waters: I love shock value, but when I'm walking down the street, I'm not thinking, "Boy, I hope I see a wreck!" It's just that if something out of the ordinary happens, it gives me something to talk about with my friends. That's why when I hear assassination news, I have very mixed feelings. I call everybody and there's an adrenaline rush, you know. I'm not glad the person was shot, but I have no control over it, so I might as well be a ghoul. I think everybody is, but nobody admits it. They wouldn't show Reagan getting shot, over and over, in slow motion and from every angle, unless people liked watching it. I mean, if they'd sold tickets to Jonestown, they could have sold it out. I hate television. I can't stand watching it. The only time it's fun to watch is when the pope's shot or something. I mean that's what it's for—national emergencies. If I could have a good time watching television, I would, but I sit and frown when I'm watching it. TV never makes me laugh. I'm against free entertainment; I think you should have to go out to see something. That's part of the ritual of it. I think video itself is ugly. If you're home, you should read.

MacDonald: But you say your goal is simply to make people laugh. TV seems to make people laugh.

Waters: Not the kind of people I care about! And I want to make them laugh in a theater, not in their houses. It's just too easy to turn on the television. You don't ever think with it on. If you watch TV all the time, you might as well be a heroin addict; it's the same thing. You make an effort to go see a movie. In the theater you have to watch the movie to know what's happening; with television you can talk on the phone, you can eat, you can read, you can do anything. Another thing I have against television is what it does to people's behavior in movie theaters. Now when I go to a movie, people just sit there and talk like they're watching in their living rooms.

MacDonald: I found *Polyester* weaker in terms of its impact than the four films that preceded it.

Waters: Right.

MacDonald: There's much less gross humor. The Divine character is a whiner and a wimp.

Waters: I didn't want to make the same movie again. I was getting bored, and I figured if *I* was, the audiences were certainly going to be. And I wanted to be able to reach a wider audience, not because I want to make a million dollars, but because I want to infect them. I saw *Polyester* with a much wider audience in Baltimore, where it did incredibly well with people who had never come to my films before. They're as appalled as people were with *Pink Flamingos*. I think it's reverse snobbism to keep making films for the same audience. But I hardly think it was that safe a bet—making a movie with Tab Hunter and a three-hundred-pound drag queen and Odorama and trying to make it go with a mass market. Originally it was not the idea to open it at fifty theaters, but the theater chains saw it and they all wanted it, so we figured, why not take the gamble? The reason I'm trying to reach more people is because I want to keep making movies, and I want them to look better. Some people say, "I miss that it's technically bad." Well, I think that's ludicrous.

I suppose the only way I have left to really shock anybody is to make a kids' movie. Which I might do.

MacDonald: Was Odorama part of the original idea?

Waters: Yeah. It's just another joke. I knew it from the two Smell-o-vision movies, *The Scent of Mystery* and another one. It never worked: they had to send these big machines around to the theaters, and they couldn't get the smells out of the air conditioning. But I liked the idea. Odorama is the same kind of gimmick as eating shit was. People remember it; they take the card with them. I think the movie would play fine without it, but the first time I saw an audience of five hundred people scratching the cards, I couldn't believe it. I was like the doctor in the movie: "It works! It actually works!" I'm always trying to think of ways to get people to come see my movies. I don't care whether they like them or not, but I want them to come.

MacDonald: How did Divine feel about playing this kind of role?

Waters: I think it would've been a real mistake for Divine to play the same role again. He'll end up as Charo if he does the same thing over and over. At first he was nervous because he depended so much on that shock kind of thing; he was so used to that, knew how to do that. But I think once he got into it he liked it because it was a challenge. I think he's real good; he's gotten good reviews. Many people who have not seen the other films have no idea it's a man. When it was over, we told the man who mixed the movie, and he said, "I am stunned."

I had no idea how critics would react to this film, and all the critics in Baltimore who always hated my films liked it. *Time* liked it. *Newsweek* liked it. *People* liked it! The house record for an opening week at the theater in Baltimore was $9,000; we did $18,000. The second week we did $20,000, which means that it got great word of mouth. There were families. There were old people, black people, a totally different kind of audience for me. But I want to reach those people. Nobody made me do this movie. It wasn't like a producer said, "You can't have this"; it's the movie I wanted to make from the beginning. I felt that with *Desperate Living* and when I wrote my book, I closed one chapter in my life. I love that chapter, but I want to do something different.

MacDonald: How did you come across Tab Hunter?

Waters: Oh, I always liked him. He was my idea of the perfect movie star. I called him up and I said, "I have this script." I sent it to him and he said he loved it. He said, "Let me wear burgundy polyester." I said, "I've got to tell you, your leading lady's a man," and he said "So what!" He was real nice to work with and just laughed about the whole thing. He got along very well with Divine and I was thrilled. I thought it was kind of a coup to get him.

MacDonald: The man who plays the husband is very good, too.

Waters: The last thing that he had done was Dr. Dolittle in a dinner theater. He's nothing like that character in real life, but he had fun playing a pig.

MacDonald: Are you working on a new film?

Waters: I've been traveling with *Polyester* for three months. I'm going to start writing soon. I want to do a film with Divine as triplets. You know, have scenes where they talk and everything. My production manager said he's going to quit if I do that.

MacDonald: You did some of that in *Female Trouble*.

Waters: Yeah, but not a whole movie. The germ for the new plot is just festering right now. The disease hasn't struck.

Bruce Conner

Bruce Conner is one of the anomalies of the American cinema. He is a distinguished avant-garde filmmaker who doesn't make psychodramas, trance films, structural films, diaries, or experimental narratives. His output is tiny—on the average, less than one short film a year—yet his name is nearly inevitable on any list of major avant-garde figures. He rarely shoots his own footage, choosing instead to collect and combine bits of old science films, TV advertisements, whatever, using only the simplest equipment, yet no one seems able to imitate him successfully. Conner uses unmanipulated, often well-known pieces of music for sound tracks, yet his editing transforms the conjunction of image and sound into an entirely new form; it is always as though the music were written for the film. His films are absolutely distinctive, yet his range is broad. Most memorable, perhaps, are the Bosch-like vision of modern progress in *A Movie* (1958), the rollicking rhythmic intensity of *Cosmic Ray* (1962), the complex social commentary on the Kennedy assassination in *Report* (1963–67), the outrageously funny juxtaposition of Biblical narrative and Bob Dylan's "Rainy Day Women #12 & 35" in *Permian Strata* (1969), the heart-rending contemplation of Marilyn Monroe in *Marilyn Times Five* (1969–73), the stunned fascination with the atom's explosive force in *Crossroads* (1976), the haunting dreaminess of *Take the 5:10 to Dreamland* (1976), the nostalgic portrait of the American Midwest in *Valse Triste* (1977), and, most recently, the foreboding humor about American social conventions and militarism in *Mongoloid* (1978) and *America Is Waiting* (1981). But whatever the subject or the mood of particular films, the driving force in Conner's work seems to me to be an ecstasy that is generated by his being able to recycle even the most banal commercial and industrial film imagery into new works that are not only dense and sophisticated but also accessible to almost any viewer.

I talked with Conner, who is also an accomplished sculptor and graphic artist, in August 1981. Conner had stipulated in advance that he wanted to confine the interview to recent films, but our discussion ranged back and forth from recent to earlier work.

MacDonald: I hadn't realized until recently that you're a sculptor and a painter as well as a filmmaker.

Conner: Some people think of me as a filmmaker and don't know me as someone who does sculpture, and there are people who are familiar with my drawings, but have no idea that I've done collages.

MacDonald: When the American Federation of Arts "History of the American Avant-Garde" programs were first shown in the seventies, I remember reading a review by Andrew Sarris in which he said that if *A Movie* is an example of the best avant-garde comedy, then the avant-garde is in terrible shape.

Conner: People who have seen that program or rented it have told me that it takes all the joy out of the films. Of course, that's basically what's happened during the last ten years anyway—all these film classes, film courses, people getting masters and Ph.D.'s in making movies. When I started making movies, there weren't any film classes. Now people are learning to despise Maya Deren because they *have* to look at her films. I think the thing I dislike most is that filmmaking has been coopted by the education industry. But I don't know why Sarris felt he should take anybody at their word that *A Movie* was supposed to be a comedy.

MacDonald: When I was looking at your films this summer, it struck me more and more that to reduce them to comedy or to political statements is to miss the point. They strike me as being about rhythms. There are funny moments and politically suggestive moments, but the amalgam of music and image is so tight that the films are almost like objects. They create experiences that I find very hard to turn into statements about what this means or what that's about.

Conner: I'm reluctant to try to typify any of my films either. People seem to use categories because of the form that film reviews or commentaries take. When I talk about films, I usually talk about the process I went through making them, things that happened before or after, or the way they affect other people. I think of screenings as part of the process. Each time a film shows, it's a unique event because there's a different setting and circumstances and the audience is different. Just changing the volume control from treble to bass changes the whole character of how the sound relates to the picture.

MacDonald: Your films are often very dense, which makes what you're saying especially true. When I first saw *Mongoloid,* I looked at it one way, but with repeated viewings I've come to see more and more of the imagery. Each viewing tends to foreground different elements of what's there.

Conner: Well, I try to make films that have a character that can be conveyed in one viewing. Hopefully, there are other things that work on the viewer the second time, the third time, the fifth time. Most of my films are very short. If you blink too much, you miss most of the movie. Many of the people who seem attracted to my films are people who have had the opportunity to see them more than once. I do try to check out what happens with an audience when they look at the films. Of course, it's gotten to the point where the filmmaker practically has to go along with the films for them to be shown. If you don't come in person, many places won't show your films.

MacDonald: Have you assumed that people would look at your films on a rewind, as well as watch them projected?

Conner: I look at them on the rewind.

MacDonald: There's a very dense passage about two-thirds of the way through *Mongoloid.* It took me a day to note down all the little one-frame, two-frame, three-frame bits of material. I couldn't believe how much happened in thirty seconds.

Conner: I don't necessarily intend that you see everything that's going on. If I made films with the idea that people were going to look at them on a rewind, I wouldn't have much of an audience. Sometimes it's just the rush of images that's important.

Part of the creation of the sequence you're thinking about happened during the process of collecting film. I snip out small parts of films and collect them on a larger reel. Sometimes when I tail-end one bit of the film onto another, I'll find a relationship that I would have never thought about consciously— because it doesn't create a logical continuity, or it doesn't fit my concept of how to edit a film.

Mongoloid was made two or three years ago, but a lot of the material in it is ten or fifteen years old. Some of the sequences were in their present order on the reel of films I had collected.

MacDonald: When you're making a film, do you find that certain groups of images are coming together and then decide on a piece of music that will work with them, or does the music come first?

Conner: It works every which way. Sometimes the music comes first, sometimes the music appears while I'm working on a film, and sometimes the music's added later. One piece of music may become dominant, or in some instances music is written as a collaboration while the film is being composed. Right now, I feel kind of fed up with it. I have *America Is Waiting* and another

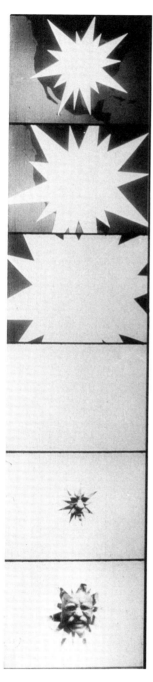

Frame sequence from Conner's America Is Waiting *(1981).*

film that I've worked on with music by David Byrne and Brian Eno. They're both good films, but I've had to rework the soundtracks. The quality and character of sound in 16mm is such a problem.

I did try working with some sound tracks when I went to Film in the Cities in St. Paul, Minnesota. I played around with a Steenbeck [a motorized flatbed editing table that is particularly helpful in editing sound and image efficiently], but it seemed far too easy, like I could turn out movie after movie with it. I use a very primitive process that I developed myself, which I'm sure film students would never aspire to as a way to make movies.

MacDonald: Your films *feel* handcrafted.

Conner: They're a little bit folksy, and they can fall apart too.

MacDonald: You mentioned that music had been composed for some of the films. Patrick Gleeson composed the music for *Crossroads*. . .

Conner: The first part. He did *5 : 10 to Dreamland* as well; he had made the music and thought it would work for me, and while I was listening to it the first time, I started to envision imagery to go with it. The music seemed like a dream and, immediately after I heard it, I described some of the scenes I was thinking about. I said, "Let's play it again and see how long it is." It was 5 minutes and 10 seconds, and Patrick said, "Take the 5:10 to Dreamland." (I had told him about seeing dreamlike images appearing and disappearing.) So the main catalyst for that film was the music. I had been collecting the images for years and had no idea what to do with them.

Sometimes it seems a mystery to me what images should be in a film. I collect all kinds, and then I can't understand why I thought I would want to use them. Sometimes I'll be editing, and I'll throw away a strip of film only to find—if I can retrieve it from the wastebasket—that it's the image that makes the whole movie work. Sometimes one image is required to pull everything together; sometimes I can't finish a film because I don't have that one missing key.

MacDonald: Where do you find what you use?

Conner: I've gathered a lot of film footage from educational films. People have given me footage. I don't really care to collect any more. Since about 1965 color has taken over, and I don't use color film, so, stylistically and subject-wise, I'm virtually locked into making "period pieces." There's a stylistic character to films made before then. A lot of the material I use could have been photographed by the same cameraman; particularly in educational films there's a format, a style, that is not a personal style. After the sixties commercial filmmakers were influenced by independents and decided to let their personalities show in the camerawork and direction. Generally I find that useless for my purposes.

MacDonald: Do you avoid color because color film degenerates so quickly?

Conner: No. There are enormous jumps in the color from one color film to another. If I'm cutting from one shot to another and I want to imply a continuous space, it's harder to do if the sky in the background is blue in one shot and pink in another. Even skin color changes enormously. In black and white you can imply that a figure walking down a road is the same person who walks through the door of a house, even though the scenes may be from two different films—you're not distracted by the color. Your attention moves in the direction of the action. If somebody's wearing a dark jacket in one image and a dark sweater in the next, it's easier to disguise the difference and convey a continuity. But if in one image it's a dark blue jacket and in the next it's a maroon sweater, the disparity is emphasized. I try to make separate things become one.

MacDonald: Both *Take the 5:10 to Dreamland* and *Valse Triste* are sepia-toned. Did that have to do with conveying a nostalgic feeling?

Conner: It was a gratuitous addition. When Patrick made his soundtrack for *Take the 5:10 to Dreamland,* he used birdcalls, which, for some reason, didn't sound like birdcalls when they were transferred onto an optical sound-track. They were distorted noises. The best we could do was make an electro-print sound track [a film printing system used on the West Coast that shortens the usual process of making prints: a print with an optical track (standard American movie projectors have optical sound) is generated directly from mag film (16mm film with a magnetic track), eliminating the usual intermediary step of making an optical master from the mag film and then generating optical prints from the master.] Everytime a new print was made, therefore, we had to make a direct copy from the magnetic soundtrack. Color film gave the sharpest, clearest sound. Since black-and-white film hardly ever looks like black and white when it's transferred onto color, tinting was necessary. It seemed to me that the appropriate color was sepia, but I wouldn't have thought about making a sepia-toned print if that situation hadn't occurred. *Valse Triste* seems an extension of *Take the 5:10 to Dreamland.* I chose to make it sepia-toned, too, even though it didn't have the same sound problems. The two films go together as a pair.

MacDonald: They're edited very differently. In *Take the 5:10 to Dream-land* we see a series of disparate, rather static, images. *Valse Triste* is also very quiet, but in a number of sequences you choreograph movement through a series of images. *Take the 5:10 to Dreamland* is one of the quietest films I've ever seen; it tends to put me into a state of being half awake, or half asleep.

Conner: That's my intention. I was trying to deal with that state without making a totally boring film. I don't know if you run into many filmmakers who are concerned with whether or not they're boring their audience. It seems to me that a number of established filmmakers don't take boredom into consideration; they expect the audience to make quite a few steps up to them.

Valse Triste and *Mongoloid* were the last films I made before *America Is Waiting.* They have entirely different audiences, as far as I can see. *Mongoloid* is popular with younger crowds—the people who are putting on film society programs. It's rented a lot but doesn't get much commentary in writing. *Valse Triste* gets more commentary in writing; it's shown in film festivals and purchased for audiovisual collections. It seems popular with people my age. It's a nostalgic treatment of their own childhood. Recently a review about it in *Film Comment* said it was the best film at the New York Film Festival, including all the feature films.[1] The reviewer was my age. Often the audience for *Valse Triste* doesn't see any humor in *Mongoloid,* and the people who are interested in *Mongoloid* couldn't care less about *Valse Triste.*

MacDonald: I have a nine-year-old and an eleven-year-old, and when I was looking at *Mongoloid* this summer, they would come running whenever they heard a note of the soundtrack. They would ask over and over, "When are you going to show *Mongoloid* again?" I wasn't sure why they were so taken with it, but they couldn't stay away.

Conner: It's got a lot of funny stuff in it. It think it's a fascinating movie for kids, but I'm not sure how many kids are going to be allowed to look at it. As far as I know, it's not on kiddie programs at museums.

MacDonald: Something that's struck me about your films, and *America Is Waiting* certainly adds to this, has to do with advertising. Everybody knows the power and subtlety of advertising, yet it's studied very little. Your films are some of the few I know that are as dense as ads. Obviously they're not selling anything, but, like ads, they hit you on many levels at once. The similarity seems clearest to me in the subtleties of rhythm. What do you feel about that kind of media manipulation? Is it something that you've been particularly conscious of and have learned from?

Conner: Cosmic Ray and *Looking for Mushrooms* [1965] used to get rented by advertising agencies. . .

MacDonald: Cosmic Ray was the first film that made me conscious of the similarity.

Conner: So in a way, I might be guilty of some of that tendency in ads to get as much information as possible into a short period of time. I'm aware of the way that people are manipulated by television advertising, so much so that I can't stand to watch the stuff. My wife and son seem to be oblivious; they find it difficult to understand why I don't want to watch television. I destroyed my TV set two years ago. I only got another set a couple of months ago—except now we're using it as a movie center. We rent videotapes of movies instead of going out to a theater. An hour of commercial television is just about all I can take. It's not just the manipulation in the commercials; it's the manipulation in the programming itself that gets to me.

MacDonald: I read recently that by the age of twenty-one the average American has seen something like 350,000 ads. What seems incredible is that

1. Elliott Stein, *"Valse Triste," Film Comment,* vol. 14, no. 6 (Nov.–Dec. 1978), p. 56.

America's younger generation in Conner's America Is Waiting *(1981).*

despite seeing all these little films, we develop almost no film education from the experience.

Conner: It's affected the way that people make movies. When I was a kid going to movies in the 1940s, I'd see scenes where somebody walks in the door, explains why they are in the room, and so on. Then they walk out of the room. It was very theatrical. Now people take it for granted that you'll make a jump cut from one place to another. I don't think it necessarily represents an independent development in filmmaking style; I think it has a lot to do with television. When people turn the dial, they jump from the middle of a love story into a commercial into a coming attractions into something else.

In between the commercials they're selling products, too. Most of it's nasty and aggressive, and I take it as a personal assault. I couldn't kill my TV set just by kicking it; I had to use a hammer. That's dangerous. Electricity is stored inside TV sets, so even when they're unplugged, there's enough power to electrocute you. I was watching the news. It started out with President Carter obviously lying, followed by the secretary of state lying, with even less attempt to cover up. This was followed by a national television anchorman expanding the lie, and that was followed by our local commentator. . . . By then I'd kicked the thing off the stand.

I couldn't get my wife and my son to stop watching TV. I found it particu-larly insulting when I was in the next room working on a film to have this television set in the other room perpetually throwing out garbage while my own films haven't been shown on television after all these years! And the only way the TV people have ever approached me is to say, "We'll be pleased to show your films for free and make you famous." Famous enough to do television commercials, I guess.

MacDonald: Another thing that the new films make me wonder about is whether you've studied music—you're very attuned to the subtleties of the music you use. When you decide to use a specific piece of music—"America Is Waiting" or "Mongoloid," for example—have you studied it for awhile?

Conner: I haven't had a formal music education. My attitude towards music education is pretty much like my attitude towards most other art or film education. I never believed those little black dots meant music, so I never learned to read music, though I can decipher it a little if I put my mind to it. But I listen to music quite a bit, and I play around with the piano. Back in 1959 or 1960, I performed with Terry Riley and LaMonte Young and other musicians who were doing experimental music events. I performed in a John Cage piece for amplified toy pianos. The only requisite for being a performer was that you had to own a toy piano. They had charts. I was standing next to a fairly well-known experimental composer who was moving his chart around and doing all sorts of calculations. I never quite understood what the relationship was between that chart and the music, but I managed to play my piano, and it sounded just right.

I do listen to the music that's used in my movies many times, and often I use music that I've known for a long time—*The Pines of Rome* by Respighi, *Sketches of Spain* by Miles Davis, Ray Charles's "What'd I Say?" I usually start by timing the music with a stopwatch. Then I time individual phrases, and once it's transferred onto magnetic film, I can time it exactly, frame for frame. I worked with magnetic film for the first time on *Crossroads.*

MacDonald: In some of the films, it's as though you're a visual percussionist playing with the other musicians. I noticed that especially with *Cosmic Ray.*

Conner: In 1967 I gave up filmmaking because I was working on a light show at the Avalon Ballroom. There were about seven of us—Lenny Silverberg, Howard Fox, and Ben Van Meter are the names I remember. We had overhead projectors and slide projectors, strobe lights and 8mm projectors, 16mm projectors, film loops, and a 180° screen. We projected images every night for live jazz and rock. After a while I couldn't see myself spending six months editing a five-minute movie that would end up being shown in a place where everybody had to sit still and look at a little rectangle. From 1967 until 1976 I made only two films: *Permian Strata* and *Marilyn Times Five.* But, yes, I'm very interested in music. I listen maybe five or six hours a day. I have a familiarity with the different historical periods of classical music, plus ethnic musics from around the world and the different developments in jazz, rock, and blues.

MacDonald: By the way, is that really Marilyn Monroe in *Marilyn Times Five?*

Conner: Well, I understand that it may not be. I tell people that while it may or may not have been Marilyn Monroe in the original footage, it's her now. Part of what that film is about is the roles people play, and I think it fits either way. It's her image and her persona.

MacDonald: What else did you do in that gap between 1967 and 1976?

Conner: I did an enormous number of drawings. I gave advice to other filmmakers. I would find locations for people who were shooting in Los Angeles and in San Francisco. Dennis Hopper asked me to help with *Easy Rider.* I worked on *The Hired Hand* with Peter Fonda for awhile. I gave Dennis an enormous amount of advice on *The Last Movie;* most of it was designed to keep him from making the film too obscure. I thought it could be a better movie and at the same time be commercial, but he was intent on making an "artistic" movie.

MacDonald: The films you made once you started to make films again seem very different from your early work, which involves syncopation and a barrage of imagery.

Conner: The character of some of the earlier films was economically determined. I couldn't afford to buy editing equipment, processing, and all that sort of thing. I had an enormous amount of time to spend editing, so I edited the hell out of them. My early films were unique. Nobody was making films like *Cosmic Ray* with lots of fast editing and jump cuts. Later I figured that I had done that; I was tired of it.

MacDonald: I was talking to Robert Nelson recently, and he talked about how impressed he was by your work when he was starting out and how he was strongly influenced by you. I can't think of early filmmakers whose work is particularly like yours. Were there people who had a lot of influence on you, or did the films grow mostly out of collage work?

Conner: A Movie started from seeing *Duck Soup.* There's a war going on, and the Marx brothers are surrounded in a farm house. Groucho says, "We need help," and all of a sudden you see soldiers and airplanes and dolphins and giraffes and everything else running to help them. I saw that movie when I was sixteen.

For a long time, also, I was involved in film societies. It was difficult to see experimental films or surrealist films or silent films or foreign films except in that context. Now the independent film societies have disappeared. I think the main reason is that government funding has put money into nonprofit organizations that show films at museums and colleges where the programmers don't pay attention to the audience. They destroy the audience. The Cinémathèque has programs where five people show up. You can't pay for film rentals that way; you can't build an audience. Independent films are ending up as just teaching tools for film classes.

And "coming attractions" influenced me. It seemed so extreme that people would accept them on their own terms mainly because they were throwaways, unimportant. If you take the point of view that "coming attractions" are not a throwaway, that they are intended to be seen exactly the way they are, you find there's an emotional purpose and context to the way they're made. There might be a scene of Barbara Stanwyck yelling at a man, "I hate you! I hate you! I hate you!" and she'd slap him, and the next shot would be a train going off a cliff. You'd see that kind of combination of images every week at the movie theater. So to me it seemed perfectly natural.

I made my first movie the way I did because of economics. I wanted to make a movie and I couldn't afford a movie camera. I started fabricating a movie in my mind in the early fifties; it would have scenes from *King Kong* and Marlene Dietrich movies, all sorts of things, combined with soundtracks. It was just a fantasy. When I started making movies, I found out how difficult it was to get your hands on anything like that, how expensive it turns out to be. So I gathered a lot of the movies that were sold at a local film supply store. I had no idea then that *A Movie* was going to turn out the way it did. I just started putting pieces of film together and running them on the projector. I'd turn on the radio and whatever was on was assumed and accepted as the sound track. One time it was *The Pines of Rome,* which coincided with what is now the last two or three minutes of *A Movie,* and I decided to use it.

Anyway, the economics of it was that I could buy a 16mm hundred-foot silent condensation of a Hopalong Cassidy movie, about two-and-a-half minutes long, for $3.00. If I shot that much film and had it processed and printed, it would cost $12.00 or $13.00. I bought condensations of films that I knew had action. Of course, that something was condensed down to one hundred feet meant it had all the most visual material in the first place.

MacDonald: You've recently collected your individual films onto reels for distribution.

Conner: There's a collection of eight films, a collection of seven films, and a collection of six films. I organized them so that all of my movies would be available in one of those three contexts. When I program my films, I put the shorter pieces that have rock-and-roll sound tracks first. Then I move into something longer—*Report* or *A Movie* or *Marilyn Times Five.* By that time, the mood has changed. I always conclude those reels with *Take the 5:10 to Dreamland* and *Valse Triste.* It's mainly a matter of pacing. If I started out with *5:10 to Dreamland,* I think there'd be uneasiness and moving around and coughing and commenting on the film. I find the most difficult reception for my films is when they're stuck on a program with other people's films— sandwiched between a George Kuchar film and somebody else's.

MacDonald: When I was looking at *Crossroads,* it seemed less edited than almost any of the other films.

Conner: Well, it has twenty-six different shots.

MacDonald: It's all of the same explosion?

Conner: Yes, viewed from different places.

MacDonald: Would I be right in assuming that what drew you to the explosion was not so much the literal meaning of nuclear warheads as the fact that they release tremendous forces in a very visible way?

Conner: It's just fascinating footage. I saw a lot of it when I was thirteen. At that time I thought I would see even more of it in the future, but it turns out that people are not really allowed to see very much of it. I waited to see the footage again, but nobody brought it out. One reason I make a movie is that if I don't, I won't get to see it.

MacDonald: Where did you get the footage?

Conner: The National Archives. You could make *Crossroads.* It's copyrighted, but I think I only own the splices. The copyright is mainly to protect the musicians.

MacDonald: You mentioned being tired of saving footage. Are you thinking of shooting new material, or of giving up film altogether, or . . .

Conner: No, I'm not planning to shoot my own footage. I'm not sure if I'm going to make movies or not. Movies are a rich man's toy. I can sit here and cut out pictures for collages, or get a pencil and a piece of paper and do a drawing. Even a three-minute movie may end up costing thousands by the time prints are made. David Byrne and I expected that the record company would want to use *America Is Waiting* as a promotional film. They didn't. Their lawyers said that they could be sued by the people who own the pictures that I used for the film. But even if they were going to use it, they wouldn't pay me anything because they only make promotional films for music that is already a hit—to make it a bigger hit. They don't invest money in any promotional film except in-house productions. If a musician or a group sponsors a promotional film, the company will distribute it, but they won't pay anything for it, and they won't charge anyone for using it. One of the reasons I wanted to do *America Is Waiting* was that it seemed possible to finance another film like it, which turned out not to be true.

MacDonald: Are there filmmakers working now who you admire or learn from?

Conner: There've always been lots of filmmakers whose work I've liked. But I don't go to movies anymore. I don't particularly like going out to movie theaters. I think I've seen enough movies. I've bought some videotapes. I've got *Citizen Kane, Frankenstein, King Kong, Duck Soup, Animal Crackers, Night at the Opera, The Man Who Knew Too Much* . . .

MacDonald: The early one or the more recent?

Conner: The early one. Disney cartoons. There are a few others I'd like to get my hands on: the 1930s Buck Rogers serials. In my 16mm collection I've got lots of movies by Stan Brakhage. I've got a bunch of his 8mm films. I've got one Shirley Clarke movie—*Bridges-Go-Round*. I have two films by Dean Stockwell. I have some educational films, some early Flash Gordon serials, a Buck Rogers serial, about five or six Laurel and Hardy comedies, Buster Keaton, Charlie Chaplin, some very odd 1940s musical interlude movies. And Betty Boop cartoons. I love Betty Boop. I don't know if that answers your question or not. I like old movies. I don't think I like new movies very much at all.

Robert Nelson

In one sense, Robert Nelson's films seem very diverse; they reject conventional film expectations in a wide range of ways. *Plastic Haircut* (1963), *Oh Dem Watermelons* (1965), and *Confessions of a Black Mother Succuba* (1965) are anarchic comedies reminiscent of the surrealist film avant-garde of the 1920s. *The Great Blondino* (1967) is a symbolic dreamlike picaresque narrative. *The Awful Backlash* (1967) is a fourteen-minute single-shot meditative film. *Bleu Shut* (1970) has serialist, formal dimensions related to Frampton's *Zorns Lemma* and Murphy's *Print Generation*. *Suite California Stops and Passes: Part 1* (1976) and *Part 2* (1978) are a portrait of California with diary and landscape elements. But regardless of their differences, the most interesting Nelson films share an enthusiastic, deeply felt humor that seems to be a function of Nelson's assumption that if the collaborative process of filmmaking is pleasurable enough, the energy generated by the process will fuel the resulting films.

Early in his career, Nelson collaborated with friends and colleagues in the San Francisco art scene: with composer Steve Reich on *Plastic Haircut, Oh Dem Watermelons,* and *Thick Pucker* (1965); with William Allan on *The Awful Backlash* and *War is Hell* (1968); with the San Francisco Mime Troupe on *Oh Dem Watermelons* and *King Ubu* (1963); with painter William T. Wiley on *Plastic Haircut, The Great Blondino, The Off-Handed Jape* (1967), *Bleu Shut,* and *Deep Westurn* (1974); and in more recent years with students and colleagues at University of Wisconsin–Milwaukee on *How To Get Out of a Burning House* (1979), and *Hamlet Act* (1982). The most interesting of the results are indices of the pleasure Nelson and his collaborators took in being together to make these films. Nelson's work implicitly critiques both the conventionalized rhetorical structures of commercial cinema (a form of stylistic "seriousness" necessary to maintain an audience large enough to sustain cost-intensive film production) and the metaphysical angst and formal solemnity of some critical films. For Nelson, making film art seems to imply a commitment to open expression of the joy of life, and especially the joy of making films—even when the films include serious themes.

Oh Dem Watermelons is Nelson's most memorable early film. It begins with an annoying, nearly two-minute shot of a watermelon positioned on grass as if it were a football set up for a kickoff. Finally, a foot kicks off the watermelon/football and, with it, the film: we hear "Follow the bouncing watermelon" as a chorus launches into "Oh Dem Watermelons," a send-up of Stephen Foster songs and of the racism in some of them. A cut-out watermelon helps us follow the words, which are printed on the bottom of the image, though after a while the watermelon flies out of control.

During the remainder of the film we watch the Mime Troupe do just about anything one can imagine with watermelons: they are thrown off roofs, trampled, shot, smashed by construction machinery, used erotically by a naked woman, and disemboweled. After "Oh Dem Watermelons" has been sung, *watermelon* is sung over and over, like a chant. Various details in the film make clear that the watermelon is a symbol for racist stereotypes—such as the watermelon-eating Negro—but instead of polemicizing about the issue of race, *Oh Dem Watermelons* seems to suggest that a first step in dealing with racial denigration is for all of us to have a good laugh at the idiocies we sometimes find our society and ourselves participating in.

While *The Great Blondino* includes a good bit of humor, the raucous comedy of *Oh Dem Watermelons* is less evident. The film refers to Blondin, the nineteenth-century magician and acrobat whose trips across Niagara Falls on a tightrope became legendary. In *The Great Blondino* the Blondin figure pushing a wheelbarrow through San Francisco becomes a symbolic individualist moving through a pop landscape, following his own intuitions, a figure suggestive of Nelson himself: as Blondino explores the Bay Area, Nelson explores a wide range of filmic materials, processes, and perspectival conventions. In fact, *The Great Blondino* can be seen as Nelson's first major attempt to come to terms with his new status as celebrity filmmaker artist. Nelson was establishing himself as a filmmaker just as San Francisco was being transformed by influences from the Orient and by a variety of American political developments. Blondin seems to represent Nelson, a person moving through this strange new world, working to maintain his balance on a celluloid tightrope.

The Awful Backlash is simultaneously one of Nelson's simplest films and one of his most suggestive. The camera is mounted so that we can see, in close, a fishing reel that, at the beginning of the film, seems impossibly tangled. During fourteen minutes of continuous shooting we see William Allan's hands slowly, carefully untangle the reel and roll up the freed line.

William Allan's hands untangle an impossibly tangled fishing reel in Nelson's The Awful Backlash *(1967)*.

Soon after Allan is finished, the film ends. *The Awful Backlash* was an outgrowth of Nelson's friendship with Allan and, on one level, is a document of Allan's skill as a fisherman. But it is also a filmic meditation on patience and on the nature of the film experience. While the "backlash" of the title is primarily a reference to the tangled fishing line, it also suggests a stylistic backlash on Nelson's part: a moment of serenity after the exuberant miscellany of his thirteen previous films. And it predicts (with implicit good humor) the reaction of some viewers.

Nelson has always been open to the work of other filmmakers. The wild montage-collage of *Confessions of a Black Mother Succuba* is indebted to Bruce Conner's films, as *The Awful Backlash* is—at least in a general sense— to Andy Warhol's experiments with film time and real time. *Bleu Shut* reveals that Nelson was in tune with the developments that led to what came to be called structural film. *Bleu Shut* is organized according to a series of grids: imagery is presented within numbered, minute-long segments (a tiny clock with a minute and second hand is continually visible in the upper right corner of the frame). After a brief, quirky prologue, a woman's voice (Dorothy Wiley) announces a game and other upcoming events. The game begins with a photograph of a boat (apparently taken from a magazine) and, superimposed, a series of what we assume are boat names. On the sound track we hear two voices (Nelson and William T. Wiley) discussing which of the names is the correct one for the boat we see. At the end of the minute, a buzzer sounds, and the "correct" name is revealed and the emcee and the two contestants discuss the outcome for a few seconds. The remainder of this second minute is footage of blues musicians. During the rest of the film we see eleven more boat pictures and sets of names; after each post-buzzer discussion we see a different kind of filler: a looped image of a dog barking and unbarking, a bit of an old silent porn film with ludicrous new intertitles, a brief montage of footage from several classics. The film concludes by returning to the kinds of imagery seen in the prologue. Nelson's bizarre conglomeration of imagery, the amusing conversations between the emcee and the contestants (only in *The Off-Handed Jape* is Nelson and Wiley's pleasure in each other's company as infectious), and the wit of the boat names—all of which were invented by Nelson—make *Bleu Shut* a remarkable experience. And when one realizes that the entire game is a ruse—is "bleu shut," "bull shit" (see Nelson's comments on the film in the following interview)—one is face to face with the power of language and of certain ways of structuring time and "information."

If Nelson's early films reveal an exuberant, light-hearted confidence, the series of strange, largely unmemorable films Nelson made in the years after *Bleu Shut*—such as *King David* (1970), *Worldly Woman* (1973), *Rest in Pieces 74* (1974)—suggest that he had become troubled. Even the most enjoyable of the films of this period, *Deep Westurn* (1974), is a form of gallows humor occasioned by the death of a popular San Francisco art patron. To a degree, Nelson pulls out of this troubled period with his longest film, *Suite California Stops and Passes: Part 1* and *Part 2*, an expansive, rambling, often diaristic work, divided geographically. *Part 1* centers on southern California: it includes a mock foreign-film border intrigue filmed at the U.S.–Mexico border, an automobile trip through and out of Death Valley, a long single-shot record of a line of people waiting to see *The Godfather*, a visit to Will Rogers' home, and, at the end, diverse bits of found and photographed footage. *Part 2* centers on central California, particularly on San Francisco and the Sierra Nevada: it begins with archival footage of the old Sutro Baths and the original Cliff House and with home-movie footage of a Christmas pageant Nelson's daughter is in, followed by more home-movie footage of the Nelson family at Christmas, a passage about the Golden Gate Bridge, panoramas of San Francisco from one of the hills, montages of old home-movie footage of the Nelson children, and (in "Fourth Movement: Deer Hunt") a remarkable passage for which Nelson reedited old home movies of various deer hunts in the Sierra Nevada into a single beautiful, nostalgic hunting trip. *Suite California Stops and Passes* is sometimes lovely and inventive, sometimes humdrum, often melancholy. It communicates something of the feel of California, of the size and diversity of the state, and of the personal history of a man who has lived there and loved it for much of his life.

Since finishing *Suite California Stops and Passes: Part 2*, Nelson has completed one student film and an unusual adaptation of a portion of *Hamlet: Hamlet Act.*

I talked with Nelson for the first time in August 1981 in San Francisco. In April 1982 we recorded a second conversation in Utica, and during the fall of 1982 and the winter of 1983, we exchanged voice tapes, filling out our discussion of the films. Our original interview (*Afterimage,* summer 1983 and October 1983) included more extended discussions, especially of recent films.

MacDonald: I know very little about the art scene in the mid-sixties in California, but I've always assumed *Plastic Haircut, Oh Dem Watermelons,* and *Confessions of a Black Mother Succuba* were tied to things going on there.

Nelson: Definitely. I came on the art scene in San Francisco in about 1956 or 1957, when I went to the San Francisco Art Institute to take a painting course. I'd already graduated from college as an art major, but I'd never really connected to an art scene. The Art Institute (then called the California School of Fine Arts) was very energetic, and the students were doing exciting work. I think some of it came down through Clyfford Still, who had carried the torch from New York. The whole scene was really cookin'. I got excited about it and became a painter and a beatnik.

San Francisco had always been the center of interesting activities, but at that point, the Zen Center was established, with Suzuki Roshi. The literary scene, the beatniks, Lawrence Ferlinghetti, and City Lights Bookstore—all that was in San Francisco. The city was being validated as an art center in a larger context than anybody had felt before, though a few older artists from around the area were already recognized: Diebenkorn, for one, and Parks, and Bishoff.

So going back to your question, I'd say that everybody knew something was going on, but nobody I knew imagined what would actually happen in the sixties explosion. Haight-Ashbury, the neighborhood I'd spent my life in, was an ordinary neighborhood in the fifties. The drugs and the Age of Aquarius and the flower children and the love generation transformed it before my eyes. But many of the people who were already in the art scene, who were just a little bit older, kept some distance. They'd already formed their own alternate lifestyles. To the extent that their lives overlapped with what was happening in the mid-sixties, they were a part of it, but they were already there when it exploded. The hippies didn't have an art scene because they didn't make a distinction between art and everything else in life. Wait, that's too flip . . . psychedelic art—poster art and all the rest—did have a lot of influence.

Anyway by the time 1963 came around and I was shooting *Plastic Haircut,* I'd already spent several years as an aspiring painter, had had a couple shows, and so on. *Plastic Haircut* was made before the Haight-Ashbury explosion, but after the San Francisco Mime Troupe had been formed by Ron Davis. They were living in poverty conditions but had great energy and zeal for their theater activities. They'd set up headquarters in an abandoned church in the Mission District. Their *Ubu Roi,* with costumes by Bill Wiley, set some kind of high water mark for me. Their pieces sometimes played to fifteen or twenty-five people, but the people who went knew they'd been to a play. Boy, did they know it! And they liked it, too.

So Ron Davis and Wiley and Bob Hudson (a friend of Wiley's and mine, a well-known sculptor at this point) and I decided to make a movie. I'd seen a few avant-garde films, so I already knew you could do anything you wanted. John Collier, Jr., a neighbor of mine and friend of many of the local artists, had offered to loan me a camera, which meant all the ingredients were there. For me the primary ingredient was a kind of comradeship. The three of us had a great good time shooting *Plastic Haircut.* I had 2,000 feet of film after we shot it, and it looked very poor—only because it was so repetitious and long; the individual shots looked good. I struggled with the footage for weeks. No matter what I did, it seemed boring. In desperation I started cutting the shots shorter and shorter, and when I saw the energy that put into the film, I had my first real revelation about cutting.

I should mention Steve Reich here. I believe he was driving a cab at that time. I immediately enjoyed who he was; he did a sound track for *Plastic Haircut.* It was the first tape piece he ever did. At that point I didn't know how to do a mix once the quarter-inch stuff was transferred. Not being smart enough to know how to seek the solution, I put the film together in a way that put Steve's track over the black leader, not the image. I've been disappointed ever since. I was a completely untrained filmmaker then. I'd never gone to any filmmaking classes. I just had the good fortune of knowing somebody who had a camera and offered to loan it to me.

MacDonald: *Plastic Haircut* reminds me of Méliès; it's frontal.

Nelson: That was primarily because of the space we were in. I think *Plastic Haircut* was unconsciously influenced a little by *Un Chien Andalou.* I was trying to look at films that were interesting but looked uncomplex enough technically that you could imagine yourself doing them. Bruce Conner's *Cosmic Ray* and *A Movie* were very innovative, I thought.

MacDonald: One image from *Cosmic Ray* is in *Confessions of a Black Mother Succuba.*

Nelson: Well, I was so struck by Conner's work at that point that I had to resist copying it. But I would cop out. That's one of the reasons I don't show *Confessions,* although I still like it in a lot of ways. I think I'm going to re-edit it one of these days. Conner's were the first independent films that really made me say, "Yeah!" You could see that they were made for a few bucks, which was the first definite proof to me that something I could connect with as a filmmaker could be done outside of Hollywood.

MacDonald: Had you seen any of Sidney Peterson's films? There are things in your early films that seem reminiscent of *The Cage* and some of his other work.

Nelson: I saw *The Cage* and Peterson's other films somewhere around that time and definitely liked them, but I had already made four or five films. Peterson made his films at the Art Institute, too. I don't know what vibes came through the locality, but I can see the connection in sensibility. The only other films I was really interested in at that point were Hollywood films and European films—in other words, theatrical movies.

The strongest influences on my own work have generally been through my closest friends. I've had plenty of teachers and plenty of influences—too many to name, actually. I've also learned a few things by just following my nose.

MacDonald: There's an exuberance about your first three films, and especially *Oh Dem Watermelons.* They suggest a filmmaker who's just getting into film and wants to try everything for the pleasure of it.

Nelson: The artists I knew at that time felt pretty genuinely that if the process got too heavy or ponderous or worried, if you weren't having a good time at least part of the time, something was wrong. We were bent on having a good time.

MacDonald: Oh Dem Watermelons is usually considered a send-up of racist stereotypes. I wonder if you felt this at the time. If I didn't know what context that film came out of, it would be hard to tell which side of the issue it was on. I showed it to a class not long ago and a black woman got very offended. She felt that it was an instance of the stereotypes rather than an attack on them. I had the same feeling about the way women appear in *Black Mother Succuba,* but several women I showed it to surprised me. . . .

Nelson: They thought it was OK. Well, I don't think my attitudes were all that pure. In the last few years I've been taught a lot about my sexist ideas, but I've never been a terrible sexist because I had a mother who was a powerhouse. I don't take women for granted. That's not a great thing on my part; it's just an accident of birth.

I probably felt that *Oh Dem Watermelons* was an instance of stereotypes, but of stereotypes that were already passé, repressed. Racism is usually repressed, and for most people the only way the stereotypes are let off is through jokes and carefully shared innuendoes. Blacks with watermelons was already a little too gross for public consumption in mixed company in an art form, but when the boys were having a drink at the bar it wasn't too gross by any means.

My view was that stereotypes in themselves can't say anything: they obscure rather than reveal. To present them blatantly, in a context that made them confrontational, seemed to me a way of being bold and daring (which I didn't mind doing at that particular time) *and* a way of creating a lure for racist projections. I can understand people getting upset, but the film is about being on a razor line. Because you can't add all the images together into a conclusive point of view, the film becomes what you project into it. I'd never have chosen to stand up on my own and be a spokesman on racism. But it was offered to me as an opportunity, and I thought it was a good opportunity.

Ron Davis was and is a very active political person. That's how the San Francisco Mime Troupe got going as street theater. He and Saul Landau were making *A Minstrel Show* (*Civil Rights from the Cracker Barrel*) was the subtitle), which was designed to be a shocking confrontation of racial issues. For that time it *was* shocking. It was based on the old-time format of minstrel shows, with song-and-dance men playing the banjo and wearing blackface. The updated version would confront people with the racism inherent in our culture.

Right after *Plastic Haircut* was finished, or around then, Bill Graham, the film entrepreneur, who had recently emigrated to California from New York City, had become the Mime Troupe's business manager. He was in charge of the general hustle. Meanwhile rock and roll was developing. I met Jerry Garcia and Phil Lesh, who were then in a band called the Warlocks—later to become the Grateful Dead. A benefit was put on for the Mime Troupe. They hoped to be able to make five hundred bucks, at $2.00 a head I think it was. As I remember, the Warlocks played, maybe the Jefferson Airplane or Marty Balin, too—I can't remember for sure. Anyway, it turned out to be the first total mob scene I saw in San Francisco. There must have been two or three thousand people. It was a stunning, overwhelming success, packed body to body with people in some kind of strange new ecstatic frenzy. Very shortly thereafter, competing with one or two other hustlers who had seen the writing on the wall, Graham had the Fillmore Auditorium, which had been standing dark. Overnight that whole scene was born. From my point of view, it was almost instantaneous. Old icons were tumbling and floating downstream; other gods were disappearing over the horizon. It was an astounding continual shock, and people came—young people, bigger crowds, still bigger crowds— all dancing in the streets and taking acid and being transformed by it.

Ron asked if I would make a short intermission piece for *A Minstrel Show*. All I knew was that the show was about blacks and whites. The deal was that they'd pay all the costs.

I had the idea of using watermelons and a general idea of the approach. Saul Landau, Ron Davis, and I met once or twice, and both of them, especially Landau, fed ideas into the scheme of the movie. We shot it in a couple of weekends. The theme of black-white race relations was inherent in the assignment. I couldn't, or wouldn't—I don't know what the difference is—make some kind of diatribe on the subject of race. The only thing I could imagine doing was making something that would be shocking in how it would meet the issue, but fundamentally ambiguous. The film demonstrated the forbidden and didn't say anything about it afterwards, which I think is what I can praise about it.

A bouncing watermelon leads the audience in song, in Nelson's Oh Dem Watermelons
(1965).

Then Steve Reich came through with a great sound track.

MacDonald: Did you show *Oh Dem Watermelons* a lot when it first came
out, other than in connection with *A Minstrel Show?*

Nelson: Oh yeah! It was a big hit! It won a prize at Ann Arbor and was
shown all over the place. It even had a couple of theater runs.

MacDonald: I'm struck by how early some aspects of it are: that long take
of the watermelon at the beginning, for instance. The idea of sustaining a shot
for a long time came to be very common, but this was 1965. I assume you
were trying to structure the film in ways that would be a shock to standard
pacing.

Nelson: I was trying to drop standard limits from my imagination, to be
alert to when I would say to myself, "Well, it should be this way." I tried to
think structurally, like I would about a painting. You spend ten years struggling with blank canvas, trying to learn how to approach *this* blank canvas or
paper or whatever—how to make a mark and what to do subsequently. For me
it was part of the same practice. I imagined that that long take of the watermelon would build up such a tension that when the movie finally got going, it
would be like a release—you'd just roll downhill to the end. Maybe the idea
of a long shot was somewhat daring, but it wasn't new. *Oh Dem Watermelons*
is really a primitively made film. Almost every inch of footage that was shot is
in the finished film.

A couple of times I've seen black people upset with *Oh Dem Watermelons,* and many times I've seen people wondering, "What was *that* about?" But then, on the other hand, one of the best compliments I ever had (and not too long ago) was after I had seen Peter Kubelka's *Unsere Afrikareise* again. I was stunned by how it held up and what a beautiful film it was and the editing mastery of it and the power of its indictment of these Austrian business bureaucrat pigs, whoever they were. I was talking to somebody after the film and I said that it was, at that moment, the only powerful political statement from the avant-garde film scene I could think of. (I don't mean to say that there are not political implications in many films, but I meant a film that vivifies what some perhaps already know and what others may not already know.) And this person said, "There's one other: *Oh Dem Watermelons.*" I was surprised, pleased, and grateful.

MacDonald: What contact with black people did you have prior to making *Oh Dem Watermelons?*

Nelson: When I was in high school, I became very interested in blacks and black culture. Blacks seemed to have a maximum of what I most wished I had: I was not cool as a teenager, and I wanted to be cool. I came from an ethnic family, very collective people who hung out together, and I wanted desperately to get away from that. The most attractive and scary thing in the world around me was "blackness." By the time I was sixteen years old, I was a fan of Sugar Ray Robinson, and I drew a picture of him defeating Tommy Bell: Bell is collapsing and Robinson still looks good, having just backed off. It's a pretty good drawing.

A few years later I was an encyclopedia salesman. We sold almost exclusively to poor people in housing projects. I was too innocent to know I was preying on anybody. I was just trying to get into what was going on. For me it was a great treat to be able to go into thousands of homes and make friends with people in about two minutes. And if you had to sell them something, that was just part of the big con that was going on anyway, or so I thought. So I spent a lot of time in dank and sometimes swank and sometimes funky and sometimes fuzzy apartments, sometimes with single people and sometimes with couples and often families and sometimes with more than one family, and sometimes in steamy kitchens and sometimes in apartments where it seemed like the windows had never been opened—just talking to lots and lots of folks.

When I was growing up, the Fillmore district was the black hot spot of town, the place where you didn't dare go. But there I was, climbing through the casbah of the Fillmore district, through apartments behind apartments, back down through alleys and up another set of stairs, with people crawling around everywhere. It was like being in Turkey or Marrakesh. I loved it.

Also, before that time and during that time, I was listening to soul music, to the stations way down at the end of the dial. I went to black bars sometimes, and I liked the challenge of that environment. I had some awareness of racism, and was confronting it in myself and in others. I was very interested in how the negative projections worked, but on a personal level I was involved in an idealization of blackness.

But actually, now that I think about it, it all started much earlier. When I was five years old, I started listening to the Joe Louis fights on radio. My dad and I would sit in the kitchen. It was the only time my mother had to tiptoe around in our house. I can still remember all the way back to the Carnera fight (1935) and the Max Baer fight, and details from both Schmeling fights and on up through Louis's whole career. You could say Joe Louis was a watermelon seed for me.

MacDonald: Two other films from 1967 that seem very early in terms of what they're doing formally are *The Awful Backlash* and *Hot Leatherette.* By the way, what is "hot leatherette"? What's "plastic haircut"?

Nelson: A lot of my titles are absurdist. I think "Plastic Haircut" was Wiley's idea. Some titles you recognize as correct immediately. "Hot Leatherette" is a reference to cars, leatherette being an upholstery material.

MacDonald: I love *The Awful Backlash.* It's obviously a document of somebody untangling a fishing line, though ironically that was the second thing I thought about. When I first saw it, I had already gotten interested in a particular group of films, often made by filmmakers early in their careers. Each film uses a single continuous shot (or the illusion of one) from a single camera position. Larry Gottheim's *Fog Line* and *Blues,* J. J. Murphy's *Highway Landscape,* and Hollis Frampton's *Lemon* can serve as examples. In almost every case, the subject being photographed becomes a metaphor for some aspect or aspects of the film process itself. *The Awful Backlash* is the earliest of these films I know of. When the line is untangled, the film ends: its "line" has been untangled and rolled onto the take-up reel.

Nelson: The original idea was primarily Allan's, and I immediately liked it. He's an expert at everything regarding fishing, because he's been doing it all his life. He's good at untangling a backlash, and he also knew how to make a tremendous one. We've gone salmon fishing together a couple times. From the beginning the idea was that the film would be real time: he'd keep untangling until he got it all cleaned up and that would be it. We just mounted the camera and got the focus set. You can think metaphorically about the film in all kinds of ways. That openness was appealing to me.

I'm going to put another sound track on it.

MacDonald: I was just going to ask you about the sound. It's put together in a way that makes the viewer aware that it's faked. When you move back and forth between your mumbling and the sound of the reel, the seam is very noticeable.

Nelson: A lot of the elements in those early films are there because I didn't know any other way to do things. I still don't know that much, but I know a lot more than I did then.

MacDonald: What are you going to do for a new sound track?

Nelson: I don't know. That's one of the films in the pile I want to work on.

MacDonald: I don't often hear anybody talking about changing their old films.

Nelson: The fact that no one else does it doesn't bother me a bit. I can see real simple ways to improve many of those films, so why not?

MacDonald: In the early years were you and Gunvor collaborators?

Nelson: When I met Gunvor, we were both art students. I had never had any direction. She knew she wanted to be an artist—meaning primarily a painter, I guess—from the time she was twelve. She was a much more developed artist than I was at that point.

MacDonald: You met her when?

Nelson: In 1955 or '56 I think; we were married in 1958. We were both painting students when we met. Later we lived in Spain for a year, had a good year there painting. Then we came back to the U.S. and built a house and kept painting on the side. We also made a film together for her parents about building the house. We made another film about a year later (1961, I think), when we were in the house. That was an edited film, mostly camera edited, and scripted. We were making a parody of *Last Year at Marienbad,* called *Last Week at Oona's Bath.* Primarily it was Oona, who was under a year old, and quite a bit of Gunvor and some of me. We took turns using the camera. After that, I started getting more interested in film. By the time I made *Oh Dem Watermelons,* I was sailing on film. Then Gunvor got together with Dorothy Wiley, and they made *Schmeerguntz* (1966). It's a knockout. And that's her first film! I mean it goes way past *Plastic Haircut.* And she's been cranking them out ever since. But as it turned out, Gunvor and I never worked together on films after those first two.

MacDonald: I've read that *The Off-Handed Jape* was shot very quickly.

Nelson: Yeah, in a couple of hours. A couple of weeks later we did the sound track in an hour or so. We did two full takes, and I used some of each.

MacDonald: That film is often funny in an unusual way. What strikes me as funniest are the moments when the voices on the sound track are saying things to "Dr. Bird" or "Butch Babad" which they obviously can't hear. It's only funny because we know that the voices are in a totally different time and space. It's a two-cushion laugh: the two of you laugh about what you're saying about what you're seeing, and we laugh at, and with, you.

Nelson: Not many people even know about that film, but I like it too.

MacDonald: Grateful Dead was made on an optical printer?

Nelson: A homemade optical printer, the first one I knew of in San Francisco. It was built by a filmmaker named Lauren Sears. The Grateful Dead wanted a film as a warm-up, and they wanted the sound to be a piece out of their record. That's another film I want to rework: years ago Jerry Garcia gave me a great tape, an original piece of their music, which I'd much rather use.

MacDonald: The year 1967 was very productive for you. There's *The*

Awful Backlash, Hot Leatherette, Grateful Dead, The Off-Handed Jape, and
The Great Blondino.

Nelson: Oh Dem Watermelons got so much recognition—all of a sudden
five or six letters a day were coming in. I saw my name in *The Village Voice.*
It all seemed so easy that I got energized and made a whole bunch of films in
the next couple years, *Blondino* being the best of them, I think.

MacDonald: What led you to center the film around Blondin? When I first
saw it, I thought of Ferlinghetti's poetry; he uses an image of a high-wire artist
as a metaphor for the poet, the creative spirit.

Nelson: One of the things that has always been in my mind has been *not*
making a film that expresses a meaning that I could already express, but
instead to let the thing itself find out what it is. When we made *The Great
Blondino,* the only thing Wiley and I had agreed to do was to make a film.
Finally it got down to "OK, let's start Saturday." Then it was "I'll buy some
film, but what are we gonna film?" We knew we wanted to use some of the
objects and paintings in Wiley's studio, and while we were talking, he was
standing in front of a big painting he'd made of the Great Blondin crossing
Niagara Falls on a tightrope. If I remember right, I said, "We could make it
about a tightrope walker." I wasn't even serious, but Wiley took it seriously,
and then all of a sudden I took it seriously, and then Dorothy Wiley came in
and said, "I can make a suit like that," and I said, "OK, let's get Chuck [Bill
Wiley's brother] to be Blondin." So we had a character with a wheelbarrow—
Wiley made a wheelbarrow—and after that we'd just meet on weekends and
shoot whatever we could think of. There were only the vaguest ideas about
what might happen narratively. The structure or narrative or poetic framework
came in the editing.

MacDonald: How long did it take?

Nelson: I think we shot it in six or eight sessions. We'd work on weekends,
though as usual it wasn't really work. We had a good time. Lew Welch, Bill
and Chuck Wiley, and I would go all over town. Off camera we were usually
hysterical. It was wide open. We all knew each other well, and no one was too
precious about their ideas. Everyone could go, "Boo! Not that," without anyone's feelings being too hurt. No one was afraid to say—no matter how dumb
it might sound—"Let's do this!" One of the things that came up that way was
"OK, he's balancing on a tightrope; we'll have him fall." Then we thought,
"Let's have him get up." We figured we could use it anywhere in the film. The
rebirth implication is there, but it wasn't an idea we were going for.

It was almost a year before I finally edited it. I had no idea what to do.
I kept knowing I would get to it, and finally, still without knowing what to
do, I just dove in and started mixing the footage with TV outs and other material. As I was working on it, I could see a kind of story evolving, so I went
with that. After a while it seemed to be making itself, telling a story in some
crude episodic way.

Chuck Wiley as Blondino in The Great Blondino *(1967), co-made with William T. Wiley. Photo by Jack Fulton.*

MacDonald: War Is Hell seems almost a complete change from *The Great Blondino*.

Nelson: That film got made because a man came to San Francisco from New York with a Ford grant to get a bunch of artists to work in a TV studio to get the San Francisco art scene linked up with the media. The idea was that artists could use the facilities at KQED and make whatever they wanted. There were some poets, painters, and couple of filmmakers. I got invited, but I was just leaving for Europe and reluctantly turned it down. I asked Bill Allan if he was interested, and he got on the project. I was gone for almost a year, but when I came back the project was still going, so I hooked up with it again and started working with Bill. There was a big problem: the director was saying, "Anything goes." But in fact, unless it looked psychedelic, he didn't want it. This double-message situation put Allan and me into a reactionary frame of mind, and we began to think what might be the furthest thing imaginable from what this guy wanted. We came up with a black-and-white World War I narrative movie. We got into it and had a good time. The hospital scene was just hilarious when we were doing it. When we got the film back, we were startled: it looked like maybe we were trying to be serious.

MacDonald: I assumed that since you made it in 1970, it was an anti-war film.

Nelson: No, not at all. It's not pro-war either. I'd say it's more about romantic movies and also about art. The art part may be antiwar if you trace it far enough—but I wouldn't bet on it. Any fantasy that either of us had was supported by the other . . . we followed one another like the blind leading the blind.

MacDonald: Bleu Shut is a hard film to ask questions about. Is the naming game a device to hold it all together?

Nelson: The first thing I knew I wanted in the film was a clock. Before I even knew what film it was going to be, I thought it would be a half-hour long and that it would have a clock in the upper right-hand corner. That suggested segments in one- or two-minute lengths. And then I had this peyote experience in San Rafael. I was walking down by the yacht harbor watching boat salesmen taking families of people around the boats, as if they were housing tracts. Kids were whining, "Oh I don't like that one, Mommy, the one with the red kitchen is much better." These were people with absolutely no connection to boats or water—it was ludicrous. I had an enormous revulsion about it all, and I thought to myself that this shallow bullshit would someday have to be smeared out—boats jammed with conveniences just to make them salable to people like this! Later I could only look at the situation humorously. I couldn't use my condemnation to make a film—it's just not my way of expressing myself. Somehow it got connected to these ludicrous boat names. I made up all the names and set up a game. I got a bunch of objects from around the house and put them on a table, and I laid out each list of boat names face down. I'd turn one over and pick up an object—an ashtray, for example—and we'd talk about *that*. We didn't have the pictures of the boats yet. Then later I took pictures of boats out of yacht magazines. It seemed too long to go thirty minutes with just that idea, so it occurred to me to use the checkerboard arrangement and to include all this other material in a discontinuous way that would be like turning the channel on TV. TV is a reference, but the film is not centrally about TV.

MacDonald: It's also easy to deal with *Bleu Shut* as a satire of the educational process. When I showed it to a class recently, people had their notebooks out and were taking down the "correct" names of the boats.

Nelson: You can see a boat in a harbor and have one reaction to it, walk around and see the name and have a different reaction. The boat feels one way if it's called the *Mary Jane;* it feels another way if it's called *The Weekender*. It *looks* different. For me those names, and the kitsch mentality they reflect, are appealing and repulsive. Since you can feel both ways about them, there's an edge, and that edge appeals to me.

MacDonald: Because of the clock, there seems an implicit connection between school examination experiences and the film.

Nelson: The clock came out of my own arduous struggle to sit through a lot of independent movies. I often have a powerful urge to look back to see how much is left on the reel. When I succumb, the reel always looks *huge*! I put the clock up there so that no one would have to turn around.

MacDonald: King David, Worldly Woman, and *Rest in Pieces 74* feel like troubled films.

Nelson: After making all those films in the sixties, I went through a very difficult period. I was having what I guess is a somewhat conventional crisis. For those so afflicted, there's a point after some years where the meaningfulness of what you're doing disappears, and there's this desert that has to be crossed: you either continue somehow or you don't. What got you high before has evaporated; whatever energy was inspired by the medium itself is gone. Plus you don't want to repeat anything you've done. I felt very empty at that point.

MacDonald: Deep Westurn was made in 1974, during the same period, but it looks as though it could have been made seven years earlier.

Nelson: Deep Westurn was as easy to shoot as *Off-Handed Jape*. I see it as related to *Off-Handed Jape* partly because it's another collaboration with Wiley, although it's also a collaboration with Henderson. Henderson had the idea of the chairs and pushed getting the film made. Bill Geis—a sculptor—is the fourth guy in the film. We fell over on the chairs fifteen times or whatever. When we looked at the footage, the falling seemed a little too slow. I tried a jump cut to make the chairs fall faster, and it immediately picked up the energy, so I left the footage chronological and made a cut in the middle of each motion.

A boat and possible boat names, the "correct" boat name, and beans and weenies, from Bleu Shut *(1970).*

Do you know the background to *Deep Westurn*? There was a patron of the arts in the Bay area named Sam West. He'd pick unknown young artists and buy paintings and sculptures. He bought paintings from Wiley and Allan and Henderson, paintings and sculptures from Geis and from Hudson before anyone else knew about them. They've all had big careers since, but West's thing was to be in on it first. He got a whole house full of good artwork very cheap, and he made friends with all the artists. He was a hard-working dentist with a big practice, and a colorful guy. He had a taste for the bizarre, and he liked West Coast art. Sometimes he traded: Wiley's whole family had I don't know how many years of free dental work.

All of a sudden, to everybody's shock and surprise, he committed suicide. It was a combination of personal problems and health problems, I think, and it was a jolt. A party was held for him, at Bob Hudson's studio. Everybody had a good time—in West's honor. Sometime later, the Saturday came when we were getting together to make the film. The original idea had nothing to do with Dr. West, but the timing finally brought us there.

Another thing was that about a month earlier Henderson had gotten some quarter-inch plywood and sawed out some tombstones. He handed one to each of us and said, "Make your own tombstones." We decided to finish them before that Saturday. I was the only one desperate enough to put my full name on it, half hoping I'd be planted under it soon. So there we were: we had these tombstones, it was near the occasion of Sam West's death, and Henderson had the idea of falling over on the chairs. We just had a good time and did the movie. Wiley came up with the title "Deep Western" [deep West urn]. It encoded some of the information that was in all of our lives at that point.

MacDonald: I like the film, though I think it's important to know about West.

Nelson: Interesting maybe, but not important. The film should work without those specifics. The problem, it seems to me, with the kind of homemade movies we're talking about is that it takes years to know how to look at them. It takes maybe ten or fifteen years to know how to listen to jazz, for instance. Finding anything interesting in pocket-money movies is an acquired taste, and takes at least as long. You need a trained audience. You can't get a hundred people at the mall and show them independent films. Some are entertaining enough, but overall they're not that easily accessible. People have to submit themselves to the experience for quite some time to be able to drop their expectations about what movies are. They have to assume some responsibility as an audience.

When I say "they," I definitely don't mean to exclude myself. When I first saw independent films, I thought that just about all of them were garbage. Even now I dislike most of them. It took me many years of seeing Brakhage films before I could see *any*thing in any of them, and I mean *anything*. Now I think some of those same films are masterpieces. As I've gotten older, I've come to feel that I don't have to bring what I want for *my* films with me when I'm an audience.

If I were deprived equally of theatrical films and independent films for a long enough time, my hunger probably would be to see independent film. If you go to see an independent film, it may very well be, or even probably will be, like others you've seen. But the chance is there for a new experience, and when you get it, you prize it more. The illusion is that your relationship to it is more personal, more real. I think you feel that connection more in independent films because of their low-budget funkiness: the person behind the camera, the arrangements that were made to have the film happen are more evident. When the magic works, it's a bit more of a miracle.

MacDonald: People tend to miss the humor and the sensuousness of independent film. To me *Wavelength* seems at least as sensuous as it is intellectual.

Nelson: Well, it's also true that you've often got to sit with yourself for a while, and that's hard on people too.

MacDonald: Right, although nearly all films have slow moments. In *Wavelength* the action is so skeletal that the periodic references to traditional narrative—the women who come in and leave, the guy coming in and dying, and the discovery of the body—are pretty funny.

Nelson: Not only that, people are still talking about *Wavelength*—since 1968!

I admire Michael Snow as an artist and filmmaker. He's done as much as anybody I know in the whole film scene, and he continues to make really exquisite works. In general, though, I like expressionist pieces more than formalist pieces—reckless wild chance-taking more than intellectual control. Snow is the exception. So is Ernie Gehr, and there are lots of exceptions.

If a film is strictly formalist and very serious and seems to be addressed to filmmakers rather than to whoever wants to look at it—that bothers me. It often seems like somebody is admiring the art scene—or the *idea* of being a filmmaker—too much, rather than just thinking of film as a medium that can allow them to sing their song or see if they have a song to sing. Snow can do it because he never loses his sense of humor. And he stays in front of the pack. A new Snow film is a new experience.

Manuel DeLanda's *Raw Nerves* is interesting in that regard. The Lacanians are impressed because DeLanda's references to Lacanian psychoanalytic theory are correctly presented. Usually the theorists assume a superiority over the filmmaker because they can project and extract meanings the innocent, primitive filmmaker doesn't even know about. But DeLanda very specifically and deliberately signals that he knows exactly what he's doing. At the same time, the film has a lot of power and energy and is entertaining and funny—the elevator sequence, for example. It draws on enough things besides film theory that it's interesting even if you don't tune into that level. That's an achievement.

But finally, for me, it's humor that saves many of these works. If the vision is intense enough, anything is grist for the mill. Except for film theory. It's the only thing in the world that film *can't* feed on. The food of film theory is films. If filmmakers start going to film theory for what to do next, it's like they're eating their own caca.

MacDonald: Between 1970 and 1975 you made very little film. *Suite California Stops and Passes* came out in 1976 and 1978. Were you working toward that film for a long time?

Nelson: During that period I kept shooting a lot of stuff, but it didn't have any context. Finally I began to think of it as having something to do with California. Most of *Part 1* was shot after I had the idea; and then for *Part 2* I used a lot of old family footage.

MacDonald: The section in *Part 2* about the hunting trip is a knockout.

Nelson: Thanks. Some people hate that part—I've had some of the coldest audiences! On the other hand, when I showed it at Madison, I could feel that the audience was with it. It was just one of those nights. That was the first real good audience experience I had with that film. It doesn't have the kind of force *Watermelons* has. If you don't go with it, you can easily hate it. When I saw it at the Whitney, it seemed raw and hairy and rough, and sickeningly sentimental. In New York City its West Coast informalism was hard to sit through.

MacDonald: Part 2 is much more personal in terms of your own background.

Nelson: When I was making that home-movie footage, I never dreamed I would use it in any of my films. But once I got into the idea of *Suite California,* I began thinking of different kinds of history and their intersection.

MacDonald: They connect in interesting ways. The man at the beginning who worked on the Golden Gate Bridge . . .

Nelson: That's my father.

MacDonald: Oh yes? When we see him talk about the bridge with the bridge in the background, we're looking at a historical documentary. Later, when we see him in a home-movie context, it's hard to recognize him as the same person.

Suite California is such an unpretentious film. It seems right on the line between art and whatever it is that we do when we make snapshots and home-movies. To be somber about it, to intellectualize it, seems a little too heavy. Sometimes I get the feeling that for you the worst thing of all would be to be pretentious.

Nelson: I'm definitely not interested in passing along intellectual information about California. There's plenty of that everywhere. I'm trying to get at some feeling state.

MacDonald: What led to the making of *Hamlet Act*? It seems very different from your other work, more openly serious, academic. It's based on

Shakespeare and set in what is obviously a college drama context. It's less intimate, less wide-open than any previous film of yours that I can think of.

Nelson: As an independent filmmaker and artist, I *can* be very different. That's the freedom one has being outside of the commercial machinery. What I want is relative to the conditions I find myself in. I'm not interested in repeating myself. All the films are different. This is *more* different. It goes into the areas you mentioned—academe, Shakespeare, verbal narrative—where practically the whole dramatic content is in language. The approach is very different because the problems are different. On short notice I found myself team-teaching a class with Joe Chang, who'd written the script. I read it and liked it. Once I went for it, I just wanted to follow my nose.

I could never have imagined myself doing Shakespeare. But *that very thing* attracted me to the project, which is another similarity with many of my other films. If someone says, "How would you like to do Shakespeare," and I immediately guffaw and cough and say, "Of course not!"—I'm piqued in a very special way. I had the same kind of experience when I realized that for some reason I was absolutely refusing to consider the home-movie footage I used in *Suite California* as film material. As soon as I noticed that, I became interested in using the home movies.

When I first got to University of Wisconsin–Milwaukee, I often felt like a Swedish carpenter or something because I was so inarticulate, so informal in my thinking, relative to real scholars. Some artists don't want to know what they're thinking about; others do. We don't need artists to filter everything through some conceptual framework, through some giant intellect. It's like weight lifting. If you work out on your intellect, you can make a great big head. You can deal conceptually and structurally with language zap, zap, zap, and you can find the logical flaw anywhere. That can be interesting and good, but speaking for myself, I wouldn't want to give up real life for it.

When it comes to working on a painting or a film or anything, the intellect can sometimes give you a supplementary reason for what you're doing, but what you're really looking for is some kind of response where the film is speaking to you as you're working on it. That response is perceptible not through analysis but through immediacy. That's what I like about film, what I want to follow in film. After twenty years in film, it seems clearer to me than ever that if the thing is alive in some way through all the processes, you're not in control—you don't know what it's going to be. You might have intuitions or expectations, but what actually is happening is not totally in your control.

MacDonald: Some people do make films that they're really involved with but that they totally control.

Nelson: Kagemusha, the Kurosawa film, is a great epic film, and pretty much every millimeter seems controlled, but that's masterly, exquisite control. It's great storytelling. He has to be one of the greatest storytellers in the world, and I guess that takes enormous control. I like to work out of control most of the time, in that sense at least. The thing stays more alive for me. By the time it's finished, it's like discovery. My way of working is like jazz or improvisational music. Kurosawa's is like scored music. He makes the score—that's where his art is—and then he must have managerial and executive skills and communicative and inspiration skills to get all the technicians to do it exactly right. Technicians are the ones who need control. Artists are people. Sometimes they're technicians too . . . but the art part, where it all comes from, that's out of control.

Babette Mangolte

Babette Mangolte's contributions to recent independent filmmaking are of two kinds. She is best known as the accomplished cinematographer whose formally elegant camera work has been important for a number of the seminal films that critique commercial film rhetoric, in particular the highly determined rhetoric used to reflect and to construct our sense of gender difference: Yvonne Rainer's *Lives of Performers* (1972) and *Film About a Woman Who . . .* (1974), Chantal Akerman's *Jeanne Dielman, 23 quai du commerce, 1080 Bruxelles* (1975) and *News from Home* (1977), Jackie Raynal's *New York Story* (1979), Anthony McCall, Claire Pajaczkowska, Andrew Tyndall, and Jane Weinstock's *Sigmund Freud's Dora* (1979), and Sally Potter's *The Gold Diggers* (1983). Less well known is Mangolte's work as a filmmaker on four interesting feature films—*What Maisie Knew* (1975), *The Camera: Je,* or, *La Camera: I* (1977), *The Cold Eye (My Darling, Be Careful)* (1980) and *The Sky on Location* (1982)—the first three of which are sophisticated investigations of cinematic point of view.

What Maisie Knew is a fifty-eight minute, black-and-white mixture of formalism and narrative, in which James Barth, Jerry Bauman, John Erdman, Philip Glass, Epp Kotkas, Kate Manheim, Saskia Noordhoek-Hegt, Linda Patton, and Yvonne Rainer appear as characters in a series of sketches. Since their conversations are not presented to us and since we learn nothing about them in addition to what we see, we do not feel we know them in the usual narrative sense; we observe them, mostly at a country home, conversing, cooking, walking, running through a field, having sexual encounters, playing parlor games. The unusually low camera position draws attention to the point of view, especially when characters are apparently looking for Maisie. If one

Delphine Seyrig as Jeanne Dielman in Chantal Akerman's Jeanne Dielman, 23 quai du commerce, 1080 Bruxelles *(1975), camerawork by Babette Mangolte. Photo by Mangolte.*

knows the Henry James novel (*What Maisie Knew*) about a young girl's adjustment to her parents' divorce and to their involvements with a series of lovers (the novel is told in the third person, but entirely from Maisie's angle of view), one can at least tentatively identify the point-of-view character. And yet to assume simply that the activities are presented as seen by a young girl hiding around the house is to ignore a good deal of what the film shows us. Near the beginning, for example, we see a long, apparently single-shot image in which, at first, the screen is almost pure white. As the image slowly darkens—actually, fog is clearing—we are able to identify the space as a room. At one point we see what looks to be cigarette smoke entering the image from just outside it; later, a dog walks through, exiting into the foreground beneath the camera. A distant violin accompanies the imagery. It is a haunting passage, which functions primarily as a formalist moment: we become conscious of the camera as camera, doing things only a camera can do.

The pace of *What Maisie Knew* is often reminiscent of long structural films like Michael Snow's *Wavelength* (Mangolte shot a segment of Snow's "*Rameau's Nephew*" . . .). But her film's stunning romantic and erotic moments, its humor (especially when Rainer and Patton mime a series of adjectives beginning with *s: spooky, slinky, snoopy,* and so on), and its general look help to maintain the viewer's attention.

The Camera: Je presents several workdays in the life of a still photographer. The eighty-eight-minute film divides into several distinct sections, two of which are quite long. Again, we see all the action from a particular point of view, that of a still photographer we never see, though we feel her behind the camera. Approximately the first half of the film is devoted to a series of photo sessions in each of which a man or a woman (and in one instance, two men) pose for portraits. We see these sessions from the point of view of the still camera on its tripod, as though we are seeing what the photographer sees through the camera as she makes images. (Even when we hear Mangolte move away from the "still camera," this point of view is maintained, as though she is primarily conscious of how things will look in the finished photographs, no matter where she is in the room.) For the most part, the sitters look at the camera, and us, as they and we tensely await the loud clap of the shutter and the black frame used to simulate the exposure being made. The portrait sequence is followed by a long, hand-held, single-take, sync-sound shot during which Mangolte walks along Lower Manhattan streets until she reaches a particular building. A direct cut brings us inside, where another brief photo session is held: the photographer shoots one, then two men, who walk, then freeze, then walk across a large loft space in front of a background of gridlike windows. Later, she walks home through the now-dark streets.

During the second of the longer sequences, the photographer walks around Manhattan photographing buildings, streets, windows, and talking to herself as she works ("Relax . . . relax . . ."; "There! There!"). Throughout this passage, the camera is hand held—it sweeps this way, then that, looking for images to record. At the end of this passage, the photographer returns, burned out, to her apartment. During a short final sequence, she shows and discusses her recent work with a friend (John Erdman). We see proof sheets of outdoor shots and several large multiple-image photo-constructions that include some of the images we "saw" the photographer make during the portrait sessions.

The sense of a person working at art comes across powerfully in *The Camera: Je*. There's nothing at all of the photographer as romantic figure here; instead, we follow the exhausting, time-consuming procedure of pursuing images. In fact, what many viewers would probably consider the film's primary weakness—its tendency to repeat a limited number of activities for too long—is precisely the point: the inspiration for doing film or photographic art may be mysterious, but the exertion it necessitates is not—though one would never guess this from most presentations of artists working.

Although the autobiographical sources of *The Cold Eye (My Darling, Be Careful)* seem implied by the final title credit—"My darling, be careful/ (an education re-visited)"—Mangolte's third feature is the most overtly fictional film she's directed. Here, the action is presented consistently from the first-person camera's-eye view of a young painter, Cathy Digby, whose face and body we never see, though we do hear her voice (Kim Ginsberg). Though the structure and the formal means of *The Cold Eye* are almost minimal, the film develops considerable subtlety and complexity. For one thing, though we see all the action from Cathy's point of view, we do not always align with her.

In fact, I find nearly all the people Cathy talks with more interesting and pre-possessing than Cathy, whose constant self-questioning often seems as self-righteous as it is self-defeating. Further, our restriction to Cathy's point of view results in our having no "objective" standard against which we can measure the truth or value of what her interlocutors tell her or of what they say about each other. On first viewing, we do not know what Cathy will see next, and even once we have found out, we do not know if these events result in Cathy's changing her approach to art or life. What we do have is a sense of the difficulties—personal, social, and aesthetic—that any young artist must face.

In one important sense, Mangolte's first three features—and *The Cold Eye,* most clearly—suggest solutions to a dilemma that has troubled many film-makers: how can one portray a female protagonist without participating in conventions that offer the female image to the viewer as an eroticized object? By using the first person, Mangolte puts us in a position of identifying with female protagonists—or at least of seeing the world from their point of view—rather than gazing *at* them. We are intimate with these women, in a new way.

Mangolte's fourth feature is a lovely, easy-to-watch exploration of the landscape of the American West, much indebted (as the credits indicate) to Barbara Novak's *Nature and Culture* (New York: Oxford, 1980), an authoritative study of the Hudson River School of nineteenth-century American landscape painting.

Mangolte and I talked in September 1983.

MacDonald: When I finally got to see the films you've done since *What Maisie Knew,* I was very impressed—and amazed that I'd heard nothing about them.

Mangolte: It's partially because of me, but it's not just me. The distribution situation for independent film has changed quite a bit in the last few years. There are fewer outlets now, I think, and more competition than there used to be. When I finished *Maisie,* people wrote me letters and called me up. I did not have to do any work. The film was shown at the Whitney for two weeks, which helped a lot. John Hanhardt did not like *The Camera: Je,* my next film, but Larry Kardish did, so it was shown at the Modern. That's the only time it was ever shown, actually—except for French television. It was co-produced with money from French television. I really did not push to show *The Cold Eye* in New York. Actually, I did not even make an attempt. I was scared. I have great problems with *The Cold Eye.* I have great problems with all my films. The only one I really like is *The Camera: Je.* Also, *The Cold Eye* was not finished when I started *The Sky on Location*. I had gotten the money for *The Sky* from German television when I was still editing *The Cold Eye*. Between the preparation of one film and the finishing of the other I had two things going on together for six months. The work on *The Sky* was by far the most time consuming I have ever done on any film, and it cost more money, so I had to earn more to make up the difference. I'm still not quite recovered financially, or in terms of fatigue. So I have not done anything about the two films.

MacDonald: I find *Maisie* interesting as a demonstration of some of the voyeuristic aspects of film. Sometimes in the middle of an erotic scene or a scene that seems potentially erotic, a door closes in our face. We're simultaneously titillated and aware of our own voyeurism.

Mangolte: That's not at all the way I ever thought about the movie. Not at all. Basically everything in the film got there in a haphazard way. I kept shooting for about a two-year period, one weekend every six months or so. I had no idea where the film would go. There was just that central idea, given by the title—the little girl, Maisie, behind the camera. Originally my idea was to take five women I had worked with and who were friends of mine and make one ideal woman. That was the idea of the close-up camera movements on the parts of the body at the beginning. The legs are Kate's; the eyes are Yvonne's; the hands and arms are Saskia. Those were the best parts of their bodies, or some of the best anyway. The early shot of the fog inside the room, washing everything out and slowly disappearing was also done on the first shoot. I had a beautiful loft just at the corner of Duane and Greenwich. A certain light came in there in the late afternoons, and with the fog it was wonderful to see, but what was the meaning? By the way, I got the idea for the fog by going through a catalogue from Camera Mart. I paid $15.00 to rent the fog machine for a weekend.

When I looked at the footage I had collected, I thought, how can I bring some sense into it? I started with the fact that you do not have to have a complete progression of events to have a narrative line. Even if you have just bits and pieces of narrative elements, things will gel if you place them in a certain order. There is no real necessity for Kate to go into the garden and be dressed up by the man you see here and there on the edge of the frame. And Yvonne and Linda miming the meaning of adjectives starting with *s* has no real necessity either. It's just another game. And there are elements that are representations of moments in relationships: the couple walking together, kissing, and so on.

MacDonald: And the whole thing coheres, at least to a degree, because we're so trained to find narrative that we project a coherence onto these disparate fragments?

Mangolte: Exactly, exactly. I think there is no way an audience cannot see a film as a coherent whole. You can see it as messy, but you will always find a common factor to bind everything together. So that was the assumption I worked with. I did not really care about the details of what was seen. I just invented the action to fit the bodies and performing abilities of the people I used in the movie. That element of haphazardness, of chance, was part of the conversation going on around me in the early seventies. It's very much what Yvonne's dance group, Grand Union, was involved with.

MacDonald: What Maisie Knew reminds me of Rainer's *Lives of Performers* (1972), which was the first film you shot in this country. It too combines diverse subject matter and uses some of the same people.

Mangolte: Lives of Performers is a more original film. And it's more like scene after scene, each with its own structure and center. *Maisie* is a constant flow of haphazardness, which is really what I don't like about it now. To a degree *Maisie* is entertaining and pleasurable to watch. There are breathtaking moments, like that early shot with the fog, and what I call the slow kiss: Philip and Epp stay still and kiss for two minutes, thirty seconds (it was shot on a one-hundred-foot roll of film and I timed it), then slowly drop out of the frame. And I think the double-door shot is a great moment. But there are many other things I *don't* like. They're nice to see once, but they don't really have any weight.

MacDonald: Had you read a lot of film theory when you were working on that film?

Mangolte: Yes and no. I have friends who are film theorists, and I hear their conversation. But I'm not well cultivated in film criticism or film theory. I'm not interested in it. I used to be very interested in going to see film, and that's still the case, but for the last four or five years I've been working so much that I almost never have time. When I was doing *Maisie,* I was going to see every independent film showing in the city. I saw the cycle at the Archives [Anthology Film Archives] several times, and I was always going to the Modern to catch a film. When I was still living in France, before going to film school, I did one thing from 10 in the morning until midnight, for about two years: I looked at film. I'm a film buff basically, but not a film theorist at all. My insight that *Maisie* would work no matter what I did was an idea that can come to somebody who has been to so many films that what's on the screen no longer makes any difference; it's the film fact, the process of looking at film, that is your concern.

What I'm disturbed by in *Maisie* now is that it makes sense only if you look at it as a film about point of view and tactics of narrative. That was the way I conceived it. I was totally immersed in the formalism, the structuralist attitude of the period, and I'm certainly very grateful for it. But I'm not thinking about film in that way any more, at least for my own films.

Because of my work on other people's films as a cameraperson, I'm very trained in seeing things on a formal basis. That's the way I earn a living. But I have to disengage myself from that training to be able to work on a film that

The room with the fog, from Mangolte's What Maisie Knew *(1975). Photo by Mangolte.*

will be interesting to me or to write the scripts I want to write. And I'm looking for a viewer who likes new territories. I'm sure I've benefited greatly from
working with the people I've worked for as a cameraperson. I've gotten to see
what I like and what I don't like. Being a cameraperson has given me an ease
with the medium that other filmmakers don't have. I do pretty much everything in my own films, the camerawork and the editing—though I would
gladly relinquish the editing to somebody else. My experience gives me confidence that I can improvise when I'm on the set. I can make decisions quickly.
I don't have to get my ideas across to a cameraperson. That's comforting, and
I think I owe it to having been a cameraperson for filmmakers who have standards, who try to make above-average films. Had I worked on commercial
film or industrial film or advertisements or exploitation features, I think I
would have been totally blocked. I would have always been thinking only in
terms of effect.

 MacDonald: What is it about *The Camera: Je* that makes you like it better
than your other films?

 Mangolte: I think it's my most original film in terms of form. It's also
about my deeply felt involvement with still photography. But I think what
makes the film original is also its problem: the first part (the models sitting for
portraits) and the second part (shooting on the street in New York) ask the
viewer to interact in two different ways with what's presented. In general,

people get lost because of that shift. The shift to outdoor open spaces was meant as a release from the confinement of the portrait sittings. But the release is short-lived. From enclosure you go to the anxiety of multiple choices and total scatter. The sound in the city is particularly chaotic.

MacDonald: I had trouble with the second part. I assume it's about what it means to be a photographer and to try to figure out what to shoot.

Mangolte: It is, yes. The first part is about control, and the second is about impulse.

MacDonald: But I wasn't sure that I ever really deciphered what made one view the shot that was taken rather than another. In the first part that was a little clearer to me. I could understand more of what the photographer in the film (you) were trying to get and why you would shoot when you shot.

Mangolte: The first part is so much about the concentration involved in doing portraits. It's all very tightly knit together, and one of the reasons it could be was that each time I put in the black frame to simulate the shutter effect, I could cut. I shot much more of the models than you see, but because of that black frame I could cut inside a given shot. From a ten-minute scene I ended up having three or four minutes that seem to be continuous, real time, even though they aren't.

For the second part, when I go out into the city, I did not have that as an option because of the constant motion of the traffic and the passers-by and because of the camera movement—the camera never stops. So there was no way to remake filmic time, and the second part is looser because of that.

MacDonald: I noticed that every time the "shutter" interrupts the image, there's a moment immediately afterward where the image looks like a still photograph.

Mangolte: That's happening on purpose. I directed the actors to do it. It comes from my experience of taking still photographs. I never know for sure until I see a contact sheet whether I have taken good photographs. But in general I know when one is really going to hit the mark and be interesting, because right after that split second when you don't see—which is just the moment when the shutter is open and the picture is taken—you see an imprint like a still photograph. This is very subjective on my part. My experience with still photography is not at all doing faces, portraits; I've mostly done dance or theater work—photographs of people in motion basically, and sometimes in very fast motion. But I have always had the sense that even when I keep watching the dance movements, if I have just taken a good photograph, I see that image as a still.

MacDonald: The section between the two parts, where the people walk and then freeze in that room with the grid windows, is like Muybridge. The minute the people stop, the scene looks like a film of a still photograph. Everything flattens.

Mangolte: That's my homage to him, actually.

I like *The Camera: Je* because I think it succeeds in making visible an experience most people who are not still photographers have never had. It's more interesting than *The Cold Eye* or *Maisie,* which are too formal.

I didn't take myself seriously as a filmmaker until I shot *The Camera: Je.* I said to myself, "I'm a good cameraperson. I have no problem organizing people and things and making things occur, even with very little money. Now I have to express something." Like everybody else, I went directly to my most immediate experience. One subject I felt had not been really treated in film, at least not recently, is the process of work. That became the idea for *The Cold Eye* and *The Camera: Je.* I wanted to show the concentration one has in working.

MacDonald: That comes across very much in the pace of *The Camera: Je.* When you come back at the end of the film and say, "I'm burned out," the viewer thinks, "Me, too." It feels like a lot of work walking around the city making those images.

Mangolte: Also, I put that line there because I was in a shadow area and kept the camera rolling as we went into the sun: that part is overexposed by about three stops. The film is literally burned out. Sometimes I have this immature pleasure in literalness. It drives some people crazy. They think it's too self-indulgent, not serious and self-critical enough. I'm very much against self-criticism as part of the film content. It's too sixty-ish for me. What I think has been missing in film recently is what you found in classical cinema, what you find above all in Renoir and in John Ford, who are the two classical filmmakers I like the best: I'm talking about a trust, a belief. It's not there any more in a lot of independent cinema. I think it was there in the early Brakhage, and probably is still in Brakhage now. But it's not the case in the generation of independent filmmakers of the seventies, who are absolutely preoccupied by the necessity of being self-critical. Their work is often referential to other films, to film itself. They don't try to have a content that is outside the filmmaking process. They think they cannot be true to filmmaking if they don't constantly rethink the filmmaking process or something like that. The way this is expressed is very academic; it seems so flat; it's so uninteresting.

But that's not the only ground on which I object to that attitude. I think what bothers me in it is that films are generally an hour to an hour and a half long. And even that is a very short time to be able to have a discourse that is at the same time self-analytical *and* positive. I think that most of the work that uses tactics of disjunction in terms of sound and image and of discourse totally loses impact and credibility, because the films work much faster than your brain can work. The viewer just gets the surface of things, which don't sink in on an emotional level somehow. You are left with cynicism or in-jokes. I don't think I make films—thank god for me—in which the audience has time to really be critical of the film as they are seeing it. They just feel the fascination, the impact. Now impact is very strange. It can work negatively very strongly and positively very strongly—depending on who you are addressing. But it involves the fascination of somebody looking—not looking at *film*—looking in general, with intense concentration. Half the cognitive process is looking. It's that which is at stake I think, more than the fact of *film* technique or theory. I was interested in creating that fascination all through the seventies, but I'm changing now. Looking at film more and more on the TV screen, where the visual is singularly lacking, I think you can't any more conceive films as the ideal tool to simulate perception.

MacDonald: The sound in *The Camera: Je,* particularly in the first part, is very powerful. The shutter of the still camera sounds like a guillotine.

Mangolte: It's powerful because before it there's almost total silence. The shutter resonates in that very boomy room, and also I use many modulations of "silence." For the outdoor section, the shutter was recorded outdoors. I think the sound outdoors is very good, too. What I wanted to create—I don't know if it's perceivable by anybody but me—is that when the camera (and the photographer) turns 360°, the sound is changing. I have noticed the difference in sound even when I stand in one place and turn around. The sound has such perspective in the city, and it varies in relation to the size of the buildings and the width of the street. So I used these tiny differences in constructing the soundtrack, which was all done after the fact but recorded at the same place and at the same time of day that I had actually shot the pictures.

MacDonald: I like *The Cold Eye* best of all your films.

Mangolte: I don't know if I should be so negative, but there are many things I don't like in *The Cold Eye.* I produced the film on my own, and I didn't have much money, so I had to shoot very, very, very fast. I had to cut corners. I should have taken more time, in particular with the scene of Allan, which was shot in a weekend. We should have had at least four days. It's about forty-five minutes of the final film, and I never had time to do more than a second take, and not that much time to rehearse, and so on. The acting style ends up a bit haphazard; it varies a lot from one performer to another.

MacDonald: For me—at least in this film—the failures of the acting tend to work for the film. People don't talk perfectly when they speak to us, and we don't speak perfectly to them. The film reflects that, without seeming to try too hard at it.

Mangolte: I don't mean that the actors did a bad job. Actually, some of them did very well, considering that they're not movie actors. George Deem is not a performer at all; he's a painter. I used him because I thought he was visually fit for the part, and he brought himself to it, adding to the text, and so on. Some of what he says is not really understandable because the rhythm of the language is not there. I think that has to do with me not really being at ease in English. Not that I'm not fluent in English, but I speak with a very strong accent, and so I could not help the actors as much as I should have been able to. Saskia, who was the only professional actor in the lot, is pretty good, and

Illiana (Saskia Noordhoek-Hegt) talks to Cathy in Mangolte's The Cold Eye *(1980).*
Photo by Mangolte.

Ela and Jim did their own directing as far as voice was concerned. I directed
their facial expressions, positions, and things like that. But with Allan it didn't
work out as well as I would have liked. I failed there.

The film was written in such a way that I could not change the order of the
scenes, except for one: what is now the first scene, Cathy working alone in her
studio. Originally that was meant to be at the end of the film. The first scene
was to be Allan, but since that scene did not turn out so well, I was afraid I
wouldn't be able to convince the viewer that the camera was the point of view
of a specific person. I decided to impose Cathy's presence first, which was a
much better move as things worked out.

MacDonald: I can't think of any other feature-length film that stays consistently within the point of view of a character for the entire film. A lot of
people—Stan Brakhage, most obviously—have made films where the camera
is their eyes, or an approximation of them. But that's different from what you
do. Here we see from a fictional character's point of view.

Mangolte: There are examples in classical cinema: Robert Montgomery's
Lady in the Lake (1946), though there you see the point-of-view character in
reflections in mirrors. Originally I had a scene in which Cathy calls Allan, and
you see her reflection in the pay phone. I shot at least five or six takes. But it
did not work well.

290 A Critical Cinema

MacDonald: Another thing I think is really interesting about *The Cold Eye* is the way in which you capture what it must be like to function as an artist in Lower Manhattan.

Mangolte: Yes, I think it does document that pretty well.

MacDonald: There's a subtitle at the end, "an education re-visited," which implies that you see the film as having to do with what you went through when you were first in New York.

Mangolte: Very much so. The character of Illiana is based on a friend of mine who functioned for me a little bit like Illiana functions for Cathy.

MacDonald: I was thinking of Cathy's intense self-questioning about what an artist can do that's worth doing. I see the film as providing not only Cathy's point of view (in general, as well as in the literal sense), but a second, more fully accomplished point of view. Cathy may not be sure what's worth doing, and who she should learn from; but since the film itself *is* finished, it posits another person—the filmmaker—who has gone further than Cathy has yet been able to. It reminds me of Hemingway's "The Snows of Kilimanjaro," a story about a writer who didn't get his writing done, told by a writer who clearly did.

Mangolte: I don't personally identify with the film at all on that level. What is somewhat autobiographical in the film has to do with the relationships and the interchange between generations—not at all the questioning of what to do. That questioning is very American. It's not at all like that in Europe, where people always assume that art is important. Artists don't have to defend their position, and being an artist is not a move that implies a separation from the main culture.

MacDonald: I assume it's not accidental that we meet the character of Gertrude, a critic who knows everybody, in the same scene where we see Annette Michelson.

Mangolte: Oh, Annette is the model for Gertrude. She has been very influential to my life and is definitely one of the reasons I came to New York in the first place—and one of the reasons I met Yvonne and shot *Lives of Performers.* She has done a great deal for me, and she's a good friend. I owe her a lot, and I think my tribute to what I owe her is only partially evoked in the kindness Gertrude shows to Cathy when she's being a pretty unbearable character.

MacDonald: At various times in *The Cold Eye,* the sound and image aren't quite synced. Is that on purpose, or . . .

Mangolte: No, no. One scene—the sculpture gallery scene—was shot before I wrote the script. I recorded the lines many, many times and tried to fit them with the picture as best I could, but it's not very well done, unfortunately. It's meant to be sync.

Also, everything in the studio when Cathy is painting was shot silent and synced afterwards. The paintbrush sound does not work at all. I did it myself at a sound studio, but I was too pressed for time and did not do a very good job. It's also unfortunate that the sound level is mixed too high. If I had had the money, I would have redone it after hearing the optical.

The great interest of the movie for me is in the editing. Again, because I did not have much money, I cut corners. I should have added more cutaway shots. I did not have much material to work with. The finished film is about a third of what I shot. When I edited, I wanted to be sure that when Cathy was looking away from the person she's talking with and letting her eyes move around whatever space she's in, the objects she sees would not be thought of as metaphors for the ideas expressed in the conversation. It was really an exercise in making neutral shots that would still give you a sense that Cathy's visual instinct is working. That was thrilling to try, and some of it really works nicely, in a nonobtrusive manner. It gives you a sense of how you keep on working even when you're listening to somebody else.

Another thing I do like about *The Cold Eye* is that it's ninety minutes long and just the right length. Mostly people are annoyed by it but not bored, whereas they are strongly bored by *The Camera: Je* and by *Maisie,* which is unbearable to watch now. I think the reason *The Cold Eye* is not boring is that the system of cutaways works to keep your attention. You don't have the sense of very long takes because the film is edited with the rhythm of the sentences in mind. In general, a cutaway happens in the middle of a sentence, not after a period or when there is a change of idea.

One thing that I have always been very, very concerned about in my films is the density of things. There should be no slack moments. The structure has to be very tight, very locked in, so that you maintain the concentration of the viewer, that fascination I'm interested in. *The Cold Eye* is packed.

MacDonald: The Cold Eye seems at least as Jamesian as *Maisie.* Nearly the whole film is a series of complex verbal interactions, all seen from a very particular point of view. How familiar are you with James?

Mangolte: Before I came here, I had read quite a bit in French. My mother bought me *What Maisie Knew,* and I read it when I was fifteen. I was very struck by the book. I had also read *The American, The Bostonians, Portrait of a Lady,* other things. The first book I read in English was not James, but Jane Austen's *Pride and Prejudice.* That was in 1975. I reread *What Maisie Knew* in English when I was working on the movie, and I had also my French copy. I can read it in English with no effort now.

MacDonald: Another element that reminds me of James is that although the other characters are looking at Cathy as though she were us, there's a considerable disparity between Cathy and us. James does a similar thing in *The Aspern Papers,* where we come to dislike the narrator who is telling us the story.

Mangolte: That's one of the reasons the film can be awkward to look at. You can't really identify with Cathy. Even if you're willing to accept what you see as what she sees, it's much more difficult to accept her speech as your speech. You are forced to separate from it, and yet you still have these people confronting you, looking at you as if you were Cathy.

MacDonald: That particular sort of complexity is very common in novels, but it's still very bizarre in films.

Mangolte: I've always been interested in exploring what makes you go to see movies, and what exactly is happening when you are sitting and looking at the screen. What is your position in relation to the screen? How much are you in it? How much are you out of it? You yourself are not part of the action, and yet, when people on the screen look at you, you are forced into a direct interchange with them. Basically I wanted to explore that interchange.

MacDonald: My original interest in interviewing you had to do with my continually seeing films that were interesting both conceptually and visually and then finding out you were cameraperson. I think I sense a general personality in your camerawork: it's very direct and very sensuous, but nonromantic, at least in the conventional sense of romantic.

Mangolte: I think that evolved with Yvonne and Chantal. I don't know exactly. I do think all the films have a look that comes from my doing the camerawork—even though the personalities of Yvonne and Chantal or Richard Foreman [Mangolte shot Foreman's *Strong Medicine* (1978)] are totally different, and even though Yvonne and Chantal come from two different cultures altogether.

And the lighting: I'm more preoccupied by lighting than by camerawork actually. Why this is so, I don't know exactly, but I think it relates to that clarity and trust I see in Renoir and in Ford—their realism. I'm not interested in manipulation of imagery at all. I'm not interested in optical work, in rethinking an image through change of speed or reframing. I find that totally boring—though as an audience I can be very taken with such films and like them because they show me things that I would not have seen otherwise.

I like many kinds of films. I admire Welles, for instance: in particular, *Citizen Kane* and *Touch of Evil*. But just as an audience; Welles does not feed me anything as a filmmaker. For me it's too visually expressionistic. It's so extremely composed for effect that I get bothered and bored. It's not a neutral way of looking at things, an average way of looking at things, which is basically the way I conceive what camerawork is about, especially in my own films. Now when I work with somebody else, I do what they want, and if they don't know exactly what they want, I try to feel intuitively what they need.

I like to do exercises that copy somebody else's work. For instance, it was a great thrill to do that scene based on *Lulu,* by Pabst, in Yvonne's *Lives of Performers.* That was Yvonne's idea, and I think it was a brilliant idea. We restaged stills taken from that movie. We used the characters of Yvonne's movie, but we redid the lighting and composition and so on. That was really pleasurable to do, and it is perfectly integrated into *Lives of Performers.* As an audience I really like to watch it. But I would never think of doing that myself.

From Yvonne Rainer's Film About a Woman Who . . . *(1974), camerawork by Mangolte. Photo by Mangolte.*

The same thing goes for Brakhage's work. I really respect him as one of the greatest American filmmakers. But I'm not really fed by it. I think the sensibility is too idiosyncratic. I like more "selfless" work. Brakhage's films are very rich and bring something to everybody who looks at them with some attention, but somehow for me his work does not have the impact of the simplicity of Ford or Renoir, that immediate visual impact, that cannot be cumbersome or affected or overly formal as it is to a degree in Welles, or Eisenstein, or in Yvonne's films. Of the filmmakers I've worked with, Chantal has it, especially in *Jeanne Dielman.* . . .

Actually, I'm in an intermediary period right now. I think that film as a sensory experience, which starts with *2001* and *Wavelength,* is over now. I don't know which way to go, but I felt all during the seventies that what was missing in the current cinema was that directness.

MacDonald: I think of the shots of the woman's lips in *Sigmund Freud's Dora* as extremely direct and powerful. That's the main image I remember from that film.

Mangolte: It's a spectacular and yet very simple image. But that's really Anthony and Claire and Andrew. They wrote the script and designed every shot. I did not do anything, except one thing (and it's proof that I'm very crafty). We shot it in a very fine grain reversal stock. I think few people have done such beautiful color work in reversal. I'm very proud of that. But as far as the design and the kind of image it was, that was written into the film. Many of the strong images in Yvonne's films also were totally designed by Yvonne. So it's unfair to give me credit; those images are the imagination of the filmmakers.

Yet, I think there is a look that belongs to me as a cameraperson. There is a precision in my work, especially in the light and the containment in the framing. When you look at work done by the same filmmakers with other camerapeople, that precision is not there.

MacDonald: The Sky on Location has to do with the physical shape and expanse of the West, not with its human geography.

Mangolte: From the beginning the film was meant to be without any people at all. But after I saw the footage from the summer, I said, "That's unbearable; I need to have once or twice an element of scale." Because everything appeared to be at the same distance. Whether you use a telephoto shot of a mountain or a wide-angle shot, you're always very far away from the mountain, if you see it at all. If you are on it or near it, you see only a section of the mountain. The space is so open that there is never any foreground to give you perspective. That's what fascinated me in the subject matter. I thought about it in 1975 when I went on a bus tour to visit the West. The other thing the film was about from the beginning was the difference in color from north to south—geography made visual through color and light. I discovered that the light shifts so radically that a certain element of drama was possible.

The Sky is not about nature as backdrop but more about the idea of wilderness, which I've discovered is so ingrained in American culture but totally bewildering to Europeans. I don't even know a French word you could use to translate the idea. I am Americanized enough now to identify with it. Traveling alone or with one assistant through those places helped me understand. But Europe lost the sense of wilderness centuries ago. It's so much more crowded per square mile. There is no area that is not put to some use and that is not crossed by many roads. Even the tops of the mountains are not really secluded.

MacDonald: Did you use three narrators in order to make sure the film wouldn't be seen as a diary? The multiple narrators detach it from you.

Mangolte: The idea of having three narrators was part of the film originally. I wanted three voices, only one of which would be mine. I was the foreigner. Also, I think it's important to justify the possible naiveté of my "discovering" something that is second nature for Americans. What's interesting is that most of the early writing about the discovery of that land was done by people like me, coming from Europe, people for whom that space was amazingly different. So I feel an element of identification with the first settlers.

There are some mistakes in the narration, but nothing intentionally false.

Of course, all the information is false in a sense because it's schematic, too much about details, and you're well aware of that. So there is a kind of fighting with the text, which, like the text in *The Cold Eye,* is very dense and very much articulated. It works a bit like Cathy's comments in *The Cold Eye.* You are in the same scene, and there is somebody speaking "for you," but that person is not really you. You struggle with the information addressing itself to your intellect at the same time that you are seduced by the visuals. I think that's where the dynamism of the film lies, in that disjunction between the studio aspect of the voices commenting after the fact (even when they actually speak very literally of what is in the frame) and the presence of the actual landscape itself.

MacDonald: How much time did you spend traveling?

Mangolte: About three and a half weeks for the summer, about twelve days for the fall (considering the success of the fall, that was the most economical part of the shoot; I got really wonderful material there), and two weeks for the winter. The spring was really a big failure. I traveled more than for any other season, and I never got what I wanted. I did two shoots in the spring: one for about two weeks in April, and one for about two weeks in May. I was always too late or too early. In the fall and winter everything went well, and even in the summer. I was in Glacier Park *one day* and got that snowfall—just what I wanted. Altogether I drove close to 20,000 miles. I was always trying to make sure I would take a road that would lead me to something interesting, even though I couldn't be sure: I was always taking the road for the first time.

The landscape has a clear homogeneity, as far as color is concerned, because I kept everything in the order of the shoot. I shot many areas I did not use, but I did not shift order, except in the spring material shot in the Cascades. For people who know the landscape, the film is very coherent. It really does show the progress of going on a route that is basically logical. That was important to me.

MacDonald: Do you think of yourself as both a filmmaker and a still photographer?

Mangolte: No, not at all. I think of myself as a cameraperson. I went to film school, and when I left film school, I worked as a film editor for a while. Finally I stopped, because I wanted to be a cameraperson. In France there is really no way to combine two different careers. People don't take you seriously. I decided if I wanted to become a cameraperson, I had to stop being an editor. So I saved enough money to be able to do that, knowing that I would probably be unemployed most of the time, at least for awhile.

Originally I came to New York just for two months, to see Brakhage and Snow films. I had heard their names but had never seen their films. I stayed because I also discovered dance and theater. The only way I could make a living originally was to work in a photo darkroom. I had done that in film school, and it's something you can do, even if you don't speak English. Darkroom work is relatively easy to find, and I'm very good at it, so it was easy for me to find a job. That's how I became involved. I still do photographic work, but I'm not really a still photographer. Or I don't feel I am somehow.

The photographs I took on my own were of theater and dance pieces that were fascinating to me. It became an important part of my first years in New York. Since I have been involved in doing films, I've had practically no time for still photography.

There is also a great difference between working on film and working on photographs. When I work on a film, I find it difficult even to make production stills. I do many different activities and pretty much everything can be combined, with an effort, even on a twenty-four-hour basis. I can teach and then go back to my studio and think about my film. But it's very hard to distract yourself from shooting with a movie camera and suddenly take a still camera and think about doing photographs. It's a totally different relationship with visual material. The process of doing camerawork for film is totally about being constantly, constantly focused—on the shot you are doing now and the one you are going to do just after. You want to speed the work process and make sure you don't have everybody standing around waiting for you to set up the camera and the lights. The way you feel time passing in still photography is very different. It's not motivated by a clock. On the contrary, it's very relaxed and instinctive. It's only if I'm very relaxed and very nonfocused that I'm able to take pictures. You can make still photographs one day, and the next day be shooting a movie, but you need a period in between; you cannot just shift from one to the other.

Another thing: still photography is like instant gratification, while film is not. When I take pictures, even if it turns out that I'm not very satisfied, the visual impact of what the photograph could be, as I'm shooting, is already gratification. And that evening I can process the film and the next morning do the contact sheet: I can see everything in front of me. And there's lots of choice. You don't have to care about the money, because you don't spend that much. You can overshoot; you can be extremist; you can try things; you can be sloppy—because you always have thirty-six exposures and usually need only one or two good ones. Basically there's a carelessness about still photography which is satisfying.

You cannot afford that in movies. Being an independent filmmaker is so full of frustration, because in general you work against yourself in terms of money, against your own interests. You don't have the money you need, and the compromises you make hurt your film. Because you never pay them enough, you work always with the sense that you are exploiting the people working for you. You work much more slowly than you should because you have to stop and start over again, so you lose your concentration, and have to remotivate yourself. To do a film that is only an hour and a half of visual and sound information, you spend two years of your life.

George Kuchar

During the fifties, when he was still in his mid-teens, George Kuchar and his twin brother, Mike, were regularly at work on the roof of their Bronx apartment building, dressed in their parents' clothes, producing, directing, and performing with their friends in a series of bizarre 8mm melodramas. In *The Naked and the Nude* (1957), *The Slasher* (1958), *The Thief and the Stripper* (1959), *I Was a Teenage Rumpot* (1960), *Pussy on a Hot Tin Roof* (1961), *Born of the Wind* (1961), *Lust for Ecstasy* (1963), and other films, their considerable knowledge of Hollywood and their determination to make real movies even if they didn't have the money allowed them to transcend adolescent parody. By the sixties the films were being screened in downtown Manhattan art houses and recognized as landmarks in what Jonas Mekas was calling the New American Cinema.

In 1965 George—the brothers were working independently of each other by this time—shifted to 16mm and made the near-feature-length *Corruption of the Damned,* which was followed by his first 16mm color film: *Hold Me While I'm Naked* (1966), a seventeen-minute self-reflexive examination of himself as a young, frustrated filmmaker who suspects that most everyone is having a better time, a sexier time, than he is. *Hold Me While I'm Naked* is a sophisticated and memorable film by any standard, and its remarkable sense of color and design seems more impressive—and more prescient of new wave style—every time I see it. In fact, there's been an unfortunate tendency to see Kuchar's subsequent work as a failure to live up to the promise of *Hold Me While I'm Naked:* Kuchar sometimes introduces himself to audiences as a filmmaker who's considered "all washed up."

The truth is that Kuchar has continued to be a remarkably productive filmmaker during the years since *Hold Me While I'm Naked*. He has made, or appeared in, more than sixty films, and if some of this work is undistinguished, a considerable portion of it is first-rate. For me the best work includes a number of the funky melodramas that are the Kuchar staple—*Knocturne* (1968), *The Sunshine Sisters* (1972), *Back to Nature* (1976), *A Reason to Live* (1976), *The Mongreloid* (1978), *The Oneers* (1982), *Cattle Mutilations* (1983)—and several overtly diaristic and documentary works: *Encyclopedia of the Blessed* (1968—a film about Kuchar's friendship with Red Grooms and Mimi Gross), *Wild Night in El Reno* (1977—Kuchar has been known to vacation in El Reno, Oklahoma, to enjoy the wild thunderstorms there), and his documentation of George Segal at work, *House of the White People* (1968). Kuchar has always had an audience. There is a cult following in San Francisco and New York; Madison, Wisconsin, boasts the official Kuchar fan club. For most of those who know the films, Kuchar is, above all else, a camp humorist. Audiences guffaw at the ludicrous costumes and sets, at the outrageous over- and under-acting, at the zoftig leading ladies and the geeky leading men, at the absurd plots and the cheap, raucous mise-en-scène, at the overly melodramatic music. That this sounds like a description of John Waters's approach is no accident: according to Waters, "George and Mike Kuchar influenced me more than anybody."

Because the narrative situations in George Kuchar's films resemble the conventional situations of commercial movies and TV—especially romances, soaps, horror, sci fi, and suspense films—there is a tendency to assume that the relationship between Kuchar as producer-director and his films is basically the same as the relationship between Hollywood producers and directors and their films. In one sense this assumption is correct. Kuchar is in charge of the films he makes: he writes the characters' dialogue, explains how he wants the actors to play their roles, and so on. And yet, the immense financial discrepancy between Kuchar's films and the big-budget Hollywood products they seem to mimic has resulted in an essential difference. Because Kuchar does not pay his casts and crews, he has needed to rely on friends and family. I'm tempted to say he's been *forced* to work with people he knows, but what may originally have been a matter of necessity has become his consistent choice. At various times his reputation has probably been strong enough to earn him a chance to make big-budget films, but his decision has always been to allow the films to emerge as amateur productions out of his everyday life. While Kuchar brings a thorough awareness of the gestures and means of conventional commercial fiction film to his productions, the results are as diaristic as they are fictional. The environments in the films and the faces, bodies, and gestures of Kuchar's actors may seem bizarre, even outrageous, in their failure to live up to the standards implied by the filmic forms Kuchar is using, but these are, in fact, the real people and places Kuchar knows, and the stories they enact are based on Kuchar's experiences. For years I was troubled by my

From the Kuchar Brothers' I Was a Teenage Rumpot *(1960).*

inability to remember which Kuchar titles go with which Kuchar films or even to remember one film as distinct from another. I can see now that my diffi- culties have a good deal to do with the films being for Kuchar periodic re- leases in a continuous psychic flow. The conventions of commercial movies provide a formal structure.

One might ask, why bother with the ludicrous, campy sets and costumes? If the films are episodes from a dramatized diary, why not let everyone look themselves—why design costumes and sets at all? Well, for one thing, as Kuchar seems fully aware, everyday life can no longer be detached from the imagery that commercial film and television provide in such abundance. When we look in a mirror, our vision is powerfully informed by media stan- dards we cannot escape: we see so many perfect-looking, perfectly dressed people in films and on TV that we cannot help judging ourselves according to those standards. Even when we don't try to look like the stars, we find our- selves dressing in clothes modeled on theirs and making gestures and setting goals reminiscent of theirs. Surely one of the psychologically destructive ironies of contemporary life is that our attempts to be entertained provide us not only with the thrill of identifying with this or that fantasy life but also with a continuing reaffirmation of our personal inadequacies.

Kuchar's characters are everyday people like ourselves. Some of them are very attractive: Donna Kerness's sultry, sensual presence invigorates a num- ber of the mid-sixties films. But, even as we respond to Kerness, we recognize that she wouldn't do for conventional film and TV: she's a bit too chunky. And Kerness is the exception. By and large, Kuchar's people are average-looking, and when we see them magnified by camera and projector, their "inade- quacies" become more fully the subject than the narratives that the characters are supposedly engaged in. The films' sketchy plots are pretexts that allow us to watch the performers' and characters' funny/sad attempts to live up to the standards of perfection that the media Industry provides, as they struggle with the complex, frustrating shocks and mysteries of human experience.

While the gap between the high-tech Industry product and Kuchar's "imi- tations" tends to create humor, it also educates the eye. Once I had laughed at Kuchar's uses of Hollywood sound and image conventions, I found that the absurdity of many of these conventions was more evident than ever before. In *The Mongreloid* we see Kuchar and his aging dog, Bocko, "reminiscing" about the experiences they've been through together. Again and again, pas- sages of typical movie music (borrowed, like so much of Kuchar's music, from commercial movie sound tracks) abruptly begin and end, dramatizing the "inner significance" of the memories in the typical Hollywood manner. Because of the unusual brevity of these passages of music, however, we feel the abruptness of their beginnings and endings more than we would if the passages were longer, more precisely conventional. As usual, we laugh at Kuchar's revision of the convention. But once I had seen *The Mongreloid* several times—and numerous other Kuchar films that use sound conventions in a similar way—I saw the imitated commercial gesture more clearly as the absurd manipulative cliché it is. The more I have watched Kuchar's films, the more alert I've become to the grandiose silliness of much of the language of commercial cinema and of a mass viewership that has collaborated with Hollywood to accept the most absurd renderings of experience as believable images of a way of life to be defended at all costs.

Nowhere is Kuchar's method of turning convention on itself more evident than in special effects. In several of the forms of commercial cinema and TV that Kuchar uses as raw material—sci fi and horror, most obviously—special effects are crucial: if they don't work for the audience, the films fail. Whole industries have grown up to provide big-budget films with believable fantasy environments and frightening transformations. One would think, therefore, that an amateur with a few hundred dollars would avoid trying to compete with the commercial product on this level. Yet, special effects are common in Kuchar's films. The 8mm *A Town Called Tempest* (1963), for example, includes an elaborate tornado sequence. On one level the storm is very funny because we can see immediately that Kuchar is using cheap plastic models and drawings. And yet, because this scene is developed with all the seriousness and detail of a special-effects scene in a sci-fi epic, the effect is multileveled. What is most remarkable about the tornado scene is that, to a surprising degree, it does work: Kuchar's awareness of the correct positioning and development of such a scene, his obvious determination to overcome financial limitations, and his apparent faith in the viewer's good will toward his considerable efforts give the tornado sequence a charming, if campy, grandeur. Similar special-effects sequences are used in a number of Kuchar's recent films; the most memorable one dramatizes the epic journey of the American pioneers in *The Oneers*. The use of dime-store toys and a Woolworth's painting on velvet to re-create an epic sylvan scene in the manner of the Hudson River School and of a flying saucer "flying" by means of a perfectly visible string to represent the arrival of pioneers from other worlds are less elaborate than the tornado sequence, but they are very funny and, in one sense, more acceptable than the special effects of Hollywood films. Hollywood's full effort goes into making its fantasies have the power (and residual impact) of real experiences. Even to substantiate historical topics, the Industry relies on special effects rather than on research. As a result, the most ludicrous "myths" become American society's sense of its own history. But in *The Oneers* Kuchar does just the opposite. He presents the usual clichés but "substantiates" them with special effects that are humorous rather than awesome, and that have the residual impact of undercutting Hollywood's fabrications rather than history itself.

I would contend that Kuchar's approach to film is an attempt to humanize and democratize a medium that conventionally has been *for* the people (to a degree at least) without being *of* them or *by* them. One of my favorite moments in Kuchar's films is when a character enters a bathroom and finds a turd in an unflushed toilet. (The discovery is sometimes punctuated by loud melodramatic music.) On one level, these moments are catalysts for undergraduate hilarity, reminiscent of Divine's eating poodle shit at the end of *Pink Flamingos*. But on another level, they are potent satire. Our experience of watching the "intimacies" of countless characters in film and television melodramas without ever seeing them deal with a reality as fundamental as taking a crap has made us vulnerable to Kuchar's gesture. And the implications are disturbing. In reality we see shit in toilets daily—it is one of the few things we automatically have in common as human beings—and having a look at what we produce is interesting, informative, and potentially healthful. It is only other people's shit we find revolting, a reaction we consider a civilized given. But by making an everyday process something to be completely hidden from each other at all costs, we become characters in a sanitized soap opera, imprisoned by our dependence on privacy and by the resulting fear of life in public spaces. Once one has seen one of Kuchar's prefabricated "turds" and laughed at that melodramatic music, however, this horror of others is one degree less powerful.

George Kuchar has shown that interesting, enjoyable, technically intelligent films with a creative, distinctive sense of color and design can develop out of communities of everyday people working together. He has demonstrated again and again that his commitment as a director is not the exertion of power, not the control of other people nor the aggrandizement of himself, but rather an attempt to work with whoever is available and willing, to do the most interesting film possible. In Kuchar's world anyone can, and should, be a movie star; everyone can use movies as a vehicle for self-expression and interaction. Yes, some of Kuchar's films are boring and unaffecting; in fact, as much as I like them, an hour's worth is usually plenty. And yet, that hour's worth of Kuchar is more fun and considerably more humane than the big-budget Hollywood films I've been throwing my money away on.

I talked with Kuchar for the first time at his home in San Francisco in 1981, then again, in upstate New York in the fall of 1983, when he was on leave from his teaching job at the San Francisco Art Institute. At the time, he was recovering from a serious injury to his foot, sustained during the shooting of the Boston Movie Company's *Screamplay,* in which he plays a central role.

MacDonald: These days any number of independent filmmakers are trying to move into, or toward, the kinds of films the Hollywood industry is built on, and I'd guess they're having to work hard to learn the standard syntax of commercially viable feature-length narratives. You seem to have known since you were fifteen just how to make a Hollywood film, and yet you're not in Holly-wood. Why not?

Kuchar: Well, I dunno. I don't have much interest. If I make a picture, I like to have a good time, and if people were depending on too much money, I'd get scared. I think my films would wind up in the red. Plus going to work: I hate the idea of going to work. You go to work and you have to do a good job and be professional. You have to go to meetings. It's kind of scary; it takes the fun away from it.

MacDonald: But in a certain way your films are totally professional.

Kuchar: Yeah, that's true. But I might have a built-in destruct mechanism when it's considered work.

MacDonald: Has anyone from the Industry ever approached you?

Kuchar: Well, a lady from Paramount wanted to see the films. She acted like it was going to be my big break or something. So I did send films, but they sent them back real quick, COD. [laughter] The lady sent a little card: "Thanks for sending your films, glad to know your work." And that was the end of *that*. I don't know, it's probably not my calling anyway. There are a lot of people making movies there, and they make very good movies too. I like starting from scratch, starting my own studio and stuff like that. It could change—who knows?

MacDonald: Some independent filmmakers would probably feel that having to go to class and make films with students is less than a perfect situation.

Kuchar: Oh yeah? I gotta earn a living somehow.

MacDonald: But you seem to really get into it.

Kuchar: Well, I have to; I gotta earn a living. It's a little like going to Hollywood: you work with a crew; you do have to explain to them what the picture's supposed to look like. But it's only for three hours—you go in there for three hours, and you get out. You can try to pass on information, but you don't have to be too professional. The school supplies some of the money, and you put in some of your own. I suppose it is like going to work, but it's only six hours a week, instead of 8-, 9-, 10-, 12-hour days. Plus you can make a film any length you want. My pictures are like Hollywood projects but on a small scale.

MacDonald: When we were talking yesterday about *The Wizard of Oz,* about how the make-up used in that film hurt people's faces, your reaction seemed to indicate that the worst thing for you would be to have any-body get hurt during the process of making a movie, either physically or psychologically.

Kuchar: Yeah, I don't think it's worth it. It is just a movie. I don't see why anybody should get hurt. But people are always emotionally hurt. That's one of the horrible things about filmmaking. They get their roles confused. Some-times they think you have them pegged psychologically and that you're type-casting them. And the people they're acting with can be callous, too.

MacDonald: Are you hard to work with?

George Kuchar directing Symphony for a Sinner *(1979).*

Kuchar: No, I don't think I've ever been. People sometimes complain that I'm too easy. They usually make fun of me. I'm always saying, "Excellent!" "Very nice!" They say, "We know it wasn't—it stunk!" [laughter] This is the cast!

But with movies you can put somebody's performance together. So, big deal—they stink one moment: you just look through the viewfinder and find out where they stink, and instead of doing the whole scene over again, you redo that part from a different angle and splice it together. Since nobody's getting paid anyway, why should they be put through a horrible mill and suffer to try to make it perfect?

MacDonald: Do you have trouble with cast members feeling that, since pretty much anything is OK, there's no reason to do a good job?

Kuchar: They can do a good job, but they don't have to suffer through it. Some people do a good job, some people do a lousy job. Those who do a lousy job you cover up. Either you don't show their face too much, or you have them wear heavy make-up.

MacDonald: Often you seem to want actors to do lousy performances. In *Cattle Mutilations* David Hallinger seems so awkward about his own performance that it's hard to remember his character.

Kuchar: I wanted to use David because I was borrowing his camera for the sync sound parts. Otherwise it's just not fair. And I like him. I think he has an honest face, like Rock Hudson. Rock Hudson was considered a lousy actor, but they gave him roles. Douglas Sirk said he just had something about him that was honest.

When you went to movies in the old days, there was rotten acting, and you said, "That's a rotten performance." But sometimes even when it's rotten, there can be something interesting about it. And it's part of making pictures!

MacDonald: A few years ago I was doing some research on Erskine Caldwell. He wrote *God's Little Acre, Tobacco Road,* and was wildly popular in the forties and fifties. When his books were coming out, they were assumed to be comedies. Everybody dealt with them as though they were comedies, even though *he* never thought they were comedies. He always thought you could laugh or you could cry at them. Whatever emotion you had was up to you. But from his point of view, the books were realism. Do you think of your films as comedies?

Kuchar: I never say I'm going to make a comedy. The pictures have comical scenes in them. I laugh at scenes even when I'm making them. Picture-making is hard work, and you want to have a good time, so sometimes you do scenes where you have a good time. But I never tackle a film like it's a comedy. In fact I suffered through most all of the pictures. I mean making them I had a good time, but most of them were based on terrible experiences. I was a miserable wretch during certain periods, and those periods are documented in the movies.

MacDonald: In some of the films, that personal dimension is really obvious; in others, less so. It's very obvious in *Hold Me While I'm Naked.* It's less clear in *Cattle Mutilations.*

Kuchar: Yeah, but I'm taking an enema in *Cattle Mutilations.* That may just give you a hint! [laughter] Anyway, I never shoot a film like it's a comedy. I might laugh through it, but I never label it a comedy. Sometimes the subject matter is pretty serious. When the Film Forum showed my films recently, I didn't want to go to the show, because I was afraid. But my friend, Ellen, said, "Ah, let's go," so I went. There were people there, which sort of surprised me. And it looked like a new audience, new people, and they were getting a kick out of it. But I was suffering.

I was reading this book about St. Martin de Porres, from Peru. He was a mulatto who became a saint. He helped the sick and had this life of suffering. And he also made himself suffer. He used to have people beat him. It was a strange mixture of pain and suffering and religious ecstasy and healing and crazy miraculous stuff. I was interested in that, and when I went to see my movies, it was the same thing. I'd remember what happened during the period when I was making certain scenes, and how my life was going then—it was such a horrible tragedy; it was so awful [laughter]—and people were laughing.

I'm not saying that actual moviemaking is suffering. Moviemaking is very interesting; you really feel alive.

MacDonald: But you have to suffer in order to create the energy you need to make movies?

Kuchar: Yeah. Isn't it weird? I have a whole career based on suffering.

MacDonald: I always enjoy your films, but I don't remember them as separate from one another. They feel like some kind of continuing, externalized diary.

Kuchar: I know what you mean. It's a continuing saga. It's not good to have new traumas, of course, but it's good for films. Pictures certainly cost more than they bring in. They may make some money over the years, but it takes ten years sometimes. You probably have to have a psychological motivation just to keep things going. And making movies is a good way to meet people. In a way it's your whole social life. You don't like to say that too much, because then people see your life too clearly, even though you mask the images somewhat.

MacDonald: Do you make one of your own films a year and one class film?

Kuchar: I have to make two class films a year. I'll make those and then feel guilty because I haven't made any of my own, so I'll have to make one or two of my own.

MacDonald: What's different in making your own films and the class films?

Kuchar: I allow things to pass in the class films that I would not do nowadays in my own films. Certain performances and the cheapness of sets. Class films can really stink and you can really play it up. The class films are more like a throwback to my 8mm days. In a way I sort of like it. You're working with new people all the time, and you've got to invent new stuff.

MacDonald: I like a lot of things about your work, but my favorite is the extravagant miniatures you build for the big special-effects scenes in some of the 8mm films. The tornado in *A Town Called Tempest*, for example. There are some of those scenes in recent class films. The waterfall scene and the images of the gunfight in *The Oneers* are terrific.

Donna Kerness and Hope Morris enjoying the passion the filmmaker cannot, in George Kuchar's Hold Me While I'm Naked *(1966).*

Kuchar: Yeah. You know why I did those scenes in *The Oneers*? I didn't want to be in the classroom with those people. They were nice, but some of them were a little scary. I don't know, they were either too loud or too aggressive. They frightened me. I had to teach them, but I didn't want to be in a room with them, so I said, "Let's go up on the roof." So we went up on the roof and brought little toys up. My brother had one of those black velvet paintings in the house. He wanted the frames for his own paintings, and he'd throw away the paintings. When it came time to shoot, I said, "Don't throw away this painting; I want to take it to class." And I had some dolls in the house. So I'd bring all these things up on the roof and do scenes with *them,* because the students were a little scary. We had to do something. The class is three hours, and we had to keep busy. Then later it got better, and occasionally we went downstairs. You have to work, and you have to adjust yourself to the working conditions and the people you're around.

MacDonald: I'm not sure I can always tell the difference between the class films and your own. I assumed that *The Oneers* was a class film and that *Cattle Mutilations* wasn't, but I wasn't sure.

Kuchar: Oh, that's good. Usually people say they don't like the class movies because the people are hamming it up too much or something but I like the class movies. *Boulevard Kishka* is a class movie. And *How to Chose a Wife*— they spelled it wrong; they're always spelling things wrong. That's one of my favorites.

MacDonald: Are certain films—class films or others—rented much more often than others? I assume *Hold Me While I'm Naked* is the most popular film.

Kuchar: Yeah. And *Reason to Live.* Something about that movie seems very controlled.

MacDonald: The shots of San Francisco are beautiful.

Kuchar: Yeah. I was using FX (400 ASA film), and I wanted to take advantage of it by shooting when there wasn't much light. A lot of that film is supposed to be at dawn, but I couldn't ask Curt McDowell to get up at dawn to do scenes, so we did them at twilight. There's a little more traffic in the street, but it looks nice. I always like the way cities sparkle at twilight, and I wanted to get that on film. Luckily they're coming out with all those new filmstocks; that inspires you.

MacDonald: Which other films are popular?

Kuchar: Well, *The Mongreloid* is getting to be a big hit. The one with my dog, Bocko. *Back to Nature*—did you ever see that one? I like that one. Some people like it; some people don't. Sometimes people say, "That could have been a good picture if you'd developed the relationships." I'm not interested in developing the relationships. It couldn't be more boring to me to develop a relationship. You can see that they're crackin' up. I wasn't interested in getting together with a writer—yuck!—who wants to do that?

Back to Nature began as a vacation film. It's two vacations put together. Before I moved out of my old apartment, I decided to take some footage of it. That was combined with some fill-in scenes. But I didn't want to have to make up a relationship—not for a ten-minute movie. How stupid can you get? I mean, if somebody else wants to write and develop a relationship, they can develop a relationship. But if you're going to make a movie, you don't have to do that old thing. You'd be sitting there writing, and it would take you a year.

MacDonald: Most of the more serious films do involve relationships, but mostly you dramatize the moment when somebody discovers that their lover is with another person, or some other shock. You seem interested in moments of powerful emotional turmoil, moments when people are thrown into themselves and are not interrelating very much. They're like zombies walking around, taken up with the pain inside themselves.

Kuchar: You just do certain scenes that interest you, know what I mean?

MacDonald: When I was talking to Bob Nelson, he said that you have "taste," which allows you to tread the line between depicting grossness and being gross. He felt that you transform repulsive material into charming material, while people who try to imitate you often end up making films that are repulsive and gross.

Kuchar: Yeah. The subject may be kind of gross, but I like to film it in the most beautiful way—not just nice shots of grossness, but, you know, by just filtering the subject through me and through the camera, it should come out a little attractive.

MacDonald: I can't think of anybody whose sense of color and design is quite like yours. Are there filmmakers who have been useful to you in developing this look?

Kuchar: Well, I don't know. If you use color film, sometimes the colors just turn out crazy. You go to a house to shoot, and you can't change much around—it's somebody's house—so you shoot, and the colors turn out strange because of the way the film is printed or something. But you use it—that's the scene. Maybe my films look the way they do because everything *else* is color-corrected. Hollywood films are all color-designed and color-corrected. But in mine, nothing's color-corrected. Strange colors bounce on somebody, and you leave it in. Sometimes at the lab they apologize for the colors being weird, and usually I say, "Oh no! I like it. Leave it like that."

Of course, when you're filming, you have to think in terms of composition and movement. I enjoy that part very much. The subject can be kind of horrible, but I enjoy setting it up and photographing it, and if I see a certain color in there, or a lamp I like, I turn the light on—because you have to enjoy the photography element, and then it'll turn out kind of nice-looking.

MacDonald: Your films age well. When I first saw *Hold Me While I'm Naked,* the color and design looked outrageous, but now it looks really beautiful. New wave dress and punk film have made it look good again.

Kuchar: Yeah, that's right! *Devil's Cleavage* has a revival now because of the punk thing. They like the heavy make-up and the costumes, and they like the subject matter. It's real loud. When it first came out, some people liked it, some didn't. Then it hit a period where everyone thought it was a grotesque horror. And now it looks good.

MacDonald: Your films are a little like John Waters's in that sense, except that you're not trying so hard. In his best early stuff he's working like crazy to shock you, to gross you out, and he definitely does it.

Kuchar: Well, you can offend an audience. It doesn't matter. After a while you probably get mad at audiences and purposely want to make something horrible. At least you get a reaction. I don't mean that the audience is the enemy, but it's a very good thing if people hate your films, if you get bad reviews. It helps you to go on. Nothing's more crippling than a good review. It makes you real tight inside. So it's good if you're not neglected but also if you're not too well liked.

MacDonald: I've always figured it would be the other way around.

Kuchar: No, no. You have to get bad reviews, so that you say, "I'll show them, the sons of bitches. They thought they could crush me!" Know what I mean? But maybe as you get older you get more sensitive.

MacDonald: I'm surprised that nobody's thought of blowing up some of your films to 35mm and distributing them. Would you want that?

Kuchar: No. Nobody signed releases. Nothing's legal. [laughter] So the hell with it.

MacDonald: But they probably would sign releases.

Kuchar: No, my pictures weren't made for big things. If I was to make a picture for big distribution, I'd have to start from scratch and know I was going to make it for big distribution. Even people who run festivals, who say, "Well, he's made a feature film now—this will be his big break," take a look at the film and say, "Forget it!" I don't know if anybody could tolerate the films big like that.

MacDonald: I think a film like *Corruption of the Damned* would be pretty amazing in 35mm.

Kuchar: I don't know. It has intertitles. People aren't going to pay to look at intertitles again. Plus, the sound fidelity was hideous. I've got to do a remake of that film because I spliced it wrong and it fell apart.

I Married a Heathen, a class movie, showed at a regular theater once. It was so unabashedly awful. We did our best to make this drama, but there were just too many words in it, and the scenes were kind of long, and the sets were just sheets hung up. A woman was supposed to be living in a condominium apartment. We had outside shots of a condominium. Then it switches inside, and it's like she's in a tent! And the characters look over each others' shoulders to read the dialogue, which was scribbled on blackboards. One of the guys who operated the theater had liked the theme: people come to San Francisco, wanting it to be a place of new beginnings, and it turns out to be a rotten hellhole. He very much liked that, so he decided he would play it. And people came in off the street and saw this movie.

I got into that project because we'd done two class movies before and we had used black-and-white and color and special effects, and the new term was coming and the students said, "We've got to do something new; let's do sync sound, a talkie. Maybe it will take place at a party." And I said, "It's a great idea. Make a talking picture." So we had to do it. I wrote a screenplay, and I wrote too much—too much of a talkie, page after page after page. But there was no stopping, so we did it. And that comes across, I think—that these people *had* to make a movie, for some reason they were being forced to, and they were doing the best they could. And the audience accepted it after a while, maybe because the movie theater itself, the Roxy, is kind of like a long tunnel, and it's in a crappy neighborhood. It's got a certain flavor that matched the movie. In a posh theater those films would be disgusting.

MacDonald: Do you spend a lot of time maintaining films? Are the 8mm films taken care of?

Kuchar: Well, the originals are in my mother's closet. I have such a backlog now. Some of the newer films are in labs, and sometimes I get terrified that the labs are going to throw them out or that they've lost them. Or that they're charging me money for them—then I'm afraid to check if they still have the films. So maintenance-wise, I'm completely terrified. I have no money to replace prints, or I keep saying I have no money to do that because I spend the money on other things, or I'm making a new picture, so I let everything fall apart.

Once this guy came from Italy and he wanted to see the 8mm's, and I said all right and took them out and realized that some were in horrible shape. So I eventually re-edited them and did titles. Sometimes you get depressed and you say, "Oh, they're going to fade" or "There's going to be a fire in the house and they'll be destroyed," and you start worrying about that and then you don't want to make movies anymore. You wonder why you're doing it; it's all going to rot anyway.

MacDonald: You do a lot of acting in other people's films. When did you start that?

Kuchar: In 8mm. I used to photograph Mike and he used to photograph me, so I've been in and out of films for thirty years.

MacDonald: In those days did other people use you in films?

Kuchar: Yeah, my friend Larry Liebowitz from the Bronx. He was interested in cannibalism and he made special effects like they're doing now in the splatter pictures—he started that twenty-five years ago. And then I acted in Bob Cowan's 16mm movies. When I went to San Francisco, people put me in movies. I enjoy the acting. I wonder if I would rather go to Hollywood as an actor.

MacDonald: It would be the same tension, wouldn't it?

Kuchar: I don't know. I have more interest in going there as an actor. I would have no problem with that. As a filmmaker, I think I would be rebellious. If I was told, "Come down, you don't need a screen test, just come down and be in this picture," I could do it. But I couldn't do the normal route of acting. I couldn't go through auditions. I would have to be wanted. [laughter]

MacDonald: What was your role in the film you were shooting when you hurt your foot?

Kuchar: I was in the picture *Screamplay,* by the Boston Movie Company. Rufus Butler Seder is the director. I played the role of a manager of an apartment building in Hollywood, a greasy ex-weight-lifter or wrestler who lost his shape and is frustrated about it and always sort of horny, always trying to make it with the girls in the place. He falls in love with this nice young actress, but she's not interested in him and rejects him. He's a vigilante type, angry all the time. I tried to get into the role. I had seen Richard Gere in *Breathless,* and I had this inspiration that I wanted to be like Richard Gere, so I got a tan when I went to Colorado, and I was going to do weight lifting and get into shape. Then I read in the script that I'm supposed to be falling apart and that I hate my stomach because it's getting too big, so I said, "Why the hell bother?"

When I got on the set, I decided I was going to be OK: I wasn't going to fall apart ahead of time. I was going to be a together person. Then the night before my big scene, I fell apart as usual. I was just a wreck. I knew my lines and everything, but I went through the thing in a daze, and I thought I was absolutely awful and felt so sorry for them having paid the airfare to get me out there to do the scene. I was just so hideous, and I knew I said the lines horribly. Then nobody said anything. I thought they were too embarrassed to tell me how horrible it was. I went to a restaurant with people on the crew and said, "Oh, I apologize—I was so spaced out," and a girl said, "Whatever you did, keep on doing it; it was good." I said, "It was good?" Then the next day the director said it was really good, and I said I thought it was miserable.

It was constantly like that through the whole picture. I was always just hideous.

MacDonald: Are you believable as a heavy?

Kuchar: That's what I mean. One morning I got up and I didn't feel mean at all, and I knew I was in trouble. I could not do this scene. And these people on the set were younger than me, and here I was, a forty-one-year-old, about to have a big breakdown and run off the set in tears. I went behind the set and slapped myself across the face as shock therapy, and said, "Get a grip on yourself! Get a grip on yourself! You gotta do this scene and you're not going to crack! It's too ridiculous!" Some way I got through it, and I did the big scene and it actually turned out pretty good; I really look furious. They were all happy, but I said to myself, "I can't go through this trauma every time the camera's going to roll; I'll be dead before the picture's ended!" And sure enough, I ended up in a hospital!

MacDonald: When you were in New York during the sixties, you were one of the fixtures of the New York scene. Were you in contact with people like Jack Smith or Ken Jacobs whose work yours might be grouped with, or with Michael Snow or Ernie Gehr?

Kuchar: Well, we'd meet now and then. It was never a closely knit group. It was people who did work and knew about one another and occasionally got together and then called it quits. They'd be cordial. But it was a bunch of volatile people, some of them nuts—know what I mean? Very rarely did you have a get-together. I remember one at Robert Breer's house. There was a bunch of filmmakers, but then one critic and one star started having a battle in the kitchen.

You had a sense of unity that was sort of nice, but then of course everybody was so different. It was no big school of filmmaking. Jonas Mekas was writing about films, and everybody wanted to get in the paper and be mentioned, and there were hard feelings and stuff like that. In a way it was like a scaled-down, miniature version of Hollywood.

MacDonald: Have you kept up with any of these people?

Kuchar: I saw one of Snow's films recently, the one on sound . . .

MacDonald: "Rameau's Nephew" . . . ?

Kuchar: Yeah, that's it. That was very good. It had very good parts. I always like his stuff. He's got a sense of humor.

MacDonald: Do you show a lot of other people's films in your classes?

Kuchar: When they come as visiting artists, yeah. I can't rent them; we don't have enough budget. I have a collection of films that people gave me for acting in their films. Some Bob Cowan pictures, a Michael Zuckerman movie, a Barnie Blech picture—a lot of people who don't get shown too much. And I have a collection of movies I bought. *Zippy's Beach Adventure* (a chimpanzee makes mischief) and stuff like that. For my birthday somebody gave me a dramatic documentary about the Boston Tea Party. All the colors have faded; there's only browns and reds. And it's so horribly stilted. I play that in class. The students sit through that junk, and they see a different aspect of film. There are whole courses where you see regular films. But you can't see *Zippy's Beach Adventure* anywhere else, and *Perrot and the Vacuum Cleaner,* which is about this little puppet that shows you how to work a vacuum cleaner . . . unbelievably boring and unique.

What the hell, you can see all the classics, and you can get sick to your stomach seeing all the great stuff. And it is great stuff. But you see enough of that. You've got to see the other petty, garbagy junk that's around, stuff that's been made and neglected, awful stuff. It's like a shot in the arm. It's fun to look at, and it often ends up being a new trend, a new style. The classics are great pictures, but enough is enough. You've got to have your system flushed out now and then. Am I going to show the students *Potemkin* and then talk about our class movies? With the kind of words I use and *my* accent? It'd be like a sacrilege or something. I can't do that, and I don't want to do it. I'd be putting on an act.

It's stupid anyway. Renting movies is expensive as hell, and you can put that money into *making* a movie. The students are stuck with me for three hours, so I try to take them out and work. Most people are very afraid of the camera because it's technical equipment, and usually the people you get cameras from are rather intimidating; they like to badger big words around, and you think you have to know everything about the camera. It's too terrifying. Then you realize that the damn camera is made so that anybody can take the stupid movie, or you get a $2.00 book on how to make movies. Anyway, it's so simple, it's almost dopey.

MacDonald: Are there kinds of films or specific films that are popular or critically respected that you can't stand? What makes for a film that you don't like?

Kuchar: I don't like an ugly film. A film that looks like it was made by an ugly person, with ugly intentions.

MacDonald: Do you have an example?

Kuchar: Let's see. What did I hate? I guess I go blank. I like *Gandhi* and *The Return of the Jedi.* They ain't ugly pictures. I liked *Cat People.* I didn't think that was ugly; some people did. I can't think of a film I hated. I think George Lucas quit because he was tired of being hated. People hate you just because you make films. They hate your movie so they hate you. Isn't that awful? I never want to get into that. Big deal—it's only a movie. Why should you hate the person who made it? That's why I don't like going to those independent film showings with the filmmaker there; there's always hate-filled people in the audience. [laughter]

I thought John Landis made an ugly film: *An American Werewolf in London*. I had to walk out. I don't walk out of horror movies, but this one had this horrible edge to it. He seems like a nice happy-go-lucky guy, but he seemed to take delight in mowing down the families and in shooting up his television and furniture and in stabbing the nurse and in having that nice looking guy go through the tortures of a man turning into an animal. I don't mind images that are kind of ugly, like in Carpenter's *The Thing*. I like that film. The people were so human. They were overly stoned and had lost their brains, and they couldn't battle this thing from outer space that was all sharp and all points and all bristly, a horrible-lookin' thing. They were just these overly mellow potheads, stuck in the Arctic, trying to battle this thing. Something very human about it. But with some other directors I sense something of a brutishness.

MacDonald: Do you go to a lot of horror films?

Kuchar: Not any more. My heyday was the rubber monsters, the patently fake rubber monsters. I always liked that. And the lousy acting. And the black and white.

In some of the horror films my students take me to now, the grisliness of the killings is never matched by the motivations of the people, so it gets to be kind of funny. They're so grisly that I can't get into it; I laugh. But the students get affected by the new films the same way I was getting affected when I was going to see those rubber monsters: they're cringing and saying how horrible it is.

MacDonald: Women, often older women, are important characters in a lot of your films. Your mother is in *Hold Me While I'm Naked* and other films, but I have no sense at all of your father. Were you close to him?

Kuchar: Not that close. He was my father. And I was his son. [laughter] And he was very nice. He was interested in electronics, and he drove a truck. And he was interested in movies, the more erotic aspects of movies. The same way in painting. He was interested in history, in the world war he had been through. His experiences were so totally different from my experiences. Eventually, after I left home, we got to know each other a little better. But we were such different people—just the family kept it together. We never got to know each other, or if we did, it stopped at an early age, and we went our separate ways. My father used to work nights and sleep days, so everytime I'd be home, he'd be asleep. The only time we'd get together as a family was dinnertime. Once he took me on his truck, and that was nice. He might have wanted to get out of the house more than be with us, know what I mean? When you've got two twins in the house, it's kind of noisy. And me and my brother probably wanted to be away from the family. It was up to my father and mother to get close—they were married to one another, right? He was only in one shot in a movie, in 8mm home-movie footage of a funeral that I eventually spliced into *A Town Called Tempest*. But he was all right.

MacDonald: One situation I really like, which shows up in a lot of the movies, is the one where a character comes into a bathroom and there's shit in the toilet. Your films are the first I've seen that include that reality in a way that helps the viewer to think about it and deal with it.

Kuchar: It is a big chunk of your life. When I used to go to movies, scenes like that were always absent. Nobody ever went to the bathroom. I guess I rebelled against all those movies where you never saw a turd. Also, making movies you get kind of devilish after awhile. Right? You have your little quirks, and you have to have a little fun. So you might want to make a turd and place it in the bowl. Things like that. The turds in my pictures are never real. Except for a dog turd one time. I like to make them fake. And sometimes you get carried away, but then you realize that people are greatly affected by the image on the screen.

MacDonald: Especially by that one!

The enema scene in *Cattle Mutilations* is shocking. The viewer is literally as horrified as the woman.

Kuchar: Yeah. Well, nobody wants to see me taking an enema. It's the last thing in the world they go to the movies and pay money to see. They'd rather look away. I don't blame them.

I wasn't supposed to be the one taking the enema. It was supposed to be Michelle [Inouchi]. In the scene now there's a guy on the telephone, listening. I leave the phone off the hook and say, "Wait a minute." The way it was supposed to be, the guy on the other end would hear Michelle taking the enema, and he would get excited—by hearing a lady taking an enema. And then he'd be repelled at his arousal at this kind of thing with the lady.

This was Michelle's first big talking picture, and one day I said, "Well, Michelle, this week we're going to do your enema scene." And she was horrified, she was so horrified. I saw her face drop, and then I realized, how awful! She wants to be an ingenue, and attractive, and she's going to take an enema? I was quiet for about ten minutes and just did small talk, then I said to her, "Michelle, you're not going to have an enema scene." I said, "*I'm* going to do the enema," and suddenly I felt very relieved. She was *immensely* relieved. And I felt very free because then I knew I could do all kinds of horrible special effects. I would be free to do that, whereas with Michelle I would have limited it. Then I realized when I was doing the picture, no, I didn't want to go too overboard. So, instead of her taking an enema and the guy on the other end of the phone hearing her getting an enema, he just hears her throwing up and *me* taking the enema. She discovers me and gets sick, and he hears both of us—and seems to get turned on.

MacDonald: Have you had censorship trouble with your films?

Kuchar: Well, once in Boston, in the sixties, they closed the theater just because of the title of *Hold Me While I'm Naked.* People get offended all the time, even nowadays. Audiences like to feel offended or they're not getting their money's worth. They watch too much television—television is about as bland as you can get. They think these are made-for-TV movies, where you're not supposed to be offensive. That's ridiculous. So stay home and watch television. They've got whole committees made not to offend you, and one letter gets sent in to television and they change the whole concept of the program. It's preposterous. Audiences talk in movies more nowadays, don't they, because of TV. Even underground films. They have no respect anymore. Thank god for Dolby sound, because they're blabbering a mile a minute. That's why you've got to make loud films and big music tracks and keep the sound track blasting: to drown out all that blabbering.

I think there's a whole new trend coming. There's going to be movies shown where the filmmakers don't get paid and the audience doesn't pay; they go in and they get food and drink. And maybe there's a band that plays afterward. A nice friendly atmosphere. I think the hour-and-a-half programs are going down the drain. Going to them is like going to a strange mausoleum. The life has gone out of it. It's no fun anymore. In San Francisco they have some of these alternative kinds of theaters. You go in and they have clams and spaghetti cooked up. You have that and then you go and see a ten-minute movie and you come out and there's a band. Storefront galleries like in the old days are opening up. They have home-movie night, they have Super-8 night, and they have strange other programs. There's a certain life to it because it's in a neighborhood. Things are kind of primitive, and it's really fun.

MacDonald: I think of the original audiences for Méliès's films or for Edwin Porter's or Winsor McCay's as being similar to the new audience you're talking about.

Kuchar: Yeah. Going to pictures should be a big lively thing, not a dead event. Maybe you've got to go to a movie with nothing but people you know—close friends. The well-known places now—the big commercial movie houses and the established independent film theaters—are like funeral parlors where they're playing the corpses on the screen.

Diana Barrie

By definition, a commercial producer or director cannot long entertain the idea of making films simply for pleasure, with no concern about the size of the audience that will pay to see them. Money has been invested, and there must be a return on that investment if the filmmakers mean to continue to work. For Diana Barrie, however, making films is itself the goal and pleasure. As a result, she is not well known even in the experimental/avant-garde film world, though she has been making interesting films since the early 1970s, and though these films are unusually relevant to recent thinking about alternative forms of film: the relative potentials and limitations of Super-8 and 16mm, the cinematic construction of gender definition, and the relevance of early cinema and pre-cinema for recent experimental/avant-garde film. The lack of public awareness about her work not only does not seem to trouble Barrie, but it may be premeditated. Stan Brakhage explains that when he "asked Diana Barrie if I couldn't write something on her films *The Annunciation* and *Sarah's Room* for distribution or program notes, she said (speaking of her sense of her contemporaries): 'No, we've taken a good look at you and your generation—and the public hassle you're having—and want to find some way to keep out of that altogether.'"[1]

Barrie's career can be divided roughly into an early Super-8 period (from the early to the middle 1970s) and a more recent 16mm period. While the 16mm films are, in my view, of more consistent interest, a number of the Super-8 films are fascinating and memorable, *The Annunciation* (1974), in

---

1. Stan Brakhage, "An Open Letter" in *Brakhage Scrapbook,* ed. Robert A. Haller (New Paltz, NY: Documentext, 1982), p. 235.

particular. *The Annunciation* is part of the tradition of the visionary film defined by P. Adams Sitney (1974). Using the traditional Annunciation story and
symbolism so fascinating to early Renaissance painters, Barrie announces the
coming of a woman's vision. A plastic angel in the window heralds the coming
of the "Light" to a young woman: Barrie herself, who is both character (object of our gaze) and filmmaker (subject, through whose camera, or eyes, we
see). Since we see Barrie's vision through her eyes, we find ourselves, like
Barrie, in the role of the Virgin at the moment a New Dispensation is announced and begun. Here, however, the result of the Dispensation is not a son
conceived nonsexually by a male god, but a woman (the "daughter" of the
filmmaker) conceived by a female creator. While Christ is God's spirit made
flesh, Barrie's film image of herself is flesh made spirit: she transforms herself
into a being of light. In fact, in at least one instance Barrie images the camera
as an extension of her vagina and the means for letting the light inside woman
out. Barrie's "New Dispensation" helps to remind us of the progressive core
of what, except for Maya Deren, had been a largely male-dominated area of
American independent film; the triumph of the visionary film was its demonstration that the individual, not just the corporate interest, could and should
produce memorable American cinema. Barrie demonstrates that this field
(produced in reaction to the equally male-dominated corporate film field) can
be appropriated by—can be seen as prophesying—a woman visionary.

One of *The Annunciation*'s departures from the Renaissance paintings of
the Annunciation is the space in which the event occurs. In many of the paintings the Virgin receives the Light in a painted architecture suggestive of the
Church (and, of course, the paintings were usually in churches or church-
related buildings). Barrie's annunciation (like the original Biblical one) takes
place in a humble, personal space, or really two spaces: Barrie's apartment and the "space" of her Super-8 camera (and of our projection facility,
rendered, almost inevitably, a home-movie space by the showing of a Super-8
film). Indeed, Barrie's Annunciation can be seen as resulting from the discovery (by an economically disenfranchised sex) of the potentials of a new, comparatively inexpensive film technology.

Barrie's decision to devote herself to 16mm seems to have resulted literally,
from her fall from innocence about the problems of the smaller gauge. The
16mm films differ from the Super-8s seemingly because of the difference in
gauge. In contrast to the hand-held personal intimacy of the Super-8 films, the
action in the 16mm films has more the feel of spectacle: the camera is still and
events are enacted in front of it, *for* it rather than *with* it. Or *on* the film itself:
the comparative solidity of the larger gauge (and the fact that one can make
good 16mm reduction prints from 35mm) has allowed Barrie to explore the
possibilities of directly painting and scratching the imagery, techniques with
which she shows remarkable dexterity.

My Version of the Fall (1978) stands in relation to Barrie's 16mm work the way *The Annunciation* stands in relation to her Super-8 films. In *My Version of the Fall,* Barrie is again the object of our gaze. Unlike the earlier film, however, *My Version of the Fall* does not present events in the "first person": there is a detachment here between the camera eye and her eye. And yet Barrie's gorgeous, intricate hand-coloring and scratching infuses what we see with an intimacy (a homemade feel) equal to that created in *The Annunciation.* While *The Annunciation* uses the metaphor of the Annunciation and a gestural, rhythmic style reminiscent of Brakhage, *My Version of the Fall* alludes to the earliest filmmakers and uses a serialistic structure to address film's place in the history of imaging of women. The film begins with various forms of complexly worked leader and credits, followed by a long, continuous, hand-colored shot of a woman (Barrie) smoking "luxuriously," an image strongly reminiscent of early Edison and Lumière films. Then, in an exquisite hand-colored and scratched passage, Barrie appears as a wizard who does a series of magic tricks and transformations reminiscent of Méliès. The smoking woman is then repeated, this time in reverse and hand-colored differently, and after this passage comes *the end* and a repetition of the countdown leader, now printed upside down and in reverse. Then we see the entire series of images a second time, beginning with the leader and *the end* upside down and reverse, followed by the smoking woman, by the Méliès magic tricks, by the smoking woman in reverse, and by the credits and the countdown leader right side up.

As is true in *The Annunciation,* Barrie once again uses elements of male-dominated film history in a way that redeems what is wonderful in the early films without submitting to those elements that may have been detrimental to women. The Lumière pleasure of being able to look carefully at a documented activity and the Méliès pleasure in magic and color remain, but the implications of the particular actions we see reverse the early conventions. The smoking woman is reminiscent of traditional film images of the "fallen woman," though in this instance the woman-creator has redeemed her own "fall": it is obvious that we are looking at a woman pretending to smoke luxuriously, a woman pretending to be "The Fallen Woman" or "The Smoker" and implicitly laughing at the silliness of such a stance—a positioning with regard to the camera that is reminiscent of the Lumières. In other words, we see a document of the pretense, not an illusion. In the wizard section, a woman creates a male (with the intervention of a devil figure) and subsequently makes him disappear, a reversal of the pattern so effectively exploited by Méliès and the other early trick-film directors.[2]

An even more interesting reversal is suggested by the film's serial structure. Méliès's innovations are usually seen not only as the elaboration of film magic but also as a crucial part of the development of extended, conventionalized

---

2. See Lucy Fisher, "The Lady Vanishes," in *Before Griffith,* ed. John L. Fell (Berkeley: University of California Press, 1983), pp. 339–54.

Barrie as wizard in Magic Explained *(1980).*

narrative from the Lumières to Méliès to Porter to Griffith. During recent years, as we have come to explore this development more carefully, we have begun to consider the degree to which "progress" has depended on the exploitation of women. In fact, we can easily image conventional film narrative as a period of phallic thrusting toward the goal of climax: the attainment of a reward in the form of romance with a woman. In this context, the progress from Lumière documentary to Méliès magic is in reality a fall—a fall from film's original potential to have been a progressive force in Western culture's imaging of women. But Barrie is not interested in eliminating the history of film: to eliminate the past is to impoverish men and women filmmakers and viewers alike. The structure of *My Version of the Fall* implicitly allows for all the central creative urges that have found release in the documentary tradition and in the tradition of film magic (both as sci fi and horror special effects and as used by the surrealists and the visionaries: Deren, Anger, Brakhage, et al.). But the film allows for these urges without assuming that they must express a fundamentally phallic system of organization. The "goal" of Barrie's *Version* becomes the experience of a symmetrical system within which considerable pleasure is available, not just one time as an adjunct to the economies of a plot's forward thrust, but slowly, over and over, for the magic itself.

In the films she has made since *My Version of the Fall,* Barrie has continued to exploit—with considerable effectiveness—her interest in a variety of forms of film magic. For *The Living or Dead Test* (1979), she painted and scratched onto passages of film leader and tiny bits of found footage that are arranged rhythmically into peculiar stanzas. *Magic Explained* (1980) plays with a set of traditional symbols that appear frequently in Barrie's work—and that are familiar from Maya Deren's *Meshes of the Afternoon*—in a manner analogous to Méliès's play with people and objects; the imagery is exquisitely hand-scratched and hand-painted. *Stay Awake Whenever You Can* (1982) is a dramatized sci-fi narrative which looks like Conner-esque found footage.

I spoke with Barrie in December 1984 and May 1985; we subsequently filled out the interview through an exchange of voice tapes.

MacDonald: Nineteen seventy-four seems to have been a big year for you. *The Annunciation, Night Movie # 1 (Self-Portrait), Dear Diary Volume 1, Portrait of Pamela, For the Dead Angels, Auto-Graph, The Red House, Sarah's Room,* and *Night Movie # 2 (Flashlight)* are all dated that year.

Barrie: Well, actually those are dates of completion. I was shooting before that. I started shooting *The Annunciation* in 1972. I edited it for a year.

MacDonald: The Annunciation seems an inversion of those fifties and sixties films by Brakhage and other men who saw themselves in mythic terms as questing toward vision. Here you seem to be announcing the arrival of a woman's vision. You were a student at the Art Institute of Chicago. Did you study under Brakhage there?

Barrie: He didn't really teach filmmaking. He taught a film history course. The people teaching film production were John Schofill (aka John Luther) and George Landow—I don't know what he's calling himself these days [Owen Land]. Brakhage would come in every two weeks to teach. His was actually the first film course I took; I took production later. I had been studying still photography long before that. I didn't intentionally do the kind of film you mention. I shot all of the footage first with no particular idea in mind at all, and then I studied it. The intention came afterwards when I saw the possibility for that idea.

MacDonald: It's a really dense film, and very beautiful.

Barrie: Yeah, it is. My main discovery at that time was what you could do on a cut. I was paying real careful attention to the small rhythms in a shot.

MacDonald: I like that little focus passage before the body of the film. It helps you get the projector adjusted, and it's also an annunciation of *The Annunciation* and its new "focus" on a woman filmmaker.

Barrie: I decided to use a focus image after seeing how Brakhage's scratch credits were too brief to allow the projectionist to focus the films. But the problem is that my focus shot is so long that projectionists keep going back to get the focus perfect, and at the last minute, they throw the film out of focus again.

MacDonald: Were you consciously playing on your name, Diana, in *The Annunciation*? In classic literature Diana and the Virgin Mary were sometimes closely related.

Barrie: If you read *The Great Mother*[3] you find out that almost any classical woman's name—Diana or Mary, any name that's not a recent invention—goes back to the root Inana, the Great Mother. So, yeah, I knew about that. My father picked my name out, and he was very careful to explain to me that it was the name of the goddess of the moon. That was something I thought about, and it led me to be interested in reading mythology.

MacDonald: You're very physical in that film, involved with yourself as a physical, sexual being, but usually the Annunciation is seen as a spiritual infusion.

Barrie: If you see those things as separate. I don't. I guess that's part of my point in naming it *The Annunciation*. The problem with recent religion, as opposed to what may have existed a long time ago, is that the Goddess—the Great Mother—has been divided into two parts: the spiritual, which is good, and the physical, which is evil. That's happened to the male image too to some extent, but not quite as drastically as it has to women.

MacDonald: I assume that from a Catholic standpoint *The Annunciation* would seem salacious.

Barrie: That particular dynamic didn't enter into it for me, because I wasn't raised as a Catholic. I didn't feel that I was committing sacrilege. It's funny because when I've shown that film to classes, I've always had to explain what the Annunciation means. Even Catholic kids don't have that background. I picked it up mostly from art history. I had a whole collection of prints of paintings of the Annunciation when I was shooting the film.

MacDonald: The Annunciation is a very tight film, whereas other early films seem much looser.

Barrie: The Annunciation dealt with an overall theme. Some of the others were consciously trying for a rhythm that was not as regimented. The diary films are the ultimate in looseness. When I look at them now, they seem very ephemeral. Sometimes I can understand what I was doing and sometimes I can't. When I work on something that's very structured, at a certain point it becomes boring to me. I can make something really tight so that nothing happens by chance and everything is on the beat. But you don't discover anything that way. So for a while I'll work more loosely and just let things happen.

---

3. Erich Neumann, *The Great Mother* (Princeton: Princeton University Press, 1963).

MacDonald: Did you feel that you were being outrageous in the early films? In *Night Movie # 1* you make love with the camera. I found it very erotic.

Barrie: Well, I wouldn't show that stuff to my parents, but they haven't seen any of my films, except *Magic Explained*. They think everything I do is weird anyway.

I showed *Night Movie # 1* to a class when I was in Iowa, and it was a real problem. They just couldn't cope with it. They couldn't separate the image from me personally. Obviously when I made that film, I was presenting a sexual aspect of myself, but once it's a film, it's not me anymore: it's a picture that happens to be a woman. It is erotic, but it's not me personally inviting someone to be erotic with me. Lately I don't show that film much.

I'm working on something now that's a lot more outrageous than *Night Movie # 1*. It won't be pornographic when it's finished, but if you looked at it now, well, it's pornography. I'm making the film, but I don't know if I'll ever show it because overt sexuality is a real problem now for mixed audiences. If I don't show the film, it won't have to do with being criticized for making pornography; I'm worried about it reflecting on me personally, in the sense of seeming to be an invitation. I wouldn't want to show it at a screening I was at. I think I'll have James Brown on the sound track, one of those songs that hits you only below the waist. It'll be a funny film, I hope.

MacDonald: The diaries and other films as well—particularly parts of *Night Movies* and *Auto-Graph*—put the viewer into an unusual situation. This sounds a little silly to say, but in *Dear Diary Volume II* [1975], when you're playing with the cat, I feel as though I'm inside the camera, or that I'm one of your toys, and we're all playing together in your space. Were you consciously trying to create an unusually intimate environment for the viewer?

Barrie: Thinking back about those films now, what is most apparent to me is my obsessive self-absorption: there's no distance between me and what was made. But at the same time, making the films was always an abstract activity. I wasn't trying to record something about my life. I was more interested in exploring the way that the camera recorded things and the kind of reality that the camera would set up, a reality that was different from day-to-day life and different from the reality you might make by creating a painting or a still photograph. I agree with you about the sense of space that's involved in the films, and it seems specifically located in the films I did in Super-8 and 8mm. They all have that in common, to greater or lesser degrees. I would attribute it partly to my unconscious, personal way of handling the camera as an object. Super-8 cameras are small; they have automatic light meters. You don't have to think a lot about technique. Super-8 is about the closest you can get to having a camera built into your body. In the 16mm films I have a much greater sense of the camera being a tool for recording a spectacle or with which you can make an abstract pattern.

MacDonald: The diaries reveal many of the kinds of mysterious, magical details you use in the more tightly constructed films. One of the most obvious of these is the circular reflection that happens on the lens of the camera when you point it in the direction of certain kinds of lighting. You seem very consciously involved in trying to bring that reflection in as a motif.

Barrie: If you're interested in filmmaking and also in symbolism, it's natural to make connections between the images that are a consequence of the way light reacts with the camera. Since medieval painting there's been a vocabulary of symbolism about light. That circle can easily be compared to a halo, which indicates a certain kind of spiritual presence.

MacDonald: Dear Diary Volume II includes a shot from Deren's *Meshes of the Afternoon* that you allude to later when your hand reaches in for a flower.

Barrie: The single most important experience I had with any film was with *Meshes of the Afternoon,* which was like a moment of awakening for me about the possibility of making films. It had a lot to do with Deren's films dealing with images that I was already interested in and had been exploring in still photography and painting, and also with the maker of the film being a woman.

MacDonald: You were almost totally involved with Super-8 for almost ten years, and then . . .

Barrie: My camera died.

MacDonald: That was it?

Barrie: Yep. I had to get a new camera. Also, it was very hard to get people to show Super-8 films. And the lab services for Super-8 are pretty abominable, and the projectors are bad. It got to be too frustrating, and I felt that I didn't have a whole lot of choice if I wanted to make edited films and show prints. So I made a fairly conscious shift, although I do have a lot of Super-8 footage, hours of stuff, which at some point I plan to edit.

MacDonald: Letters from China [1975] is the earliest 16mm film you show [two earlier films—*Untitled* (1970), hand-scratched and hand-colored on black leader, and *Hand-Maid # 2* (1975), another hand-scratched and colored film made to run backwards and forwards—are listed in Barrie's filmography]. When I first looked at it, there seemed to be nothing there, but the next time, it seemed complex and interesting.

Barrie: At the time when I made that, I was hearing voices. I was a little bit borderline out-of-it. At first it didn't bother me to hear voices, but later on it frightened me quite a bit.

MacDonald: Were you under a lot of stress?

Barrie: Yeah, I think so. My life had gone through a lot of changes and I flipped out for a while. I wasn't hospitalized, but there were about six months when I was having a great deal of difficulty coping. I was relatively happy, but everything was weird. About two years before I started making films, I had a very serious falling-out with my mother and was virtually kicked out of the house. Not that I shouldn't have been, but up until then I'd led a pretty shel-tered existence. And in the space of one evening I was on my own.

MacDonald: What year was that?

Barrie: Nineteen seventy-one. There were the normal sorts of adjustments, and trying to finish school and moving. After I graduated, I moved to Texas, and then back to Chicago, and then to Tucson, and then to California, and then to Iowa. I was moving every six months. In Iowa I had this full-time teaching job, and suddenly people are evaluating me, and oh god, Iowa is pretty conservative. That was the breaking point. I felt really isolated. I made it through, but it was bumpy.

MacDonald: Letters from China has an unusual structure. There's a lot of repetitive material, then there's a long single-take shot of you slowly going into the pool, then finally getting out and coming around behind the camera to put your hand into the frame just at the flares. Having that long, unedited pas-sage seems an inversion of the standard commercial tactic of building to a heavily edited climax.

Barrie: There are certain thematic connections all through—about colors and flares and the water—that might only be clear to me. Also, my other films had used lots of quick cuts. I was thinking of different kinds of rhythmic struc-tures, and I wondered what would happen if I put a whole single-shot roll in there. I had figured out a certain way to put a film together, which had to do with classical structure. When I was in grade school and high school and mostly through college, I studied piano and singing. I didn't do composition, but from performing the material I had a pretty good idea of classical struc-ture, which is to have an introduction and then a body (and sometimes a chorus) and a climax. Having understood traditional structure, I wanted to see what I could do that would be the opposite but would still structure time in an interesting fashion. The people who were making the so-called structural films were doing that, too, but in a more obvious way. *Letters from China* is harder to follow because it doesn't agree with what you're expecting it to do. It's harder for me to follow, too. I think a lot of Brakhage's films do a similar thing to what I was trying to do. I have to be in a really good mood to look at his films, and when I am, I'm bowled over. But if I'm the least bit anxious, that doesn't happen.

MacDonald: Day Dreams [1977] has a rather musical structure.

Barrie: The optical printer is an obvious analogy to the piano: with both you're dealing with discrete units, frames and keys. That film is like music in a certain way, classical music, but it's certainly not the first film where I was thinking about musical structure. When I was making *The Annunciation,* I was definitely thinking about song structure.

MacDonald: When I first saw *My Version of the Fall* and *Magic Explained,* I was struck by the obviously painstaking, intricate work necessary to do the frame-by-frame painting (and scratching) of the photographed material. After that screening, someone asked you how you got the quality of the colors—or something like that. It's a natural response because the films are visually quite spectacular (I always hear oohs and aahs when I show them). But you seemed frustrated that the question was about technique rather than about content.

Barrie: I wasn't really frustrated. I was nervous. And it's boring, because that's what I get asked *every single time.* To me, it's pretty apparent how the film is done—but then, I did every frame, so maybe that's not fair. In any case, that part of it doesn't interest me, either in my films or in other peoples'. Well, it interests me, but I rarely find it necessary to ask, "How did you do that?" Once you have a little understanding of film technique, it's not that hard to figure out how someone does something.

MacDonald: In one sense, the color in *My Version of the Fall* and *Magic Explained* is reminiscent of George Méliès's films. But while his films were hand-painted, their color is uniform. Your films are different because you tend to change the color, at least in parts of the image, frame by frame, so that the viewer experiences subtle subliminal effects. Sometimes the imagery is silvery, iridescent; sometimes there's a barely perceptible flickering effect.

Barrie: Part of the fun of hand-coloring is working from frame to frame. Otherwise there's not a whole lot of reason for working that carefully. Of course, when Méliès did it, that was the only way to make a color film.

MacDonald: My Version of the Fall seems to be about the historical move from the Lumières to Méliès. The long, continuous shot of you smoking in *My Version of the Fall* is reminiscent of the earliest Lumière films. In fact, when I first saw it, I seemed to remember a Lumière or an Edison single-shot film about a woman smoking, though I've not been able to locate the film.

Barrie: I think I had seen an early film like that, but I can't swear to it. I did choose the image because it seemed like one of those first films. There was something archetypal about it. Certain activities seem more filmic than others, and that's something the early filmmakers went about discovering.

MacDonald: The passage where the female figure creates a man out of a small pyramid, on the other hand, is like the actions in a Méliès film. *My Version of the Fall* seems to suggest that a development that has usually been seen as progress in the development of narrative was actually not. You repeat the whole structure twice; the first presentation of the imagery is immediately followed by the same material presented in reverse order. The "end" of both presentations (including the double appearance of *the end*) is the *middle* of your film. This suggests a reversal of standard assumptions about moving from A to B, which I'm guessing you see as a male-developed, phallocentric form of narrative, a male co-option of what film can do.

Barrie: Well, I think the film works that way. I don't know that that's what I had in mind when I was making it. I worked on the film at a much more abstract level. Its meaning is becoming clearer to me now.

When I made the film, I had no idea of a title. Even when I had edited the

Barrie in My Version of the Fall *(1978).*

images and had finished the process of coloring, I didn't know what the title
was going to be. I was sitting there at my desk, and this little voice said "My
Version of the Fall." I felt weird about it, but that was the correct title. A lot of
the things in the film happened that way. I didn't so much decide on the images
as allow them to take place.

MacDonald: When you were working on the film, were you thinking specifically about Méliès and the Lumières?

Barrie: Definitely. Particularly about Méliès. I first saw Méliès's films
when Brakhage showed them to our class at the Art Institute. I had never seen
any before, and I was very impressed by them. I had always been attracted to
magic tricks and the combination of magic and film.

My running the film forwards and backwards had to do with the magic of
reverse, something I've been fascinated by since I was in grade school. I think
it was my third grade teacher who would always promise that if we were quiet,
she would show one of the films backwards at the end of the class. She kept
that promise running for a whole year and then never did it! In *My Version of
the Fall* I worked out my obsession about that experience.

MacDonald: You're one of the few filmmakers I know of who's interested
in reverse. Tom Chomont's *Space Time Studies* does some interesting explorations of it, but there aren't a lot of other films that do.

Barrie: Cocteau did a lot with reverse. I saw his films in Brakhage's class, too, and really loved them. It's rather obscure, but the scene in *Magic Explained* where the gloves go on is lifted from *Orpheus,* where Cocteau has surgical gloves go onto the hands.

I was thinking the other day that when you're picking out things that will be interesting in reverse, a certain kind of image works better than others. In order for it to be apparent that an action is happening in reverse, there has to be some kind of physical force or gravitational pull. I was thinking about the connection between time and gravity. I've had an idea for a long time to do a film completely in reverse. A narrative film, not just objects or simple actions. There'd be characters in it, and the cutting would be conventional, narrative cutting but with all the shots in reverse. In spite of this, somehow time would flow forward. I haven't really hit upon a story that would work that way.

MacDonald: One of the things that you seem to be interested in is energizing areas of film that are normally thought to be marginal. The tiny dots and circles scratched in the upper right hand corner of some of the frames of *My Version of the Fall* are a good example. Normally, the only time you see those circles is when a reel is nearly over: they're a signal to the projectionist that we're supposed to ignore. But in *My Version of the Fall* you use them in such an intricate way that even though my first reaction was "Don't look at that," I couldn't ignore them. But I'm still puzzled.

Barrie: Well, it's kind of for humor, although it's a *real* obscure joke. But projectionists laugh. Their impulse is to shut off the projector at that moment. There's a funny story about that film. When I was in Milwaukee, I was asked to show some films on a program on a local public TV station, as part of a series of interviews with local filmmakers. They taped two of my films—*My Version of the Fall* and the *The Living or Dead Test*—which I thought would be pretty readable on TV. While the films were being taped, I was with the technician, so I explained to him exactly where the film began and where it ended. When he taped it, I could hear him laughing because *he* knew that things were being shown in the film that ordinarily he would be expected to cut out. Then a couple of days later when they aired the tape, they showed the first half of the program and announced that I was to be next. The first title of the film came up and then, just before the countdown leader started, the screen went blank. About ten seconds later, it went back on, and then it went out again. Then there was a pause where nothing happened at all. Finally they put on some other film, some filler, that had nothing at all to do with my film. They had failed to instruct the technician on duty that night as to what to expect. So the joke was fully carried out because he shut the film off! After my initial shock, I was rolling on the floor. But no one else got it.

MacDonald: Your care with leader is distinctive, too.

Barrie: That has to do with the way I approach two-dimensional work. I pay a lot of attention to the edges of a piece and to its framing. I decorate the frames I put work in. One of the things I really hate to see is a drawing that's in a matte and a frame. You're supposed to see the matte and frame as neutral. You're supposed to ignore them. But I can't. I find them real disturbing unless they're part of the piece. And my approach to film is the same. The leader is part of the film. I don't think that's as true in *Stay Awake Whenever You Can.* The leader and the titles are more conventional there. But then, the film itself is deliberately conventional.

MacDonald: Certain presumably symbolic objects or images—question marks, pyramids, the infinity symbol [∞], for example—appear in your films over and over. The pyramid appears in *Stay Awake Whenever You Can, My Version of the Fall,* and *Magic Explained.*

Barrie: Those are also elements that I've used in a lot of my two-dimensional work. I'm interested in the idea that certain kinds of magical symbols may have some kind of inherent energy and that over the centuries, instead of the forms being used as symbols for certain ideas, the forms came first and the ideas developed out of the energy contained *in* the forms.

MacDonald: You mean that the symbolic meaning resulted from people trying to explain why the forms had the power they did?

Barrie: Right. Or that just by their manipulating a form, the energy would come out of it. When I do two-dimensional work, as I stare at a particular sheet of paper with some marks on it, other marks will, in my imagination, appear automatically. That process was very important in a mural I did in Milwaukee in 1984. I had a certain space to fill up. The first step was to order the wood that would fill the space, which because of standard measurements for boards, came out to be twelve sections. It so happened that those pieces had a certain shape; they were taller than they were wide. They were about the shape of human figures. And so I placed a human figure in the middle of each space. I knew that the extreme ends and the center were the points where there would be some kind of energy, just because of the shape of the thing, so I decided that on the extreme ends I would have these two figures that I think of as guardian angels. And in the center, I put the two figures of a king and a queen. The other characters proceed in from the edges or out from the center: one side is male and the other female, more or less, although many of the figures are rather ambiguous. But a lot of the piece evolved from the basic physical shape that I had to deal with. Then within the individual panels, I laid down a piece of clothing to form the body of each figure. When I got to the very last figure, I had penciled in the outlines, and there was this lo-o-o-ong space available. And while I was studying the space, a shape just popped into it: a sword. It fulfilled the requirements of the space but it also had some kind of symbolic meaning that made sense with the figures I had painted. So it was a process of formal elements suggesting, or generating, content.

Stay Awake Whenever You Can is arranged in a similar way, though it's not as obvious there. The film begins with the character falling asleep and ends with him waking up. The other things are evenly spaced out within that frame.

MacDonald: Harry Smith's films use symbolic details in a similar way.

Barrie: Oh, I love him. His films are wonderful!

MacDonald: I'm never sure whether I'm supposed to understand the specific meaning of every symbolic detail in his films or whether the more general moods and developments are the issue.

Barrie: I think Harry Smith probably has a definite idea about every detail of his films fitting into some system that doesn't necessarily have to do with film at all.

MacDonald: I have that sense with Kenneth Anger.

Barrie: Oh, definitely.

MacDonald: Have you seen a lot of Anger's work?

Barrie: I've seen all of his films. The Art Institute had a collection, and you could check out the films and look at them, study them. And they were shown frequently in the classes.

But I was interested in using symbolic objects long before I saw any of their films. In grade school, I was interested in being an archeologist. I've done a lot of reading about mythology and stuff like that. I've always been interested in ancient Egyptian work.

If I *have* a system, it is not as clear as it is for Smith or Anger, but all of my details do have certain meanings. If you pick a certain symbol, say, the moon, it has many different possible meanings. You can take it and put it next to some other things that also have several possible meanings. And what happens is that when you put them together, certain meanings drop out just because they don't make sense in this context. The remaining meanings will interact with each other to suggest something that they wouldn't suggest apart. Sometimes I'll put things together and not think too carefully or consciously about what they might mean; I'll put them together and *then* find out what they mean.

MacDonald: I'm not clear about the implications of the title in *The Living or Dead Test.*

Barrie: It's taken from a book of magic tricks. I collect various things to make collages out of, to put in the boxes I make, and I had a collection of five or six little magic trick books. That was one. I liked the title. And then I thought it made some sense in that my idea was that the film is a test and if you get it, then you're alive, and if you don't get it, you're dead. It's deliberately intimidating in a certain way because I don't think you *can* get it. There's nothing to get that's specific enough to be called a test. It's a little bit like those tests that you have in a dream.

MacDonald: In *Stay Awake Whenever You Can* we see a male protagonist getting ready to go to bed, filmed in a manner reminiscent of conventional suspense thrillers and horror films where normally a woman would be the object of the viewer's gaze. The mood of the film is mixed: the found footage feeling is humorous, but the way in which the camera presents the guy and the mysterious events that occur in his bedroom, the strange "dream" voices, are familiar from scary films. If I showed the film to my twelve-year-old, I'm sure it would scare him. I assume you meant to create an inversion of the convention of seeing women as the center of such filmic structures.

Barrie: That entered into it. Another consideration was the context in which the film was made. I taught this class where the focus was to make a film. Since I was paying for all the materials, I set it up so that it would be my film. I came into the class the first day with a basic framework: there would be this person who fell asleep and had dreams; and I suggested certain themes for the dreams, themes having to do with beings from outer space intruding upon the dreams. By the end of the film, it wouldn't be clear when he was asleep and when he was awake. The dream elements would start to intrude into what we would think was his waking life. I asked the students to make suggestions for the content of the dreams, which they proceeded not to do. So at that point I thought, "Well, if they don't want to do it, I'll just make up everything."

A lot of the content of the dreams came from my thinking about dreaming and from my keeping records of dreams. When I made my notes, I was trying to pay attention not so much to the content of dreams as to their formal qualities: for example, what things would happen as I was falling asleep or waking up, how were the dreams seen, and how did the process of remembering the dreams work? One of the things I noticed was that when I first started keeping a dream diary, it was relatively easy to remember stuff. But after several months, perhaps because of the content of the dreams and whatever unconscious problems I was trying to work out at the time, my dreaming unconscious would get more devious. I would wake up and all I would be able to remember would be, say, a shape or a color. In order to retrieve the dream content as I was waking up, I would think about that shape. Then as I thought about it, all during the day actually, little bits of the narrative structure would come back to me. So what I wanted to present was a series of different kinds of dreams. Some of the dreams are more abstract than others. And also, as the night progresses, the dreams change: at first they seem to be speaking to what's happened right before the person went to sleep, whereas toward morning they become more obscure. The content is still there, but it's jumbled and there's not as much of a narrative structure.

As I was trying to choose the protagonist for the film—I thought focusing on a woman would be a good thing to do. But then I also thought that if I did that, it would become very difficult for me to be objective about it because it would become much more like a self-portrait, it would be autobiographical. So I picked a man in order to get some distance from myself. And in a way I make him into an object, which is the reversal of convention you're talking about.

MacDonald: You capture the sort of wide-eyed, zombie look that Conner finds in outdated commercials and educational films. The film doesn't feel acted in the present at all. And yet the viewer is always very conscious that it isn't found material. When the man turns on the radio, we hear contemporary music.

Barrie: The lighting helps it to look like found footage. Part of the reason is that when I shot the film, I was—for reasons of economy—using some high-contrast print stock for the black-and-white material. In order to have things visible with that stock, you have to light it in a particular way. If an object is in the foreground and another is moving behind it, you light the shot so that the object in the foreground is dark and the one in the back is light, or vice versa. You have to do that in order to have the edges or contours of the objects visible. You want to achieve "readability" rather than beauty. It's the kind of lighting that you get in industrial films and in the stuff that's shot for television. I wasn't specifically thinking about found footage so much as a certain kind of stylelessness. I wanted to make it look neutral.

MacDonald: Has Conner's work been important to you?

Barrie: I own prints of three of his films: *Looking for Mushrooms, Breakaway* (the one with Tony Basil), and *Mongoloid.* We traded some prints. I've seen all his films many times. On the subject of erotic films—I think *Cosmic Ray* is a great example, and it's *funny* too.

MacDonald: Stay Awake also reminds me of George Kuchar's films. I'm thinking of the operation scene with the screaming in the background.

Barrie: [laughter] That's a lot like some of his stuff. Pretty tacky. It's obvious that nothing is really happening there, but it's icky anyway, especially when the doctor lifts out that gigantic calf's liver. I had to sew several pieces of liver together for that scene. It was fun.

MacDonald: Is *Stay Awake Whenever You Can* the first time you've done your own sound?

Barrie: It's the first time that I had an opportunity to use sound-editing equipment. Up until then I'd been making silent films, mainly out of necessity. The sound in *The Living or Dead Test* was on the original film. I edited it by painting out parts of the soundtrack. I made that when I was in Iowa and didn't have access to any sound equipment other than a cassette tape recorder.

MacDonald: Your films are not screened often. Are you uncomfortable showing them?

Barrie: No. It has more to do with the amount of effort involved in putting together a show and with the expense. If you're going to distribute your films, you have to have several prints of each of them. It's gotten to the point where I really can't afford that. It took me four prints of the last film to get to the stage where I had one print with correct color balance. I could spend my money on that, but given the return that you get from having shows, it becomes a real question. And I've been ambivalent about it anyway. I screen films when somebody asks me to do it, but I don't go out of my way to get shows. You can get as well known as Brakhage and still not be able to make ends meet with your films. I've thought about it a lot: why do I do this if I can't make it pay for itself? The justification for it is a little unclear.

Also, distribution is not the primary gratification that I get from film. My interest is more in making film. As long as I can afford to do *that* and not worry too much about public distribution, then the films will be there. If at some point it becomes feasible or I decide that I should become committed to showing films, I can still do it. But I won't fall apart if people don't see them now.

Manuel DeLanda

A few years ago I attended a conference on film theory, along with several dozen theorists, critics, and filmmakers. The daytime sessions involved the time-honored tradition of reading papers that were long, highly theoretical, and written in complex, publication-bound prose, which would be difficult enough to follow in print, and they were presented at sessions to which the general public had been invited. Whatever the quality of the papers (and I'm sure it was very high), the process itself seemed the epitome of elitist mystification.

Manuel DeLanda, whose penchant for performance is obvious to anyone who has seen him present his films, provided one of the few memorable interventions into this process. DeLanda read a very long paper, full of seemingly accurate references to distinguished theoreticians and philosophers, in highly technical prose. He suggested that the coherence of theories need not be respected and that the point was to excerpt whatever elements of theories suited one's purposes. His own purpose seemed to be to confuse things as thoroughly as possible. By the end of his torturous reading, I hadn't the faintest idea whether DeLanda's own theory was coherent or even if it made any sense at all. He had used a forum supposedly designed for the exchange of ideas and information against itself and, as far as I could tell, had mystified a considerable number of the mystifiers.

This subversion of the process he is involved in is characteristic of DeLanda's life and work. He is fully conscious that by working as a commercial animator for corporate interests and making subversive, anarchic films that revel in ideas anathema to the corporate mentality, he is having it both ways. This schizoid existence not only fails to pose a dilemma for DeLanda, but it

One of the redesigned cigarette ads documented in DeLanda's Ismism *(1979).*

seems positively a cause for celebration, demonstrating that no matter how much the forces of repression would like to simplify and standardize human existence, they always fail because of an inevitable human need to subvert institutional power.

Nearly all the DeLanda films now in distribution are student films made when DeLanda was studying at the School of Visual Arts in New York (Annette Michelson, P. Adams Sitney, and Amy Taubin were on the faculty). The two earliest films—*The Itch Scratch Itch Cycle* (1976) and *Incontinence* (1978)—reveal DeLanda's exploration of a variety of filmic options. In *The Itch Scratch Itch Cycle,* a scene of a man confronting a woman about the man who has just left their apartment is filmed over and over, each time in a radically different way but always in bright, brash colors. *Incontinence* begins with a couple reading a passage from Edward Albee's *Who's Afraid of Virginia Woolf?* Although the passage is read continuously and the characters are edited as though they were conventional characters in a single location, they change identity and location. Ultimately, the reading degenerates into gibberish as one man (Professor Momboozoo, aka Joe Coleman) whirls wildly in pixilated motion from one location to another, while another (Henry Jones) seems to move at normal speed through the same spaces.

Ismism (1979) is an informal but impressive record of DeLanda's street art, in particular his graphically remarkable redesigns of cigarette advertisements at the entrances of subway stations (he was busted regularly during the period when he was "defacing" the signs) and of graffiti work he did under the tag *ismism,* including several colorfully painted statements about language: "UN-CONSCIOUS DESIRE EXPRESSES ITSELF THROUGH GAPS IN THE FLOW OF LAN-GUAGE/SLIPS OF THE TONGUE/LAPSES OF MEMORY/DREAMS/JOKES/GRAFFITI/TRANSGRESSIVE ERUPTIONS OF HUMOR" and "UNPLUG YOUR ORGASM FROM THE MACHINE/USE ILLEGAL SURFACES FOR YOUR ART/LET THE SLANG OF YOUR DRIVES DRIVE LANGUAGE CRAZY."

DeLanda's most accomplished film is *Raw Nerves* (1980), a brief (thirty minutes) film noir in which we watch a private eye try to solve a mystery in a labyrinthine factory-laboratory. The film combines a raucously colored, expressionistic mise-en-scène, long, flashy, optically printed wipes, and the funny, raw language of the Bogart-style narrator, whose voice, we find out at the conclusion of the film, does not belong to the tough-guy protagonist we have been watching (but whose lips we never see in sync with the dialogue), but to a woman! The narrator supplies the moral: "Never trust a first-person pronoun."

Since *Raw Nerves* DeLanda has made only two short films: *Harmful or Fatal If Swallowed* (1982), an abrasive, wildly anarchic montage of scenes filmed on lower Manhattan streets, and *Judgement Day* (1983): in extreme close-up we watch roaches die, crushed to death by a (human) monster in a roach motel, as we listen to their shrieks of pain. Most of his time has been spent working on a 3-D animation program for home computers.

I spoke with DeLanda in September 1982 and again in August 1984. My wife, Pat O'Connor, was present at the second session.

MacDonald: I know nothing about you previous to your leaving Mexico in 1975.

DeLanda: In Mexico I was your typical hippy—into drugs, rock and roll, cars, long hair, that type of thing. I studied graphic design in a media arts program at *Universidad Iberoamerica,* but after two years I dropped out. I had always been into drawing. We used to live in the suburbs, and my father would take us to the countryside to paint watercolors. My father was a cartoonist; he drew the Mexican Spiderman and the Mexican Plasticman back in the 1950s. In retrospect I can see that his style was very expressionistic, and the lighting on his album covers and in his comic books was very cinema noir. A lot of good Mexican art is very expressionistic; the big murals are closer to the German tradition than, say, to French surrealism. Mexican expressionism is very powerful, it uses lots of colors, it's very sensual—which you can see in my films. *Raw Nerves* is like a Mexican cinema noir film. My mother was an actress in a lot of the Mexican films of the fifties. Her parents were stand-up comedians; in fact, she was born on the road. She and my father met when they were working on the same film. At the time, my father had probably the first Mexican electric guitar group.

When I was in high school, I did psychedelic drawings. What else! Everybody was doing San Francisco-style psychedelic drawings. Later on you would go to a hotel in Oaxaca and do magic mushrooms. The walls in the hotels there were covered with wild psychedelic stuff. People tripping would start a piece, then, later on, other people would do a little more. I dropped out of graphic design school because of psychedelics. I wasn't living with my parents anymore. They kicked me out of the house when I was eighteen after finding two hits of acid, so I had to go to work. I found a job as a graphic designer, and one day, by chance, the place where I was working got a big job: a logo for the new Mexican national TV. It was a rush job so they didn't just have the main designers work on it, they let everybody try. And I won. From then on I had a better position.

Tripping got me into philosophy. Psychedelic drugs are a philosophical question. Is the new dimension you discover always here but invisible without the drugs? What *is* the nature, the type of being of that experience? The way I would have phrased it then is that once you eat mushrooms and a half hour goes by, you don't know if you ate the mushrooms or the mushrooms ate you. You are in *their* world, a totally alien world to you, and you can *see* that it's a world. We used to buy lots of mushrooms—more than we could eat! We would eat some and then, while tripping, watch the rest. They had brought us to *their* dimension. I saw the drug experience as having political significance, as being superrevolutionary somehow. I was real naive, but immediately I felt, "This is *it*! A total denial of what we've learned."

After a while I quit my graphics design job and started my own little studio with a couple of friends. We did logos. At the same time, we bought a Super-8 camera. I'd gone to London for about a month to see a brother who was studying there, and I saw a student Super-8 show. I remember close-ups of naked feet splashing in food or paint—stuff like that. I thought they were really funny, and they were cheap to make. I came back all excited, and we did a film. I got the idea for the guy changing voices at the end of *Raw Nerves* from that film. During the whole first part you see a guy and you hear a voice-over. You're sure the voice is his, but in the second part all you see is a woman talking with the same male voice, now in lip sync. So actually the voice didn't belong anywhere. The voice was saying this existentialist stuff I was into then, lines like "To be conscious is to be conscious of something" and "To be conscious of something is to be conscious of being conscious of something."

Then there was another film, which involved hand-drawn wipes. Unfortunately, I don't have a print of it anymore. A friend and I did it; he kept the original, and I kept a print, which I lost. The only part I still have is now a scene at the beginning of *Harmful or Fatal if Swallowed:* a guy is eating pizza, and then you see this weird image—a chicken leg being pulled out of its socket, in reverse—which you can't figure out at first. That film was full of handmade special effects.

In my first two 16mm films—*Incontinence* and *Itch Scratch Itch*—I was still doing hand-painted effects. All the wipes are hand-done. Even in *Raw Nerves* two scenes are hand-done. If you really watch for it, you'll see pieces of paint that came off during the printing, on some frames. It looks nice. All the rest of the effects in *Raw Nerves* were optically printed by Bill Brand. I designed the wipes and animated them and then made male and female loops, which he printed with his optical printer.

By this time my father was freaking out. He told me one day (he has money), "I want you to get the piece of paper that says you went to college. Choose wherever you want to go—just get the piece of paper." So I said, "What about New York?" He paid for my school here (the School of Visual Arts) and gave me some money for an apartment. I was able to live with the little money he used to send, so I didn't have to work. I did the typical thing of making an apartment out of found furniture and all of that. What was real good about it was that he was putting money into the films I was making at school. That's how I was able to make them. Of course, later he couldn't believe he'd given money to make *those* films.

Harmful or Fatal if Swallowed was made out of the films that were my first-year projects: the first was called *Shit* [1975], the second was *Song of a Bitch* [1976] (I didn't know then that you don't pronounce *song* the same way you pronounce *son*!). Both were overlong. I thought of them as tributes to records that had played an important part in my psychedelic phase. *Shit* is an homage to Frank Zappa's "We're Only in It for the Money"; *Song of a Bitch* is an homage to Captain Beefheart. I showed them at Anthology Film Archives one time, and after that, nobody wanted to show them anymore. I found out later that those records had been out of it for years—passé.

MacDonald: When was the Anthology screening?

DeLanda: Nineteen seventy-seven. I came to the States to start school in the fall of '75, and I had finished those two films by the fall of '76. Then I did a real short 16mm, which was called *Saliva Dildo* [1976]. For that I shot Henry Jones (he worked as production manager on *Incontinence* and *Raw Nerves*) so that he moved along a street at what looked like normal speed, while everything else moved superfast. Later we did the same effect for a scene in *Incontinence*. Henry has that film. Then came *Itch Scratch Itch*.

MacDonald: Itch Scratch Itch feels like a student film—a very good one.

DeLanda: All my films, with the exception of the Super-8 material used for *Harmful*, were student films. For *Harmful or Fatal if Swallowed,* I wanted to make a film out of *Shit* and *Song of a Bitch* but without Zappa or Beefheart—with my own track. There was great material in those films, like the scene with the naked man. I used to walk around every morning with my camera and experiment with walking towards people and harassing them, doing weird things to them. I would also try to catch the events I saw happening. This naked guy was one of those. There he was, and I couldn't believe it. I let him come towards me and followed him with the camera. Then I ran ahead of him a couple of blocks to where I saw these two women sitting in a park. I zoomed into them and focused and zoomed out—so I knew they would be in focus. Then I waited for the guy, and when he reached the women, I zoomed in, waiting for a response. They stand up and start screaming! And then, I don't know how, I pan the camera and see the guy putting his clothes on, and then I pan back to the women. It looks staged.

So *Harmful* was made out of that old material, but it's a totally new film. I showed it as a Super-8 first. Jim Hoberman saw the Super-8 version, and he chose it as one of the ten best films of the year,[1] which was pretty amazing for a Super-8. That prompted me to blow the film up to 16mm and do a new sound track.

MacDonald: When did you do *Ismism*?

DeLanda: I was doing graffiti throughout the period when I was first in New York. *Ismism* came about when I started taking this class with P. Adams Sitney. I filmed my graffiti as my term project for him.

MacDonald: How did you come to center on cigarette advertisements?

DeLanda: Well, they offered the best target. I don't think it was related at all to cigarettes; it was just that those ads used faces. After looking at a normal ad for a while, you would feel that it was a composite face, not a real face. There was something subliminal about it. And since there were so many of these same faces around the city, you would inevitably memorize them. You'd be walking around and see this flesh-toned blob two blocks away and *know* it was the same guy you saw two blocks back. The faces were haunting me, so they were the perfect target. I could attack one neighborhood and leave a twenty-block area full of monsters. It was like the Winston effect of bombarding you with the same face, same face, so you would recognize Winston Winston Winston—but turned around. I probably helped them sell cigarettes. My monsters would definitely call people's attention to the ads.

MacDonald: But you use the idea against itself. When I see the distortion of the face, I read it as a comment on smoking—as if smoking makes you a monster.

Harmful or Fatal if Swallowed and *Ismism* seem more political than *Itch Scratch Itch* and *Incontinence*, which seem more involved with trying out formal filmic options.

DeLanda: I also had definite political intentions when I made them. At the time, I was getting into film theory. I'd read Noel Burch's discussions of two rhetorical figures that started with Griffith and then took over. One of the two

---

1. See *Village Voice*, Dec. 30, 1981.

was the shot-countershot editing technique, which allows you to feel the set as a four-walled enclosure—as opposed to a stage set seen from the front. A second rhetorical figure he identified, as I remember, involved making two heterogeneous spaces seem homogeneous so that narrative could be extended. The way I understood it was that realistic, narrative film had instituted itself as a form of power against a background of all the early experiments. This one form became dominant and relegated the rest to a ghetto area, which became the avant-garde.

In *Itch Scratch Itch* I was beating the shit out of shot-countershot. I used it in the most bizarre circumstances, so that the device didn't work anymore or so that I could teach something about how it works. *Itch Scratch Itch* uses a four-walled set, which we built. The film starts with a figure-eight dolly that reveals that this is a space "for real," and from then on, that space is destroyed in different ways. The first variation is wipes, where you see both shot and countershot simultaneously, and the space gets flattened. The next variation is shot from an impossible angle, from an angle where you know there's a wall. Another variation is a normal shot-countershot, but I start with a real tight close-up of the mouths and then pull out to a normal angle: by breaking up the relative plausibility of the framing, I undermined the convention—or thought I did. In still another variation you get the two angles cut at different rates, which again puts the rhetorical figure into crisis by forcing it to work in circumstances it wasn't designed to operate in.

MacDonald: Itch Scratch Itch has a double impact on me. On one hand, there's a very traditional, soap-operatic situation and also a fundamental human situation: Am I secure in my relationship with my lover or spouse or am I not? Once you're old enough to know you might not be, you never know whether you are. At first I felt that what was happening in *Itch Scratch* was what you describe: the destruction of the viewer's ability to follow the original narrative by presenting it in ways that undercut conventions. But then I found that the narrative always did mean exactly the same thing to me; no matter how you presented it, it still encoded the same situation. What I was left with is that *Itch Scratch* is both a narrative film, with characterization and other standard commercial conventions, *and* a reaction to narrative.

DeLanda: If you want to break up narrative space, you first have to create a narrative, even if it's very naked and very stereotyped. If I had shot *Itch Scratch* so that the actors addressed the screen, breaking up the narrative space in all sorts of familiar, avant-garde ways, I would have constructed an avant-garde space that was flat from the start. I didn't want that, I wanted a bare-bones scene that I could proceed to destroy.

Incontinence is about eye-matching and action-matching. People jump out of the frame and land as different people. I connect all the different spaces in the conventional ways, but the spaces are so disjunctive that the usual techniques don't quite work. I mean they do, but in a way that reveals something about them. Ironically, when I used to show those films and talk about them, people found that the editing techniques were the least interesting part; they thought I was being too academic.

Raw Nerves was born as another exercise. This time I was going to test crosscutting; but in the process of writing the script I realized that there were certain formal similarities between my explanation of how crosscutting worked to create suspense and certain ideas in psychoanalysis. So I thought, instead of doing a film just about crosscutting, why not move more toward content? I didn't want to do something that was *about* psychoanalysis, the way *Sigmund Freud's Dora* [by Anthony McCall, Claire Pajaczkowska, Andrew Tyndall, and Jane Weinstock, 1979] is. I like some parts of that film, and I think the people who made it are real smart. But to do a didactic, documentary-looking film was the last thing I wanted. And I did want to do a film noir. I'd seen my first film noir here in the States—I'd never seen one in Mexico—and it blew my mind.

MacDonald: Which one did you see?

DeLanda: Kiss Me Deadly [by Robert Aldrich, 1955]. I became a noir addict. There was a noir retrospective at the Thalia, and I went all the time. I found noir a great model for my thinking about power. I love the psychologically unbalanced noir hero; you never know what to expect from him. He doesn't get involved in the plot because of his thirst for justice or anything like that. He's not really a hero; he's more an anti-hero. But he's stubborn, and everybody around him gets killed—his best friend gets killed, the girlfriend gets kidnapped—just because he's real nosey. In the best noirs, he doesn't even win, and *he* may get killed. But what's great about it is that he's able to infiltrate the Big Plan in the process. Mr. Big is always surprised to see this stupid asshole coming from nowhere, fucking up the whole thing. He's been protecting himself from the other Mr. Bigs, and all of a sudden this little guy comes out of nowhere, moves in sideways, infiltrates, and destroys the whole scheme.

Raw Nerves was my thesis film. All of it was shot at SVA, using the same corridor over and over, but lit differently.

MacDonald: I figured you'd found an abandoned building.

DeLanda: No, that was the school. I liked working there because there was something oppressive about the building. They permitted graffiti in one area, where the lockers were, and that area was covered in an almost baroque way with graffiti over graffiti over graffiti—twenty, twenty-five layers. You'd go to the other parts of the school and they'd be all clean—it was funny. I did some of the obscene diagrams for *Ismism* in the illegal area one day. It was nice to see everybody coming out of class looking at these big dicks and tits and stuff.

I never had a guru at SVA. I guess that was healthy. Well, I was very close to Harry Smith for awhile. I used to go to his house to study the Cabala—very informally because the guy's real nuts—a kind of mad archivist. He has these great books and great records. And he does extremely meticulous paintings, all related to the Cabala. Anyway, I hate the idea of gurus—that's the point. I hate the idea of masters who have followers. What's great is to equip kids with their own critical apparatus; then they can add all the pieces together and make their own stuff.

MacDonald: But that statement goes both ways. If you want to "equip" people with "a critical apparatus," you've already got a program set up. Even to teach students not to need gurus, you've got to be a guru.

DeLanda: Or some sort of anti-guru. I guess what I would say is "Rip me off. Don't listen to me as a person telling you the Truth; see me as somebody who's been accumulating this knowledge and who you are going to rip off." At the same time, when I say "Rip me off!" I don't mean to be totally severe. You also have to learn to maintain alliances; you can't just go around ripping everybody off. If you're going to rip them off, you have to give something back. I like the relationship of accomplices.

It was fortunate that SVA had a lot of theory-oriented people. Reading theory (Barthes's *Sade, Fourier and Loyola* was important for me) was like a short cut; it put me on the right track. Also, I was introduced to avant-garde film early in my first year by Joan Braderman, Amy Taubin, and P. Adams Sitney, and to the alternative spaces where avant-garde films are shown. When I did my films in Mexico, I had no idea where I was going to show them. I was just making films.

MacDonald: Not long ago people talked about structural films being non-narrative. A film was either narrative and commercial or formal and non-commercial. What seems increasingly clear to me is that most films, or all films, are both things all the time. Michael Snow's *Wavelength* (1967) is a formal film, but it's also a narrative film: life goes on outside the windows, people come in and out, things happen. The narrative level may not be what we see when the film comes out. At first we notice what seems unconventional, but as we move away from that moment and its context, the originally-less-visible conventional elements of that film become more visible.

On the other hand, people used to talk about how viewers of a conventional film became so totally enveloped in the narrative that they weren't aware of the film's formal dimension; they "forgot" they were looking at a film and got carried away. But that's ridiculous. The audience goes to *Jaws* knowing it's a horror film using a rubber (or whatever) shark. Every time the director can scare us *anyway,* we laugh. We are fully conscious that tricks of composition and timing have surprised us as usual.

Raw Nerves makes that schizoid dimension of the film experience very dramatic. We're involved in trying to figure out the cinema noir situation: how this guy got into this fix (and wondering if we missed something), *and* we're involved with all these bizarre graphic transitions, the wild colors, and so on. It's like 3-D, where you're involved with the formal (using clumsy glasses to produce a formal effect) because you want to experience the narrative level completely. To me the active interplay of the formal and narrative levels of your films and your obvious awareness of it gives your work its particular power.

DeLanda: I think *Raw Nerves* is the first of my films that fully achieves that double nature.

MacDonald: What have you been doing since *Raw Nerves?*

DeLanda: I've been doing 2-D graphic design—logos mostly—for TV stations and shows, and I've been designing artists' tools for making 3-D animations on a computer. I've also been working on four films: *Judgement Day, Porking Jesus,* a sequel to *Raw Nerves,* and very recently *My Dick.*

My work on my 3-D programs has taken most of my time. In fact, I quit my 2-D graphics job for a while to work on it. I call my system a landscaping system. It allows you to construct, building by building, a 3-D city. And once you finish, it allows you to travel *through* this landscape in any way you want. Once you approve the basic motion and the basic shapes on the screen, the computer can draw every frame. The program is designed for artists who don't want to think about math.

My system isn't smart enough yet to surprise me. I want to get to the point where I can build in a little intelligence so it can come up with something that does surprise me. For example, I'd like to be able to tell it, "These are the rules to create an art-nouveau type of door. Now combine the rules and throw some dice and come up with an art-nouveau door." I want to be able to turn a corner and find things I've never seen.

The politics of the home-computer industry are very interesting. If you think about capitalism as trying to oppress more and more people, this industry is a mistake. Hippies started the whole thing: the people who sold Apple were a bunch of semi-anarchic scummed-out tinkerers who got high and put together a machine that started a whole grass-roots industry. Right now, for a hundred bucks, you can buy a computer that has the computing power that IBM had in the early sixties. Among the early manifestations of how revolutionary this could be were the phone freaks. Do you know about them?

MacDonald: No.

DeLanda: Well, an interesting chapter of the story (the whole story starts back in the fifties) begins in the late sixties with a kid named Joe Ecresia, a blind kid with perfect pitch. He collected phones of all kinds, and maybe because he's blind and sound is his only source of information, he develops this love affair with telecommunications. He starts out by trying to communicate with his lover, through whistling. He learns all the tones that Ma Bell uses as a code to indicate to the computer that a long-distance call is supposed to be taking place and "whistles" his way around the country. He was so naive and innocent that when he'd run into trouble with connections, he would call up the phone company and say, "Listen, you have problems on the line between

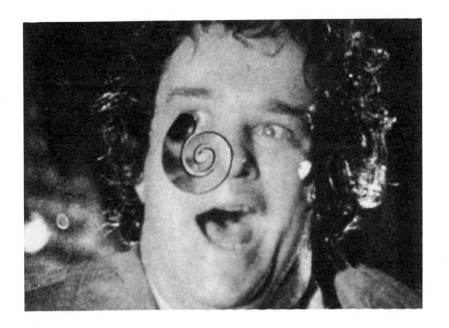

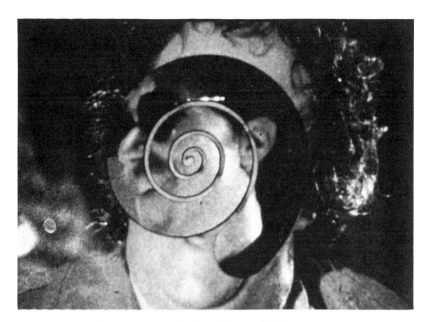

One of the optical wipes in DeLanda's Raw Nerves *(1980).*

Milwaukee and Madison," or whatever. After a while the phone company started verifying that there *were* problems on these lines. So they'd go and bust him. Instead of thanking him, they wanted to put him in jail. But by the time they did that (this is in the early seventies), he had already passed the secret to all these nonblind, less-naive kids who didn't have perfect pitch. They built little boxes that could put out perfect tones. They'd go to a pay phone and dial an 800-number or a rent-a-car or motel reservation number, and while the telephone was dialing, they would beep—"doot doot doot"— and be on their way to Paris. They could call somebody in Paris if they wanted to, but after a while you run out of friends in Paris to call. So they would stand in two adjoining public phone booths and dial an 800-number, then—"doot doot doot"—Paris—"doot doot doot"—London—"doot doot doot" . . . around the world, and the last number would be the booth right next to the one they were phoning from. They would start talking to each other with a 10-minute delay.

Of course, everybody was after them. In fact the main phone freak—his name was Captain Crunch—ended up in jail, and he got the shit beat out of him because all the inmates wanted the secret. Everybody had to go underground because the private detectives from Ma Bell were after every phone freak in the country. Now, imagine what happens when these tinkering-oriented, pervert people with computers get started!

The way I like to picture it is that when they sell you a computer, they sell you a machine that's only half hardwired. A toaster, a TV set, a radio are 100-percent hardwired. All you can do is turn them on or off, turn the volume up or down. Everything is decided for you; you have a minimum of options. A computer is different. Half the computer is abstract. You can construct a million different machines out of the computer by designing a million half-softwired pieces that complete it. It's really a new type of machine. As a way of producing special effects, it's not hardwired. If you can come up with the effect in your mind, then you can do it: you can take the frame and process it, even if everything you're stretching or shredding is happening in live action.

The networks use $300,000 machines, like the Quantel Mirage or the ADO by Ampex, to do their effects—the flip-frames everybody's using, for example. But those machines can only do limited things, and once you run out of them you cannot start inventing your own effects. My machine can stretch a live-action face so that it looks like a Lucas Samaras Polaroid.

MacDonald: The redesigned poster faces in *Ismism* seem a precedent for this.

DeLanda: I'm obsessed with the human face. I do a lot of real tight close-ups in *Itch Scratch Itch,* too. Actually, the army has the most fantastic computer animation stuff for training pilots. They put you in this thing that from the outside looks like a gigantic blender. Inside, everything looks like an airplane. They've built all these computer-generated landscapes based on satellite photographs of the Earth, and you "fly" through a detailed simulation of the real world. You can even get lost. They run missions just to keep morale up. You're flying over Libya, and all of a sudden you see Libyan planes coming at you, and you shoot the missiles at them. It's not like videogames; here the missile actually follows the trajectory it would follow if you were flying at that speed.

O'Connor: And later, I suppose, they can get the pilots to do what they want them to do because the real thing seems as unreal as the simulation.

DeLanda: Exactly. Reality is transformed into a spectacle. I just came back from a computer graphics convention in Minneapolis. The Japanese are doing incredible stuff. They discovered that instead of trying to reproduce a plant already full grown, it's much easier to design the seed and a program to simulate growth. You actually grow the plants inside a computer.

MacDonald: Soon DNA will be used as a means of growing characters!

DeLanda: The line between reality and simulation is getting more blurred everyday. We're already blurred by TV and movies. It's very hard to relate to an event like the killing of a president as anything but a spectacle. You see it on TV first, replayed from all the angles.

So anyway, I still like making art. I get off on showing my films and being praised, or whatever. But I get more gratification out of thinking that the art that's going to be produced in ten years is going to be produced on *my* machines. I'm going to be producing not only things that people can consume, but machines that people can use in production.

MacDonald: Let's go back to the films you've been working on. *Judgement Day* is the film where you smash the roaches in the roach motel. It's pretty hard to watch.

DeLanda: That film looks simple, but it took me months to shoot. Everyday I'd check the roach motel, but the roaches would be too numbed by the poison to move: there was no action. So I had to collect roaches and drop them into the scene—among the other sick and dead roaches—when I was ready to shoot.

MacDonald: Wasn't that film originally called *Massive Annihilation of Fetuses*? Why did you change the title?

DeLanda: Two reasons. First, Joan Braderman hated it. (We've known each other for ten years. She's helped me a lot with the films—the title *Raw Nerves* was her idea). It was a quote from Jerry Falwell, and she was afraid the film would be seen as an endorsement of his ideas about abortion. Second, as I filmed the roaches dying, the religious implications became real obvious. Though I harrass and kill them in all sorts of ways—burying them in a glob of three-colored toothpaste, drowning them in honey, smashing them with a Godzilla-looking pliers, cutting them with scissors and knives, and finally burning them—all the destruction descends from above, like a series of divine retributions.

MacDonald: The sound track is very disconcerting.

DeLanda: That was just me and Joan yelling, screaming, but I layered the track with four slow-motion recordings, all offset from each other, and four fast-motion recordings, also offset. It sounds like weird human screams, and it humanizes the roaches: the screams seem to come from them. I also "humanized" them by decorating the roach motel, with a Lifesaver here and an M&M there—in the macro lens it looks like the roaches' modern art.

MacDonald: How did you decide on the title *Porking Jesus*?

DeLanda: That project was originally called *Fucking Jesus Christ in the Ass*. I thought *Porking Jesus* was a better title because it included the element of pork, which is a forbidden meat for some people. I've got to buy an inflatable doll, which I'm going to dress like Jesus Christ, and that doll is really going to get it. I went to a nuns' elementary school and a Jesuit high school, so I have plenty of shit to get rid of. Also, Jesus is such a *heavy* presence in Mexico. When you're a kid and go to church, Jesus Christ isn't a nice, gentle-looking guy; he's this ugly guy who got the shit beat out of him. You really feel guilty: who *did* this to him? It's real sadistic and masochistic at the same time. That's implanted in my brain, and unless I do a movie to exorcize it, its going to stay there. That film will be Super-8, a real home movie. On 14th

Street there are all these Puerto Rican religious houses that sell the most bizarre Jesus Christs. I'm going to go there and buy a bunch of them. I'm not sure whether I'll do that one before *Public Enema*. I just got a NYSCA [New York State Council on the Arts] grant to do *Public Enema*, and I have limited time to use the money.

MacDonald: Public Enema is the sequel to *Raw Nerves*?

DeLanda: Yes. It's going to be a mirror image of *Raw Nerves*. In *Raw Nerves* everything happens inside, in a very claustrophobic space; in *Public Enema* everything is going to happen outside. In *Raw Nerves* the guy gets in trouble because he knows too much. He sees a scribble on the wall; he doesn't know what it means, but he knows he knows too much. In *Public Enema* he's going to wake up with his voice back, but now he won't know who he is. He'll have lost his identity. He's going to get in trouble again, but this time because he knows too little. He'll come in contact with bag ladies and street people.

Around here there are these loony bag ladies and street writers who spend all day drawing diagrams and talking about Nixon and Watergate and the U.N. conspiracy. That fascinates me. In fact, in *Ismism* the phrase "Open up gaps" in the second series of spray-painted titles is written on top of a vast map of power relationships that one of these loonies made. His name is Butterball; he's my favorite because he's *monumental*. He doesn't do little pieces; he does entire *blocks* of maps and symbols. He's a super anti-Communist and he hates all religions: the Nazis, the Christians, the Jews—every group is the enemy. Apparently he was raped when he was a Boy Scout by a Boy Scout leader or something; he *really* hates the Boy Scouts! Lately, he's been sending letters to everybody.

O'Connor: Where do you see these letters?

DeLanda: He pastes them up all over the place. I just peel them off walls. I collect them. He's fantastic. Harry Smith is an admirer of Butterball. He's been following Butterball for a long time. Before Butterball started doing the letters, he used to do things directly on the sidewalk with a special ink. I was doing graffiti at the time, and I remember how hard it was to do a piece six feet long without getting caught. This guy would do whole block-long sidewalks in ink that would last forever.

Anyway, in *Public Enema*, the bag lady gives the guy a map and a big kiss—to transmit herpes or some disease. There is a very close tie between the plague in the Middle Ages and power mechanisms in society. The first real display of power in the sense of controlling populations and closing down towns, as far as Western civilization goes, had to do with epidemics. Now New York is in the middle of an epidemic—AIDS and herpes—which nobody understands. AIDS almost looks like a conspiracy to eliminate homosexuals. It's like some Midwestern mad scientist was playing around with viruses and came up with one that kills mostly homosexuals and people from Haiti. Of course, other people are getting killed by AIDS too, but mostly because they get blood transfusions from somebody with AIDS. What do homosexuals and Haitians have in common? Probably one of these crazy street people will come up with the connection.

MacDonald: Several of your films have dealt with the underworld. In fact, your own career—half commercial artist, half graffiti artist—seems to embody the overworld/underworld idea.

DeLanda: Right. Underneath this building [on E. 46th St.] are all the Grand Central tunnels. There are secret societies and all sorts of shit going on down there. Actually, I don't know if they're still there, but they used to be—in abandoned tunnels, particularly in this area because around here there are subways *and* trains *and* all the tunnels that were never finished. There's more than the cockroaches and rats down there, that's for sure.

In *Raw Nerves* the central character was a private eye; in the sequel he'll be a public "enema." I'm playing on the word *enema* because the way in which the asshole, the actual organ, has been viewed has had a big effect on society. Privatizing the shitting function, as opposed to its being more of a collective thing—making it into *your own business*—in some theories anyway, has served as a model for the modern individual. I'll play on the word *asshole* and *enema* and on *getting rid of waste*. There's going to be a relationship between the guy's asshole and the city's "asshole."

MacDonald: Will *Public Enema* look like *Raw Nerves*?

DeLanda: Public Enema is going to have even more special effects than *Raw Nerves.* In fact, the whole thing is going to be special effects. I don't want any "regular" shots. The basic special effect is going to be similar to the wipes in *Raw Nerves,* but instead of having the two combined images of different locations, the two interwoven levels of imagery will be two images of the exact same scene, two or three frames away from each other. I'll use complex patterns that will make the whole frame undulate. Basically, the guy will move along, and it will be as if pieces of his flesh stretch and come loose, get left behind. But at the same time you'll *see* a face and landmarks you know: Chinatown, the Brooklyn Bridge, skyscrapers. It will be a superstylized, expressionistic film noir, but also supermodernized and computerized.

I'm going to design the structure of the film, and then I'll let my friend Professor Momboozoo (his real name is Joe Coleman—a completely crazy, unclassifiable guy from Connecticut) flesh it out. That's pretty much how I did *Raw Nerves.* I wrote the structure and then gave Joan Braderman, Paul Arthur, Bill Coleman, and Momboozoo different scenes to flesh out. Momboozoo and I have been together a long time. He was in *Incontinence*: he was the one who jumped all over the place singing "Who's afraid of Virginia Woolf, Virginia Woolf," and he was the corpse in the closet in *Raw Nerves.* He wrote the first scene where the spiral is coming out from the face: "It was like the face of an acromegaly victim growing bigger and uglier. . . ." He knows all these cryptic words. He's also a cartoonist (he does comic books and covers for *Screw*) and a painter (he does extremely detailed paintings of catastrophes and cruelty). His blow-up act is famous: he puts the equivalent of $100 worth of firecrackers on his chest (with some protection, but not a lot), ties everything to a single fuse, gets dressed, and goes out. He'll find a bar or a party, walk in, make his presence felt by insulting or harassing people; then he'll light himself up and explode. You'd swear the guy is dying.

O'Connor: He makes you feel real sane, doesn't he?

DeLanda: He's like a shrink. A few hours with him and you come out feeling "Oh, I'm so normal!"

Momboozoo hates everything that's fake. He's never used fake blood. If he needs blood on his face for a particular performance or something, he breaks a bottle on his face. That's how he started the Kitchen performance. And he had this wound and a cigar, and he put out the cigar *in* the wound. You should have seen the audience. Also for that performance he bought a freshly decapitated pig's head and cow's head, which we were wearing later on while we were throwing animals at the audience. I rented a double-barreled shotgun for him, and he chased everybody around with it—including the organizers. After you see this guy perpetrating all this violence on his own body, you don't know if the guy is putting real bullets in the gun.

I have a new Momboozoo story.[2] He calls me up one day. It's full moon, and he wants me to videotape this performance he wants to do on the West Side Highway at Spring Street, where apparently demonic or satanic ceremonies have been going on. He says, "We're ready tonight for a *big* thing." I can never say no to this guy, and I always get in trouble when I'm with him, but that's the way it is. He says, "I'll pick you up in half an hour." He arrives with this van, with a dead dog in a barrel in the back, and a big fish, and his firecrackers on—the whole thing. He drives to this place, and it's got an open front; it's *outside*. I say, "We're going to get busted here, man!" He hangs the dog from the ceiling, and he paints the chest white with red voodoo symbols on it. Disgusting. Then he makes the fish stick out of his pants as if it were his dick, and he starts carrying on. He's about to cut the dog open and start playing with the organs when the cops arrive. As far as the cops can see, we might have a human body hanging from the ceiling. They walk into the place and go, "What the *fuck* is *this*!" Meanwhile I'm using my little video spy camera— you don't need to look through a viewfinder or have light—to shoot the whole thing. Five minutes later there are eight cop cars.

They finally take us to Port Authority. It was supposed to be *our* performance, but instead the cops put one on. Everybody in the place goes nuts. All the cops are having a great time, barking and howling. Every new cop that walks into the place is welcomed by somebody: "You're not going to *believe*

2. The original tape recording of this story was included in *Spiral*, No. 3 (April 1985), a stereo tape issue.

this." One cop tells me, "Don't say anything till your lawyer comes; I'm a dog lover. I'm going to get you for this." We're really nervous, because they have $2,000 worth of video equipment, and I don't know what they're going to do. But at the same time, we can't stop giggling. They're calling their lawyer friends, and you hear these incredible discussions: "This has *got* to count as cruelty to animals." "You can't be cruel to a *dead dog*!" "There's something here about sexual intercourse with animals." "But they weren't having sexual *intercourse* with a fish; they were just having sexual *contact* with a fish!" "OK, so look it up!"

They had to make sure we hadn't fucked the dog, and at one point we see this cop walking out of the dog room, removing this weirded-out rubber glove from his hand, giving us this dirty look, and saying, "Nothing in there." They started calling us the Fish Fuckers, and they'd walk into our cell and say, "I've been with the New York Police Department for twelve years, and I've never seen anything *this sick*!" And, of course, Momboozoo was very happy to hear it.

We ended up at 8:00 in the morning at the captain's office. The captain's calling the DA to see if he wants to prosecute. And I just keep quoting him Buñuel and Dali, and saying, "Listen, in the 1920s they were getting away with it, and this is 1983." Finally we get off. Because we were white, for one thing. Three months before, a black graffiti artist had been strangled by the cops for painting little things on the wall. So the color of our skin certainly helped. And because we were artists. I had to show up the following day with proof that I had shown my movies at the Whitney Museum. It was the funniest thing walking into the same place with this little invitation to a show at the Whitney. And with a receipt for the dog: we had to prove we had not stolen the dog. We ended up getting away with it for $175: $100 for possession of firecrackers, and three $25 summons for trespassing. They gave us back all the equipment, but they'd erased the tape. I'd shot the whole bust. But they'd played back the tapes and they saw themselves, and they knew it was the hottest tape.

MacDonald: Who got the third trespassing summons?

DeLanda: Momboozoo's wife. Nobody can believe that this girl married this guy. She's into B-movies and monsters and stuff like that, but she's not like him. But he did teach her to blow up. In fact, at the Kitchen performance she was sitting in the audience. When he blows up, she stands up as though hypnotized and blows up too.

MacDonald: You remind me of Buñuel's *The Discreet Charm of the Bourgeoisie,* where the rich people are simultaneously lawmakers and enforcers *and* the drug connection they're in charge of wiping out.

DeLanda: I think it's just that people are complicated, and class structure is, too. The usual idea is that the class in control has a pretty clear idea of what it's doing. But I think that, in fact, the capitalists have to play it by ear, day by day. That's what Foucault says about the Panopticon, the advanced prison designed by Jeremy Bentham. As impressive as the Panopticon looks, it doesn't quite work. It has to keep exercising power over its prisoners *every day*. If it lets go for one day, they're gone. In other words, it's not that a conspiracy has already worked and we're living in an Orwellian society. Undoubtedly the capitalists have all kinds of things under their control, but the project as a whole is something they have to play by ear every day. All sorts of things continually resist that control. In fact, the oppressive power is there all the time *because* those points of resistance keep resisting.

Morgan Fisher

Since 1968, Morgan Fisher has been making films that provide informed, witty discourses on the apparatus of film production. To date he has completed twelve films—*The Director and His Actor Look at Footage Showing Preparations for an Unmade Film (2)* (1968; two versions of this film were made, but Fisher distributes only the second), *Documentary Footage* (1968), *Phi Phenomenon* (1968), *Screening Room* (1968), *Production Stills* (1970), *Production Footage* (1971), *Picture and Sound Rushes* (1973), *The Wilkinson Household Fire Alarm* (1973), *Cue Rolls* (1974), *240x* (1974), *Projection Instructions* (1976), and *Standard Gauge* (1984)—each of which creates intensive conceptual involvement with fundamental filmic questions, often by placing the viewer's usual ways of thinking about the cinematic apparatus into crisis.

Production Stills may be the most elegant of Fisher's early films. In a single continuous, roll-long shot, we see at first a blank screen (actually a portion of a white wall) and a flash of light; then, after thirty seconds or so, hands enter the image and mount a black-and-white Polaroid photograph in the center of the image: this photograph, and the seven that are subsequently mounted, one at a time and in the same way, reveal the procedure whose results we are apparently seeing. The first Polaroid is a long shot of four people and a large camera rig; in subsequent Polaroids we see this impressive set-up from a variety of angles. Throughout the film we hear what we assume are the sounds of the procedure. As simple as *Production Stills* may seem in comparison with conventional films, it is capable of confounding our filmic assumptions and the categories we normally employ to describe film experiences. *Production Stills* is a single unedited shot, and yet, each new Polaroid

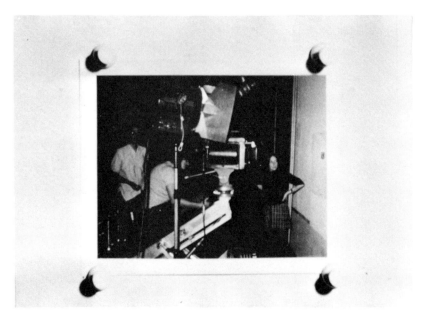

Frame enlargement from Fisher's Production Stills *(1970).*

"shot" reveals a different aspect of an ongoing procedure: the result is a film that is simultaneously unedited and "edited." The film is both "minimal"—it is one continuous, roll-long shot of eight Polaroids—and "maximal"— Fisher uses a sophisticated, Industry-grade camera set-up (a Mitchell on a Moviola crab dolly on a soundstage). The Polaroids are black-and-white and the wall on which they are mounted is white, but the fingers that we see for a few seconds mounting each image are in color: the film is simultaneously black and white and color. Fisher has made an obviously noncommercial, avant-garde film, and yet his means—the Industry equipment, the crew, and, of course, the making of production stills—are those developed by the commercial industry: *Production Stills* is simultaneously an avant-garde and an Industry film.

Each of Fisher's films foregrounds a different set of procedures, pieces of equipment, and issues in ways that generate conceptual ironies and paradoxes. In *The Director and His Actor Look at Footage Showing Preparations for an Unmade Film (2),* we see two men (Fisher and Paul Morrison) in various production stages of a film, which, judging from the title, never got made. And yet, every process we see "documented" in the film posits another process (or processes): the process of looking at footage in the screening room that opens the film, for example, is available to us only because Fisher made footage of himself and Morrison looking (or supposedly looking) at footage and subsequently looked at that footage and made it into a portion of the film we are watching. *Documentary Footage* confronts the conventional distinction between documentary and dramatization; *Production Footage* centers on the differences between working with a studio camera (a 16mm Mitchell) and a more mobile hand-held camera (a 16mm Eclair); *Picture and Sound Rushes,* on the relationship between sound and image; and *Screening Room* and *Projection Instructions,* on the apparatus of the projection space.

Even *Phi Phenomenon,* probably the sparest of all Fisher films is, for all its apparent simplicity, dense with idea. In *Phi Phenomenon* we see a continuous, stationary shot of the face of an institutional clock, exactly one roll of 16mm film (approximately eleven minutes) long. The clock does not even have a second hand! The film is silent. In any conventional sense, there is simply nothing to look at: we can merely feel that time is passing. For lack of anything else to occupy the eye, we may try to perceive the minute and hour hands moving—they are, after all, the only parts of the image we know are in motion—but no matter how hard we try, we cannot see the hands actually moving; we can perceive only that each time we focus on them, they *have moved.* When we remind ourselves that the phi phenomenon is "the psychological perception of motion which is caused by the displacement of two objects in quick succession in neighboring positions"[1] and that it is one of the two basic mechanisms (the other is persistence of vision) that enable us to see the motion in motion pictures, a series of ironies and paradoxes becomes apparent. Fisher has made a movie that doesn't "move," in the normal sense of the word, about one of the mechanisms that allows us to see those forms of motion that are *not* evident in *Phi Phenomenon.* Yet to say that the film doesn't move is not accurate either: we can see that it is a motion picture and that it is documenting a moving object. Since we know the clock is moving only because we can see, from minute to minute, that the clock hands are in a new position, we are experiencing the phi phenomenon in "slow motion," not as a means to an end, as in conventional film, but as an end in itself.

Of course, as soon as one tunes into the conceptual dimensions of *Phi Phenomenon,* the film's original "emptiness" becomes an instance of the deadpan humor evident throughout Fisher's work. (For my first experience of *Phi Phenomenon*—and of Fisher's films, for that matter—I drove two hundred miles, to Buffalo, New York. I was late arriving in town, found my way to the SUNY–Buffalo campus, ran frantically from building to building trying to find the screening room, and tore into the theater just before the lights went down . . . to find myself staring at an institutional clock. At the time, it seemed outrageous—and outrageously funny—but since then, I have noticed that the "normal" film experience is not always so different: much of what we hurry to pay to see is little more than minutes going by.)

After *Projection Instructions* Fisher presented several film installations—

1. James Monaco, *How to Read a Film,* rev. ed. (New York: Oxford University Press, 1981), p. 445.

Installation view from Fisher's Southern Exposure, *a continuous-loop film installation (1977).*

Southern Exposure (1977), *North Light* (1979), *Passing Time* (1979), and *Color Balance* (1980)—but he did not finish another film for nearly ten years, until *Standard Gauge*. Using scraps of 35mm film collected while working in the Industry—over the years he has worked on a variety of commercial films—Fisher fashioned a poignant, autobiographical 16mm review of his 35mm filmmaking experiences. Using bits of leader and other throwaways, Fisher wittily dramatizes the fragility of the film medium and the nature of his position as an experimental/avant-garde filmmaker vis-à-vis the Industry.

I first spoke with Fisher in August 1981 at his home in Santa Monica. Subsequently, we exchanged many drafts of the interview before it achieved its present form.

MacDonald: I was surprised to learn that you had worked on commercial features with Roger Corman and Haskell Wexler.

Fisher: I would have thought it was apparent from my films that I had some kind of relationship with the Industry at the practical level. The Industry has always been important for me. I became interested in filmmaking in the middle sixties, when *Film Culture* presented articles about the New American Cinema and films made in Hollywood on an equal footing. In the same issue were stills from *Flaming Creatures* and the opening sequence of *The Naked Kiss,* where Constance Towers beats up her pimp. That was a golden moment. The unifying idea was that of being an artist in film, no matter where. There was also the implication, which I think is correct, that what independent films and commercial films have in common is as important, or perhaps more important, than what divides them. Soon afterwards the critical politics of the magazine shifted, and except for some old films that were enshrined in history, commercial films were dismissed as being unspeakable. This is an orthodoxy that I feel hasn't done much good. In my work I have tried to acknowledge the unalterable fact of the Industry, which there is no getting around, and to maintain an openness toward what it is and what it has given us. I regard the Industry as a source of ideas and material, as a subject, and in some ways as a model, even though I also criticize it.

But at any rate, during the early seventies I worked as an editor on low-budget features. I was the second editor on *The Student Nurses* [1970] for which Roger Corman was the executive producer. It was his first film, I think, after he formed New World. But I worked under him, not with him, since I saw him only when we screened the cuts. Later on I was the editor of an independent feature called—it had three titles—*The Second Coming, Blood Virgin,* and *Messiah of Evil,* the title under which it was finally released [in 1975]. It was a horror film, need I say, and was intended as a straightforward exploitation programmer. I did some second-unit directing, and I also had a bit part in the film opposite Marianna Hill. (She had been in *Red Line 7000* and later played the wife of Fredo in *The Godfather II.*) In my scenes with her I play an assistant in an art gallery. She comes in looking for her father, a painter who's gone mad and has vanished, and I try to throw her off the track. I wear the same suit that I later wore in George Landow's *On the Marriage Broker Joke* [*as Cited by Sigmund Freud in "Wit and its Relation to the Unconscious" or Can the Avant-Garde Artist Be Wholed?*].

Messiah of Evil had a commercial release, but it was withdrawn after an abbreviated run because of legal problems. In Los Angeles it played at a big popcorn theater downtown, where for the first and only time I saw the film with a real audience. The atmosphere was similar to the theaters on 42nd Street. I sat behind a large woman whose responses to the film were quite vocal. When I had done my scene I was nervous, so I was pale and my voice trembled. But it turned out that these seeming flaws in my performance fitted perfectly with the spooky weirdness that was the intended effect of the scene. When I came on the screen, I had the pleasure of hearing this woman in front of me say, in this genuinely feeling tone, "That guy gives me the creeps."

I've heard a rumor that the film was rereleased under still another title, but again only briefly. I don't think it's in distribution anymore. Among people who've managed to see it, it's become something of a cult film. In a poll published in *Film Comment* in 1976, several dozen British film figures, mostly critics, were asked to name their twelve favorite films of all time, and two of them mentioned *Messiah of Evil*. Someone else named *Eadweard Muybridge, Zoopraxographer* [1975], the documentary by Thom Andersen that I worked on as editor and general collaborator. The Muybridge film was also listed by two critics in the 1976 *Sight and Sound* poll of the ten best films released that year in Great Britain.

For Haskell Wexler I was a stock footage researcher for a couple of weeks, for a feature that never materialized. It was supposed to be the next film after *Medium Cool*. I was looking for scenes of people dying violent deaths, and one of the shots I found was in Bruce Conner's *A Movie*, the execution scene where the man is sitting in a chair with his back to the firing squad. According to the microfilm at the stock-footage library, he had been the warden of a prison in fascist Italy. The motif of fascism in *A Movie* is very pronounced, but in anything I've ever read about the film, that's gone unmentioned. It's an extremely powerful and seductive film. People must realize what it is they're responding to and don't want to face it in the film because that would mean having to face it in themselves. And *A Movie* is the one independent film that everyone likes. The film plays on destruction as spectacle, and it's haunted by a kind of dreadful euphoria, and Mussolini is in the film, dead. And the music, *The Pines of Rome* by Respighi, is related to fascism, and in a double sense. As I understand it, Respighi was associated with fascism at the level of organized politics, though whether as a matter of expedience or out of conviction, I don't know. And the music is program music, which can be called fascist in an extended or poetic sense (if that isn't a contradiction), since it's intended to describe specific scenes, that is to say, to pre-empt your reaction to it, to control you, because there is only one correct response.

Conner's method as a filmmaker—found footage and collage—is one of the subjects of a film I'm working on [*Standard Gauge*]. It's an autobiographical sketch of the time I've spent in the Industry, organized around pieces of 35mm film that I've scavenged over the years. It's all found footage, but instead of being brought to life by projection, as in Conner's films, it's presented as inert material, as separate strips of film. It's like show and tell, a picture album with an extended commentary. The material is vastly miscellaneous so it lets me talk about all kinds of things, but the underlying subject of the film is the Industry.

MacDonald: You're making it in 35mm?

Fisher: No, it's in 16mm, but all you see are pieces of 35mm, one after another. It'll be a little bit like *Production Stills* in that it's literally a spatially

"SCENE MISSING" (which is cut into an Industry workprint when there's an insert to be added later on) becomes its opposite in Fisher's Standard Gauge *(1984).*

and temporally continuous shot, within which a series of disjunctive visual events is presented.

Another of the film's subjects is gauge and what it implies: the complex of economic activity that gives rise to an Industrial standard and afterwards is a further consequence of that standard, and the fact that gauge unifies films of every kind. Gauge is one of the unexamined facts of film. There are only a few gauges, and every film is on, or in, one or another of them. No independent filmmaker, however committed to the ideal of the personal and the artisanal and the poetic, makes his or her own raw stock; you work with what large-scale Industrial enterprise gives you. There are organizations such as the Society of Motion Picture and Television Engineers that exist for the sole purpose of setting dimensions and standards for the Industry, and they set these standards to the thousandth part of an inch. Every film is embedded in, or interwoven with, the same material form. As Bruce Conner has shown, this means that any film can become a part of any other film in a way that is utterly direct. The material sameness of all film and, as a corollary, the sameness of the process by which it is presented to us, namely projection, have theoretical implications that should not be overlooked.

And since the film will show you pieces of film, strips of translucent celluloid, it brings up the question of film as an object. Unlike videotape, for example, film has a dual identity. When you look at a piece of videotape, no information is visible; it's encoded within the material in such a way that it can be interpreted only by a machine. The format of film is equally prescribed, but if you pick up a piece of film, there's something to look at. Film can to some degree be read, experienced directly, without a machine, at the level of inert material. An awareness of the material base of film dominates our thinking about it. Sprocket holes are not a part of what we see when a film is projected, and yet we know they're there. They are, in fact, the universal emblem of film, as almost every film festival poster attests. And yet sprocket holes don't stand just for the physical medium but for the idea of movie-ness in the broadest sense: theaters, projection, sitting in the dark, the succession of frames, watching an image, *any* image, the entire potential of film.

MacDonald: A number of your films foreground equipment, often Industry-level equipment, as a subject. In *Production Stills* you use a Mitchell, an Industry camera; *Production Footage* presents an interaction between two kinds of 16mm cameras and the filming conventions that each implies; in *Cue Rolls* we see a synchronizer; in *240x* you use a cel punch and an Oxberry animation stand; and in *Documentary Footage* the woman uses a tape recorder. You seem very involved with machinery, though in a very different way than, say, Léger or Eisenstein.

Fisher: Machines are what make movies. And, as Thom Andersen points out in a long and fascinating essay that is on its way to being published as a book, film—the institution of film, the cinema—is itself a machine, a process of production whose product is none other than its audience, us. If—as I do— you want to take film itself as your subject, I think it's natural to approach it through equipment, because any single piece of machinery can be made to stand for the entire system of machines and what that system is capable of doing.

But even in films that do not actually depict production, filmmakers sometimes choose their equipment as a way of dramatizing their position with respect to the politics of practice. For example, when Godard was shooting the episode on sloth for *The Seven Deadly Sins,* he wanted a camera that was, as he put it, "lazy." He chose, as I recall, a Debrie. To me that's more than just a joke. But this kind of thinking can easily exaggerate itself into a kind of fetishism. When I first became interested in film, the piece of equipment that was fetishized was the Bolex, the archetypal 16mm amateur camera. It was more or less the official camera of underground film. Someone would say in *Film Culture,* "I use no camera but the Bolex," as if it were an emblem of ideological correctness. There was a time when more than anything I wanted a Bolex, so that I too could be ideologically correct, but I never could afford one. In fact I've never owned any of the equipment I've used to produce my films. I've always rented or scrounged what I've needed. In its own mild way, I think it's just as much a polemical position not to own equipment and to get what you want only when you need it as it is to always have your Bolex ready at your side. It implies a different relationship to the act of production.

A lot of my films are shot in sync, and when you work in sync it's easiest and simplest to use professional equipment. It would be perverse to do anything else. And within the category of professional equipment that's portable and simple to operate, there isn't much choice. An Arriflex, or an Eclair, and a Nagra are pretty standard.

The point of *Production Stills* was to replicate the situation of production that is standard in the Industry, or even to overstate it. It was necessary to have a camera that looked like a studio camera, so I used a Mitchell. But in fact even if the idea of the film hadn't required using it, a Mitchell still would have been the best choice. The film was shot on a soundstage, where the ambient sound is negligible, so it was necessary to use the quietest camera possible. An Arri or an Eclair is quiet enough shooting on location, but on a soundstage, even if you use a barney, you still would probably hear camera noise. Not so with a Mitchell in a blimp. It's a camera that's designed for only one purpose, and it does not compromise.

The 16mm Mitchell is an old camera, which made it all the more perfect for *Production Stills*. For me, older equipment is closer to the idea of "the movies." A Mitchell BNC or a BNCR, which are both 35mm cameras, are relatively old-fashioned and conservative designs, but I think of them as emblems of the Industry, the old Industry, Hollywood in its days of glory. For all I know, a Panavision camera might be a better piece of equipment, but it just isn't the same.

MacDonald: The Director and His Actor . . . originates in narrative, but the formal strategies you use—building the film up from roll-long units, jump-cutting, and multiple points of view—and your inclusion of film equipment produce a very unusual kind of narrative.

Fisher: Narrative filmmaking was my original interest, and it is a continuing interest. I make no apologies for it. It's always been a part of my work, however obliquely. In fact if there were no narrative filmmaking and no Industry, I don't think I could do work. I don't mean this in the obvious sense: that—as would certainly be the case—without the Industry, and industry in general, there would be no film or equipment and hence no independent filmmaking (in that respect we are all at the mercy of industrial capitalism, whose sympathies and motives are directed elsewhere). I just mean that for me the Industry is a point of reference and a source, in both a positive and a negative sense, something to recognize and at the same time to react to.

The Director . . . acknowledges the inexorability of the Industry and of narrative, the form the Industry depends on. As much as I like conventional narrative films, narrative is tedious and unsatisfying in a short film because it can't give you the complexity in form and characterization that you need for a narrative to fulfill itself. At best what you get is an elementary story, so all a film like that tells you is that it wants to grow up and be a *real* narrative, a feature-length film. In a short film that derives from narrative, the complexity has to come from somewhere else, so it's almost necessary to take an attitude toward narrative, to play off of the way it works in longer films. The last two segments of *The Director* . . . consist of two parallel series of stills. I took the first series, and the actor took the second. The first declares by means of a title that it is to be understood as a photographic storyboard, a film in schematic form, and it's a particularly bathetic and simple-minded film at that. The second series is presented simply as a succession of stills taken by the actor in accordance with his own wishes. His reasons for taking what he does are not clear, whereas mine are a foregone conclusion. Because the actor was, so to speak, free; his set of stills is elusive and mysterious; mine, because I was a slave of the film's construction, are pedestrian. But the mere fact that the pictures he takes are then presented in succession invites the viewer to narratize them, to draw connections and supply coherence, an invitation that is reinforced by their being presented in parallel with the first sequence, which explicitly announces itself as a film, however rudimentary. The set that I took is foreshadowed by the same scenes presented in live-action, so it's familiar, but when you see the actor's set, you're seeing it for the first time.

In fact, within the framework of the film the actor's choices of what to photograph came first and determined the geography of the film. I and my assistant followed him with the movie camera. The film is built up from his decisions, and yet the pictures he takes are the last thing the film shows you. Or to relate the film's construction to the rules of classical editing in narrative films, the last sequence gives you the reverse angles that are implied in the earlier segment where we take the pictures. Sometimes in the first sequence you see the actor pointing his camera offscreen, but the shot you expect to come next—the reverse angle showing what the actor is pointing his camera at—doesn't occur. Instead, the film saves up all the reverse angles and gives them to you at the end. You do finally get the information, but drastically postponed from the moment when by convention you should receive it. So the film disobeys the law of the reverse angle, but in so doing it conforms to another conventional device of narrative construction, that of suspense: you are caused to want information, the information is withheld from you as you wonder how and when it will be given to you, then you're told, and it's over. So *The Director* . . . acknowledges one part of the conventions of the Industry even while it works against another part.

MacDonald: I'm intrigued by *Screening Room,* which I've read about but never seen. There, too, the conceptual design seems more nearly the work than any specific enactment of it.

Fisher: I would put it the opposite way: that the full import of the underlying idea can be grasped only by seeing the concrete and topical qualities of any correctly executed version or, to use the word I prefer, *state*. Or even better, the film can best be understood by seeing two different states, so that despite their depicting different places, you see how they are both the same film.

Screening Room is a special case of normal theatrical projection. It's best when it's shown in a conventional movie theater, with a proscenium arch, a raked floor, fixed seats, and a projection booth. It starts with a title card, it has a beginning, a middle, and an end, and it relies on normal projection. So in those respects it's a conventional film that's meant to function within the situation of classical projection, but it's also about the limits of that situation. It lies just short of the point where regular projection passes over into an installation-like situation. The film consists of a tracking shot into the theater where the film is going to be shown. As the camera enters the empty theater, the projector is on, but without film in it, so that on the screen there's just a rectangle of flickering white light. The camera stops at the back of the theater, then centers that rectangle. And then there's a slow zoom into the center of the screen. When you're watching the film, you recognize that you are approaching the very building in which you are sitting as you watch this image, and then you see the interior of the theater itself, and finally, as the camera zooms into the empty rectangle of light, representation is dissolved into material. Once the shot is within that rectangle, it becomes a picture of an empty screen, a picture of nothing, that is to say, clear film, not a picture of anything, but just material.

I made the film for the first time in 1968, and of course it has to be made again for each different place it's shown. Each state is materially a different piece of film that registers a different image at a different time, but it's always the same film because the organizing principle, the spatial syntax, is in each instance the same. And because each state is specific to a particular location, the film can be shown only there—and of course never broadcast on television. The title card of the film always includes an announcement to that effect, specifying the one place it can be shown and prohibiting broadcast, like a legal notice.

MacDonald: Production Stills defies conventional distinctions. It's one continuous take, and yet we see a series of Polaroids, each of which contains information that is comparable to a shot. We know it's a color film, since the hand that comes into the frame is color, but since everything else is in black and white, we tend to forget about the color when the hand is absent.

Fisher: That's the method of the film: contrast, or if you like, contradiction. The same thing is true of how the space is treated. The camera's field of view is extremely shallow and extremely small. What you're looking at is a piece of cellotex that's about two feet in front of the camera, and the field of view about four inches by six inches. The stills are introduced one after the other into this tiny space, and they offer a progressive revelation of the much larger space that, as the soundtrack has already told you, has been there all along. And in contradiction to the sharply confined visual space in front of the camera, you're aware of an acoustical space that is extensive, a good part of a soundstage.

MacDonald: Were you taking the pictures yourself?

Fisher: No, I wanted to question the conventional ideas of authorship in filmmaking by showing that it was possible to make a film that was my own even while giving up control over every detail of how the frame looks. Within the limitation that the photographs had to be production stills, the photographer, Thom Andersen, was free to interpret the situation as he chose. The ostensible subject of the film is production stills, but the specific topical details that the stills show, their texture, and the visual sensibility and thought that they embody—most of what the film gives you to look at, in other words—were all determined by someone else. As you suggest, the series of stills are shots that amount to a movie, but its director wasn't me, it was Thom Andersen. I was just the producer. But I did in fact take the last photograph, so that Thom would appear in the film.

MacDonald: All your films strike me as being very witty, and sometimes very funny, in a subtle way. In *Production Stills* there's this incredible array of equipment, and instead of being directed toward some extravaganza with lavish sets and a cast of thousands, it's trained on a piece of cellotex and some black-and-white Polaroids.

Fisher: Again, it's contradiction: an Industry production of a non-Industry film. The film presents the basic model of production in the Industry, albeit in 16mm: a Mitchell on a Moviola crab dolly on a soundstage with a Fisher boom for the mike and a Nagra recorder. All that was missing was a Worrell geared head. I did my best to find one, but had to settle for an ordinary friction head. Not that I would have made use of the capabilities of a geared head: there's no panning or tilting, just as the dolly remains immobile. The film also presents the division of labor and the hierarchy of functions that occur in the Industry: producer, director, director of photography, sound recordist, production assistants.

Production Stills presents the allure of the Industry, while at the same time it takes an attitude toward the Industry by misappropriating its resources. The film is a deliberate underutilization of the equipment that its production uses and depicts. I once showed the film to a normal movie audience, and all they were interested in was how much the equipment was worth. I think they were reacting to what they perceived as my wasting an opportunity: this glamorous equipment thrown away, so to speak, on such a simple film. But if it wasn't that, their reaction at least suggests one of the sources of film's power to fascinate. At any rate, the film's refusal to take advantage of the capabilities of the equipment is a way of criticizing the use that is customarily made of it, just as the film's refusal of production values and its visual poverty are ways of obliquely suggesting other kinds of poverty in products of the Industry.

MacDonald: In *Picture and Sound Rushes* you seem to suggest that sync sound is the primary situation of film.

Fisher: It has always been an axiom with me that sync sound is the basic condition of motion pictures.

MacDonald: You mean in terms of their primary effect on audiences?

Fisher: I mean that's what film *is,* the recording of image and sound in synchronization. Some independent filmmakers regard sync with suspicion, but, as far as I can see, for no other reason than that it's the foundation of commercial filmmaking. My own choice in the matter is plain: you can use the technical attributes and resources of commercial filmmaking while refusing to fall in with the uses to which those techniques and resources are customarily put. In fact you can use them to illuminate and criticize Industry practice itself. I find that choice preferable to letting the Industry drive you into reaction. Why, because the Industry depends on sync, should you feel that the technique has been preempted, that you have no choice but to make a silent film? That's not making a choice, that's letting a choice be taken away from you, retreating before an assertion of cultural and economic power and trying to make a virtue of it—as if that distinction in and of itself could enable you to claim a substantive difference or a kind of purity. It is a difference, but not necessarily a substantive one. And although silent film is certainly simpler, it is not, by any historical or technical standard, purer. The reaction against sync is a particularly pernicious form of entrapment because it means that you are almost automatically accepting consignment to a minority practice. And the effectiveness of minority practice and its place in the larger world are serious questions. I'm all for film at the level of the personal and the poetic, but these questions do need to be thought about. Because it's much more expensive to shoot sync than silent—not just twice as expensive but several times more so—it's tempting to make silent films for economic reasons alone, which is the worst reason of all. That's not an assertion of creative freedom, but an acceptance of being reduced to the margin. I do acknowledge that there have been great silent films made within the last twenty years. They are able to defeat the possibility of sound; although silent, they are whole films. I'm thinking, of course, of Brakhage and some of the structuralists. But these filmmakers do not have illusions about their audience.

As the Industry has shown, sync is an extremely powerful technique. And it is not necessarily tainted merely because the Industry has relied so heavily on it. Why acquiesce in the Industry's claim on it? Why give up so easily, and for poor reasons? Better to reclaim it, so that it can be redeemed and enlisted in the cause of other ways of thinking and other values.

MacDonald: I think I agree with *Picture and Sound Rushes* more than I agree with what you're saying, because *Picture and Sound Rushes* says that

Fisher in Picture and Sound Rushes *(1973)*.

one relationship between image and sound, sync, may be primary in our thinking, but that all are of equal weight.

Fisher: In a quantitative sense that's what the film says, but that's a consequence of its formal composition, which is designed above all to place sound on an absolutely equal footing with picture. In the film I begin by explicitly stating that I regard sync as the primary case, and I use Industry terms like "MOS," "wild," and "rushes," so the film points to the Industry, whose foundation is sync. But the film is certainly not a catalogue of the entire range of sound-image relationships that are found in the Industry. There's no post-synchronization of sound effects, no looping, no narration, no interior voices, and no music. Instead, the film limits itself to the elementary case of double-system sync and permutates the four combinations that it makes possible. So it uses the basic production techniques of the Industry, and uses Industry terms, but it juxtaposes them with other ways of thinking. For example, I may call it MOS, but it's left silent instead of having sound added to it, which in the Industry is invariably the fate of picture material that is shot silent. The same is true of the wild sound; it's left to stand by itself instead of being joined to picture, as in the Industry it always would be.

In the Industry there's sometimes a tendency to treat the recording of production sound less critically than the recording of the image; if the sound doesn't come out right, you can always save the scene by looping it, and you can always go back and record more wild sound. There's confirmation of this unequal relationship in the credit sequences of commercial films; the director of photography is always given a prominent place, and the sound recordist is buried in a list with the hairdresser and the wardrobe person. *Picture and Sound Rushes* criticizes that attitude by explicitly elevating sound to an equal standing with picture. Sound and image are present in equal quantities, and there is just as much wild sound as there is MOS. And since the film was done as one continuous act of production, it's out of the question that the sync sound would be dubbed or the wild sound recorded at a later time. The sound recordist and the camera operator are partners; each is exactly as important as the other.

And juxtaposed with these concerns is something I call the "null case." It's the absence of both picture and sound, an empty screen and a track that is silent, the two voids that the Industry has dedicated itself to filling. And yet the film offers that condition as being on a par with conventional sync, MOS, and wild sound.

In the Industry, rushes aren't just the result of each day's shooting; they're also the raw footage and sound from the entire production, before it is edited into a film. Rushes are just the beginning of post-production, the phase where you decide what to use and what to discard and where a movie is given its specific shape: you decide to the frame where to get in and out of every shot and where to begin and end each piece of music. It takes months. But as soon as *Picture and Sound Rushes* was synced up, assembled in the form of rushes, it was finished. What's more, films made in the Industry—and most made elsewhere, for that matter—invariably consist of only a fraction of the footage that was shot, but as its title suggests, *Picture and Sound Rushes* includes everything that was shot and recorded.

`MacDonald:` Your insistence on sync sound as the absolute in film means you eliminate everything before the late twenties, and furthermore, you don't take into account that most of what presents itself as sync is not really sync at all, but a facsimile of sync.

Fisher: I'm not talking about history, I'm talking about the present and my own work. I'm simply explaining my strategies and suggesting that other people in independent film might want to think about some of these questions. I'm certainly not saying that everything made before the sound era must be consigned to oblivion or regarded as inadequate.

In the Industry, sync is the law, but it's a special and conventionalized kind of sync. No doubt you're correct in saying that a lot of what passes for sync in Industry films is not production sync but a construction of it. The appearance of sync in car chases and similar sequences is only created by the earnest drudgery of sound effects editors. But the fact that it's obligatory for tire squeals and gunshots to be added to picture that is shot silent only confirms my point: in a film made in the Industry, when you see something that you know makes a sound, you have to hear it. And dialogue scenes—human beings talking to each other, the heart of movies—are almost certainly shot in sync. What else is a soundstage for? And when it's not possible to do production sync, prodigious energy is expended to construct the appearance of sync: looping, a Foley stage, and squads of effects editors. But it's always conventionalized sync, flawless and under total control; it seals out the larger world in order to make you a captive of a kind of narrative that is equally a convention.

By far the most significant and constructive use of sync in current film occurs in the work of Straub and Huillet. In fact, their films embody solutions to some of the questions I'm trying to raise. Production sync is the foundation of their work. Their films depict human beings, whether actors or people being themselves. Those people speak, and the sound of their voices is recorded synchronously with the movement of their lips. What is registered by camera and recorder is the appearance of the normal; seemingly a conservative strategy, yet their films are models of correct practice. I think that to Straub and Huillet sync sound represents a convergence between technique and morality. The camera's gaze is directed on a unity, and it is a moral duty to preserve that unity. People must speak for themselves, just as the equipment and material must speak for themselves. So for Straub and Huillet the beginning of film is a commitment to the literality of how the camera and recorder transcribe the scene to which they are witness. The unity of sound and image produces an authenticity and clarity that makes it possible for their films to go on and do very complicated things.

The vocal technique of the performers is a crucial part of their films. Much of the power of *From the Cloud to the Resistance,* for example, depends on the specifics of vocal performance: different accents, inflections, textures, how the words are shaped and given weight. It's essential that you see those people in the act of producing the words that you hear, that you see them engaged in vocal labor, so to speak. The actors are somehow able to turn speech into material, something ponderable, and the effect is sublime.

One hazard of shooting sync on location is extraneous noise in the background. By the standards of the Industry—sync as a self-contained ideal—it's an intolerable flaw that has to be eliminated by shooting the scene over again or by doctoring the track during post-production. But Straub and Huillet accept such intrusions as a way of emphasizing the origin of sound and image in a specific moment of production that has been transcribed by machines. It's part of their larger strategy, that film is not a system of illusion but a system of materials that represent. By the simple device of using sync in this literal way, Straub and Huillet rehabilitate it, and at the same time they criticize the use that has customarily been made of it.

MacDonald: I can see the argument that the use of both sound and image is an axiom of film, but I'd still say that sync is not fundamental to the system to the degree you believe it is. Music and film seem fully as basic as synced voice and image. People speak for themselves in a wide variety of ways, not just when we're looking at their faces as they talk. Chaplin's work and Keaton's prove that. And I don't agree either that human beings talking to each other are *the* heart of movies. There are several, perhaps many, "hearts." The crucial moments in horror films, to take one instance, usually don't center on talking people.

Fisher: Again, I'm talking about the present. Movies made in the Industry tell stories. The stories are about people. That's what movie stars are for. Showing people talking to each other within a construction of convention-alized sync and conventionalized editing techniques is one of the basic ways a movie gains a hold on its audience. Beyond that, what I'm trying to say is very simple. We are at a particular moment in history. What should independent film be trying to do? In what direction lies the greatest opportunity for discovery and progress? One thing to do, instead of straining to extend the technical means of film, is to rediscover old techniques, to use what is already known in new ways. The Industry has relied on sync from the beginning. Partly for this reason sync has come to be regarded as intrinsically conservative, in the sense that a film that uses it can be only a conservative film, just another movie. But in fact this is not so, as the films of Straub and Huillet demonstrate. Sync can be translated into other contexts and used in ways that diverge from the conventions of the Industry and can in fact criticize them. This is equally true for the conventions of continuity editing, as Straub and Huillet demonstrate in *History Lessons*. In films made in the Industry the technical means and conventions conceal themselves. The consequences are the appearance of inevitability and the regulation of the audience's reactions at every moment. In the work of Straub and Huillet, on the other hand, you're able to think about what you see because you're shown how you see it, instead of having the film think it for you.

But the important point is that Straub and Huillet use sync of a kind, and continuity editing of a kind, and they accept some of the production standards that are the norm in the Industry, such as filming at twenty-four frames per second, keeping the image in focus, using normal lighting ratios, and shooting with the camera on a tripod. I think the potential for progress in film is far greater in this direction—one that uses some of the techniques of the Industry and so is seemingly conservative—than it is in the direction of technical manipulations of the kinds that are usually associated with experimental film.

MacDonald: For a long time there was an assumption that film and language didn't belong together. Murnau tried to eliminate intertitles, filmmakers were criticized for being literary, and so on. But it seems implicit in your work that language is as much an automatic part of the system as sound is. In many of your films there's a printed text. Sometimes it's very obvious, as it is in *The Wilkinson Household Fire Alarm* and *Projection Instructions,* and sometimes it's very subtle, as in *Cue Rolls:* other than those moments when the white leader moves through, everything in *Cue Rolls* seems completely still, except that we can see that the footage counter is moving; we can't read it, but we know that it's a text, if only in the most rudimentary sense, and this tiny textual motion alters our understanding of what we see. The Xeroxes of the Maltese cross in *240x* are also a kind of text, as is the face of the clock in *Phi Phenomenon.* Even the unusually long titles of *The Director and His Actor Look at Footage Showing Preparations for an Unmade Film (2)* and *The Wilkinson Household Fire Alarm*—the film is only one and a half minutes long—draw further attention to language.

Fisher: It's asking a lot of a simple word like *text* to comprehend all those different instances, and I don't know about your suggestion that what you call text is comparable to language, or at least implies it. But nonetheless your observation is basically correct. I feel that language, in the strict sense, absolutely belongs in film. And you're correct in saying that my insistence on language parallels my insistence on sound. One implies the other; they go together. Like sound, especially sync sound, language is a resource, an extremely powerful one. Why renounce it? A flight from language is the same thing as a flight from sound into silence and has the same consequences. Declining to use language means you accept the use that others make of it. Why deprive yourself of a voice?

MacDonald: The text of *Projection Instructions* creates a three-way relationship. By reading the text on the screen—the orders *you* are giving—our attention is focussed on the projectionist.

Fisher: It's really not me giving the instructions, it's the piece of celluloid in the projector, whose shadow the projectionist is looking at. But you're right that the audience is made aware of the projectionist. That's really one of the points of the film. And furthermore I think the audience's awareness is sympathetic, not the hostile kind that occurs when a conventional film is out of focus or there's a sloppy reel change. On those occasions the projectionist is regarded as nothing more than some anonymous mechanic who's failing to do his job. But in *Projection Instructions,* I think the audience is in sympathy with the projectionist because he's perceived as being tyrannized by the film's unrelenting demands. At bottom, the film is simply a score, and the projectionist is the person who performs it. The audience is watching a performance where they can see the score at the same time that they see the performer's interpretation of it. But the film reverses the usual relation between score and performer: the score is visible, but the performer, enclosed in the projection booth, is not. And even if there's no booth, the performer is still behind the audience instead of in front of it.

In *Projection Instructions* I wanted to play against the idea of the visual as the essential attribute of film. All you see are words, and all you hear are words. Like *The Wilkinson Household Fire Alarm,* it's a case of redundancy,

Instructions to the projectionist, from Fisher's Projection Instructions *(1976).*

but still more literal and hyperbolic: the words on the screen are exactly the same as the words on the track. Yet it's a work that could be realized only as a film, and it's a very film-y film.

Above all, the film raises questions about the projector as the last in the succession of machines through which film comes to us. A lot of attention has been given to the camera as an interpretive instrument. But the projector has remained enshrined as an objective, almost scientific, instrument. Normal projection is a hidden assumption even in the few examples of avant-garde work that have taken projection as a subject, where, for example, the projector serves as a device that extrudes light or inflects the space through which the beam passes before it strikes the screen. Even then, the projector's autonomy as a mechanism that functions by itself remains inviolable. There's obviously nothing wrong with conventional projection, but still I find it strange that work of every kind, including advanced work, relies on a single standard of correctness. I wanted to see what could be done by bringing that standard into question: there is no one correct way to show *Projection Instructions.* It is, so to speak, an objective film, one that gives the projectionist the chance to be an interpretive artist.

MacDonald: I've seen Ken Jacobs do performances with projectors, but he's one of the very few exceptions to what you're saying that I know of.

Fisher: Even that's a little different. The piece of his that I recall most vividly required two projectors, two prints, and an auxiliary shutter mechanism, and I think each member of the audience watched the film through a polarizing filter. And Ken Jacobs himself was the projectionist and operator of the special shutter. Even if the technical apparatus were simpler, I think the central element would remain Ken Jacobs as the interpreter of the material, the filmmaker as a performing artist, performing a work that he alone can present, that is unimaginable without his being there. That piece is more about Ken Jacobs as an interpretive paleographer of images than anything else. *Projection Instructions,* on the other hand, accepts the mechanical limitations of normal projection even as it calls into question the conventions that have arisen from them. The film requires only the irreducible minimum that is necessary to present any film: one film, one projector, one projectionist. I drop the film in the mail, and it can be shown anywhere there's a 16mm sound projector and someone who knows how to run it. One of the things the film does is to rediscover this anonymous attendant, so it's best when the film is projected by anyone but me.

MacDonald: In two films—*Picture and Sound Rushes* and *Documentary Footage*—we don't actually see a text, but we see someone read one.

Fisher: In *Picture and Sound Rushes* I wasn't reading a text; I was improvising from notes. That accounts for my awkward delivery. Some people think it's just hilarious, but however embarrassing it is to me, my performance gives the film a pathos that contrasts with the rigidity of its timetable format. In *Documentary Footage* the woman first reads a list of questions into a tape recorder, then plays back the questions and improvises her answers to them. One way the film achieves its effect is through the interplay between the questions, which are brief and exact and come at regular intervals, and her spontaneous answers.

But *Documentary Footage* and *Picture and Sound Rushes* are similar in that both of them set a task for a subject within a closely controlled situation and then record the subject's performance, like a scientific experiment. They draw from psychological testing and instrumentation photography, even to the extent that in both of them there's a timer.

MacDonald: There are wonderful moments in *Documentary Footage.* Did you direct the woman in any way?

Fisher: Not at all, except to the extent that I composed the scheme for the film, and she created her performance in response to it. In the second half of the film, there was an alternation between questions and opportunities to answer them. So there were open spaces within which she was free to respond, and she filled them with her own inventions, with herself, really. She rehearsed operating the equipment and moving to her mark, but that was all. She knew in advance that the questions would be about physical appearance, but she didn't actually see them until the shot began. Then she was on her own for eleven minutes. She did things with her face and gestures that a director could never imagine, much less achieve through building and controlling a performance. I had total confidence in her, and she gave a brilliant performance. She had real star quality. In that respect it's a conventional film. I wanted to do it on the first take—that was related to the idea of accepting her performance as she gave it—and that's what happened. We did a second take for protection, but she had given everything to her first performance. I got the second take developed but never had it workprinted.

MacDonald: She goes through a complete change in body language and mood, and everything has to do with her position with regard to language.

Fisher: Your observation is literally correct. Her performance is shaped by where the language is coming from or where it's being directed, that is, who she thinks is asking the questions and to whom she in turn addresses her answers. The questions come back to her from the tape recorder in her own voice, but the author of the questions is me, so the interrogator has a compound identity. Partly as a result of that, she directs her answers to different listeners: herself on the tape, me on the tape as the author of the questions, the tape recorder itself, the camera, me operating the camera, and sometimes the audience that she knows will ultimately see the film, as if it's asking the questions. These shifts give her performance a lot of its energy and charm.

MacDonald: One last question: many filmmakers are deeply—I could say obsessively, but this *is* a serious problem—involved in protecting their prints from damage. When I asked you the other night whether I had scratched *The Wilkinson Household Fire Alarm,* you didn't seem particularly concerned.

Fisher: How can you fetishize a print? I mean, people do, but you have to fight against it, otherwise you live in fear. A brand-new print is one thing, but the print you mentioned is ten years old. After all, it's the nature of movies to wear out. They're presented to us by a machine that sooner or later destroys them.

Filmography

The following listing is as complete as I am able to make it. Each film's title is followed by the year in which the film was completed, the film's gauge, the length of the film to the nearest quarter minute, and finally by an indication of whether the film is black and white or color or both, and silent or sound. (When more than one film was completed in a single year, I use the order that the filmmaker has approved.) In parentheses I have listed primary rental sources for good prints, often using the following abbreviations: AFA (American Federation of Arts, 41 East 65th St., New York, NY 10021), BFI (British Film Institute, 81 Dean St., London W1V 6AA), CC (Canyon Cinema, 2325 Third St., Suite 338, San Francisco, CA 94107), CFDC (Canadian Filmmakers Distribution Centre, 299 Queen St. W., Suite 204A, Toronto, Ontario, M5V 1Z9), FMC (Film-makers' Cooperative, 175 Lexington Ave., New York, NY 10016), LFC (London Film-makers' Co-operative, 42 Gloucester Ave., London, NW1), and MOMA (Museum of Modern Art, Department of Film, 11 W. 53rd St., New York, NY 10019). In some cases, films are available from the filmmakers. In those instances, I include the filmmaker's address only once, with the listing of the earliest of the films available from the filmmaker.

Beth B and Scott B

G-Man. 1978. Super-8mm; 37 minutes; color; sound (B Studio, 45 Crosby St. #5S, New York, NY 10012).
Black Box. 1978. Super-8mm; 25 minutes; color; sound (B Studio).
Letters to Dad. 1979. Super-8mm/16mm; 15 minutes; color; sound (B Studio).
The Offenders. 1979. Super-8mm; 90 minutes; color; sound (B Studio).
The Trap Door. 1980. Super-8mm; 70 minutes; color; sound (B Studio).
Vortex. 1983. 16mm; 90 minutes; color; sound (First Run).

Beth B

Dominatrix: The Dominatrix Sleeps Tonight (music video). 1984. 16mm; 4¼ minutes; color; sound (First Run).

Joan Jett: I Need Someone (music video). 1984. 16mm; 3¼ minutes; color; sound (First Run).

Taka Boom. In the Middle of the Night (music video). 1985. 16mm; 3¼ minutes; color; sound (First Run).

Salvation (Have You Said Your Prayers Today?). 1986. 35mm; 90 minutes; color; sound (Circle Releasing).

Scott B

The Specialist. 1984. Super-8mm; 10 minutes; color; sound (First Run).

Last Rights. 1985. Super-8mm; 15 minutes; color; sound (First Run).

Diana Barrie

Untitled. 1970. 16mm; 3 minutes; color; silent.

To Clearlight. 1972. Super-8mm; 11¼ minutes; color; silent.

Eyes Through Snow. 1973. Super-8mm; 3¾ minutes; color; silent.

A Curious Story. 1973. Super-8mm; 1¾ minutes; color; silent.

The Annunciation. 1974. Super-8mm; 8¼ minutes; color; silent (Barrie, 60 E. 3rd St., Apt. #9, New York, NY 10003).

Night Movie #1 (Self-Portrait). 1974. Super-8mm; 3½ minutes; black and white; silent (Barrie).

Dear Diary Volume I. 1974. Super-8mm; 11¼ minutes; color; silent (Barrie).

Portrait of Pamela. 1974. Super-8mm; 2¾ minutes; color; silent (Barrie).

For the Dead Angels. 1974. Super-8mm; 4 minutes; black and white; silent (Barrie).

Auto-Graph. 1974. Super-8mm; ¾ minute; color; silent (Barrie).

The Red House. 1974. Super-8mm; 4¾ minutes; color; silent (Barrie).

Sarah's Room. 1974. Super-8mm; 4¾ minutes; color; silent (Barrie).

Night Movie #2 (Flashlight). 1974. Super-8mm; 4 minutes; black and white; silent (Barrie).

Dear Diary Volume II. 1975. Super-8mm; 11¼ minutes; color; silent (Barrie).

Hand-Maid #2. 1975. 16mm; 1¾ minutes; color; sound (Barrie).

Circus Vignettes. 1975. Super-8mm; 8¾ minutes; color; silent (Barrie).

Letters from China. 1975. 16mm; 8 minutes; color; silent (Barrie).

Dear Diary Volume III. 1976. Super-8mm; 9 minutes; color; silent (Barrie).

A Song for Solomon. 1976. Super-8mm; 16¾ minutes; color; silent (Barrie).

Day Dreams. 1977. 16mm; 10½ minutes; color; silent (Barrie).

By Sea. 1978. 8mm; 9½ minutes; color; silent (Barrie).

W'loo. 1978. 8mm; 3 minutes; color; silent (Barrie).

My Version of the Fall. 1978. 16mm; 8½ minutes; color; silent (Cecile Starr, 50 West 96th St., New York, NY 10025).

The Living or Dead Test. 1979. 16mm; 5¼ minutes; color; sound (Starr).

Le Mois de Fevrier. 1979. Super-8mm; 5 minutes; color; silent (Barrie).

Night Movie #3 (The Party). 1979. Super-8mm; 4¼ minutes; black and white; silent (Barrie).
Untitled. 1980. 16mm; 2½ minutes; color; silent (Starr).
Magic Explained. 1980. 16mm; 4 minutes; color; silent (Starr).
Stay Awake Whenever You Can. 1982. 16mm; 29 minutes; color; sound (Starr).
The Garden. 1987. 16mm; 2½ minutes; color; sound (Barrie).

Tom Chomont

Diary Rolls. 1961–63. 8mm; black and white; silent.
Vowels. 1963. 8mm; 1 minute; color; silent.
The Tendency. 1963. 8mm; 4 minutes; black and white; silent (Chomont, 260 Elizabeth St., New York, NY 10012).
The Hungry Heart. 1964. 16mm; 4 minutes; color; silent.
Flames. 1965. 16mm; 6 minutes; black and white/color; silent (FMC).
Night Blossoms. 1965. 16mm; 5 minutes; black and white/color; silent (FMC).
Anthony. 1966. 16mm; 12 minutes; color; silent (FMC).
Mona Lysa. 1966. 16mm; 4 minutes; color; silent (FMC).
The Mirror Garden. 1967. 16mm; 5 minutes; color; silent (Chomont).
Jabbok. 1967. 16mm; 3 minutes; black and white; silent (Chomont).
Squills. 1967. 16mm; 5 minutes; black and white; silent.
Morpheus in Hell. 1967. 16mm; 16 minutes; black and white/color; silent (FMC).
Epilog/Siam. 1968. 16mm; 6 minutes; color; silent (FMC).
Phases of the Moon: The Parapsychology of Everyday Life. 1968. 16mm; 4 minutes; black and white/color; silent (Chomont, FMC, LFC).
Ophelia and *The Cat Lady*. 1969. 16mm; ¾ minute/1½ minutes; black and white/color; sound (Chomont, FMC, LFC).
Oblivion. 1969. 16mm; 5 minutes; black and white/color; silent (BFI, Chomont, FMC).
A Persian Rug. 1969. 16mm; 4 minutes; black and white/color; silent (BFI, Chomont, FMC).
Gloria in the Glass. 1969. 16mm; 1 minute; color; silent (BFI, Chomont, FMC).
Untitled. 1969. 16mm; 1 minute; color; silent (Chomont).
Portret. 1971. 16 mm; 3 minutes; black and white, printed on color stock; silent (FMC).
Aria. 1971. 16mm; 2 minutes; color; silent (FMC).
Love Objects. 1971. 16mm; 15 minutes; black and white/color; silent (FMC, LFC).
Onderzoek/Research. 1972. 16mm; 6 minutes; color; silent (Chomont, FMC).
Lijn II. 1972. 16mm; 1 minute; color; silent (FMC).
Re:Incarnation (co-made with Peter Erdmann). 1973. 16mm; 14 minutes; color; sound on tape (Chomont, FMC).
Bild. 1974. 16mm; 4 minutes; color; silent (Chomont).
.. 1974. 16mm; 3 minutes; black and white; silent (FMC).
abda. 1974. 16mm; 5 minutes; black and white; silent (FMC).
Rebirth. 1974. 16mm; 3 minutes; black and white, printed with color filters; silent (Chomont, FMC).
Lynne. 1975. 16mm; 3 minutes; black and white; silent.

Untitled. 1975. 16mm; 2 minutes; black and white; silent (FMC, on video from Chomont).

Endymion by Joseph Glin (Chomont was assistant cameraperson and editor and appears in film). 1977. 16mm; 9 minutes; black and white, printed on color stock; silent (Chomont, FMC).

Crosscurrents. 1977. 16mm; 4 minutes; black and white; silent (FMC).

modern art. 1977. 16mm; 5 minutes; black and white; silent (FMC).

The Heavens. 1977. 16mm; 4 minutes; color; silent. (Chomont, FMC).

Space Time Studies. 1977. 16mm; 20 minutes; color; silent (Chomont, FMC).

Earth. 1978. 16mm; 4 minutes; color; silent (Chomont, FMC).

Astral Logic. 1978. 16mm; 2 minutes; black and white, printed red and blue; silent (Chomont).

Life Style. 1978. 16mm; 3 minutes; color; silent (Chomont, FMC).

Mouse in Your Face. 1978. 16mm (3-D); 3 minutes; black and white, printed red and blue; silent (Chomont).

Minor Revisions. 1979. 16mm; 12 minutes; color; silent (Chomont, FMC).

Razor Head. 1981. 16mm; 6 minutes; color; silent (Chomont, FMC).

Couples (portraits of couples, ongoing). 1981 to present. 16mm; color; silent (Chomont, FMC).

Partial Memory. 1984. 16mm; 4 minutes; black and white/color; silent (Chomont).

Broken Heart. 1984. 16mm; 6 minutes; color; silent (Chomont, FMC).

Joe's maison. 1984. 16mm; 6 minutes; color; silent (Chomont, FMC).

Dream & Desire. 1986. 16mm; 6 minutes; color; sound (Chomont).

Eine Kleine Katzen Muziek (The Cat Music). 1987. 16mm; 5½ minutes; color; silent (Chomont, FMC).

Bruce Conner

A Movie. 1958. 16mm; 12 minutes; black and white; sound (CC, MOMA).

Cosmic Ray. 1962. 16mm; 4¼ minutes; black and white; sound (CC).

Leader. 1964. 16mm; 35 minutes; black and white; sound (destroyed).

Vivian. 1965. 16mm; 3 minutes; black and white; sound (CC).

Ten Second Film. 1965. 16mm; 10 seconds; black and white; silent (CC).

Cosmic Ray #1/Cosmic Ray #2/Cosmic Ray #3. 1965. Three 8mm loops to be shown simultaneously; continuous; #1: color, #2, 3: black and white; silent.

Looking for Mushrooms. 1965. 8mm; 50 feet (can be shown at various speeds or as loop); color; sound.

Class Picture. 1965. 8mm; 50 feet (can be shown at various speeds or as loop); black and white; silent.

Easter Morning. 1966. 8mm; 50 feet (can be shown at various speeds or as loop); color; silent.

Luke. 1966. 8mm; 50 feet (can be shown at various speeds or as loop); color; sound.

Breakaway. 1966. 16mm; 5 minutes; black and white; sound (CC).

Report. 1963–67 (various versions). 16mm; 13 minutes; black and white; sound (CC).

Report (an "entirely different film" from the previous listing). 1964–68 (various versions). 8mm; 50 feet (shown as a continuous loop and as an 8mm film); black and white; silent.

Looking for Mushrooms. 1961–67 (various versions). 16mm; 3 minutes; color; sound (CC).

The White Rose. 1967. 16mm; 7 minutes; black and white; sound (CC).

Liberty Crown. 1967. 16mm; 5 minutes; black and white; sound (destroyed).

Antonia Christina Basilotta. 1968. 8mm; 126 feet (can be shown at various speeds or as loop); black and white; silent.

Coming Attractions. 1968. 8mm; 40 feet (can be shown at various speeds or as loop); black and white; silent.

Permian Strata. 1969. 16mm; 3½ minutes; black and white; sound (CC, MOMA).

Marilyn Times Five. 1969–73 (various versions). 16mm; 13½ minutes; black and white; sound (CC).

Crossroads. 1976. 16mm; 36 minutes; black and white; sound (CC).

Take the 5:10 to Dreamland. 1976. 16mm; 5 minutes, 10 seconds; sepia; sound (CC, MOMA).

Valse Triste. 1977. 16mm; 5 minutes; sepia; sound (CC, MOMA).

Mongoloid. 1978. 16mm; 4 minutes; black and white; sound (CC, MOMA).

America Is Waiting. 1981. 16mm; 3½ minutes; black and white; sound (CC).

Manuel DeLanda

Shit. 1975. Super-8mm; 30 minutes; black and white; sound (DeLanda, 140 East 46th St., Apt. 6P, New York, NY 10017).

Song of a Bitch. 1976. Super-8mm; 30 minutes; color; sound (DeLanda).

Saliva Dildo—Premature Ejaculators. 1976. 16mm; 8 minutes; color; silent (DeLanda).

The Itch Scratch Itch Cycle. 1976. 16mm; 8 minutes; color; sound (DeLanda, LFC).

Incontinence. 1978. 16mm; 18 minutes; color; sound (DeLanda, LFC).

Ismism. 1979. 16mm; 8 minutes; color; silent (DeLanda).

Raw Nerves. 1980. 16mm; 30 minutes; color; sound (DeLanda, LFC).

Magic Mushroom Mountain Movie. 1981. Super-8mm; 10 minutes; color; sound (DeLanda).

Harmful or Fatal If Swallowed. 1982. Super-8mm/16mm; 14 minutes; black and white; sound (DeLanda).

Judgement Day. 1983. 16mm; 8 minutes; color; sound (DeLanda).

Vivienne Dick

Guérillère Talks. 1978. Super-8mm; 30 minutes; color; sound (Dick, 128 Burnham, Fellows Road, London NW3, England).

She Had Her Gun All Ready. 1978. Super-8mm; 30 minutes; color; sound (Dick, LFC).

Beauty Becomes the Beast. 1979. Super-8mm; 45 minutes; color; sound (Dick, The Kitchen, LFC).

Liberty's Booty. 1980. Super-8mm; 50 minutes; color; sound (Dick, LFC).

Visibility: Moderate. 1981. Super-8mm; 45 minutes; color; sound (AFA, Dick, LFC).

Loisaida. 1982. Super-8mm; 3 minutes; color; sound (Dick, LFC).

Trailer. 1983. Super-8mm; 14 minutes; color; sound (Dick, LFC).

Like Dawn to Dust. 1983. Super-8mm; 7 minutes; color; sound (Dick, LFC).

Rothach. 1986. 16mm; 8 minutes; color; sound (Dick).

Morgan Fisher

The Director and His Actor Look at Footage Showing Preparations for an Unmade Film (1). 1967. 16mm; 15 minutes; black and white; sound.

The Director and His Actor Look at Footage Showing Preparations for an Unmade Film (2). 1968. 16mm; 15 minutes; black and white; sound (FMC).

Documentary Footage. 1968. 16mm; 11 minutes; color; sound (CC, FMC, LFC).

Phi Phenomenon. 1968. 16mm; 11 minutes; black and white; silent (FMC).

Screening Room. 1968. 16mm; 3 minutes; color; silent.

Production Stills. 1970. 16mm; 11 minutes; color; sound (AFA, FMC).

Production Footage. 1971. 16mm; 10 minutes; color; sound (FMC).

Picture and Sound Rushes. 1973. 16mm; 11 minutes; black and white; sound (FMC).

The Wilkinson Household Fire Alarm. 1973. 16mm; 1½ minutes; color; sound (Fisher, 1306C Princeton St., Santa Monica, CA 90404).

240x. 1974. 16mm; 16 minutes; black and white; sound (Fisher).

Cue Rolls. 1974. 16mm; 5½ minutes; color; sound (Fisher).

Eadweard Muybridge, Zoopraxographer (directed by Thom Andersen, edited by Fisher). 1975. 16mm; 60 minutes; sepia; sound (New Yorker).

Projection Instructions. 1976. 16mm; 4 minutes; black and white; sound (Fisher).

Southern Exposure. 1977. 16mm film installation; continuous; color; silent.

North Light. 1979. 16mm film installation; continuous; color; silent.

Passing Time. 1979. 16mm film installation; continuous; black and white; silent.

Color Balance. 1980. Three-projector Super-8mm installation; continuous; color; silent.

Standard Gauge. 1984. 16mm; 35 minutes; color; sound (AFA, Fisher).

Hollis Frampton

A complete filmography for Frampton is included in *October*, no. 32 (Spring 1985), pp. 167–69.

Clouds Like White Sheep. 1962. 16mm; 25 minutes; black and white; silent (destroyed).

A Running Man. 1963. 16mm; 22 minutes; color; silent (destroyed).

Ten Mile Poem. 1964. 16mm; 33 minutes; color; silent (destroyed).

Obelisk Ampersand Encounter. 1965. 16mm; 1½ minutes; color; sound (lost).

Manual of Arms. 1966. 16mm; 17 minutes; black and white; silent (FMC).

Process Red. 1966. 16mm; 3½ minutes; color; silent (FMC).

Information. 1966. 16mm; 4 minutes; black and white; silent (FMC).

States. 1967, 1970; 16mm; 17½ minutes; black and white; silent (FMC).

Heterodyne. 1967. 16mm; 7 minutes; color; silent (FMC).

Snowblind. 1968. 16mm; 5½ minutes; black and white; silent (FMC).

Maxwell's Demon. 1968. 16mm; 4 minutes; color; sound (FMC).

Surface Tension. 1968. 16mm; 10 minutes; color; sound (FMC).

Palindrome. 1969. 16mm; 22 minutes; color; silent (FMC).

Carrots & Peas. 1969. 16mm; 5½ minutes; color; sound (FMC).

Lemon. 1969. 16mm; 7½ minutes; color; silent (FMC, LFC).

Prince Ruperts Drops. 1969. 16mm; 7 minutes; color; silent (FMC).

Works & Days. 1969. 16mm; 12 minutes; black and white; silent (FMC).

Artificial Light. 1969. 16mm; 25 minutes; color; silent (FMC, LFC).

Zorns Lemma. 1970. 16mm; 60 minutes; color; sound (FMC, LFC).

nostalgia (Part 1 of *Hapax Legomena*). 1971. 16mm; 36 minutes; black and white; sound (AFA, FMC).

Travelling Matte (Part 4 of *Hapax Legomena*). 1971. 16mm; 33½ minutes; black and white; silent (FMC).

Critical Mass (Part 3 of *Hapax Legomena*). 1971. 16mm; 25½ minutes; black and white; sound (FMC).

Special Effects (Part 7 of *Hapax Legomena*). 1972. 16mm; 10½ minutes; black and white; sound (FMC).

Poetic Justice (Part 2 of *Hapax Legomena*). 1972. 16mm; 31½ minutes; black and white; silent (FMC).

Ordinary Matter (Part 5 of *Hapax Legomena*). 1972. 16mm; 36 minutes; black and white; sound (FMC).

Remote Control (Part 6 of *Hapax Legomena*). 1972. 16mm; 29 minutes; black and white; silent (FMC).

Magellan. Begun 1972, incomplete. 16mm; 36 hours (approx.); color; sound. All the films in this listing from *Apparatus Sum (Studies for Magellan: #1)* (1972) through *The Birth of Magellan: Fourteen Cadenzas* (1980) are parts of *Magellan.*

Apparatus Sum (Studies for Magellan: #1). 1972. 16mm; 2½ minutes; color; silent (FMC).

Tiger Balm (Memoranda Magelani: #1). 1972. 16mm; 10 minutes; color; silent (FMC).

Yellow Springs (Vanishing Point: #1). 1972. 16mm; 5 minutes; color; silent (FMC).

Public Domain. 1972. 16mm; 18 minutes; black and white; silent (FMC).

Less. 1973. 16mm; 1 second (repeated 20 times); black and white; silent (FMC).

Autumnal Equinox. 1974. 16mm; 27 minutes; color; silent (FMC).

Noctiluca (Magellan's Toys: #1). 1974. 16mm; 3½ minutes; color; silent (FMC).

Winter Solstice. 1974. 16mm; 33 minutes; color; silent (FMC).

Straits of Magellan: Drafts & Fragments. 1974. 16mm; 51¼ minutes; color; silent (FMC).

Summer Solstice. 1974. 16mm; 32 minutes; color; silent (FMC).

SOLARIUMAGELANI. 1974. 16mm; 92 minutes; color; silent (FMC).

Banner. 1974. 16mm; 40 seconds; color; silent (FMC).

INGENIVM NOBIS IPSA PVELLA FECIT (formerly *Vernal Equinox*). 1975. 16mm; 67 minutes; color; silent (FMC).

Drum. 1975. 16mm; 20 seconds; color; silent (FMC).

Pas de Trois. 1975. 16mm; 4 minutes; color; silent (FMC).

Magellan: At the Gates of Death. Part I: *The Red Gate.* 1976. 16mm; 54 minutes; color; silent. Part II: *The Green Gate.* 1976. 16mm; 52 minutes; color; silent (FMC).

Otherwise Unexplained Fires. 1976. 16mm; 14 minutes; color; silent (FMC).

Not the First Time. 1976. 16mm; 6 minutes; color; silent (FMC).

For Georgia O'Keeffe. 1976. 16mm; 3½ minutes; color; silent (FMC).

Quaternion. 1976. 16mm; 4½ minutes; color; silent (FMC).

Tuba. 1976. 16mm; 3 minutes; color; silent (FMC).

Procession. 1976. 16mm; 4 minutes; color; silent (FMC).

More Than Meets the Eye. 1979. 16mm; 7½ minutes; color; silent (FMC).

Gloria! 1979. 16mm; 9½ minutes; color; sound (FMC).

The Birth of Magellan: Dreams of Magellan (Dream I: Matrix). 1979. 16mm; 28 minutes; color; silent (FMC).

The Birth of Magellan: Mindfall (Parts I and VII). 1980. 16mm; 21 minutes/21 minutes; color; sound (FMC).

The Birth of Magellan: Fourteen Cadenzas (Cadenzas I and XIV). 1980. 16mm; 5½ minutes/5½ minutes; color; sound (FMC).

Monsieur Phot: A Film by Joseph Cornell (incomplete). 16mm; color; sound (FMC).

R (incomplete). 16mm; color; sound (FMC).

A & B in Ontario (co-shot with Joyce Wieland, completed by Wieland). 1984. 16mm; 17 minutes; black and white; sound (CFDC, FMC).

Larry Gottheim

Blues. 1969. 16mm; 8½ minutes; color; silent (FMC).

Corn. 1970. 16mm; 11 minutes; color; silent (FMC).

Fog Line. 1970. 16mm; 10½ minutes; color; silent (CC, FMC, LFC).

Doorway. 1971. 16mm; 7½ minutes; black and white; silent (CC, FMC, LFC).

Thought (formerly *Swing*). 1971. 16mm; 7½ minutes; color; silent (FMC).

Harmonica. 1971. 16mm; 10½ minutes; color; sound (CC, FMC).

Barn Rushes. 1971. 16mm; 34 minutes; color; silent (CC, FMC, LFC).

Horizons (Part 1, "Overture," of *Elective Affinities*). 1973. 16mm; 75 minutes; color; silent (CC, FMC).

Mouches Volantes (Part 2 of *Elective Affinities*). 1976. 16mm; 69 minutes; black and white/color; sound (FMC).

Four Shadows (Part 3 of *Elective Affinities*). 1978. 16mm; 64 minutes; color; sound (FMC).

Tree of Knowledge (Part 4 of *Elective Affinities*). 1980. 16mm; 60 minutes; color; sound (FMC).

Natural Selection. 1983. 16mm; 35 minutes; color; sound (AFA, FMC).

"Sorry/Hear Us". 1985. 16mm; 8 minutes; black and white; sound (FMC).

Mnemosyne, Mother of Muses. 1986. 16mm; 18 minutes; color; sound (FMC).

Robert Huot

Leader. 1967. 16mm; 12 minutes; color; silent (FMC).

Scratch. 1967. 16mm; 11 minutes; black and white; silent (FMC).

From Loops. 1967. 16mm; 6 minutes; black and white; silent (FMC).

Spray. 1967. 16mm; 11½ minutes; black and white; silent (FMC).

Red Stockings. 1969. 16mm; 3 minutes; color; silent (FMC).

Cross Cut—A Blue Movie. 1969. 16mm; 1 minute; color; silent (FMC).

Black and White Film. 1969. 16mm; 12½ minutes; black and white; silent (FMC).

Nude Descending the Stairs. 1970. 16mm; 8 minutes; black and white; silent (FMC).

One Year (1970). 1971. 16mm; 150 minutes (or 40 minutes as a four-image work); black and white/color; silent (FMC).

Turning Torso Drawdown. 1971. 16mm; 16 minutes; black and white/color; silent (FMC).
The Sex Life of the Artist as a Young Man. 1971. 16mm; 6 minutes; black and white; silent (FMC).
Rolls: 1971. 1972. 16mm; 100 minutes; black and white/color; silent (FMC).
Strip. 1972. 16mm; 12 minutes; color; sound-on-tape (FMC).
Third One-Year Movie—1972. 1973. 16mm; 70 minutes; black and white/color; silent (FMC).
Accentuate the Positive. 1973. 16mm; 5 minutes; black and white; sound (FMC).
Face of Faces. 1973. 16mm; 3 minutes; black and white; sound-on-tape (FMC, LFC).
Diary Film #4—1973. 1974. 16mm; 50 minutes; color; silent (FMC; also available from Huot in a two-monitor video version, R.D.1, Box 41, New Berlin, NY 13411).
Beautiful Movie. 1975. 16mm; 5 minutes; color; silent (FMC).
Diary 1974–75. 1975. 16mm; 80 minutes; color; ambient sound from 6 radios (FMC).
China 1978. 1978. Super-8mm (presented with slides, music, and live commentary); 50 minutes; color (FMC, Huot).
Fades and Close-Ups. 1978. Super-8mm; 7 minutes; black and white; sound (FMC, Huot).
Super-8 Diary 1979. 1980. Super-8mm; 200 minutes; black and white/color; sound (FMC).
Erotic Trilogy. 1980. Super-8mm; 11 minutes; black and white/color; sound (FMC, Huot).
Cum Foo. 1980. Super-8mm; 12 minutes; black and white/color; sound (FMC, Huot).
Diary 1980. 1981. Super-8mm; 180 minutes; black and white/color; sound (Huot).
Dr. Faustus' Foot Fetish. 1981. Super-8mm; 22 minutes; black and white/color; silent (FMC, Huot).
1983 Diary. 1984. Super-8mm; 55 minutes (five projectors); black and white/color; sound (Huot).
Kai Study. 1984. Super-8mm; 3 minutes; color; sound (Huot).
Hollis Frampton 1936–84. 1984. Super-8mm; 9 minutes; color; sound (Huot).

Taka Iimura

Junk. 1962. 8mm; 12 minutes; black and white; sound-on-tape.
Iro ("Color"). 1962. 8mm/16mm; 10 minutes; color; sound (FMC, LFC).
6 × 6. 1962. 8mm/16mm; 16 minutes; black and white; silent.
Dada '62. 1962. 8mm/16mm; 10 minutes; black and white; silent.
DeSade. 1962. 8mm/16mm; 10 minutes; black and white; sound.
Love ("Ai"). 1963. 8mm/16mm; 12 minutes; black and white; sound (CC, FMC, LFC).
Onan. 1963. 16mm; 7 minutes; black and white; sound (FMC).
Upside Down ("Sakasama"). 1963. 8mm; 15 minutes; black and white; silent.
The Masseurs. 1963. 8mm/16mm; 15 minutes; black and white; silent.
Peep Show ("Ukiyo Ukare"). 1964. 8mm/16mm; 5 minutes; color; silent.
The Memory of Angkor-Wat. 1964 (abandoned).
Eye Raping. 1964. 16mm; 11 minutes; black and white; silent.

The Fact (retitled *"My Documentary"*). 1964. 16mm; 2 minutes; black and white; silent.

A Dance Party in the Kingdom of Lilliput, No. 1. 1964. 16mm; 12 minutes; black and white; sound (FMC, LFC).

A Dance Party in the Kingdom of Lilliput, No. 2. 1966. 16mm; 14 minutes; black and white; silent (FMC, LFC).

Why Don't You Sneeze. 1966 (abandoned).

Rose Colored Dance. 1966. 8mm/16mm; 13 minutes; black and white; silent.

I Saw the Shadow. 1966. 8mm/16mm; 13 minutes; black and white; silent.

Yomei-Mon. 1966. 8mm/16mm; 12 minutes; color; silent (abandoned).

Alma-Ata. 1966. 8mm/16mm; 15 minutes; color; silent (abandoned).

White Caligraphy. 1967. 16mm; 10 minutes; black and white; silent (CC, FMC, LFC).

Shelter 9999. 1967. mixed media installation with film, slides, sound-on-tape; 60 minutes; black and white/color.

Camera Massage. 1968. 16mm; 5½ minutes; black and white; sound.

Camera Massage No. 2: Virgin Conception. 1968. 16mm; 22½ minutes; color; sound.

Camera Massage No. 3: Summer Happenings, U.S.A. 1968. 16mm; 27½ minutes; black and white; sound.

Flowers. 1968. 16mm; 11 minutes; color; silent.

Flower Orgy. 1968. 16mm; 10 minutes; color; silent.

Face. 1969. 16mm; 20½ minutes; color; sound (FMC, LFC).

Filmmakers. 1969. 16mm; 28 minutes; color; sound (FMC).

New York Scene. 1966–70. 8mm (shown on two projectors simultaneously); 40 minutes; black and white/color; sound-on-tape.

Dead Movie (later revised and retitled *Projection Piece*). 1968. 16mm film installation; continuous; no projection; silent.

Three Colours. 1968. 16mm (three loops projected simultaneously on a single screen); continuous; color; silent.

Circles. 1969. 16mm (20 to 30 3-minute loop films projected on several projectors simultaneously); continuous; black and white; sound.

I Love You. 1970. 16mm; 8 minutes; color; silent.

Film Strips I (*"Eye for Eye"*). 1970. 16mm; 12 minutes; black and white; sound (FMC, LFC).

Film Strips II (*"Tooth for Tooth"*). 1970. 16mm; 12 minutes; black and white; sound (FMC, LFC).

Buddha Again. 1970. 16mm; 17 minutes; color; sound (FMC).

In the River. 1970. 16mm; 19½ minutes; color; sound (FMC).

Shutter. 1971. 16mm; 25 minutes; black and white; sound (FMC, LFC).

Projection Piece. 1972. 16mm film installation using two continuous loops; black and white; silent.

Models, Reel 1 (includes "2 Minutes 46 Seconds 16 Frames"; "Timing 1, 2, 3, 4"; "Time Length 1, 2, 3, 4"; "Timed 1, 2, 3"). 1972. 16mm; 43 minutes; black and white; sound (FMC, LFC).

Models, Reel 2 (includes "Counting 1 to 100 or Xs"; "A Line," Parts 1, 2, 3; "To See the Frame, Not to See the Frame"; "Seeing, Not Seeing"). 1972. 16mm; 44 minutes; black and white; silent (FMC, LFC).

Loop Seen as a Line. 1972. 16mm film installation using two continuous loops; black and white; silent.

Timing 1, 2, 3. 1972. 16mm film installation using one continuous projected loop and a wall-mounting of the same material; black and white; sound.

Minutes and Seconds. 1973. 16mm film installation using two continuous loops; black and white; silent.

+ & −. 1973. 16mm; 26 minutes; black and white; sound (FMC).

1 to 60 Seconds. 1973. 16mm; 30½ minutes; black and white; silent (FMC, LFC).

Parallel. 1974. 16mm; 28 minutes; black and white; silent (FMC).

Film Installation. 1974. 16mm film installation using no projector; continuous; black and white; silent.

1 Sec and ∞. 1975. 16mm installation using 2 continuous loops; black and white; silent.

24 Frames Per Second. 1975, 1978. 16mm; 20/12 minutes; black and white; sound (FMC, LFC).

Sync Sound. 1975, 1978. 16mm; 12/9 minutes; black and white; sound (FMC, LFC).

One Frame Duration. 1977. 16mm; 12 minutes; black and white/color; sound (CC, FMC, LFC).

MA ("Intervals"). 1978. 16mm; 21 minutes; black and white/color; sound (FMC).

Topological Space. 1979. 16mm film and video installation using two projectors; continuous; silent.

Repeated/Reversed Time. 1980. 16mm; 12 minutes; black and white; sound (FMC).

Talking in New York. 1981. Super-8mm; 18 minutes; color; sound.

Talking Picture (The Structure of Film Viewing). 1981. Super-8mm; 15 minutes; color; sound (FMC).

George Kuchar

The Naked and the Nude (co-made with Mike Kuchar). 1957. 8mm; 30 minutes; color; sound.

The Slasher (co-made with Mike Kuchar). 1958. 8mm; 20 minutes; color; sound.

The Thief and the Stripper (co-made with Mike Kuchar). 1959. 8mm; 20 minutes; color; sound.

I Was a Teenage Rumpot (co-made with Mike Kuchar). 1960. 8mm; 12 minutes; color; sound.

Pussy on a Hot Tin Roof (co-made with Mike Kuchar). 1961. 8mm; 12 minutes; color; sound.

Born of the Wind (co-made with Mike Kuchar). 1961. 8mm; 20 minutes; color; sound.

A Woman Distressed (co-made with Mike Kuchar). 1962. 8mm; 15 minutes; color; sound.

Night of the Bomb (co-made with Mike Kuchar). 1962. 8mm; 15 minutes; color; sound.

The Confessions of Babette (co-made with Mike Kuchar). 1963. 8mm; 15 minutes; color; sound.

A Town Called Tempest (co-made with Mike Kuchar). 1963. 8mm; 30 minutes; color; sound (CC).

Lust for Ecstasy (co-made with Mike Kuchar). 1963. 8mm; 45 minutes; color; sound (CC).

Anita Needs Me (co-made with Mike Kuchar). 1963. 8mm; 15minutes; color; sound.

Tootsies in Autumn (co-made with Mike Kuchar). 1963. 8mm; 15 minutes; color; sound.

Lovers of Eternity. 1964. 8mm; 30 minutes; color; sound (CC).

Corruption of the Damned. 1965. 16mm; 55 minutes; black and white; sound (CC, FMC).

Hold Me While I'm Naked. 1966. 16mm; 15 minutes; color; sound (CC, FMC).

Leisure. 1966. 16mm; 9½ minutes; black and white; sound (CC, FMC).

Mosholu Holiday. 1966. 16mm; 9 minutes; black and white; sound (CC, FMC).

Color Me Shameless. 1967. 16mm; 30 minutes; black and white; sound (CC, CFDC, FMC).

Eclipse of the Sun Virgin. 1967. 16mm; 15 minutes; color; sound (CC, FMC).

The Lady from Sands Point. 1967. 16mm; 10 minutes; black and white; sound (CC, FMC).

Encyclopedia of the Blessed. 1968. 16mm; 42 minutes; black and white/color; sound (CC, FMC).

House of the White People. 1968. 16mm; 17½ minutes; color; sound (CC, FMC).

Knocturne. 1968. 16mm; 10 minutes; color; sound (CC, FMC).

Unstrap Me. 1968. 16mm; 77 minutes; color; sound (CC, FMC).

The Mammal Palace. 1969. 16mm; 31 minutes; black and white; sound (CC, FMC).

Pagan Rhapsody. 1970. 16mm; 23½ minutes; color; sound (CC, FMC).

Portrait of Ramona. 1971. 16mm; 25 minutes; color; sound (CC, FMC).

The Sunshine Sisters. 1972. 16mm; 36 minutes; color; sound (CC, FMC).

Devil's Cleavage. 1973. 16mm; 122 minutes; black and white; sound (CC, FMC).

I Married a Heathen. 1974. 16mm; 55 minutes; black and white; sound (CC).

The Desperate and the Deep. 1975. 16mm; 21 minutes; black and white; sound (CC).

A Reason to Live. 1976. 16mm; 30 minutes; black and white; sound (CC, FMC).

Back to Nature. 1976. 16mm; 10 minutes; color; sound (CC, FMC).

I, an Actress. 1977. 16mm; 10 minutes; black and white; sound (CC, FMC).

The Asphalt Ribbon. 1977. 16mm; 20 minutes; black and white; sound (CC).

Ky Kapers. 1977. 16mm; 20 minutes; black and white; sound (CC).

Wild Night in El Reno. 1977. 16mm; 6 minutes; color; sound (CC, FMC).

Forever and Always. 1978. 16mm; 20 minutes; color; sound (CC).

The Mongreloid. 1978. 16mm; 10 minutes; color; sound (CC, FMC).

One Night a Week. 1978. 16mm; 27 minutes; black and white; sound (CC).

Prescription in Blue. 1978. 16mm; 20 minutes; black and white; sound (CC).

Blips. 1979. 16mm; 30 minutes; black and white; sound (CC).

The Power of the Press. 1979. 16mm; 25 minutes; black and white; sound (CC).

Symphony for a Sinner. 1979. 16mm; 56 minutes; color; sound (CC).

Aqueerius. 1980. 16mm; 8 minutes; black and white; sound (CC).

The Nocturnal Immaculation. 1980. 16mm; 27 minutes; black and white; sound (CC).

How to Chose a Wife. 1980. 16mm; 15 minutes; color; sound (CC).

The Woman and the Dress. 1980. 16mm; 14 minutes; color; sound (CC).

Yolanda. 1981. 16mm; 22 minutes; color; sound (CC).

Boulevard Kishka. 1981. 16mm; 20 minutes; color; sound (CC).

The Oneers. 1982. 16mm; 10 minutes; color; sound (CC).

Ms. Hyde. 1983. 16mm; 17 minutes; color; sound (CC).
The Cattle Mutilations. 1983. 16mm; 24 minutes; color; sound (CC).
Club Vatican. 1984. 16mm; 11 minutes; color; sound (CC).
Untitled Musical. 1984. 16mm; 13 minutes; color; sound (CC).
The X People. 1985. 16mm; 27 minutes; color; sound (CC).
Motel Capri. 1985. 16mm; 16 minutes; black and white; sound (CC).
La Noche D'Amour. 1986. 16mm; 18 minutes; black and white; sound (CC).
Ascension of the Demonoids. 1987. 16mm; 45 minutes; color; sound (CC, FMC).

Babette Mangolte

What Maisie Knew. 1975. 16mm; 58 minutes; black and white; sound (Circles, 713 Roman Road, London E2, England; FMC, LFC).
(Now) (or *Maintenant entre parenthèses*). 1976. 16mm; 10 minutes; color; silent (FMC).
The Camera: Je, or, *La Camera: I.* 1978. 16mm; 88 minutes; black and white/color; sound (Circles, FMC).
Water Motor. 1978. 16mm; 9 minutes; black and white; silent (FMC).
There? Where? 1979. 16mm; 8 minutes; color; sound (FMC).
The Cold Eye (My Darling, Be Careful). 1980. 16mm; 90 minutes; black and white; sound (Circles, FMC).
The Sky on Location. 1983. 16mm; 78 minutes; color; sound (Circles, FMC).

As Director of Photography

Marcel Hanoun, *L'Automne.* 1971. 16mm; 90 minutes; black and white; sound.
Yvonne Rainer, *Lives of Performers.* 1972. 16mm; 90 minutes; black and white; sound (FMC, BFI).
Chantal Akerman, *The Room.* 1972. 16mm; 10 minutes; color; sound.
Chantal Akerman, *Hotel Monterey.* 1972. 16mm; 100 minutes; color; sound.
Yvonne Rainer, *Film about a Woman Who . . . .* 1974. 16mm; 90 minutes; black and white; sound (First Run).
Michael Snow, *"Rameau's Nephew" by Diderot (Thanx to Dennis Young) by Wilma Schoen* (New York sequences). 1974. 16mm; 260 minutes; color; sound (CFDC, FMC).
Chantal Akerman, *Jeanne Dielman, 23 quai du commerce, 1080 Bruxelles.* 1975. 35mm; 195 minutes; color; sound (New Yorker).
Margaret Murphy and Lucille Rhodes, *They Are Their Own Gifts* (Mangolte shot about half the film, including sections on Alice Neal and Anna Sokolow). 1976. 16mm; 90 minutes; color; sound.
Chantal Akerman, *News from Home.* 1977. 16mm; 90 minutes; color; sound.
Richard Foreman, *Strong Medicine.* 1978. 35mm; 85 minutes; color; sound.
Anthony McCall, Claire Pajaczkowska, Andrew Tyndall, Jane Weinstock, *Sigmund Freud's Dora.* 1979. 16mm; 40 minutes; color; sound.
Jackie Raynal, *New York Story.* 1979. 16mm; 35 minutes; black and white/color; sound (Zanzibar Productions, 40 Central Park S., New York, NY 10019).
Sally Potter, *The Gold Diggers.* 1983. 35mm; 85 minutes; black and white; sound (BFI; Women Make Movies, 19 W. 21st St., 2nd Floor, New York, NY 10010).

Jackie Raynal, *Hotel New York*. 1983. 16mm; 60 minutes; color; sound (Zanzibar).

Chantal Akerman, *Un jour Pina a demandé* . . . . 1984. 16mm; 60 minutes; color; sound (French TV Antenne 2).

Jean Pierre Gorin, *Routine Pleasures*. 1986. 16mm; 82 minutes; black and white/color; sound.

J. J. Murphy

Highway Landscape. 1972. 16mm; 6½ minutes; color; sound (CC, FMC, MOMA).

In Progress (co-made with Ed Small). 1972. 16mm; 18 minutes; color; silent (CC, FMC).

Ice. 1972. 16mm; 7¼ minutes; color; sound (CC, FMC, MOMA).

Sky Blue Water Light Sign. 1972. 16mm; 8½ minutes; color; sound (CC, FMC, MOMA).

Print Generation. 1974. 16mm; 50 minutes; color; sound (CC, FMC, MOMA).

Summer Diary. 1976. 16mm; 2 minutes; color; silent (Murphy, 1320 East Mifflin St., Madison, WI 53703).

Movie Stills. 1977. 16mm; 45 minutes; black and white; silent (CC, FMC).

Science Fiction. 1979. 16mm; 5¼ minutes; color; sound (CC, FMC, MOMA).

Preview. 1980. 16mm; 3½ minutes; color; sound (CC, FMC).

The Night Belongs to the Police. 1982. 16mm; 29 minutes; color; sound (FMC).

Terminal Disorder. 1983. 16mm; 42 minutes; color; sound (Murphy).

Frame of Mind. 1985. 16mm; 80 minutes; color; sound (Murphy).

Robert Nelson

Building Muir Beach House (co-made with Gunvor Nelson). 1961. 16mm; 3 minutes; silent.

Last Week at Oona's Bath (co-made with Gunvor Nelson). 1962. 16mm; 3 minutes; silent.

The Mystery of Amelia Airheart Solved. 1962. 16mm; 2½ minutes; silent.

Plastic Haircut. 1963. 16mm; 15 minutes; black and white; sound (FMC).

King Ubu. 1963. 16mm; 5 minutes (approximate); black and white; silent.

Oh Dem Watermelons. 1965. 16mm; 12 minutes; color; sound (CC, FMC, LFC, MOMA).

Sixty Lazy Dogs. 1965. 16mm; 5 minutes; black and white; sound.

Confessions of a Black Mother Succuba. 1965. 16mm; 16 minutes; black and white; sound (FMC, LFC).

Thick Pucker. 1965. 16mm; 11 minutes; black and white; sound (FMC).

Oiley Peloso the Pump Man. 1965. 16mm; 14 minutes; black and white; sound (FMC).

Grateful Dead. 1967. 16mm; 7½ minutes; color; sound (FMC, LFC).

Hot Leatherette. 1967. 16mm; 5½ minutes; black and white; sound (CC, FMC, LFC).

The Great Blondino (co-made with William T. Wiley). 1967. 16mm; 42 minutes; color; sound (CC, FMC, MOMA).

The Great Blondino Preview (co-made with William T. Wiley). 1967. 16mm; 3 minutes; color; sound (FMC).

Half Open and Lumpy. 1967. 16mm; 2½ minutes; color; sound (FMC).

The Off-Handed Jape (co-made with William T. Wiley). 1967. 16mm; 9 minutes; color; sound (CCC, FMC).

Penny Bright and Jimmy Witherspoon. 1967. 16mm; 3½ minutes; color; sound (FMC).

Superspread. 1967. 16mm; 13 minutes; color; sound (FMC).

The Awful Backlash. 1967. 16mm; 14 minutes; black and white; sound (FMC).

Portrait of Gourley. 1967. 16mm; 23 minutes; sound.

The Beard. 1968. 16mm; 2½ minutes; sound.

War Is Hell. 1968. 16mm; 29 minutes; black and white; sound (FMC).

Bleu Shut. 1970. 16mm; 33 minutes; color; sound (AFA, CC, FMC).

R.I.P. 1970. 16mm; 22 minutes; color; sound.

King David (co-made with Mike Henderson). 1970. 16mm; 16 minutes; color; sound (FMC).

No More. 1971. 16mm; 70 minutes; black and white; sound.

Worldly Woman (co-made with Mike Henderson). 1973. 16mm; 6½ minutes; sound.

Rest in Pieces 74. 1974. 16mm; 8½ minutes; sound.

Deep Westurn (co-made with Mike Henderson and William T. Wiley). 1974. 16mm; 6 minutes; color; sound (CC, FMC).

Suite California Stops and Passes: Part 1. 1976. 16mm; 46 minutes; color; sound (CC, FMC).

Suite California Stops and Passes: Part 2. 1978. 16mm; 48 minutes; color; sound (CC, FMC).

How to Get Out of a Burning House. 1979. 16mm; 22 minutes; black and white/color; sound.

Hamlet Act. 1982. 16mm; 21 minutes; black and white; sound (CC, FMC).

Carolee Schneemann

Carl Ruggles' Christmas Breakfast. 1963. 8mm/16mm; 7 minutes; black and white/hand-colored; sound-on-tape (FMC; Schneemann, 437 Springtown Rd., New Paltz, NY 12561).

Viet-Flakes. 1965. 16mm; 11 minutes; black and white/tinted; sound (FMC, Schneemann).

Fuses (Part 1 of *Autobiographical Trilogy*). 1967. 16mm; 22 minutes; color; silent (CC, FMC, LFC).

Plumb Line (Part 2 of *Autobiographical Trilogy*). 1971. 16mm; 18 minutes; color; sound (CC, FMC, LFC, Cecile Starr, 50 West 96th St., New York, N.Y. 10025).

Reel Time (incomplete film diary co-made with Anthony McCall). 1971–72. 16mm; 60 minutes; color; sound (Schneemann).

Acts of Perception (made with workshop group). 1973 . Super-8mm; 11 minutes; black and white; sound-on-tape (Schneemann).

Kitch's Last Meal (Part 3 of *Autobiographical Trilogy*). 1973–78 (various versions). Double-image Super-8mm; 20 to 240 minutes; color; sound-on-tape (Schneemann).

John Waters

Hag in a Black Leather Jacket. 1964. 8mm; 17 minutes; black and white; sound.

Roman Candles. 1966. 3 8mm films shown simultaneously; 40 minutes; color; sound.

Eat Your Makeup. 1968. 16mm; 45 minutes; black and white; silent.

Mondo Trasho. 1969. 16mm; 90 minutes; black and white; sound (New Line, on video from Continental).

The Diane Linkletter Story. 1970. 16mm; 15 minutes; black and white; sound (New Line).

Multiple Maniacs. 1970. 16mm; 90 minutes; black and white; sound (New Line, on video from Continental).

Pink Flamingos. 1972. 16mm/35mm; 90 minutes; color; sound (New Line, on video from Wizard).

Female Trouble. 1974. 16mm/35mm; 95 minutes; color; sound (New Line, on video from Continental).

Desperate Living. 1977. 16mm/35mm; 90 minutes; color; sound (New Line, on video from Continental).

Polyester. 1981. 35mm; 87 minutes; color; sound; "odorama" (New Line, on video from Thorn Emi).

Hairspray. 1988. 35mm; 90 minutes (approx.); color; sound.

Bibliography

This bibliography is far from exhaustive. The first section includes books relevant for the general study of independent/avant-garde forms of filmmaking. The second section includes, alphabetically by filmmaker, other interviews with the filmmakers; statements and articles by the filmmakers about their own work, the work of others and about film in general; and selected critical books and articles about the filmmakers.

General References

American Federation of Arts. *A History of the American Avant-Garde Cinema*. New York: American Federation of Arts, 1976. A catalogue for a touring show.

Arts Council of Great Britain. *Film As Film: Formal Experiment in Film 1910–1975*. London: Arts Council of Great Britain, 1979. A catalogue for a show at the Hayward Gallery, London, May 3–June 17, 1979.

Battcock, Gregory, ed. *The New American Cinema*. New York: Dutton, 1967.

Canyon Cinema Catalogue #5. San Francisco: Canyon Cinema, 1982.

Curtis, David. *Experimental Cinema*. New York: Delta, 1971.

Dwoskin, Stephen. *Film Is: The International Free Cinema*. Woodstock, NY: Overlook Press, 1975.

Film-makers' Cooperative Catalogue, no. 6. New York: Film-makers Cooperative, 1975.

Ehrenstein, David. *Film: The Front Line/1984*. Denver: Arden, 1984.

Gidal, Peter, ed. *Structural Film Anthology*. London: British Film Institute, 1976.

Grenier, Vincent, Kathy Dieckmann, and John Pruitt, eds. *10 Years of Living Cinema*. New York: Collective for Living Cinema, 1982. A catalogue for a retrospective of films shown at the Collective for Living Cinema, New York, Oct. 1–Nov. 21, 1982.

Hoberman, J. *Home Made Movies: 20 Years of American 8mm and Super-8 Films*. New York: Anthology Film Archives, 1981. A catalogue for a program of films shown at Anthology Film Archives, New York, May 1–June 30, 1981.

Hoberman, J., and Jonathan Rosenbaum. *Midnight Movies*. New York: Harper & Row, 1983.

Kaplan, E. Ann. *Women and Film: Both Sides of the Camera*. New York: Methuen, 1983.

Le Grice, Malcolm. *Abstract Film and Beyond*. Cambridge: M.I.T. Press, 1977.

Mekas, Jonas. *Movie Journal: The Rise of the New American Cinema, 1959–1971*. New York: Collier, 1972.

Mekas, Jonas, and P. Adams Sitney, eds., *"The Pleasure Dome," Amerikansk Experimentfilm 1939–1979*. Stockholm: Moderna Museet, 1980. A catalogue for a show at Moderna Museet, Stockholm, Sweden, February 16–April 4, 1980.

Michelson, Annette, ed. *New Forms in Film*. A catalogue for an exhibition of North American independent film, Montreux, Switzerland, August 3–24, 1974.

Museum of Modern Art. *Circulating Film Library Catalogue*. New York: Museum of Modern Art, 1984.

Renan, Sheldon. *An Introduction to American Underground Film*. New York: Dutton, 1967.

Rosenbaum, Jonathan. *Film: The Front Line/1983*. Denver: Arden, 1983.

Russett, Robert, and Cecile Starr. *Experimental Animation*. New York: Van Nostrand, 1976.

Sitney, P. Adams, ed. *The Avant-Garde Film: A Reader of Theory and Criticism*. New York: N.Y.U. Press, 1978.

———, ed. *The Essential Cinema: Essays on the Films in the Collection of Anthology Film Archives*. New York: Anthology Film Archives and N.Y.U. Press, 1975.

———, ed. *Film Culture Reader*. New York: Praeger, 1970.

———. *Visionary Film*. New York: Oxford, 1974.

Stauffacher, Frank, ed. *Art in Cinema*. New York: Arno, 1968. A catalogue for a symposium on the avant-garde film at the San Francisco Museum of Art, 1947.

Turim, Maureen. *Abstraction in Avant-Garde Film*. Ann Arbor, MI: U.M.I. Press, 1985.

Tyler, Parker. *Underground Film: A Critical History*. New York: Evergreen, 1969.

Vogel, Amos. *Film as a Subversive Art*. New York: Random House, 1974.

Ward, Melinda, and Bruce Jenkins. *The American New Wave 1958–1967*. Minneapolis: Walker Art Center, 1982. A catalogue for a touring film program sponsored by Media Study/Buffalo and the Walker Art Center.

Youngblood, Gene. *Expanded Cinema*. New York: Dutton, 1970.

Beth B and Scott B

Marchetti, Gina, and Keith Tishken. "An Interview with Beth and Scott B." *Millennium Film Journal*, no. 10–11 (Fall-Winter 1981–82), pp. 158–67.

Diana Barrie

Barrie, Diana. Statement in "Point of View." *Spiral*, no. 1 (Oct. 1984), pp. 10–11.

Modleski, Tania. "The Films of Diana Barrie." *Wide Angle*, vol. 7, nos. 1–2 (1985), pp. 62–67.

Tom Chomont

Murphy, J. J. "Reaching for Oblivion." *Millennium Film Journal,* no. 3 (Winter–Spring 1979), pp. 122–25.

Bruce Conner

Brown, Robert. "Interview with Bruce Conner." *Film Culture,* no. 33 (Summer 1964), pp. 15–16.
"Bruce Conner: A Discussion at the 1968 Flaherty Film Seminar." *Film Comment,* vol. 5, no. 4 (Winter 1969), pp. 15–25.
Conner, Bruce. "Bruce Conner to Scott Bartlett." *Canyon Cinemanews,* no. 72–73 (1972), p. 7.
———. "Exchanges: Correspondence between Bruce Conner and Jonas Mekas." *Canyon Cinemanews,* no. 4 (1969), pp. 5–8.
Goodeve, Thyrza. "The Warp and Woof of Bruce Conner" (an interview). *Idiolects,* no. 14 (Spring 1984), pp. 40–46.
Haller, Robert. "Excerpts from an Interview with Bruce Conner Conducted in July of 1971." *Film Culture,* no. 67–69 (1979), pp. 191–94.
Moritz, William, and Beverly O'Neill. "Fallout: Some Notes on the Films of Bruce Conner." *Film Quarterly,* vol. 31, no. 4 (Summer 1978), pp. 36–42.
Reveaux, Anthony. *Bruce Conner.* A Film in the Cities Monograph. St. Paul, MN: Film in the Cities, 1981.
Tuchman, Mitch. "Bruce Conner Interviewed by Mitch Tuchman." *Film Comment,* vol. 17, no. 5 (Sept.–Oct. 1981). pp. 73–76.

Manuel DeLanda

DeLanda, Manuel. "Policing the Spectrum." *Zone,* nos. 1–2 (Summer 1986), pp. 176–77.
———. "Skin, Bodily Fluids, and Nervous System of Film." In *Cinema off y Videoarte e New York,* pp. 161–64. Genova: Bonini, 1981.
———. "Wittgenstein at the Movies." In *Cinema Histories: Cinema Practices,* pp. 108–19. AFI Monograph Series, vol. 4. Frederick, MD: University Publications of America, 1984.

Vivienne Dick

Hoberman, J. "A Context for Vivienne Dick." *October,* no. 20 (Spring 1982), pp. 102–6.

Morgan Fisher

Fisher, Morgan. "Cue Rolls." *New,* vol. 8, no. 3 (May 1977), pp. 14–15.
———, ed. Special issue of *LAICA* (Los Angeles Institute of Contemporary Art) *Journal,* no. 14 (April–May 1977). Includes "Some Introductory Remarks" by Fisher and Fisher's interview with Jack Goldstein.

Skoller, Donald. "The Fisher Phenomenon." *Film Comment,* vol. 9, no. 2 (March–April 1973), pp. 58–63.

Weinbren, Grahame, "Six Filmmakers and an Ideal of Composition." *Millennium Film Journal,* no. 3 (Winter–Spring 1979), pp. 44–46.

Hollis Frampton

André, Carl, and Hollis Frampton. *Carl André/Hollis Frampton: 12 Dialogues, 1962–63.* Edited by Benjamin H. D. Buchloh. Halifax, Nova Scotia, and New York: Press of the Nova Scotia College of Art and Design and N.Y.U. Press, 1981.

Field, Simon, and Peter Sainsbury. "*Zorns Lemma* and *Hapax Legomena,* Interview with Hollis Frampton." *Afterimage* (London), no. 4 (Autumn 1972), pp. 44–47.

Fischer, Lucy, "*Magellan:* Navigating the Hemispheres." *University Film Study Center Newsletter,* vol. 7, no. 5 (June 1977), pp. 5–10.

Frampton, Hollis. *Circles of Confusion.* Rochester, NY: Visual Studies Workshop Press, 1983. This volume includes twelve of Frampton's most important essays: "A Pentagram for Conjuring the Narrative," "Eadweard Muybridge: Fragments of a Tesseract," "Film in the House of the Word," "Incisions in History/Segments of Eternity," "For a Metahistory of Film: Commonplace Notes and Hypotheses," "Notes on Composing in Film," "Meditations around Paul Strand," "Impromptus on Edward Weston: Everything in Its Place," "The Withering Away of the State of the Art," "A Stipulation of Terms from Maternal Hopi," "Digressions on the Photographic Agony," and "A Lecture."

———. "Digressions on the Photographic Agony." *Artforum,* vol. 11, no. 3 (November 1972), pp. 43–51.

———. "Eadweard Muybridge: Fragments of a Tesseract." *Artforum,* vol. 11, no. 7 (March 1973), pp. 43–52.

———. "Erotic Predicaments for Camera." *October,* no. 32 (Spring 1985), pp. 56–61. A special Frampton issue.

———. "For a Metahistory of Film: Commonplace Notes and Hypotheses." *Artforum,* vol. 10, no. 1 (September 1971), pp. 32–35.

———. "Impromptus on Edward Weston: Everything in Its Place." *October,* no. 5 (Summer 1978), pp. 48–69.

———. "Incisions in History/Segments of Eternity." *Artforum,* vol. 13, no. 2 (October 1974), pp. 39–50.

———. "A Lecture." In P. Adams Sitney, ed., *The Avant-Garde Film: A Reader of Theory and Criticism,* pp. 275–80. New York: NYU Press, 1978.

———. "Letters from Framp 1958–1968." *October,* no. 32 (Spring 1985), pp. 25–55.

———. "Letter from Hollis Frampton to Peter Gidal on *Zorns Lemma.*" In Gidal, ed., *Structural Film Anthology,* pp. 75–77. London: British Film Institute, 1976.

———. "Meditations Around Paul Strand." *Artforum,* vol. 10, no. 6 (February 1972), pp. 52–57.

———. "Mind Over Matter." *October,* no. 6 (Fall 1978), pp. 81–92.

———. "Notes on Composing in Film." *October,* no. 1 (Spring 1976), pp. 104–10.

———. "Notes on (nostalgia)." *Film Culture,* nos. 53–55 (Spring 1972), p. 114.

———. "A Pentagram for Conjuring the Narrative." In *Form and Structure in Recent Film,* pp. 59–68. Vancouver: Vancouver Art Gallery, 1972.

———. *Poetic Justice*. Rochester, NY: Visual Studies Workshop Press, 1973.

———. "A Stipulation of Terms from Maternal Hopi." In *Options and Alternatives: Some Directions in Recent Art*. New Haven: Yale University Art Gallery, 1973.

———. "The Withering Away of the State of the Art." *Artforum*, vol. 13, no. 4 (December 1974), pp. 50–55.

Frampton, Hollis, Ken Jacobs, and Michael Snow. "Filmmakers Versus the Museum of Modern Art." *Filmmakers' Newsletter*, vol. 2, no. 7 (May 1969), pp. 1–2.

Gidal, Peter. "Interview with Hollis Frampton." *October*, no. 32 (Spring 1985), pp. 93–117.

———. "Interview with Hollis Frampton." In Gidal, ed., *Structural Film Anthology*, pp. 64–72. London: British Film Institute, 1976.

Henderson, Brian. "Propositions for the Exploration of Frampton's *Magellan*." *October*, no. 32 (Spring 1985), pp. 129–50.

Jenkins, Bruce, and Susan Krane, eds. *Hollis Frampton: Recollections/Recreations*. Buffalo/Cambridge: Albright-Knox Art Gallery/M.I.T. Press, 1984. This volume includes a detailed, annotated chronology of Frampton's life and work and a selected bibliography of works by and about Frampton.

Mekas, Jonas. Interview with Frampton in "Movie Journal." *Village Voice*, vol. 18, no. 2 (Jan. 11, 1973), p. 67.

———. Interview with Frampton in "Movie Journal." *Village Voice*, vol. 18, no. 3 (Jan. 18, 1973), pp. 70–71.

Michelson, Annette, ed. *Hollis Frampton: A Special Issue. October*, no. 32 (Spring 1985). Includes seminal articles by and about Frampton and the most complete filmography to date.

Simon, Bill. "Talking about Magellan: An Interview with Hollis Frampton." *Millennium Film Journal*, no. 7–9 (Fall/Winter 1980), pp. 4–26.

Snow, Michael. "Hollis Frampton Interviewed by Michael Snow." *Film Culture*, no. 48–49 (Winter/Spring 1970), pp. 6–12.

Tuchman, Mitch. "Frampton at the Gates: Interview with Mitch Tuchman." *Film Comment*, vol. 13, no. 5 (Sept.–Oct. 1977), pp. 55–59.

Larry Gottheim

Gottheim, Larry. "Avant-Garde Cinema—A Single Vision." *Quarterly Review of Film Studies*, vol. 1, no. 1 (Feb. 1976), pp. 88–94.

———. "Botticelli/Schoenberg." *no rose*, vol. 1, no. 1 (Winter 1976), pp. 1–6.

———. "Sound of Mind: On Iimura's *24 Frames Per Second*." In Grenier, Dieckmann, and Pruitt, eds. *10 Years of Living Cinema*, pp. 49–51. New York: Collective for Living Cinema, 1982.

———. "Sticking In/To the Landscape." *Millennium Film Journal*, no. 4–5 (Summer/Fall 1979), pp. 84–92.

MacDonald, Scott. "The Expanding Vision of Larry Gottheim's Films." *Quarterly Review of Film Studies*, vol. 3, no. 2 (Spring 1978), pp. 207–35.

Robert Huot

Huot, Robert. "Convenience, Lower Cost, Good Sound Quality, and Demystified Image: Or Why I Like Super-8 (A Testimonial)." *Cinemanews,* no. 81: 2–6 (1982), pp. 18–19.

———. Statement in catalogue for a show of diary paintings at State University of New York–Albany, Jan. 19–Feb. 15, 1976.

———. Statement in "Point of View." *Spiral,* no. 1 (Oct. 1984), pp. 8–10.

———. Statement in "Point of View." *Spiral,* no. 4 (July 1985), pp. 4–5.

MacDonald, Scott. "Surprise! The Films of Robert Huot, 1967–1972." *Quarterly Review of Film Studies.* vol. 5, no. 3 (Summer 1980), pp. 297–318.

Taka Iimura

Ancona, Victor. "Takahiko Iimura: From Film to Video." *Videography,* vol. 3, no. 9 (Sept. 1978), pp. 58–61.

Iimura, Taka. "On Film Installation." *Millennium Film Journal,* vol. 1, no. 2 (Spring/Summer 1978), pp. 74–76.

———. "Visuality and the Japanese Language." *Art and Cinema,* no. 1 (Dec. 1978), pp. 16–22.

Martinez, Charles. "Taka Iimura Interview." *Undercut,* no. 9 (Summer 1983), pp. 43–45.

Robertson, Clive. "Videoview 4: An Interview with Taka Iimura." *Centerfold,* vol. 2, no. 6 (Sept. 1978), pp. 83–86.

George Kuchar

Hills, Henry. "George Kuchar in Europe" (an interview). *Cinemanews,* no. 78:2 (1978), pp. 3–4, 28–29.

Jalbuena, Jun. "Sausages with George Kuchar, Jose Montaño and James Oseland." *Cinematograph,* vol. 1 (1985), pp. 105–11.

Kuchar, George. "Developing an Aesthetic." *Spiral,* no. 2 (January 1985), pp. 35–37.

———. "George Kuchar Speaks on Films and Truth." *Film Culture,* no. 33 (1964), pp. 14–15.

———. "How to Light." *Idiolects,* no. 11 (Summer 1981), pp. 11–14.

———. "Schooling." *SPIRAL,* no. 1 (October 1984), pp. 13–16.

———. "Tips on Directing." *Reversal,* no. 3 (Fall 1984), pp. 5–7.

Renan, Sheldon. "Interview with the Kuchar Brothers." *Film Culture,* no. 45 (1967), pp. 47–49.

Reynolds, Mike. "Interview with George Kuchar." *Cinemanews,* no. 75: 4 (1975), pp. 5–10.

Babette Mangolte

Camera Obscura Collective. "Camera Obscura Interview with Babette Mangolte." *Camera Obscura,* no. 3–4 (Summer 1979), pp. 198–210.

Penley, Constance. *"The Camera: Je/La Camera: Eye* (Babette Mangolte)." *Camera Obscura*, no. 3–4 (Summer 1979), pp. 195–97.
———. *"What Maisie Knew* by Babette Mangolte: Childhood as Point-of-View." *Camera Obscura*, no. 2 (Fall 1977), pp. 130–36.

J. J. Murphy

Murphy, J. J. "Christopher Maclaine—Approaching 'The End.'" *Film Culture*, no. 70–71 (1983), pp. 88–99.
———. "The Films of David Brooks." *Film Culture*, no. 70–71 (1983), pp. 206–12.
———. "Reaching for Oblivion." *Millennium Film Journal*, no. 3 (Winter–Spring 1979), pp. 122–25.
Peterson, James. "The Artful Mathematicians of the Avant-Garde." *Wide Angle*, vol. 7, no. 3 (1985), pp. 14–23.

Robert Nelson

Dale, R. C. "Judging a Film Festival: An Interview with Robert Nelson." *Film-makers' Newsletter*, vol. 2, no. 12 (Oct. 1969), pp. 4, 8–9.
Hills, Henry. "Robert Nelson Interview." *Cinemanews*, no. 78: 3–4 (1979), pp. 5–9.
Hoberman, J. *Nelson/Wiley*. A Film in the Cities Monograph. St. Paul, MN: Film in the Cities, 1979.
"Robert Nelson on Robert Nelson." *Film Culture*, no. 48–49 (1970), pp. 23–30.

Carolee Schneemann

Castle, Ted. "Carolee Schneemann: The Woman Who Uses Her Body as Her Art." *Artforum*, vol. 19, no. 3 (Nov. 1980), pp. 64–70.
Coe, Robert. "Carolee Schneemann: *More Than Meat Joy.*" *Performance Art*, no. 1 (1979), pp. 8–15.
Glassner, Verina. "Interviews with Three Filmmakers." *Time Out*, no. 109 (March 17–23, 1972), p. 47.
Haller, Robert. "Rolling in the Maelstrom: A Conversation Between Carolee Schnee-mann and Robert Haller." *Idiolects*, no. 14 (Spring 1984), pp. 50–55.
MacDonald, Scott. "The Men Cooperated!: Carolee Schneemann's *ABC.*" *After-image*, vol. 12, no. 9 (April 1985), pp. 12–15.
Montano, Linda. "Interview with Carolee Schneemann." *The Flue*, vol. 2, no. 3 (Summer 1982), pp. 6–8.
Schneemann, Carolee. *ABC—We Print Anything—In the Cards*. Beuningen, Holland: Brummense Uitgeverij Van Luxe Werkjes, 1977.
———. *Cezanne, She Was a Great Painter*. New York: Tresspass Press, 1974.
———. "*Fresh Blood:* A Dream Morphology." *Dreamworks*, vol. 2, no. 1 (Fall 1981), pp. 67–75.
———. "Kitch's Last Meal." *Cinemanews*, no. 81: 2–6 (1982), pp. 55–58.
———. *More Than Meat Joy*. New Paltz, NY: Documentext, 1979. This book-length documentation of Schneemann's work as a filmmaker, painter, performance artist,

and writer includes a complete bibliography of writings about and by Schneemann through the mid-1970s.

————. "Notes from First Viewing a Film by Dusan Makavejev—*W. R. Mysteries of the Organism.*" *Idiolects*, no. 8 (Spring 1980), pp. 26–32.

————. *Parts of a Body House Book.* Devon, England: Beau Geste Press, 1972.

"Through the Body: A Dialogue Between Carolee Schneemann and Amy Greenfield." *Field of Vision*, no. 4 (Fall 1978), pp. 5–8.

John Waters

During the 1970s, Waters became something of a media star. He has been regularly interviewed in newspapers and on television. The most useful and complete commentaries on his work and life, however, are his own books:

Waters, John. *Crackpot: The Obsessions of John Waters.* New York: Macmillan, 1986.

————. *Shock Value: A Tasteful Book about Bad Taste.* New York: Delta, 1981.

Index

All films are listed individually by title rather than under the filmmaker's name.

Compositor: G & S Typesetters
Text: 10/12 Times Roman
Display: Helvetica Bold
Printer: Murray Printing Company
Binder: Murray Printing Company

Hark
1-206-385-0072